W9-BAX-821

History of London

LONDON 1808–1870:
THE INFERNAL WEN

Also by Francis Sheppard

Local Government in St Marylebone 1688–1835

History of London

LONDON
1808–1870:
THE
INFERNAL WEN

Francis Sheppard

University of California Press
Berkeley and Los Angeles 1971

GEORGE M. SMILEY MEMORIAL LIBRARY
CENTRAL METHODIST COLLEGE
FAYETTE, MISSOURI 65248

University of California Press
Berkeley and Los Angeles

Copyright © 1971 by Francis Sheppard

ISBN: 0–520–01847–8
LC: 71–142067

Printed in Great Britain

To my wife
Elizabeth

Contents

List of Illustrations

List of Figures

Preface

—————————

THIS IS not a work of original research, for my personal circumstances have precluded my undertaking such a task. It is merely an attempt to describe some of the more important aspects of the history of London between 1808 and 1870, largely from those sources which have been available to me on loan from the London Library and from the Members' Library at County Hall. I am immensely grateful to the staff of these two libraries for their help.

In adding yet another book to the already vast literature on the history of London I can only plead that nobody else has hitherto ventured to cover the whole of my chosen field, at least for very many years past. There are two causes for this absence of any recent attempt at synthesis. On the one hand there is the sheer size and complexity of the subject, and on the other there is the constantly increasing specialization of historical studies. In 1801 about one in ten of all the peoples of England and Wales lived in London, and in 1871 nearly one in every seven. To try to describe this vast urban complex as a whole is evidently not a suitable subject for university research students, nor has such a venture attracted anyone else. The result of this situation has been a constant and growing stream of theses (mostly unpublished), monographs and learned articles, all dealing with particular aspects of nineteenth-century London, many of them of the highest quality, but none of them attempting to take in the whole gigantic landscape at one glance. And this in its turn has resulted in the significance of London and its place in the life of the nation being neglected by those scholars with wider horizons who attempt to synthesize the whole field of English nineteenth-century history.

I hope that someone better qualified than I will soon perform this task of synthesis more skilfully than I have been able to do here. In the meantime I wish to express my gratitude to all those writers who have covered some part of my field, and on whose work I have drawn so heavily: particularly to Professor H. J. Dyos, of the University of Leicester, a true pioneer who has opened up so many new avenues of research, and who has given me friendship as well as help; to Sir John Summerson on architecture; to

Professor Lynn Lees on the Irish; to J. R. Kellett on the impact of railways; to Professor P. G. Hall on the industries of London; to Sidney and Beatrice Webb on local government, the poor law and trade unionism; to W. T. C. King on the London discount market; to Professor T. C. Barker and Michael Robbins on transport; to Royston Lambert, Professor S. E. Finer and R. A. Lewis on public health; to E. P. Thompson on the working class; and to very many others, including my own colleagues, Peter Bezodis and Marie Draper. I am also most grateful to Brian Spencer of the London Museum for very generous help with the illustrations; to Michael Robbins for expert assistance with the railway maps; and to Marie Draper for making the index.

FRANCIS SHEPPARD
Henley on Thames

Introduction

EARLY ON a summer morning in the year 1802 the Dover coach rattled briskly over Westminster Bridge on its way out of London to the coast. Upon the roof of the coach sat a young man, gazing at the view. It was a beautiful day, and he was much moved by what he saw. By the time he reached Dover he had composed a sonnet.

> *Earth has not any thing to show more fair :*
> *Dull would he be of soul who could pass by*
> *A sight so touching in its majesty :*
> *This City now doth, like a garment, wear*
> *The beauty of the morning ; silent, bare,*
> *Ships, towers, domes, theatres and temples lie*
> *Open unto the fields, and to the sky, –*
> *All bright and glittering in the smokeless air.*
> *Never did sun more beautifully steep*
> *In his first splendour, valley, rock, or hill ;*
> *Ne'er saw I, never felt, a calm so deep!*
> *The river glideth at his own sweet will :*
> *Dear God! The very houses seem asleep ;*
> *And all that mighty heart is lying still!*

Wordsworth lived for almost another half century. He spent most of this time among the valleys, rocks and hills of his home in far-away Westmorland, and only rarely came to the capital. One of his last visits, in 1845, was to take up his appointment as Poet Laureate; but he never wrote in praise of London again.

Nor was this surprising, for within the space of only two generations the view from the bridge (and from many other places in London too) had changed greatly. The air had become laden with the smoke of steam vessels, gasworks and the furnaces of a host of industrial establishments, and the snort and hiss of railway locomotives at the new terminus at Waterloo Station could constantly be heard. Downstream the noble prospect towards the City and the dome of St Paul's had been ruthlessly sundered by the brick and iron of Charing Cross railway bridge. Beneath Westminster Bridge itself still flowed the perennial river, no longer gliding 'at his own sweet will', but controlled and restricted by the great granite wall of the Victoria Embankment, along which clattered an endless procession of carriages, buses, cabs and carts, and beneath which there now extended an underground railway and two giant tunnels, one for gas and water pipes and telegraph wires, and the other for sewage. Upstream, too, the change was as great – to the left a vast new hospital, to the right a new Palace of Westminster, more embankments, more bridges. Nothing within sight lay 'open unto the fields', and even the sooty parapet of Westminster Bridge itself was new – iron in place of stone. London had been transformed.

When at last another poet did comment about London, he expressed himself in prose instead of verse. 'London and our other great commercial cities,' said William Morris in 1883, 'are mere masses of sordidness, filth and squalor, embroidered with patches of pompous and vulgar hideousness.' Whole counties, he continued, 'and the heavens that hang over them, [have] disappeared beneath a crust of unutterable grime'; the disease was spreading all over the country, 'and every little market town seizes the opportunity to imitate, as far as it can, the majesty of the hell of London and Manchester'.[1] Earth, he seemed to be saying, had not anything to show more foul than London and the great new industrial cities of England.

During the first seventy years of the nineteenth century London had changed more rapidly than at any other time in all her long history. This was the great age of the Industrial Revolution, when Britain was leading the world towards a new form of culture, lurching and bumping at first like a primitive aeroplane, but gradually gathering speed and climbing uncertainly upwards into the unknown regions of a new dimension. The familiar customs of field and village and centuries of mainly rural life receded ever farther away; precedent was no longer a guide, and in the mastery of the new element many people suffered, mentally as well as physically, and many died.

London was at the very hub of this great human experiment, and her position in it was therefore unique. For centuries she had been the capital city, the greatest port, the greatest manufacturing centre and the greatest centre of population in the kingdom, or indeed in the whole world, with the exception, perhaps, of one or two of the teeming cities of India and China. Compared with other European capitals, for instance, the popula-

[1] William Morris, *Architecture, Industry and Wealth*, 1902 edn, p. 172.

tion of London in 1810 was almost double that of Paris, while in 1821 it was four times that of Vienna and more than six times as great as that of Berlin. In Britain London's population in 1801 was more than eleven times as great as that of the second city, Liverpool. Her 958,863 inhabitants amounted to more than one-tenth of all the peoples of England and Wales, over three-quarters of whom still lived either in the country or in small towns with a population of under 20,000 each. In terms of size and numbers, London's supremacy was complete and overwhelming.

Seventy years later the position was very different. In 1871 the proportion of people living in the country or in small towns with a population of under 20,000 had fallen to little more than half the total population of England and Wales, and well over a quarter of the total population lived in large cities (including London) of over 100,000 inhabitants. But whereas in 1801 there were no towns except London with a population of over 100,000, by 1871 there were no fewer than sixteen such provincial towns, and all but three of them were in the Midlands or the north. A tremendous movement of economic power, hitherto concentrated upon London but elsewhere widely diffused throughout the whole country, had taken place, and the centre of gravity of the whole nation had shifted northward. London, formerly the hub of the nation's attention and the nation's industry, had now become almost isolated in the still preponderantly agricultural south.

For several decades the rate of growth among the great new northern towns had been much greater than in London. Between 1821 and 1831 the population of London had grown by 20 per cent, but Liverpool, Manchester, Birmingham, Leeds and Sheffield had all grown by over 40 per cent, and Bradford by 65 per cent. It was in these areas that the full force of the Industrial Revolution had made itself felt, and it was at Stockton and Darlington and Liverpool and Manchester, and not in London, that the earliest railways were built. Later in the century it was in the north, too, where the process of urbanization had advanced with such devastating speed, that many of the first tentative steps towards the solution of the ensuing social problems were taken – at Liverpool the first medical officer of health (1847), at Salford the first public library (1845), at Birkenhead a municipal park, free for all classes.

This was the great age of provincial civic pre-eminence, the age of the Manchester Free Trade School, of Leeds Town Hall and in the 1870s of Joseph Chamberlain's Birmingham. London, therefore, commanded a smaller share of public attention than hitherto. The City Corporation,

B

alone among all the great municipal corporations, was not reformed in the 1830s, and London was excluded from the Public Health Act of 1848. There was no focus for metropolitan civic pride and loyalty. Yet as always, London continued to grow – not at the vulgar upstart rate of the new northern towns, but evenly and inexorably, never, in any one decade between 1801 and 1871, at less than 16 per cent and never at more than 21 per cent. And so by 1871 her population had reached the enormous figure of over three and a quarter million. She was still more than six times as large as the second city, Liverpool, and the proportion of her population in relation to that of all the rest of England and Wales had actually risen from just over one-tenth in 1801 to almost one-seventh in 1871. In this new age of urban civilization more than a dozen great cities might share the economic power and the social problems which had hitherto belonged exclusively to the capital, but in size and wealth London still remained supreme.

On the other hand, London's importance as the capital of the kingdom and the seat of government declined – temporarily. George IV could celebrate his coronation and in his West End improvements indulge his passion for building (mostly at other people's expense) with the extravagance of a Renaissance Pope, but in an age when more and more people thought that society should be little more than a collection of private contractual relationships freely entered into by each individual, the stature of the capital city was inevitably reduced. To dismantle the often archaic economic regulations of the past and to let the nation's wealth 'fructify in the pockets of the people' became one of the principal aims of government. In 1833 the total number of civilian officials employed by the state was only 21,305, of whom over 15,000 were in the customs and excise departments; the Home Office establishment was 29. The dangers of centralization became a popular bogey. 'One of the principal things they had to dread,' Sir Edward Sugden told the House of Commons during the debates on the Reform Bill in 1832, 'was the giving too much power to the Metropolis. They ought not to lessen the influence of the Metropolis – indeed they could not do that if they would; but at least let them take care how they made the fate of the country depend on the will of the Metropolis.' Up in the gallery views of this kind were often heard and recorded by the young Dickens, who was then a parliamentary reporter, and years later, in *Our Mutual Friend*, his Mr Podsnap was to say much the same. 'Centralization. No. . . . Never with my consent. Not English.'

After reaching its climax, with most unfortunate results for London, around 1850, this feeling that the overbearing metropolis must be kept in its place gradually subsided. But even when the anti-centralization campaign was most vociferous, far more powerful forces had already been exerting themselves, largely unnoticed, in the opposite direction. The new urban age presented problems which demanded government attention, and while Parliament was still busying itself with the abolition of customs duties or the usury laws or the Navigation Acts it was also laying the foundations of a far more formidable new system of state paternalism. Factory or sanitary legislation, the reform of the prisons or the poor law, mounting concern with education, all occupied much parliamentary time in the middle of the nineteenth century, and all required administrators and inspectors for the enforcement of the new state action. By 1870 the power of London as the seat of government was increasing once again, and has continued to increase ever since.

Tension, the tension of opposing forces whose conflict achieves a precarious and constantly shifting equilibrium, is always present in some form in the life-history of any city. But in a capital city the strains and stresses are more complex than elsewhere. There is the usual tension between town and country, here enlarged to become the dislike and mutual suspicion prevalent between the metropolis and the whole of the rest of the nation, between London, the 'Great Wen', and 'the provinces', as everywhere else is patronizingly called, almost as if they were dependent colonies, to be controlled and managed solely in the interests of the capital. But in a capital city there is also an inner tension only to be found there – the tension between the government itself and the town in which it is situated. This, as much as mere superiority of size or wealth, is what distinguishes the history of London from all other English cities. For centuries the great City Corporation, embattled within the strong bulwarks of its ancient walls, and the sovereign power a mile away at Westminster had eyed each other with suspicion and apprehension, the one fearful for its wealth and privileges, the other for its often tenuous authority and physical safety. And now, by 1800, London had long ago burst beyond its ancient bastions and erupted over the surrounding country in hundreds of acres of bricks and mortar. 'What can be stable with these enormous cities?' exclaimed the Prime Minister, Lord Liverpool, as he looked fearfully out of the window of his house. 'One insurrection in London and all is lost.'

But this never happened. There were one or two small insurrections, but London was never 'lost', as were, at least once, the metropolitan cities of almost every other country in Europe. London did not become a centre of effective revolutionary activity. Paradoxically, it was her enormous size as much as anything else which precluded the emergence of such a force. Politically, London never overawed the rest of the nation during the nineteenth century, and the accession of the middle classes to power and the rise of working-class consciousness and organization were both achieved without violence on the Continental scale. It was in some degree through this striking absence of metropolitan political pre-eminence in nineteenth-century England that the social and economic problems engendered by the Industrial Revolution were not resolved in a revolutionary context – a legacy which, for good or ill, still exerts its influence to this day.

1

The People and
Government
of London

HE COLOSSAL growth of London is the central fact in the history
of the capital in the nineteenth century. We have already seen
that in terms of overall numbers the process was continuous,
the rate of increase per decade fluctuating in the years 1801 to 1871
between a minimum of 16 per cent and a maximum of 21 per cent.
This growth formed part of the enormous increase of population in the
whole of England and Wales, where the total number of people rose from
8,892,536 in 1801 to 22,712,266 in 1871. Whether this growth was due
primarily to an increase in the birth rate or to a decrease in the death
rate, or to a combination of both, and what were the causes of these
movements, are matters which are still being studied and discussed by
historians.[1] Prior to, and even for some years after, the Act of 1836 for
the registration of births, marriages and deaths, evidence is scanty and
often unreliable.

There were two elements in the growth of London's population –
natural increase (i.e. excess of births over deaths within the existing
community), and migration into London from outside. During the years
1856–70 the excess of births over deaths in London fluctuated between
24,000 and 41,000 per year, and between 1865 and 1870 the birth rate in
London exceeded the average rate for the whole of England. There was
therefore a very large element of natural increase in the overall growth of

[1] See G. Talbot Griffith, *Population Problems in the Age of Malthus*, 1967
edn.

London's population amounting to 254,000 in 1851–61 and to 332,000 in 1861–71.[1]

But London in the nineteenth century was by far the largest national centre of attraction for migrants and it has been calculated that in the decade 1841–51 (the first for which census evidence of birthplace is available) some 330,000 new immigrants came to the capital, representing no less than 17 per cent of the total population of London in 1841. In the 1850s and 1860s some 286,000 and 331,000 more immigrants arrived, equivalent to 12 per cent of the total population of the capital in both 1851 and 1861. Emigration out of London to other parts of England and Wales has been estimated at 116,000 and 160,000 respectively, and in addition an unknown number of emigrants left for Scotland, Ireland and abroad. London was in fact the hub of enormous and continuous movements of population.[2]

In the first half of the nineteenth century most of the migrants to London came from south and east England. Many of them came from the extra-metropolitan parts of Middlesex and Surrey, and from Kent, Essex, Hertfordshire and Berkshire. Beyond this inner belt there was, in the words of Professor Redford, 'a considerable influx from all the southern and south-eastern counties, the north-western boundary of active movement running from Gloucestershire through Warwickshire to Leicestershire. The counties to the north-west of this line sent a relatively small proportion of people to London; but the attractive force of the capital city was felt in every part of the United Kingdom.'[3] By the 1860s this pull was increasing significantly as far away as Dorset, Somerset and Devon, and many migrants were settling not in London itself but in the outer suburbs situated in Surrey and Middlesex.[4]

What this enormous upheaval meant in terms of individual human suffering can never be measured. Charles Dickens, whose parents removed from Chatham to Bayham Street, Camden Town, in 1822 when he was aged ten, always remembered his early Kentish childhood with 'deep, almost despairing nostalgia'. Years later he remembered how he had

[1] *Annual Summary of Births, Deaths and Causes of Death in London and other large Cities, published by the Registrar General*, 1871, table 7; *Thirty-Third Annual Report of the Registrar General*, 1872, table 12; H. A. Shannon, 'Migration and the Growth of London, 1841–1891', *Economic History Review*, First Series vol. 5, 1935, pp. 79–86.

[2] Shannon, pp. 79–86.

[3] Arthur Redford, *Labour Migration in England 1800–1850*, 1964 edn, pp. 184–5.

[4] D. Friedlander and R. J. Roshier, 'A Study of Internal Migration in England and Wales, Part I', *Population Studies*, vol. 19, 1965–6, pp. 239–79.

'thought in the little back garret in Bayham Street, of all I had lost in Chatham', and soon he was to be exposed to the full rigours of a migrant's struggle for existence in London when he began to work a twelve-hour day at Warren's boot-blacking factory at Hungerford Stairs, Strand, for a wage of 6s. a week.[1]

At this same time another migrant, William Lovett, later to achieve fame in the Chartist movement, was experiencing the tribulations which he subsequently recorded in his autobiography. Lovett was a native of Cornwall, where he was born in 1800, a short while after the death of his father. After being apprenticed in the decaying trade of rope-making he had resolved to go to London, and here he arrived in 1821, on board a small trading vessel, with 30s. in his pocket, 'knowing no one, nor being known to any'. He put up at a public house near the wharf where the Cornish vessels unloaded, and early the next morning he set out in search of work. But there was none to be had in the rope-yards, and after a fortnight he resolved 'to accept any kind of honest employment, rather than go home again without any'. One evening he met three fellow-Cornishmen, carpenters by trade, at his lodgings. 'They were, however, strangers to me, but coming from the same county, we soon became acquainted.' They agreed that although he was not a carpenter he should join them in their search for work, and that if they were successful he should do the roughest part of it and pay them half-a-crown each weekly in exchange for the benefit of their instruction. Two of his companions soon found jobs, but the third was not so successful. 'We generally got up at five o'clock and walked about enquiring at different shops and buildings till about nine; we then bought one penny loaf and divided it between us; then walked about again till four or five in the afternoon, when we finished our day's work with another divided loaf; and very early retired to bed footsore and hungry.' At last Lovett found work in Drury Lane, laying floors, but he became separated from his companion, whom the foreman refused to engage and from whom Lovett had hoped to learn the trade. Somehow he managed to keep the job and save 50s., but even then his troubles were not over, for he subsequently encountered the active hostility of the trade societies towards the employment of men who had not been apprenticed, and it was only after several years of struggle that he was eventually admitted to membership of the cabinet-makers' society.[2]

[1] Christopher Hibbert, *The Making of Charles Dickens*, 1967, pp. 30, 38, 52.
[2] William Lovett, *The Life and Struggles of William Lovett in his Pursuit of Bread, Knowledge and Freedom*, 1876, pp. 1–33.

Unskilled migrants did not have difficulties with the trade societies, but they were probably often near to starvation, as is shown by the case of a casual labourer at the Commercial Docks, recorded by Henry Mayhew around 1850. This man was the son of a small farmer in Dorset. 'I was left destitute, and I had to shift for myself – that's nine years ago, I think.' At first he had worked as a railway navvy, frequently shifting his quarters, but at last he had drifted to London, where he had got a job portering for a cousin, a grocer by trade.

> I've had my 15s. a week in portering in London for my cousin; but sometimes I came down to 10s., and sometimes to 5s. My cousin died suddenly, and I was very hard up after that. I made nothing at portering some weeks. I had no one to help me; and in the spring of last year – and very cold it often was – I've walked after 10, 11, or 12 at night, many a mile to lie down and sleep in any bye-place . . . I've thought of drowning myself, and of hanging myself, but somehow a penny or two came in to stop that.[1]

For the young migrant up from the country, with little money and nowhere to go to but the squalid common lodging-houses which proliferated in the most overcrowded districts of London, the moment of arrival was the most critical, and could determine the whole future course of his life.

> More of rustic innocence and honest purpose [wrote Lord Shaftesbury in 1847], both in males and females, has suffered shipwreck in these *lodging-hooses* than from any other perils that try the skill and courage of young adventurers. . . . The astonishment and perplexities of a young person on his arrival here, full of good intentions to live honestly, would be almost ludicrous, were they not the prelude to such mournful results. He alights – and is instantly directed, for the best accommodation, to Duck Lane, St Giles's, Saffron Hill, Spitalfields, or Whitechapel. He reaches the indicated region through tight avenues of glittering fish & rotten vegetables, with doorways or alleys gaping on either side – which, if they be not choked with squalid garments or sickly children, lead the eye through an almost interminable vista of filth and distress. . . . The pavement, where there is any, rugged and broken, is bespattered with dirt of every hue, ancient enough to rank with the fossils, but offensive as the most recent

[1] Henry Mayhew, *London Labour and the London Poor*, vol. III, 1861 edn, p. 310.

deposits. The houses, small, low, and mournful, present no one part, in windows, door-posts, or brickwork, that seems fitted to stand for another week – rags and hurdles stuff up the panes, and defend the passages blackened with use and by the damps arising from the un-drained and ill-ventilated recesses. Yet each one affects to smile with promise, and invites the country-bumpkin to the comfort and repose of 'Lodgings for single men'.[1]

The census of 1861 records that there were over 250,000 domestic servants in London, of whom five-sixths were women. The census books show that very many of them were migrants, and although their condition of life must have varied enormously, it sometimes possessed considerable advantages. The diary of William Tayler, the son of an Oxfordshire farmer who by 1837 had taken service as a footman in the house of a wealthy widow living in Great Cumberland Street, St Marylebone, shows that he enjoyed comfortable quarters, ample good food and a regular wage of £42 a year. He also had enough free time to excurse about London to see his friends and relations, several of whom had also migrated to the capital, and even, probably, to revisit his country home at Grafton. He at least did not suffer either hunger or unemployment, but he was not able to live with his wife (also a native of Oxfordshire) and three young children, whom he lodged nearby and to whom he could only pay surreptitious visits, often on Sundays when he was supposed to be at church. Even so he was fortunate, for he himself recorded that 'It's surpriseing to see the number of servants that are walking about the streets out of place.' According to his own entirely unreliable calculations there were at least 1,520 high-class servants out of work in May 1837, 'and if I had reckoned servants of all work – that is, tradespeoples' servants – it would of amounted to many hundreds more. I am sertain I have underrated this number . . . London and every other tound is over run with servants.'[2]

Of the estimated 330,000 new migrants who arrived in London in the decade 1841–51, some 8,000 were Scots, 26,000 came from abroad, and 46,000 from Ireland.[3] Irish migrants had been coming to London for centuries, but in the 1820s and 1830s their numbers mounted rapidly. The census of 1841 showed that the total number of Irish-born inhabi-tants of London was 82,291, or 3 per cent of the entire population of the

[1] *Quarterly Review*, vol. 82, 1847, pp. 142–52.

[2] *Diary of William Tayler, Footman, 1837*, ed. Dorothy Wise and Ann Cox-Johnson, in St Marylebone Society Publications, 1962, p. 33 and *passim*.

[3] Shannon, p. 81.

capital. In the years of the great famine, 1846–8, when the potato crop failed in Ireland, starvation drove many more abroad, and by 1851 there were some 109,000 Irish-born living in London. This was equivalent to 4·6 per cent of the whole metropolitan population, its highest recorded proportion. But the size of the Irish colonies was in reality larger still, for these figures exclude the children born in England of Irish parents. Professor Lynn Lees has calculated that if these children and other relatives are included, the total number of Irish in London in 1851 was 156,000, and in 1861, 178,000.

The principal centres of Irish settlement in London were in Holborn, St Giles in the Fields, Whitechapel and St Olave's, Southwark where migrants amounted to between 9 and 15 per cent of the total population of each district. These were the ancient centres of the Irish colonies, and here the newcomers congregated too, living together in the increasingly overcrowded courts and alleys often referred to as 'rookeries'. One of the most notorious of these rookeries, in St Giles's, within the area bounded by Bainbridge, Dyott and High Streets, was known (from the religion of its inhabitants) as the Holy Land, or sometimes as Little Dublin, and there were other concentrations nearby, in Seven Dials and off the east side of Drury Lane. In Whitechapel the main settlement was between Rosemary Lane (Royal Mint Street) and East Smithfield, and in St Olave's, to the east of London Bridge beside the river, where over half the people of one district were Irish-born in 1851. In the suburbs, too, there were a few colonies, notably in north Camberwell and north Kensington, where local conditions created a small market for unskilled labour.[1]

Of all the nineteenth-century immigrants the Irish were the most socially cohesive. Few of them had any love for England, they were nearly all Catholics, and they were generally poor, unskilled and often destitute. So they stuck together – at first, at any rate – mostly in the increasingly overcrowded central areas, where the chief markets for casual labour were to be found. They supplied much of the unskilled labour-force for the building of the railways, the docks and for the building industry in general. Others entered the 'sweated' trades, such as tailoring and shoemaking, while the more enterprising set up on their own account as street traders, where the forced necessity of living cheap enabled some of them to undercut even the Jews. Orange-selling was their particular speciality, and Henry Mayhew

[1] I am greatly indebted to Professor Lynn Lees for lending me a copy of her Harvard University thesis, 'Social Change and Social Stability among the London Irish, 1830–1870', 1969, from which this information is taken.

records an Irishwoman who took to this activity as saying that when her husband, a labourer, was out of work 'We don't live, we starruve. We git a few 'taties and sometimes a plaice. Today I've not taken 3*d*. as yet, Sir, and it's past three. . . . We live accordingly for there's 1*s*. 3*d*. a week rent. . . . I don't know what will become of us if times don't turn.' Indeed, of all the immigrants who came to London it was probably the Irish who suffered most severely, and it was only in the 1860s and 1870s, when the scale of the Irish invasion had greatly declined, that they were able to begin to assimilate themselves to their new environment. Today no trace of their original concentrations in Holborn and the East End survives.[1]

Where did the English, Welsh and Scottish immigrants settle when they came to London? Much would depend upon the trade (if any) of each individual migrant. Unskilled labourers would pick up work wherever they could, often gravitating to the centre, where the principal markets for casual labour were to be found. Specialists would naturally tend to go to the established centres of their own particular craft, which were usually in the inner areas. Furniture-makers, for instance, might go to Tottenham Court Road or Shoreditch, printers to Clerkenwell, shipwrights to Poplar and hatters to Southwark. But building operatives and the multitudes engaged in the service industries might find work in the newer suburbs. The physical growth of London was not simply a process of outward expansion. It was also accretive round the nuclei of ancient villages and hamlets, such as Hammersmith or Notting Hill Gate or Brixton, which generated an economic life of their own. Nineteenth-century Post Office Directories suggest that many suburbs originally had a much more independent occupational structure before the outward march of the urban frontier placed them in a position of greater dependence, and (with the exception of the Irish) many migrants from outside London evidently came direct to the suburbs without first settling in the inner areas. Often they seem to have settled in the outskirts nearest to their place of origin. William Tayler, for instance, had several relatives, including a butcher and a shoe-maker, at Turnham Green on the western extremity of London, where Oxfordshire migrants might naturally settle, and the census enumerators' books for 1841, 1851 and 1861 suggest many examples of such direct suburban settlement.

In addition to these migrations into London there was also incessant

[1] John A. Jackson, 'The Irish', *London, Aspects of Change*, ed. Ruth Glass, 1964, pp. 293–308; John A. Jackson, 'The Irish in East London', *East London Papers*, vol. 6, 1963, pp. 105–19.

internal movement from one part of the capital to another. Amidst the illimitably complex pattern of internal migration revealed by the census books, two social gradients, to quote Dr H. J. Dyos's phrase, may be discerned, 'one leading upwards and outwards; the other leading downwards, if not inwards'. The upward and outward movement had been going on since the seventeenth century, but with greatly increased momentum during the early nineteenth century. By the middle of the century the old central areas of London were no longer acceptable as places to live in, at least for those who had any choice in the matter. The railways, although largely excluded from the City and the West End, nevertheless generated a vast amount of additional road traffic, and as leases fell in more and more space was devoted to the warehouses and offices which were needed for the rapid expansion of the metropolitan business centre. Land values were rising, and commercial users had longer purses than private residents. Mortality rates in the central areas were high, too, particularly during the cholera epidemic of 1848–9. All this was in marked contrast with the cleaner, quieter, healthier and less congested suburbs. By the 1850s the outward movement had attained a scale large enough to produce a substantial fall in the population of the City itself, and of the Strand and Clerkenwell districts. In the 1860s this process had extended to the much wider area shown on Fig. 4, while the outer suburbs showed large increases of population, ranging upwards from 25 per cent growth to 175 per cent in Battersea, where the number of inhabitants rose from 19,600 in 1861 to 54,016 in 1871.

As the scale of the nineteenth-century outward migration mounted, the social differentiation of the various parts of London became more pronounced. This process was of course already of great antiquity, some of its chief causes being inherent in the topography of London. For at least two centuries the world of fashion had naturally gravitated to the districts adjacent to the royal court at Westminster, Whitehall or St James's. To the east the port of London and the waterside had equally naturally become a great centre for commerce and industry. Once established, social divisions of this kind tend to gather cumulative momentum, and in the early nineteenth century the building of Regent Street marked the final detachment of London's principal shopping centre from the business centre of exchange in the City, and its establishment in the West End.[1] Similarly the railway companies' desire to obtain access to the docks produced a maze of lines in east London, debasing the existing residential

[1] John R. Kellett, *The Impact of Railways on Victorian Cities*, 1969, pp. 299–300.

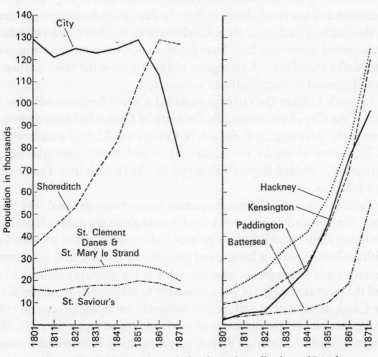

1 Growth and decline of population in various districts of London

development which they traversed; while to the west the railways were largely excluded, apart from the underground, the termini at Charing Cross, Victoria and Paddington only penetrating the peripheries of the residential districts. The westward drift of all those numerous classes able to afford to indulge their mounting social aspirations became more marked than ever, while the depopulated centre of exchange in the City formed a convenient buffer zone separating the teeming areas of the

East End from the respectable shopping and residential districts to the west.

The census books of 1851 and 1861 for a single street in Kensington, chosen at random, illustrate this process. At Royal Crescent, a range of forty-four four-storey, single-fronted houses with basements, they show a merchant and his family moving from St Pancras to Kensington, a clerk in the Court of Exchequer from Camberwell to Woolwich to Kensington, an 'owner of houses and land' from Islington to Edmonton to Kensington, a tea dealer from Bow to Kensington, and a member of the Stock Exchange from Deptford to Rotherhithe to Kensington.

In north London the railways provided a social frontier analogous to that of the City in the centre. To the north of Euston Road the approach lines to the three termini at Euston, St Pancras and King's Cross created a twilight zone of smoky marshalling yards and smelly gasworks which permanently divided Regent's Park and St Marylebone from Pentonville and Islington.

To the south of the Thames the pattern was more complicated. The river itself, the disorderly commercial development along the waterside and the low-lying land beyond, had all provided obstacles to urban growth, but with the building of new bridges and turnpike roads in the early nineteenth century rapid development soon ensued. For the railways south London had the great advantages of close proximity to both the City and the West End, and, at any rate at first, of comparatively unimpeded access to convenient termini for the discharge of goods and traffic across the river. But the area which the railways served, extending from Kent round through Surrey and Sussex to Hampshire, was comparatively small, and contained no large manufacturing towns. Fierce competition between rival companies ensued, particularly in the 1860s and 1870s, and as in so many other places much of South London was debased by a complex network of approach lines. The inner areas of Southwark, Bermondsey and north Lambeth, upon which the railways converged, suffered worst. In the mostly flat low area extending from Camberwell through Brixton to Battersea the social differentiation between one district and another was less clear-cut than to the north of the river, and only the hilly outer districts, such as Norwood, Dulwich and Sydenham, acquired a social milieu comparable with parts of Kensington or Paddington. Nevertheless some degree of social polarization between east and west, comparable to that north of the Thames, is discernible in south London, for the docks and commerce of the waterside exerted the same influence in Rotherhithe and

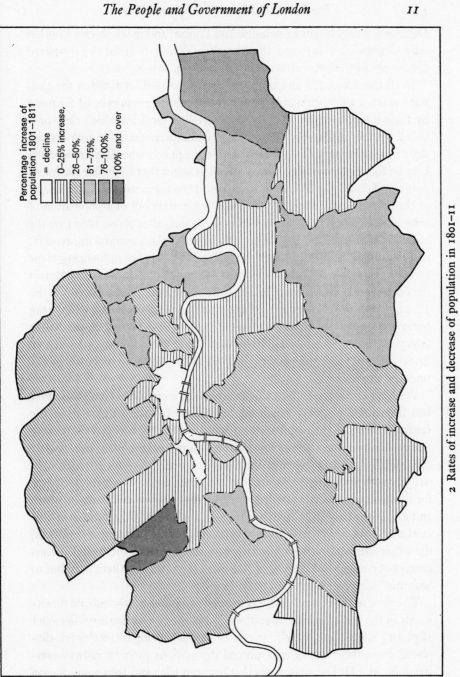

2 Rates of increase and decrease of population in 1801–11

Percentage increase of
population 1801–1811

= decline
0–25% increase,
26–50%,
51–75%,
76–100%,
100% and over

Deptford as they did in Limehouse and Poplar; and in south-east London only Greenwich village and Blackheath were able to resist the westward movement of the prosperous and the aspiring.

In all these 'upward and outward' migrations within London the railways exerted an enormous influence. This influence was exerted far more by their mere existence than by the travelling facilities which they provided. In the 1850s only some 27,000 commuters (at the most) arrived daily in London by rail, compared with the 244,000 who daily entered the City on foot or by omnibus, and Dr Kellett states that long after the introduction of cheap workmen's fares around 1860 there were still, at the end of the century, only about 250,000 rail commuters out of a population of some six and a half millions. It was only, in fact, after about 1880 that the railways, to quote Dr Kellett again, 'began to make a marked impression, in London, at any rate, upon the Victorian suburbs, influencing their social composition and their direction and rates of growth. . . .'[1] But in the central areas their impact had already made itself felt by the end of the 1860s, when they had penetrated as far as they were ever allowed into the heart of London, to Victoria (1860), Charing Cross (1864), Broad Street (1865), Cannon Street and Farringdon Street (1866), and to Liverpool Street in 1874; and this was the period of the building of much of the underground as well.

We have already seen how this tremendous incursion, allied with other less immediately apparent causes, had prompted the exodus from the centre of many of the residents who could afford to leave. But there were others who could not afford this escape. Many working men, particularly the unskilled, had to live near their work. Often they were engaged on a daily or even an hourly basis, and catching the foreman's eye might mean, for themselves and their families, the difference between hunger or worse and at least a bare subsistence. Much of the demand for labour of this kind was concentrated in or near the ancient heart of London, at the docks, the wholesale food markets, the railway termini, and all the miscellaneous centres of commercial exchange. For them there was no alternative but to 'stay put' wherever work was to be found.

The poor of the central districts were the Londoners who moved downwards in the great internal migrations of the nineteenth century. Between 1859 and 1867 alone, nearly 37,000 of the 'labouring classes' were displaced from their homes by enforced demolitions for new railway construction, and Dr Dyos estimates that between 1853 and 1901 some 76,000

---

[1] Kellett, pp. 18, 95, 365.

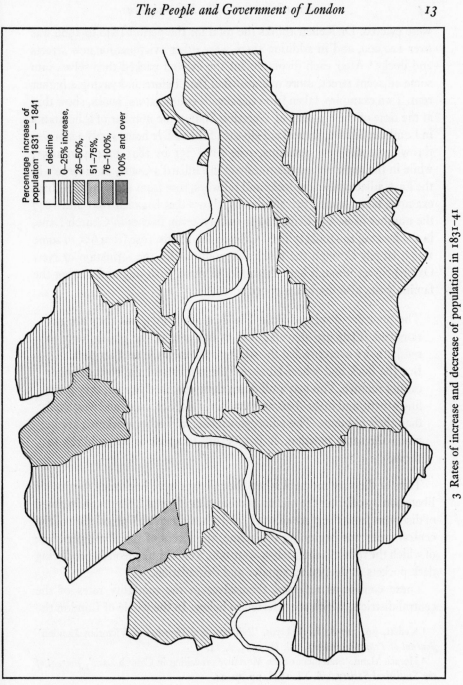

3 Rates of increase and decrease of population in 1831–41

were evicted. Dr Kellett thinks the total for the period 1840 to 1900 was over 120,000, and in addition there were other evictions for new streets and docks.[1] After each displacement the evicted packed themselves into some adjacent street, more overcrowded than before and paying a higher rent. Two examples, taken from the census enumerators' books, show that at the time of the building of Waterloo Station the number of inhabitants in Lambeth Square, a small cul-de-sac of thirty-five houses only a stone's-throw from the new terminus, rose from 351 in 1841 to 454 in 1851, while in the same period the numbers in Hilliard's Court, St George's in the East, adjacent to new docks and railways, rose from 112 to 185. A third example, taken from a private census, shows that between 1841 and 1847 the number of people living in the twenty-seven houses in Church Lane, in the heart of the rookery in St Giles in the Fields, rose from 655 to some 1,095, largely through the nearby demolitions for the formation of New Oxford Street, though here the influx of more Irish migrants during the famine years also doubtless contributed.[2]

> The poor are displaced [said *The Times* in 1861], but they are not removed. They are shovelled out of one side of the parish, only to render more overcrowded the stifling apartments in another part. . . . But the dock and wharf labourer, the porter and the costermonger cannot remove. You may pull down their wretched homes; they must find others, and make their new dwellings more crowded and wretched than their old ones. The tailor, shoemaker and other workmen are in much the same position. It is mockery to speak of the suburbs to them.[3]

Thus at the very moment when the railways were beginning to provide liberation by offering the means of domestic refuge at hitherto undreamed of distances from the place of work, and when the overall population of the central areas was beginning to decline, the forces of social compression, of which the railways themselves were one, were simultaneously producing dark pockets of deepening squalor and degradation.

These conditions reflected themselves in the mortality rates of the central districts, which are referred to below. In the whole of London the

[1] Kellett, pp. 327–8; H. J. Dyos, 'Railways and Housing in Victorian London' *Journal of Transport History*, vol. II, 1955, p. 14.

[2] Horace Mann, 'Statement of the Mortality prevailing in Church Lane', *Journal of the Statistical Society*, vol. XI, 1848, pp. 19–24.

[3] Kellett, p. 330, quoting *The Times*, 2 March 1861.

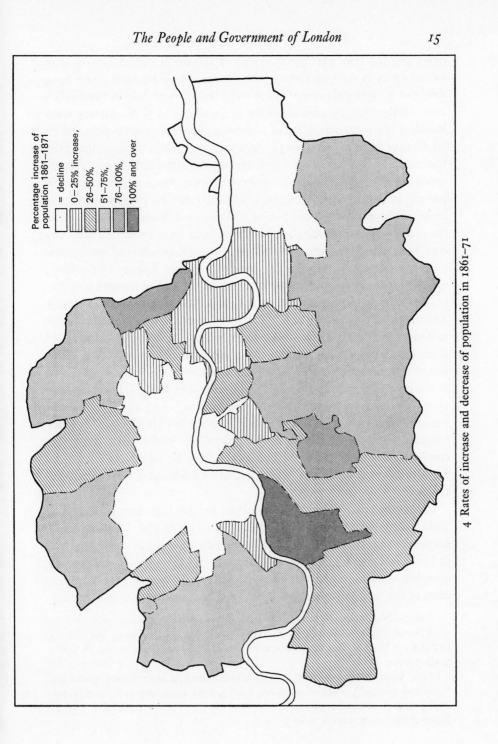

Percentage increase of
population 1861–1871

= decline
0 – 25% increase,
26–50%,
51–75%,
76–100%,
100% and over

4 Rates of increase and decrease of population in 1861–71

death rate fell from 25·2 per thousand in 1840–9 to 23·6 in 1850–9, only to rise again to 24·3 in 1860–9, the figures for all England being 22·5, 22·2 and 22·4 respectively.[1] These were the years of Edwin Chadwick's work on the sanitary administration of London and of the Metropolitan Board of Works' construction of London's sewage disposal system, which might have been expected to produce a greater fall in the mortality rate. But the figures have to be offset against the constantly rising average density of the population in the whole of London, which increased from 26 per acre in 1841 to nearly 44 in 1871. In these years, too, little progress was made in the prevention or cure of the principal causes of death. After the introduction of vaccination in 1796 deaths from smallpox, had, it is true, been greatly reduced, but there was no corresponding advance in the prevention or treatment either of consumption and diseases of the lung, which were the commonest cause of death in the mid-nineteenth century, or of measles, whooping cough and scarlatina. Recent research by Professor Thomas McKeown and Dr R. G. Record suggests that such decline of mortality as did take place may probably be attributable to generally rising standards of living, notably in the matter of diet, to improvements in personal hygiene and in the quality and quantity of the water supply, and in the case of certain diseases to a favourable shift in the relationship between the infectious agent and the human host.[2] And although the expectation of life of a male infant born in London in 1841 was only 35 years compared with 40 for the whole of England and Wales, yet at least this compared favourably with Manchester, where he might expect to live for only 25 years, or Liverpool (24), or with a dozen other large provincial towns.[3]

Contemporaries were much disturbed by the high rate of mortality among men aged over 25. At the ages of 35 to 45 the male mortality in all England was 1·346 per cent; in the Eastern counties it was only 1·035, but in London it was 1·714, a rate only exceeded in the north-western urban complex. This high rate was attributed largely to consumption and diseases of the lung brought about by the conditions of work in which many

[1] *Thirty-Third Annual Report of the Registrar General*, 1872, tables 2, 51.

[2] Thomas McKeown and R. G. Record, 'Reasons for the Decline of Mortality in England and Wales during the Nineteenth Century', *Population Studies*, vol. 16, 1962–3, pp. 94–122.

[3] D. V. Glass, 'Some Indicators between Urban and Rural Mortality in England and Wales and Scotland', *Population Studies*, vol. 17, 1963–4, pp. 263–7; P.P., 1875, vol. xviii, part II (Command 1155–1), *Supplement to the Thirty-Fifth Annual Report of the Registrar General*, p. cxxxvi, table 31.

men were employed. Much of this labour took place in the overcrowded central area, where old-established centres of small-scale industry tended to persist, and it was here that the mortality rates were highest.

In general, districts with low population densities had low mortality rates. Taking the years 1840 to 1870 as a whole, the mortality in the western and northern districts was below the average for the whole of London, while in the central and eastern districts it exceeded the rate for all London. In the southern districts it exceeded the average in the 1840s and 1850s, but fell below it in the 1860s. There were, of course, many local variations. In Hackney for instance, where in the 1860s there were still only 32 persons to the acre, the death rate was only 20 per 1,000 living compared with the average for all London of 24·3. In Lewisham, where both the density and the mortality were still extremely low, the mortality had nevertheless risen from 17 in the 1840s to 19 in the 1860s because the sanitary improvements had not kept pace with the very rapid increases of population there. But in the inner areas the position was very different. Here densities of around 200 to the acre were common, and in the parish of St Anne, Soho, there were as many as 325 in 1871. In St Giles in the Fields, where the density hovered around 220 to the acre, the annual mortality rose from 26 per 1,000 in the 1840s to 28 in the 1850s and 29 in the 1860s. In Church Lane, St Giles's, within the Irish rookery, 310 out of every 1,000 children born in the 1840s died before reaching the age of one, and of every 1,000 children aged one, 457 died before reaching the age of two. In Holborn and Finsbury, where the density was over 230 to the acre, total deaths stood at 28 per 1,000 in the 1860s, while in Whitechapel and St George's in the East, with densities of 205 and 225 respectively, mortality reached 30 per 1,000. In these and other compressed areas, life was nasty, brutish and short.[1]

The social and occupational structures of the people of London in 1851 are tabulated in the appendix on page 387. How Londoners lived and worked are subjects which will gradually emerge later in this book, but a few points may be briefly touched upon here. The tables contained in the census of 1861 reveal an extraordinary range of occupations, only to be

[1] P.P., 1875, vol. xviii, part II, p. xlv and table 56; Horace Mann, pp. 19–24; R. Price-Williams, 'The Population of London, 1801–81', *Journal of the Statistical Society*, vol. XLVIII, 1885, table C; *Thirty-Third Annual Report of the Registrar General*, 1872, table 51.

found in a capital city. There were 26,000 people engaged in the general or local government of the country, 21,000 in the defence of the country, 61,000 in the learned professions or engaged in literature, art or science, and 29,000 'persons of rank or property' – all pre-eminently metropolitan concerns.[1] In the 'domestic' class there were 23,000 in what would now be called the hotel and catering industry, plus 251,000 domestic servants. The 'commercial' class contained 59,000 engaged in buying, selling, keeping or lending money, houses or goods of various kinds, and 112,000 in the conveyance of men, animals, goods or messages. Persons engaged in art and mechanic productions covered an enormous field and numbered 207,000. Workers and dealers in textile fabrics and dress numbered 287,000, the food and drink trade and manufacture 80,000, workers and dealers in minerals 62,000, and general labourers 56,000. The largest class of all comprised 'Persons engaged in the Domestic Offices or Duties of Wives, Mothers, Mistresses of Families, Children, Relatives', 1,409,000.

There was no staple manufacturing industry in London, and the industrial structure was predominantly small in scale as well as infinitely varied in scope. Clothing, furniture-making, precision instrument-making, printing, tanning, currying, engineering and shipbuilding were all strongly represented in London, and of course building, the labour force of which numbered some 91,000 men and women in 1861. But despite the size and variety of her manufactures London was essentially a centre of service industries, and Professor Hall has recently demonstrated that in 1861 Greater London contained almost a quarter of all the workers in the whole of England and Wales engaged in the provision of services of one kind or another.[2]

Over three-fifths of all employed persons in Greater London in 1861 were concerned with supplying services for other Londoners, or for people living outside London who had personal or commercial dealings there. Some of these service workers have already been noted. Besides the civil servants and men of the two armed forces they included 13,000 lawyers, 9,000 physicians, surgeons and druggists, 3,000 ministers of religion, 6,000 artists and 18,000 teachers (of whom 14,000 were women), plus 2,000 teachers of music. Within the commercial class there were 22,000 clerks. Carriers on the roads (omnibus workers, livery stablekeepers, cabmen and carters) and carriers on the sea and rivers (including dock labourers), each with 29,000, far outnumbered railway employees, with only 8,000, and the

---

[1] These and the following figures are given to the nearest thousand.
[2] P. G. Hall, *The Industries of London since 1861*, 1962, p. 21.

messengers and porters, with 32,000, were more numerous still. There were 11,000 persons 'engaged about Animals' (mostly grooms and farriers). The food and drink trades, catering and the enormous armies of domestic servants and general labourers have already been mentioned. Not surprisingly, some 30,000 Londoners defied the census enumerators' attempts to classify them, and were entered as 'Persons of no stated Rank, Profession, or Occupation', but it is perhaps a little surprising to find that even in the great urban complex of 1861 London still numbered over 3,000 farm labourers and 32 shepherds among her inhabitants.

What administrative machinery existed for the management of this enormous concentration of population? At the opening of the nineteenth century the term 'local government' was not yet known, for government implies order, and in London order was still conspicuously absent, at least outside the City.

Within the six hundred acres of the City itself and its adjacent liberties, stretching from the Temple on the west to the Tower on the east, the ancient City Corporation reigned supreme, its existence confirmed by innumerable royal charters extending over seven centuries. It possessed wide, indefinite powers, it commanded a large and constantly increasing revenue, and in addition to possessing every known franchise and immunity within its own territories its jurisdiction extended into the surrounding counties as well. The Corporation had purchased the Shrievalty of Middlesex; it had peculiar rights in the Bailiwick of Southwark; it had a monopoly of markets (though often infringed) within a radius of seven miles; it collected coal duties over a radius of twelve miles, and it even governed the river Thames for some eighty miles from Staines to the Medway, including the whole port of London.

This extraordinary power, allied to the great wealth of many of its citizens, gave the City of London its unique independence. Although it had for centuries been the capital city of the kingdom, neither the royal palaces nor the offices of government nor the Houses of Parliament nor the royal courts of justice had ever been situated within its boundaries. Hence the centuries of bargaining between the City and the Court, privileges and immunities being constantly exchanged for money and support, until at last, with the Revolution of 1688, nothing more was left for the City to acquire. Thereafter the government ceased to attempt to intervene in the City's affairs, while the City, now replete with privilege, adopted a posture of strict defence of its established rights.

The Lord Mayor presided over the bafflingly complex internal organization of the Corporation. Beneath him stood the two Sheriffs and the four principal Courts – the Court of Aldermen, twenty-six strong and elected for life; the Court of Common Council, to which, in addition to the Aldermen, some two hundred common citizens were annually elected by the freemen ratepayers of the wards; the Court of Common Hall, comprising the Mayor, Aldermen and some twelve thousand liverymen of the City Companies; and lastly the Court of Wardmote, the foundation of the whole structure, and held separately in each of the twenty-six wards. Every ratepayer, whether a freeman of the City or not, could attend the Wardmote, and here they elected the ward officers (clerks, beadles and constables), the Common Councillors of the ward, and whenever a vacancy occurred, the Alderman of the ward.[1]

The Lord Mayor and the two Sheriffs were elected annually by the Court of Common Hall from the twenty-six members of the Court of Aldermen. The Aldermen were almost always rich and elderly, a fortune of twenty or thirty thousand pounds being deemed the minimum requisite for membership. They acted as Justices of the Peace for the City, the four Members of Parliament were almost always chosen from their ranks, and at their weekly meetings they discharged a varied assortment of business. The Court of Aldermen was, in theory, the supreme executive of the City, but by the early nineteenth century its ancient pre-eminence was being increasingly challenged by the Court of Common Council. Most of the Councilmen were retail tradesmen or ambitious attorneys, and in the second half of the eighteenth century they had gradually taken over most of the legislative and administrative business of the Corporation. This process had often brought them into conflict with the Aldermen, particularly in political affairs, where the Councilmen held more radical views, but by the 1830s the Court of Common Council had become, in the words of Sidney and Beatrice Webb, 'the supreme organ of administration, itself wielding the whole power of government, and reducing the Lord Mayor and Aldermen to a mere magistracy'.[2]

The Court of Common Council was in its turn frequently criticized and denounced by the third of the four principal Courts, the Court of Common Hall, of which all the City liverymen were members. It was in this large unwieldy body that the City's Members of Parliament as well as the Lord

[1] S. and B. Webb, *English Local Government: The Manor and the Borough*, 1908, pp. 569–79.

[2] Webb, pp. 637, 658–68.

Mayor and Sheriffs were chosen, and through this concern with national affairs the Court of Common Hall regarded itself as the political spokesman of the City. In the early nineteenth century its resolutions and addresses were almost always critical of the government (except during the struggle for the Reform Bill of 1832) but they exercised little influence in Parliament, and the Common Hall's attempts to control the Court of Common Council were no more successful.[1]

Separate from the Corporation, but nevertheless very closely associated with it, were the eighty-nine City Companies or Gilds, most of them very ancient. Admission to the freedom of the Companies was by birth, apprenticeship or purchase, no active connection with the craft or 'mystery' of the Company being required, and any freeman of a Company could acquire the freedom of the City on payment of a further fee; except for honorary freedoms conferred as a mark of distinction this was indeed the way in which all freemen of the City were recruited. Admission to the livery of a Company, the next stage in the hierarchy, was granted to such freemen as a Company might determine, on payment of yet another fee, but even then a liveryman had no share in the administration of his Company, which was entirely managed by the Court of the Company, a close body recruited by co-option from the livery. Many of the Companies were enormously wealthy, with increasingly valuable freehold properties within the City itself or in the suburbs. They conducted their affairs in complete secrecy, and in 1876 it could still be said of them that 'their real funds, which ought to have been expended under founders' wills, have been spent in dining festivities, making merry, sometimes in donations to charities or public objects, in paying large salaries, and dividing surplus property amongst members of the mystery'. The companies' 'magnificent entertainments are so many social bribes to secure friends to cover their mismanagement and abuse of the great trusts in their hands'. It was, indeed, in substantial measure through the Companies' numerous liverymen, and the lavish hospitality which they dispensed, that the City Corporation was able to exercise its all-pervasive political influence throughout the nineteenth century.[2]

The City of London was, in fact, in the Webbs' phrase, a democracy of ratepayers, a tightly knit community in which every resident householder could take an active part in municipal administration. Even in the Court of Wardmote, the oldest of the four principal Courts, but which had now

[1] Webb, *The Manor and the Borough*, pp. 616–25.
[2] Webb, pp. 579–80; 'The Government of London', *Journal of the Statistical Society*, vol. XLIX, 1876, pp. 101–3.

lost most of its ancient importance, the twenty-six wards were subdivided into 169 precincts, each with its own offices to be annually filled. There were constant meetings, mostly to transact the most pettifogging business, constant door-step gossiping and constant convivialities. Every elected representative must have known personally almost every member of his electorate. The shopkeepers and tradesmen who formed the bulk of the City's residents were both proud of and completely content with these ancient arrangements. There was no demand for municipal reform.

Yet there was another side to this happy scene of municipal democracy. There were the sewers, or rather the almost total lack of them, and the hundred and fifty slaughterhouses, many of them underground. There was Smithfield cattle market, a vile nuisance which the Corporation for years refused to remove or reform, and the City's prisons, among the worst in the whole kingdom. It might be argued that all these things were the City's own affair, but there were others too, equally discreditable, which had ramifications far beyond the sacred square mile of the City's boundaries – the repeated opposition to the establishment of new markets in the new suburbs, the neglect of the conservancy of the river, the failure to protect property in the Port of London, and, even more surprising for such a commercially minded community, the lack of any attempt before the end of the eighteenth century to enlarge the dock accommodation in the Port. The City shopkeepers were, in fact, often selfish and petty-minded. 'Counter transactions in small coins,' said a critic in 1854, 'have no tendency to give a man an enlarged view, or habits of viewing in a large sense any interests which he may be delegated to promote.'[1] It was through this lack of 'an enlarged view' that the City had ever since the seventeenth century refused to accept any responsibility for the new suburbs which were growing up all around it. By 1811 only about one-tenth of the people of the metropolis lived in the tight little municipal island in the centre. For all that the City cared, the remaining nine-tenths could be left to sink or swim as best they could.

These nine-tenths consisted in 1811 of just over one million people. The built-up area had by now extended, in varying degrees of completeness, into over ninety administrative parishes or precincts situated outside the City and within the three counties of Middlesex, Surrey and Kent. The million inhabitants of these suburbs amounted to about one-tenth of the whole population of England and Wales.

Until 1855, when the population of this vast amorphous area had

[1] Quoted in Webb, *The Manor and the Borough*, p. 692.

increased to well over two million, there was no administrative authority (except, after 1829, that of the Metropolitan Police) concerned with the whole district. At county level there were three separate benches of magistrates for Middlesex, Surrey and Kent, as well as that of Westminster, while at parish or precinct level there was every conceivable variety of local assembly, ranging from such ancient oddities as the tiny Liberty of the Old Artillery Ground near Bishopsgate, with a population of 1,428 in 1801, to the great and powerful select vestry of St George's, Hanover Square, which managed the affairs of a parish with over 60,000 inhabitants. All these local assemblies, regardless of differences in size, wealth or constitution, discharged substantially the same functions.

The Justices of the Peace did, it is true, exercise some degree of supervision over the vestries in such matters as the appointment of the unpaid parish constables, overseers of the poor and surveyors of the highways, and the inspection of the parish accounts. But by the beginning of the nineteenth century this supervision had become more nominal than real, particularly in the larger parishes, where much of the daily work was now done by paid officials. In the eighteenth century many of the Justices had been notorious for their 'trading' activities, and although after about 1780 there appears to have been some improvement in the quality of the membership of the bench, it was still possible for a man like Joseph Merceron, for many years the 'boss' of Bethnal Green, to become a Justice, and during William Mainwaring's chairmanship of the Middlesex Quarter Sessions from 1781 to 1816 widespread corruption was prevalent.

In practice the parishes were therefore left largely to their own devices in the discharge of their affairs, the most important of which were the paving, lighting and cleansing of the streets, the relief of the poor and the maintenance of the peace. The diverse constitutions of the parish vestries reflected this absence of supervision. Many of them were still, at the beginning of the nineteenth century, of the 'open' variety, where all male ratepayers were entitled to attend. These open vestries usually survived in the little parishes within the City, and in the still largely rural out-parishes such as St Pancras, where the volume of business remained small. But in the great new suburbs 'close' or 'select' vestries were more common, and here membership and power were restricted to a group of from thirty to a hundred of the 'principal inhabitants', who filled vacancies by nomination. Some of these close vestries owed their existence to immemorial custom, or to a bishop's faculty issued when the parish had been established, or to an Act of Parliament. By 1800 about a quarter of the two hundred metropolitan parishes had select vestries. Many of them were in the more fashionable western parts of London, such as St Marylebone and the Westminster parishes of St Paul's, Covent Garden, St James's and St George's, Hanover Square, where the exclusion of almost all the inhabitants from participation in parochial affairs was in marked contrast with the democratic franchise of the Westminster parliamentary constituency.

Yet the situation was in reality even more confused, for by the early nineteenth century the majority of these metropolitan local authorities had obtained their own individual Acts of Parliament and were acting under the various powers which these Acts had conferred. In 1759, for instance, the trustees of the Liberty of Norton Folgate, another tiny enclave near Bishopsgate, had obtained an Act for the better lighting, cleansing and watching of the extraparochial part of the Liberty. In 1778 a paving Act had been obtained, but the fifty commissioners nominated in this Act were quite separate from the trustees under the Act of 1759. The latter, in 1810, found it necessary to promote a second lighting Act, to which they tacked on powers for the supervision of the workhouse. Drainage, of course, was outside the purview of either the trustees or the commissioners, and a mercer living in the liberty in 1805 recalled how water used to stand three or four feet deep in the cellars of the houses, so that 'the Servants used to be obliged to punt themselves along in a washingtub, from the Cellar stairs to the Beer Barrels, to draw Beer daily for the Use of the Family'.[1]

Norton Folgate was not at all unusual in having two separate authorities to manage its affairs. In the rapidly growing parish of Lambeth, where the open vestry obtained a local Act in 1810, there were also nine separate local trusts for the lighting of different parts of the parish, while the affairs of St Mary, Newington, where there was also an open vestry, were in the hands of thirteen trusts. Sometimes the area of jurisdiction of trusts of this kind was coterminous with that of the parish in which they were situated; sometimes, as in the case of Southwark, it extended over several parishes, but more usually it extended over only part of a parish – a hamlet, perhaps, or a single estate or a square. Within the parish of St James's, Westminster, the aristocratic inhabitants of St James's Square had their own Act for the embellishment of the garden of the square. They were exempt from payment of the parish scavenging rate; instead they levied a private rate of their own and even employed their own watchmen. Naturally, the parish vestry disliked this 'contracting out' from their authority and, in

[1] *Survey of London*, vol. xxvii, 1957, pp. 18–19.

general, the more powerful and efficient the vestry, the fewer the number
of local statutory trusts with special privileges. In the well-run parish of
St Marylebone the select vestry was for many years successful in resisting
all attempts to establish any privileged statutory position within its bounds,
and was only defeated at last by the Crown itself at the time of the formation of Regent Street and Regent's Park. But at the opposite extreme stood
the neighbouring parish of St Pancras, whose extraordinary administrative arrangements provide the most startling example of what *laissez-faire*
in the suburbs of London could produce in the early nineteenth century.

During the last twenty-five years of the eighteenth century the population of St Pancras had leaped from some 600 to 31,779, and by 1821 to
71,838, of whom Charles Dickens's family, precariously solvent and living
in Somers Town for a year or two after leaving the Marshalsea prison, was
perhaps a typical example. The parish vestry was of the open variety
commonly found in rural areas, but now several hundred and sometimes
even a thousand angry and vociferous ratepayers would crowd into the
meetings held in the little medieval parish church which still stands beside
the railway lines outside St Pancras Station. There was no committee of
management, no paid staff and no local Act of Parliament. Everything was
decided, or left undecided, in public meetings, the results of elections to
the parish offices of churchwarden and overseer were frequently contested,
and in one year there were even two rival sets of churchwardens, elected by
rival vestry meetings. Everywhere inefficiency and recrimination prevailed.
But at last, in about 1802, a self-appointed reformer, Thomas Rhodes,
cowkeeper, brickmaker and great-uncle of Cecil Rhodes, appeared, determined to abolish the open vestry. He persuaded the vestry, already sus-
picious of his intentions, to agree to a parliamentary Bill which would
permit the appointment of salaried officials. But then he surreptitiously
added clauses which would have excluded the open vestry from any part in
the relief of the poor, and substituted a Committee of Guardians, 'elected
in perpetuity and self-continuing'. The vestry discovered Mr Rhodes's
machinations and the Bill was withdrawn. But Mr Rhodes then produced a
report on the scandalous condition of the workhouse – the paupers were
half-naked, although three thousand yards of linen had been bought for
their use, £200 had been spent in one year on beer for the nurses who sat up
with the sick, and at least one-third of the whole of the expenditure at the
workhouse was either fraudulent or illegal. So the vestry had to agree to a
Bill, passed in 1804, authorizing the appointment of elected Directors of
the Poor. But the Directors, once established, immediately promoted

another Bill by which they were to remain in office for life and with power to co-opt their successors. The furious fulminations of the vestry were useless: the Bill passed, and for some years the Directors relieved the poor in splendid independence and at ever rising cost. At last the vestry roused itself again and promoted a Bill for the abolition of the Directors. But the Directors replied with a Bill to extinguish the open vestry, and as open vestries were not favourably regarded by Parliament at this time, it was Mr Rhodes and the Directors who proved successful. In 1819 an Act was passed abolishing the open vestry and conferring all the powers of both the vestry and the Directors upon a select vestry of persons named in the Act and with power to fill vacancies by co-option.[1]

Meanwhile the population of the parish was continuing to grow by leaps and bounds – 103,548 by 1831, 129,763 by 1841 – new estates were being laid out – the Foundling, the Calthorpe, the Doughty, the Southampton and the Bedford, to name only a few – and in the absence of any effective parochial authority, local Acts of Parliament proliferated in corresponding numbers. Eventually there were no fewer than eighteen separate paving trusts within the four square miles of this one parish.

In the East End of London these conditions were matched, in Bethnal Green, by the rule of Joseph Merceron, originally a clerk to a lottery office-keeper, who for over thirty years corrupted and dominated the affairs of the parish. He became chairman of the watch board and the paving trust, treasurer of the parish funds, a commissioner of sewers and even a Justice of the Peace. By controlling the beer shops (of which he owned eleven and received rent from eleven more) he was always able to assemble several hundred weavers and artisans at the meetings of the open vestry, where he could 'instigate his creatures to riot and clamour, even within the walls of the church'. Whomever he nominated the vestry was sure to approve, for 'the will and opinion of the major part of the parish were subservient to Mr Merceron's views and interests for a long course of years'. But in 1809 his supremacy was challenged by a new rector. Merceron was prosecuted for fraudulently appropriating £925 of parish money to his own use, and corruptly licensing his turbulent public houses; he was convicted, fined and sentenced to eighteen months' imprisonment. But when he emerged from gaol he reasserted his old power. His son-in-law was elected vestry clerk, and he himself was re-elected a commissioner of the Court of Requests. With old age perhaps advancing he seems not to have

---

[1] S. and B. Webb, *English Local Government: The Parish and the County*, 1906, pp. 207–11.

opposed the establishment in 1823 of a quasi-select vestry, of which he and another Merceron, probably his son, soon became the leading members. He became treasurer of the watch board and the paving trust, of which he had previously been chairman, and when in 1830 another parliamentary committee investigated the affairs of Bethnal Green, all the old accusations of secrecy, jobbery and corruption were made once again. In the anarchical conditions of early nineteenth-century suburban London the Mercerons proved indestructible, and their grip on the affairs of Bethnal Green was not finally relaxed until their death.[1]

In addition to the vestries and the statutory trusts there were also the turnpike trusts. They too had been established by local Acts of Parliament, either for the formation of new trunk roads, like the Marylebone Road, or more commonly for the upkeep of existing roads which the local vestries had proved incompetent to maintain. Oxford Street, for instance, until 1721 the joint responsibility of the four bordering parishes, had been handed over to a trust which repaired the surface, but, typically, the cleansing of the surface remained the duty of the parishes. Each Turnpike Act nominated a hundred or more trustees, with power to co-opt to fill vacancies, and the cost of their works was met by tolls paid by the users of the road. By the early nineteenth century there were over fifty such trusts in the vicinity of London.[2]

Then, too, there were the metropolitan commissioners of sewers, eight in number. Until the early nineteenth century, when it acquired its malodorous significance, the word sewer meant a channel for the removal of surface water, and this was the sole function of all the commissioners of sewers, who were appointed by the Crown under the Sewers Act of 1532. In the new suburbs of London the survival of these archaic bodies was to prove a disaster for public health in the mid-nineteenth century. The Westminster commission, in 1834, had some 250 members, but the average attendance at meetings was only eleven. 'The gentlemen come in and walk out again: they are not men of business; perhaps they do not stop two minutes.' For some thirty years this commission had been controlled by two families of contractors to whom almost all the contracts for sewers were given. On average some £30,000, raised by the sewers rate, were spent each year, but until 1817 the Westminster commission did not even possess a plan of its own drains. Until about 1811 the connection of

---

[1] Webb, *The Parish and the County*, pp. 79–90.
[2] F. H. W. Sheppard, *Local Government in St Marylebone 1688–1835. A Study of the Vestry and the Turnpike Trusts*, 1958, pp. 59, 217.

bog-houses or houses of office with the street sewers was in theory forbidden in London, and sometimes actually prevented. Even in a large part of the City, including Cheapside, there was in 1844 no underground drainage; 'its nightsoil is kept in poisonous pools, of which the inhabitants pump out the contents into the open channels of the street in the night, or have them removed by nightmen'. In the same year it could still be said that 'it is not to the present day a recognized purpose of several of the principal Boards of Commissioners to protect the public health, by the *covering* of the sewers, from the noisome effluvia of a city's drainage, but only to effect the mechanical transmission of the superfluous fluids to the Thames.'[1]

This parlous state of public administration in London at the beginning of the nineteenth century arose from the indifference displayed during the whole of the eighteenth century by King and Parliament towards the actions of the various local governing authorities throughout the country. So the obligation of each individual to render unpaid service to the community – the foundation of English local administration from time immemorial – survived, and indeed in rural areas was still perhaps adequate to the needs of the times. But in London there were many parishes like St Pancras which could no longer depend for the paving, lighting and cleansing of their streets, for the relief of the poor, and above all for the maintenance of order upon the unpaid, amateur, compulsory labours of their surveyors of the highways, overseers of the poor and constables. The local Act of Parliament provided a temporary remedy for situations of this kind, and by the end of the eighteenth century the obligation of personal service had in general been superseded in the suburbs of London by the obligation to pay a rate from which contractors or salaried staff could be employed to perform the old irksome tasks. The condition of many parishes had been greatly improved in consequence, but this new system of local administration had equally severe limitations. In the first half of the nineteenth century it was to prove quite inadequate to deal with the problems of an urban community between one and two million strong. There were the problems of public health, ignored in all eighteenth-century local Acts, and the endless but now more insistent problem of pauperism. There was the constitutional problem of finding a compromise between the rowdy direct democracy of the open vestries and the self-perpetuating

[1] *Journal of the Statistical Society of London*, vol. VII 1844, pp. 157–8, 164; S. and B. Webb *English Local Government: Statutory Authorities for Special Purposes*, 1922, pp. 81–2, 105 n.

exclusiveness of the select vestries, for except in the City the idea of representation by election had not yet been applied to local government in London. These problems gave rise to another one – how to reconcile the gradually mounting intervention of the State in local affairs with the pretensions of the existing local authorities, so long accustomed to independence and therefore so resentful of any interference? And lastly, and perhaps most important of all, there was the problem of law and order.

Yet despite this formidable agenda there was no demand for municipal reform in London until the mid-1820s. Nobody quite knew how to deal with the suburbs, their unincorporated and unco-ordinated urban vastness presenting a unique and baffling problem in the life of the nation. Few people at Westminster cared much about their difficulties anyway, and fewer still in Whitehall, and so such trifling improvements in their administration as were made depended upon the equally unco-ordinated tinkerings of private Members of Parliament.

First there was Michael Angelo Taylor, son of the distinguished architect Sir Robert Taylor, to whom, presumably, he owed his ambitious combination of Christian names. After sitting in the House of Commons for thirty years without ever holding any office, Michael Angelo Taylor began to draw attention to the defective paving and lighting of the streets of London. For three years he laboured to establish one board of paving commissioners for all the streets within five miles of the centre of London. The vestries at once raised a tremendous hubbub, of course, in which every sort of well-founded objection and ill-founded prejudice was levelled at Michael Angelo's proposal, and at last in 1817 he had to be satisfied with a much less ambitious Act by which the existing laws were consolidated; no overall control was imposed on the activities of the multifarious boards and vestries.[1]

Next came William Sturges Bourne, a knowledgeable barrister, unimpressive in manner and ineffective in speech. He, too, had sat in the Commons for many years before becoming chairman, in 1817, of a Select Committee on the Poor Laws. As a member of the aristocratic select vestry of St George's, Hanover Square, he had been much concerned at the way in which in neighbouring disorderly open vestries, such as that of St Pancras, the many small ratepayers could outvote the large property owners. Parliament at the time of Peterloo did not view these primitive parochial democracies with favour either, and he was therefore successful in the promotion of two Acts, one of which restored by a system of plural

[1] Sheppard, pp. 185–7.

D

voting in open vestries the influence hitherto enjoyed by the substantial men of property. This Act applied compulsorily to all vestries outside the City of London and Southwark which were not already governed by their own Acts or peculiar customs. Most of the suburban parishes did already possess such local Acts, and were therefore unaffected, while in those parishes where it did apply the Act often led to disorderly polls in which the complicated graduated scale of voting always proved cumbrous and often unworkable.

Sturges Bourne's second Act, passed in 1819, permitted any parish to elect a committee annually to manage the relief of the poor. It was quickly adopted in several metropolitan parishes with open vestries like Clapham, Lambeth and Rotherhithe, where at first it proved very successful in reducing the amount spent on poor relief. But at best it was only a make-shift arrangement; the parish committees could only deal with poor relief, they could be and after a while often were abolished by the open vestries which had appointed them, and above all the committees were commonly (and quite wrongly) referred to as select vestries – a term which within a few years was to be widely regarded in London as synonymous with ex-clusiveness, secrecy and corruption.

Of much greater lasting importance than Sturges Bourne's efforts was the Act promoted in 1826 by Lord Lowther for the amalgamation of all the turnpike trusts in the vicinity of London to the north of the Thames. Fourteen separate trusts were superseded by a new body of Commissioners appointed by the government, over which Lord Lowther himself presided for thirty years. A staff of salaried officers headed by James McAdam, the son of the inventor of the macadamized road, was appointed, many toll gates were removed, the tolls were reduced, and in a short while the general standard of the roads was greatly improved.[1]

After the dangerous post-war years of crisis, cautious administrative re-forms of this kind had at last become possible, and by 1829 it was even possible for John Cam Hobhouse, one of the radical Members for West-minster, to mount a frontal assault on the secrecy and exclusiveness of the close vestries. The agitation of which he made himself the parliamentary spokesman coincided with the Reform Bill crisis of 1830–2, and will be discussed later in this chapter. But 1829 was also the year of the establish-ment of the Metropolitan Police, and it is now necessary to look back at the antecedents of this event.

In 1828, the year before the new police first went out on the beat,

[1] Sheppard, pp. 217, 223–5.

London was protected by some 5,500 men, of whom about nine-tenths were under the control of the City authorities and the parish vestries. In the City there was a small 'general police' of some fifty men under the immediate superintendence of the Lord Mayor and Aldermen, but there were also over a thousand beadles, constables and watchmen distributed among the twenty-six wards, so that each ward had virtually 'an independent establishment of its own'. In the suburbs there were the unpaid parish constables and the paid beadles and watchmen, some 3,500 in all, directed by over seventy vestries and trusts.[1] The constables were chosen by the Justices; they were usually petty tradesmen, and they gave their reluctant service for one year, unless they were able to hire a substitute. In times of emergency 'special constables' were often sworn in to supplement the parish constables. The beadles, decked out, frequently, in an impressive gold-laced livery, were the masters of the parish watch-house, from which they sallied forth by day to drive away beggars, prostitutes and wandering animals. But in the hours of daylight Londoners were to a large extent expected to protect themselves, and it was only at night that the watchmen, far more numerous than the beadles, came on duty. They were badly paid; often they were old or corrupt, and many of them slept or wenched in the wooden watch-boxes which were provided on each beat. They were a totally inadequate force for the prevention of crime; there was no uniformity of organization, and concerted action of any kind between the different parish vestries was quite impossible.

Government participation in the routine maintenance of order in London – as distinct from the use of troops in times of emergency – dated back to the early 1750s, when Henry Fielding, one of the Justices for Middlesex, had obtained a small grant of public money which had enabled him to recruit and pay half-a-dozen 'thief-takers' attached to his office in Bow Street. After the Gordon Riots of 1780 William Pitt had in 1785 introduced a Bill which in many respects foreshadowed Sir Robert Peel's Act of 1829. But his proposals had evoked widespread opposition, particularly from the City Fathers, who had claimed that they would involve 'the entire subversion of the Chartered Rights of the greatest City in the World', and the Bill had been abandoned. In 1792, however, an Act sponsored by a private Member of Parliament had established seven new Public Offices on the lines started by Fielding at the Bow Street Office. At each office there were to be three salaried or stipendiary Justices of the Peace,

[1] Leon Radzinowicz, *A History of English Criminal Law and its Administration from 1750*, vol. II, 1956, pp. 176–81.

with six paid constables acting under their orders. Even this measure, from which the City was excluded in order to avoid its inevitable opposition, was regarded as merely a temporary experiment; it was only enacted for three years, and was not made permanent until 1812.

In 1798 Patrick Colquhoun, the most able of the new stipendiary magistrates and author of a comprehensive *Treatise on the Police of the Metropolis*, was able to put some of the theories which he had there advanced into practice by the formation of a Marine Police Establishment for the protection of property in the Port of London. Part of the cost was paid for out of public funds and part by the West India merchants, who had been the chief sufferers in this paradise for pilferers.[1]

The efficient policing of the river was achieved because, firstly, crime had reached such a scale as almost to threaten the commercial prosperity of the nation (then at war), and, secondly, because there existed, in the West India merchants, a powerful interest capable of exerting pressure on the government to act and capable, also, of paying from their own pockets for most of the cost of the action which they advocated. Thirdly, too, it may be conjectured that the government proved unusually sympathetic because crime in the port was reducing its own revenues from the customs dues. But elsewhere in London none of these conditions prevailed – even the scale of crime had become so familiar as to excite no undue alarm – and consequently the degree of government intervention remained minimal.

In 1828 the government's contribution to the protection of London was still based on the Public or Police Offices, now nine in number, at each of which there were up to twelve paid constables acting under the orders of the stipendiary magistrates. At Bow Street the eight constables had evolved into the famous Runners, the crack force of the whole metropolis, whose members ranged all over the country and often achieved spectacular successes. They were increasingly employed by private individuals, and were well paid for their services – one Runner, John Sayer, left £30,000 – but their day-to-day duties were neglected in consequence. 'Why, Sir Richard Birnie,' exclaimed John Townsend (another successful Runner, who left £20,000) on being ordered by the chief magistrate at Bow Street to execute a routine warrant, 'I beg leave to tell you that I think it would lessen me a great deal if I were to execute a warrant upon a barber . . . after forty-six years service, during which period I have had the honour of taking Earls, Marquises, and Dukes. No, no, Sir Richard . . . don't let

[1] Radzinowicz, vol. II, p. 365.

me be degraded by executing the warrant.'[1] The Bow Street Runners more nearly resembled a disreputable private detective agency than a branch of a modern police force; they accepted rewards, they often kept information about a crime to themselves in the hope of turning it to their own advantage later, and their honesty was often suspect. Much more valuable were the various patrols attached to Bow Street, consisting of some 270 men, some mounted, whose main task was to guard the principal roads leading out of London up to a distance of some twenty miles.

The total number of constables paid for out of government funds in 1828 was 427, including 86 at the Thames Police Office, and the cost was about £35,000. All such other protection as London enjoyed was provided by the City and the parishes, by the private subscriptions of individual inhabitants who employed their own watchmen, or in the port, by the subscription of the new dock companies.[2]

This protection did not amount to much, particularly in the eastern parts of London. In the 1820s the tradesmen of Bethnal Green were so terrorized by a band of thieves that they frequently had to put up their shutters to protect their shops. This gang, sometimes several hundred in number, lurked by day in the abandoned brickfields, muddy and otherwise deserted, where they cooked their stolen food, and from which they would emerge to ambush the huge herds of cattle being driven along the main highways to Smithfield Market. The drover would be knocked on the head and the fiercest beast removed to their lair until night-fall. Then they would sally out through the unlit darkening streets, shouting and hallooing and driving the terrified bullock before them. Noise, confusion and alarm would ensue, and anyone whom they met would be assaulted and robbed. Within the space of a single fortnight in 1828 over fifty people were attacked, and one of the gang had been seen with 'nearly half-a-hat-full of watches'. Similarly in Spitalfields, a few years earlier, a crowd of two to three hundred men, motivated, probably, by economic grievance or personal grudge, had driven a bullock into a silk warehouse which contained goods worth over £100,000. The proprietor's own men had poured scalding water over the attackers; then they fired blanks, and eventually ball shot. 'A desperate contest' had ensued, which would have ended in favour of the attackers had not a posse of constables from the nearest Public Office arrived. Seven workmen were severely wounded, while 'the poor bullock was driven in so

[1] Quoted in Radzinowicz, vol. II, p. 268.
[2] Radzinowicz, vol. II, pp. 177 n., 189 n., 511–28.

desperate a manner, and goaded so cruelly, that it ran mad; and after having tossed several peaceable persons, fell down dead'.[1]

Conditions of this kind were tolerated because all Englishmen were convinced that they possessed a birthright of personal freedom from arbitrary authority of all kinds, and that they must maintain this birthright whenever it was attacked. Freedom of speech, freedom from arbitrary arrest, and the right to trial by jury would all be threatened by a government system of police, and this is why all governments from the 1750s onwards preferred to evade the problem. Committees of the House of Commons were repeatedly appointed to investigate 'the State of the Nightly Watch in London'. They repeatedly reported, as for instance in 1812, that the 'mode of watching [is] generally bad, and the men employed, both in number and ability, wholly inefficient for the purpose', and 'neither the Magistracy or the Government have at present any connection whatever with the state of the Watch, and no control or superintendence over it'. Yet no action was taken, even after the notorious Ratcliffe Highway murders of 1811, which Robert Southey described as 'events which, by the depth and expansion of horror attending them, had risen to the dignity of a *national* interest'. Tories, Whigs and Radicals in Parliament, and even the unrepresented common people outside Parliament, were all united in at least one conviction, that an improved police would subvert their ancient liberties. Even the very word 'police' was of foreign origin, hardly known in England before the middle of the eighteenth century.

When Robert Peel (not yet a baronet) became Home Secretary in 1822 – the office which he held, with one short break, until 1830 – London had in the past seven years experienced numerous political as well as criminal disorders, and the use of troops to restore the peace had become almost a matter of routine. But what might happen if the troops were to mutiny, as had nearly happened in a battalion of the Guards? The Duke of Wellington, in 1820, thought that 'either a police in London or a military corps which should be of a different description from the regular military force' was needed, and this, therefore, was one of the first questions to which Peel turned in 1822, when he successfully moved for the establishment of another select committee on the police of the metropolis.[2]

This Committee's report embodied the last, classic statement of the national antipathy for the whole idea of police. 'It is difficult to reconcile an effective system of police' – so ran the report – 'with that perfect

---

[1] *Annual Register*, 1818, p. 266; 1826, pp. 140–1.
[2] Norman Gash, *Mr Secretary Peel*, 1961, pp. 312–13.

freedom of action and exemption from interference, which are the great privileges and blessings of society in this country; and Your Committee think that the forfeiture of such advantages would be too great a sacrifice for improvements in police, or facilities in detection of crime, however desirable in themselves if abstractedly considered.'[1] Yet within seven years Peel was able to dissipate these ancient fears and prejudices, at any rate within the walls of Parliament. There was as yet no important political group which championed police reform, but criminal law reform had already been supported with some success for a number of years by a few M.P.s, led by Sir Samuel Romilly. Baffled over the police, Peel turned to this complementary problem, and by a dozen new Acts he consolidated, simplified and above all mitigated a mass of obsolete and now unenforceable legislation. Parliament became accustomed to accepting the measures of cautious reform which he sponsored, and in 1828 he was able to secure the appointment of yet another committee to look at 'the State of the Police of the Metropolis'.

By this time he had realized that to be successful he must exclude the City, with which, so he had privately confessed in 1826, he would 'be afraid to meddle'.[2] This, perhaps, was why the committee's principal conclusion, that 'the time is now come when determined efforts ought to be made to effect a decisive change', met with hardly any opposition. When Peel introduced his Metropolitan Police Bill in April 1829, Parliament was engrossed in the Catholic Emancipation question. The Bill was debated briefly, even perfunctorily, and there were only two petitions against it – one from the parish of Hackney, where the watch was exceptionally efficient, and the other from the Commissioners for paving, lighting and watching the estate of the Skinners' Company in St Pancras. In the Commons one member and in the Lords one peer objected to the exclusion of the City, but to the former Peel replied that 'the state of the nightly police there was much superior to that in Westminster', and to the latter the Duke of Wellington did not even bother to reply. On 19 June 1829 the Bill received the royal assent.[3]

The Metropolitan Police Act of 1829 proved to be a turning-point in one of the great historic processes of the nineteenth century – the elimination of riot and disorder as an endemic feature of British life. Within a few

[1] P.P., 1882, vol. iv, *Report of Select Committee on Police of the Metropolis*, p. 11.
[2] Gash, p. 492.
[3] *Journals of the House of Commons*, 1829, pp. 311, 338; *Hansard, new series*, vol. 21 1829, cols. 1488, 1752.

years the Metropolitan Police had established their authority over the streets of London, and while Nottingham Castle, the centre of Bristol and the hay and corn-ricks of Southern England blazed away during the Reform Bill crisis, order never quite broke down in the capital – a fact of far more than merely metropolitan significance. During the Chartist and other disorders of the 1830s and 1840s troops had still to be used in the provinces, but they no longer had any active role in London, where in moments of emergency the policeman's baton was less likely to provoke another Peterloo than the firearms of the army or the sabres of the yeomanry. Soon the services of the Metropolitan Police were frequently being sought for in less orderly parts of the country; its officers went to establish and train new provincial forces on metropolitan lines, and detachments of men – 2,246 between 1830 and 1838 – were temporarily posted to the provinces for the preservation of the peace in times of crisis. Between 1830 and 1850 nearly every established government in Europe was overthrown by revolution, and without the Metropolitan Police 'the tale of England's development', might also, in Professor Reddaway's words, 'have been either republican or reactionary'.[1]

But this success was not gained without cost. The Act of 1829 established a new police office with authority over the whole metropolitan area (except the City) within a range of between four and seven miles of Charing Cross. Two magistrates (or commissioners, as they were soon called) were to preside over this new office; they were to establish and administer a police force consisting of 'a sufficient number of fit and able men', who were to be sworn in as constables and who were to have the same common-law rights as the old parish constables. But the commissioners themselves were to be appointed by the Home Secretary, and everything that they did was to be under his immediate superintendence. What the Act did, in effect, was to transfer one of the principal functions hitherto discharged by the London local authorities to the central government. It isolated and dealt successfully with one aspect of local government reform because the need for action there could no longer be delayed, but by so doing it greatly retarded the reform of all other aspects of metropolitan local administration. Even this was only achieved by by-passing the main source of opposition – the City Corporation.

The Act was therefore a landmark in the history of administration as

[1] T. F. Reddaway, 'London in the Nineteenth Century: The Origins of the Metropolitan Police', *The Nineteenth Century and After*, vol. 147, 1950, p. 105; F. C. Mather, *Public Order in the Age of the Chartists*, 1959, p. 105.

1 Waterloo Bridge from Westminster Stairs, 1821

2 The Pool of London, *c*. 1801–10

(*over leaf*) 3 London in 1800

4 The Royal Mail leaving the General Post Office, St Martin's le Grand

5 Traffic on London Bridge, 1872

well as in the history of police. Only in an island entirely safe from foreign invasion could autonomy in local affairs have proceeded to such lengths as in eighteenth-century England. But now an increasingly urban and industrial society was posing new problems quite beyond the capacity of the old local institutions, and when inefficiency or danger could no longer be endured, the government was beginning to intervene. The Holyhead Road Commissioners had been established in 1815 to guarantee rapid communications with dangerous Ireland, then the Commissioners of Metropolitan Turnpike Roads in 1826, and in 1829 the Metropolitan Commissioners in Lunacy, all under government aegis of various sorts. The Metropolitan Police Act was more far-reaching in its effects than any of these earlier examples of state intervention. The transfer of responsibility for the preservation of order within the capital from the local to the central authority was the longest step yet taken, however unsuspectingly, in this direction, and provided a useful precedent at the time of the Poor Law Amendment Act of 1834 for the removal of another of the principal functions of the parish vestries, both in London and throughout the rest of the country, this time to the new centrally-controlled Poor Law Unions. And so far as London alone was concerned the Metropolitan Police Act also provided the precedent for the exemption of the City from the reform of the municipal corporations in 1835 – a precedent still followed today in any general scheme of metropolitan administrative reorganization.

But in the summer of 1829 all this was still a long way away in the future. The Act had contained no detailed regulations for the new force, whose organization and character would depend upon the Home Secretary and the two magistrates now to be appointed. Within less than three weeks of the royal assent Peel had made his selections. Colonel Charles Rowan, who had served in the Peninsular War and at Waterloo, was to be 'the Military Magistrate'. Rowan was a life-long bachelor with a wide circle of well-connected friends, fond of salmon-fishing and shooting. Now, at the age of forty-six, and seven years after his retirement from the army, he was to be in charge of the Metropolitan Police for its first formative twenty-one years. His colleague and friend throughout the whole of this arduous period was Richard Mayne, a young Irish barrister then practising on the northern circuit in England. On 6 July 1829 Peel interviewed Mayne and offered him the post; he accepted, and later on the same day Peel introduced him to Rowan at the Home Office.[1]

Within a fortnight Rowan and Mayne had produced their plan. The

[1] Charles Reith, *A New Study of Police History*, 1956, p. 130.

whole Metropolitan Police area was to be divided in military fashion into
divisions, each with its own station and under the command of a superintendent. Each division was to be subdivided into eight sections, and
each section into eight beats, with an establishment of four inspectors,
sixteen sergeants and 144 constables. There was much discussion as to
whether the men should wear uniform, and when it was at last decided
that they should, red and gold colours were at first chosen. But this decision, which would have given the force an extremely military aspect, was
at once reversed in favour of a dark blue tailed coat and trousers and
specially strengthened black top hat. Even more important to the achievement of good relations with the public were the *General Instructions*,
which were written by Rowan and Mayne, approved by Peel, and issued
to every member of the force.

> It should be understood, at the outset [state the *Instructions*], that the
> principal object to be attained is the Prevention of Crime. To this
> great end every effort of the Police is to be directed. The security of
> person and property, the preservation of the public tranquillity, and
> all the other objects of a Police Establishment, will thus be better
> effected, than by the detection and punishment of the offender, after
> he has succeeded in committing the crime.

The constable on the beat was to be 'civil and attentive to all persons, of
every rank and class; insolence and incivility will not be passed over. . .'.
He was not to interfere officiously, but when required to act he was to do
so with decision. He must at all times have 'a perfect command of tem-
per, never suffering himself to be moved in the slightest degree, by any
language or threats that may be used; if he do his duty in a quiet and
determined manner, such conduct will probably induce well-disposed
bystanders to assist him should he require it'.[1]

To recruit the several thousand paragons of honesty and self-control
required for the achievement of these ideals was the principal task of
Rowan and Mayne in the late summer of 1829. Hundreds of men attended
for interview at the hastily-established office at No. 4 Whitehall Place,
many of them coming through the rear entrance from Scotland Yard, the
street whose ancient name has now become synonymous with the headquarters of the Metropolitan Police. Retired or half-pay naval and army
officers were rejected, even for the rank of superintendent – the new force
was not to be a refuge for the middle-aged or the inefficient – but many

[1] Reith, pp. 135–43.

non-commissioned officers, unencumbered with pretensions to gentility, were enrolled, even at the low pay of one guinea a week for constables. Thus the tradition of promotion from below was established at the outset, but only at the cost of a very high turnover of recruits; by 1833, out of a total strength of 3,389 men, only 562 remained of those who had joined in 1829.[1]

By the end of September five divisions were ready to go on duty. The men paraded in the grounds of the Foundling Hospital in Holborn to be sworn in; the *General Instructions* were read out, uniforms were issued, and at 6 p.m. on Tuesday 19 September 1829, the first detachments of the Metropolitan Police marched out to inaugurate their watch and ward in the streets of London. The bucolic perambulations of the parish watchmen had ended, and within a fortnight Peel could write to his wife that he had again been 'busy all the morning about my Police. I think it is going very well. The men look very smart and a strong contrast to the old Watchmen.' The Duke of Wellington, too, was equally pleased. 'I congratulate you upon the entire success of the police in London,' he wrote in November. 'It is impossible to see anything more respectable than they are.'[2]

But lasting success was not easily won. The crisis leading up to the struggle for the Reform Bill began with the fall of the Duke of Wellington's ministry in November 1830, within only fourteen months of the first policemen going out on their beat. Not yet accepted, still less trusted by the general public, constantly attacked by the vestries upon whom fell the duty of collecting the police rate, the subject of the wildest inflammatory rumours in the press, and as yet without the steadying influence of a traditional *esprit de corps*, the police nevertheless survived, somehow, and maintained control throughout all the radical agitations of the early 1830s. They were often assaulted, and a few died. In 1833 they were subjected to three parliamentary enquiries, but their behaviour was vindicated, and soon afterwards the process of consolidation began. In 1836 the Bow Street horse patrol was transferred to the Metropolitan force and became the mounted branch; the foot patrol had already been transferred in 1829. By an Act of 1839 the river police became the Thames division under Rowan and Mayne, who also took charge of the constables hitherto under the separate control of the stipendiary magistrates; and the Metropolitan Police district was at the same time extended to include the area within a radius of some fifteen miles of Charing Cross.

[1] Reith, pp. 146–7; Gash, p. 502.
[2] T. A. Critchley, *A History of Police in England and Wales, 900–1966*, 1967, pp. 53–4.

There remained only the anomaly of the City. During the passage of the Reform Bill the Corporation had been greatly alarmed at the inadequacy of its antiquated arrangements, and in April 1832, when the two-year crisis was nearly over, it had belatedly reorganized part of its force on the lines of the Metropolitan Police. In 1837 a Royal Commission and in 1838 a Select Committee both recommended the consolidation of 'the several constabulary forces of the metropolis, including those of the city of London', and the government's police bill of 1839, as originally drafted, included clauses to this effect. But the City Fathers rose proudly to the occasion, and (according to an independent enquirer) 'every means of influence which the Corporation at large, and every class of it, possessed' were mobilized 'to avert what they considered a fatal blow at its very existence'. The government abandoned the struggle, and a separate Act was passed which established the City's own force of some five hundred men under the command of a commissioner appointed by the Corporation. 'This expensive insulation,' the same enquirer reported in 1850, was not 'accompanied by any superiority of management; but quite the reverse.'[1]

The establishment of the Metropolitan Police was the one great reform of the first half of the nineteenth century in which London showed the way for the rest of the country. By contrast, the reshaping of the administration of the capital was delayed until 1855, twenty years after the reform of every other large city and town in the kingdom. But in the late 1820s a partially successful attempt was made to abolish all select vestries, many of which were to be found in London. The movement was radical in origin, and many of its strongest supporters were drawn from the shopkeepers and small employers who abounded in London, particularly in Westminster.

The agitation seems to have begun in the parish of St Paul's, Covent Garden, where the origins and legality of the select vestry were shrouded in obscurity. In 1826 the inhabitants obtained with unexpected ease the right to participate in the vestry meetings, and three years later they obtained a Local Act enabling the twenty-pound householders to elect a standing committee in which all parochial authority was vested. Only the bias of the Lord Chief Justice prevented a similar result in St Martin in the Fields in 1827, while in St Pancras, where there were large numbers of dissenters and Irish Roman Catholics, a violent and disorderly agitation against the select vestry, established as recently as 1819, was kept up for

[1] Joseph Fletcher, 'Statistical Account of the Police of the Metropolis', *Journal of the Statistical Society of London*, 1850, vol. XIII pp. 221–67.

several years, the rallying-cry being objection to the payment of church rates for the new parish church and chapels. But the select vestries established by Acts of Parliament could only be ousted by fresh legislation, and so the agitations in Christ Church, Spitalfields, St James's, Westminster, St Marylebone and St Pancras between 1826 and 1829 all failed for the time being. They did, however, gain the sympathy of *The Times*, which described select vestries as a 'modern excrescence upon the constitution of the country', and in April 1829 John Cam Hobhouse, one of the radical members for Westminster, successfully moved for a parliamentary committee of enquiry into the whole matter.[1]

Most of the evidence collected by this committee came from the London parishes with select vestries, but discussion of the Bill providing for elective vestries which Hobhouse subsequently introduced was brought to a premature end by the death of George IV. The agitation against the select vestries, largely a London affair, became merged in the nation-wide demand for the reform of Parliament itself, and when Lord Grey took office Hobhouse quickly re-introduced his Bill. In the midst of the struggle for the Reform Bill the Whigs in the House of Commons could not afford to reject such a measure, and several deputations of Radicals from St Marylebone and St Pancras waited on Lord Grey and Lord Melbourne (who was Home Secretary) to obtain promises of their support. Murphy, the Irish boss of St Pancras, even boasted that he frightened Lord Melbourne.

> 'I told him pretty plainly what the people wanted, and what they were determined to have. Lord Melbourne said that one of these days he should have to sign a warrant for my execution for treason. I took him by the button to the window that looks out upon the park, and pointing to one of the gas columns, I said, "Do you see that gas post, my Lord?" – "I do," said he. "Well then," returned I, "long before a warrant is signed for my execution, I shall see you dangling at the lamp post!"

It was in this sort of atmosphere that the Lords, on 8 October 1831, rejected the Reform Bill in Committee. But this, too, was the climax of the vestries campaign, for in the excitement of the moment Hobhouse's Bill somehow passed the Lords. Perhaps, even, its passage was unintended, for after a rough reception from the peers it finally received the royal assent on 20 October 1831, the very day on which Parliament was prorogued.

[1] Sheppard, pp. 275-90.

But in the confusion in the Lords the word 'pounds' was introduced instead of 'persons', which turned it into a money Bill and raised a difficulty in the Commons, who were awaiting its return. Consternation ensued, 'but by some hocus pocus, nobody knows which way or how', the Bill was sent back to the Lords the same evening; 'but whether the House was sitting or whether it was not, or whether the alteration was made by somebody or nobody, altered it was'.[1] By such haphazard means was the partial reform of London's administration achieved in 1831.

Partial it certainly was, for although Hobhouse's Act gave all ratepayers one vote, and only one, in the election of their vestrymen, it was only to apply in parishes with select vestries where a majority of the ratepayers decided, by a poll, to adopt it. In London the Act was only adopted in St George's, Hanover Square, St James's, Westminster, St John's, Westminster, St Marylebone and St Pancras – all parishes hitherto ruled by select vestries, but with a strong radical element among their inhabitants. In each of these parishes a poll of all the ratepayers was held to determine whether the Act should be adopted, and this was followed by an election for the new vestry.

These events took place in the spring of 1832, during the final climax of the Reform Bill, which was no time for careful reflection. The Radicals had their own Parochial Committees, they canvassed vigorously and they presented their lists of approved candidates. They were everywhere victorious, and a reign of truly democratic economy was immediately inaugurated.

In St Marylebone the Parochial Committee met every Monday night in the Infant School in Barlow (now Cramer) Street to control the activities of their nominees on the vestry. Here 'the majority of the measures subsequently brought forward in the vestry were concocted', for the majority of the new vestrymen were both ignorant and wholly subservient to their leaders. They cut the salaries of the vestry clerk and other parish employees, they reduced expenditure at the workhouse by a third, they agitated against the new police, and through the Overseers of the Poor they 'fiddled' the register of parliamentary electors. But their favourite pastime was baiting the rector, Dr Spry, who had been chairman of the old select vestry. Much of the hatred felt for the select vestry had indeed been occasioned by the extravagance of its long-drawn out and extravagant church-building operations, a large part of which had been paid for by compulsory church rates, levied, of course, on Nonconformists as well as

[1] Sheppard, p. 296.

Anglicans. Now many of the new vestrymen were dissenters or rationalists, and every item of church expenditure was subject to their scrutiny. They objected to the use of holly for Christmas decorations – 'a relict of paganism' – to the quantity of soap supplied to the clergy – 'he did not wonder that the ministers used so much soap, for the Lord knew that they required a great deal of washing, to cleanse them of their iniquities,' declared one vestryman, or to the use of candles for the illumination of the pulpits when gas would be cheaper – 'new light is wanted in the church,' remarked another. Not content with this petty persecution, they even petitioned the House of Commons for the reform of the doctrine of the Church – hardly a matter within their purview – and the debate which preceded the dispatch of the petition presented them with a splendid opportunity for cheap jibes. 'If a man possessed great flexibility of belief and was subject to rapid mutability of opinion he might take the Apostles' Creed for his morning digestion, the Nicene Creed for his noonday repast, and the Athanasian Creed for his evening meal! And, as that Creed is difficult of digestion, I should wish him to have it at that period of the day, in order that a gentle slumber might follow.' But, of course, added the speaker, summoning up the memory of the recent episcopal opposition to the Reform Bill in the House of Lords, 'when a man is made a bishop, he has a large stomach and is well paid'.[1]

In the other parishes with erstwhile select vestries things were much the same. In St Pancras, under the corrupt rule of Thomas Murphy, they were even more extreme, and soon every person of independent mind had been driven from the vestry. But this triumph of militant parochial radicalism was comparatively short-lived. The leaders became discredited by their occasional lapses from their original pristine incorruptibility, they began to quarrel among themselves, their debates grew ever longer and more inconclusive, and everywhere the middle-class reforming fervour engendered in 1830–2 began to subside. By 1838 a few Tories – even Tories who had previously been select vestrymen – were successful at the annual parish elections, and moderation began to reassert itself.

Yet Hobhouse's Act was important, despite its limited application, despite the limited outlook of most of the men to whom it gave a measure of brief local power, and despite its failure to reform the overall structure of local government. In point of time it was the first small instalment of that famous series of statutes which remodelled the House of Commons, the Poor Law and the Municipal Corporations, and it was, too, the first

[1] James Williamson Brooke, *The Democrats of Marylebone*, 1839, pp. 32–46.

attempt by Parliament to apply the principle of direct election to the administration of the London suburbs – an attempt which was not renewed for over twenty-five years.

During this long interim period, in which the foundations of a new social and administrative order for the nation at large were being laid, London's government was almost wholly neglected, and the notion first implicitly accepted by Peel in his Police Act of 1829, that the City Corporation was too powerful even for Parliament to touch, was powerfully reinforced. At the time of the Municipal Corporations Act of 1835, by which the government of the 178 largest boroughs in the country was remodelled, a supplementary Bill to reform the City Corporation was specifically promised. But the report of the Royal Commission to enquire into the City's workings, published in 1837, did little but point out the difficulties. There was no reason, it said, to justify 'the present distinction of this particular district from the rest, except that in *fact* it is, and has long been, so distinguished'. Nor was there any reason why the suburbs should not be embodied within the original nucleus of London, as had already been done in the great provincial municipalities, unless the sheer magnitude of the change would convert what elsewhere would 'be only a practical difficulty into an objection of principle'. Clearly the suburbs should not be converted into a galaxy of new corporations in perpetual orbit around the City, but if on the other hand a single municipality for the whole capital were to be set up, 'a new and very important question' would arise, namely 'the proper division of municipal authority between the Officers of Government and a municipal body which might be established in the Metropolis' on lines analogous to those of the provincial towns. The Commissioners were, in fact, baffled, and in conclusion they could only point out, in ambiguous and not very accurate language, that the precedent of Peel's Police Act showed that there was no middle course between 'placing the whole under a Metropolitan Municipality, and entrusting the whole to Commissioners . . . under the immediate control of Your Majesty's Government'.[1]

Either alternative was equally unpalatable for Lord Melbourne, who was then Prime Minister. 'You'd better try to do no good,' he was fond of saying, 'and then you'll get into no scrapes.' Where even Peel had flinched, Melbourne was hardly the man to scale the City's ramparts. So nothing was done, and the City of London, alone among the great municipal

[1] *Second Report of the Commissioners to inquire into the Municipal Corporations: London and Southwark*, 1837, p. 4.

corporations, survived intact and unreformed – 'our corrupt, rotting, robbing, infamous Corporation of London,' in the words of Francis Place, 'a burlesque on the human understanding more contemptible than the most paltry farce played in a booth at Bartholomew's Fair, and more mischievous than any man living is prepared to believe'.[1] London had to endure the hideous challenge of cholera in 1848 before the remodelling of her local government institutions was at last taken in hand – a subject to be discussed later in Chapter 7.

[1] Quoted in Graham Wallas, *The Life of Francis Place*, 1925 edn, p. 347.

E

2

The London Money Market

I N T H E heart of the City of London stands the Bank of England. In
the 1840s the Bank already occupied its huge island site, and like a
medieval city fortress it stood secure within the enclosure of its
high windowless walls, aloof, watchful and strong. Half-a-dozen streets
converged in front of the Bank, and on the opposite side of the irregularly
shaped open space thus formed stood the Mansion House, the official
residence of the Lord Mayor, while a little to one side, between Threadneedle Street and Cornhill, an imposing new Royal Exchange was being
built to replace its ancient predecessor, recently destroyed by fire. These
three buildings completely overshadowed all their neighbours. In Lothbury and Moorgate Street and in Cornhill and Threadneedle Street, where
innumerable banks and insurance companies have in more recent years
erected their massive and ungainly palaces, the buildings were still in the
1840s small in scale and domestic in character. People still lived in the
City – 129, 128 of them in 1851, the highest figure recorded in the nineteenth century – and all the principal streets were lined with shops, many
of them for the sale of such everyday things as food and clothing. Front-
ages were still narrow, and not many houses were more than four storeys
in height. There were a few new warehouses, but even they were not
much larger than their older neighbours, and only half-a-dozen pushing
new insurance companies had as yet begun to regard the possession of
imposing offices as an advertisement for their own strength and prosperity.
Outwardly the City had, in fact, changed relatively little during the
previous hundred years. In its baffling network of lanes and alleys, workshops, offices, domestic industries, taverns and tenements all struggled side
by side for existence. Cattle were still driven through the streets to the

slaughterhouses of Smithfield. There were few sewers, and except at Fenchurch Street there were no railways.

The year 1844, when Queen Victoria opened the new Royal Exchange, marks the beginning of the transformation of the City. Within a decade the City Corporation became willy-nilly a leader in the field of public health, many of the ancient insanitary burial grounds were closed, and the cattle were at last driven out as the railways, in the early 1860s, burst in. Large new buildings to accommodate an ever-growing army of non-resident office workers reared themselves up in the principal streets, particularly in the neighbourhood of the Bank of England, while warehouses and counting houses sprouted up in the peripheries. But 1844 also had another quite different significance in the history of the City, for in that year the passing of the Bank Charter Act marked the beginning of a new epoch in the history of banking; and the City was the hub of the national monetary system. Overseas, too, the ever-growing influence of the City was extending all over the globe, and by 1858 it was stated almost as a truism that 'The trade of the world could hardly be carried on without the intervention of English credit.' And 'English credit' meant the City of London.

During the first three-quarters of the nineteenth century Britain was transforming herself into the first industrialized nation in the world. This process involved the mobilization of financial resources on a hitherto unprecedented scale, and the importance of the City of London in the economic life of the nation was therefore enormously enlarged. In 1800 the City already commanded many centuries of financial knowledge and experience, but its practices were nevertheless very different from those described some seventy years later by Walter Bagehot in his famous treatise, *Lombard Street*. During these seventy years the two principal themes of change were the development of central banking principles by the Bank of England, and the emergence of the *short-term* London money market. These two strands are very closely related, and in following their course many other gradual changes in the work of the City reveal themselves – the decline of private banks and the growth of their joint stock rivals; the establishment of branch banks, and the amalgamation of existing firms; the growth of the international money market and of investment abroad on a massive scale; and the great enlargement of the activities of the Stock Exchange and of the insurance companies (the latter being described in Chapter 5). These and many other slow transmutations constantly proceeding in the organization of trade, finance and banking all tended to produce an ever-mounting degree of concentration of business activity in the City, until by 1870 Bagehot could describe one aspect of this activity; the London money market, as 'by far the greatest combination of economical power and economical delicacy that the world has ever seen'.

At the beginning of the nineteenth century the structure of English banking was still essentially local. The Bank of England, established by Act of Parliament in 1694 as a joint stock company to help finance the war with France, had subsequently been granted a monopoly of joint stock banking. From 1708 to 1826 all other banks were forbidden to have more than six partners, and they therefore remained relatively small in resources and unspecialized in function. Throughout this period the Bank of England was a giant – the only giant – in a field restricted to small businesses, and that it also acted as the government's banker, and possessed the only large gold reserve in the country, added still further to its unchallengeable prestige. Yet despite its privileges its position remained uncertain. Was the duty of its Governor and Court confined simply to earning maximum possible profits for the shareholders in the company? Or were they to regard themselves merely as agents of the government? Most difficult of all – were they in times of emergency to use their ascendancy to regulate the excesses of the money market, and if so, how?

The establishment of local banks outside London, privately owned by not more than six partners, began in the mid-eighteenth century, and by 1810 there were said to be over seven hundred of them.[1] These early country bankers often originated in some other field of business activity – industrialists, who needed to be able to make local payments, lawyers, who needed outlets for the investment of their clients' money, or merchants and collectors of government revenue, who needed to send money up to London. In course of time they began to receive other people's money on deposit, and to transmit it, frequently to London, for investment; often these financial transactions proved more profitable than the proprietor's original line of business, which was discarded in favour of banking alone. To these functions, too, the country bankers soon added the local circulation of their own paper notes, for the deplorable state of the currency in the eighteenth century had caused a shortage in the means of cash payment. Thus by the opening of the nineteenth century many towns throughout the country had their own local paper currency,

---

[1] W. T. C. King, *History of the London Discount Market*, 1936, pp. 7–8. I am heavily indebted to King's work throughout this chapter.

backed and issued by a privately owned local bank which was in regular correspondence with an agent in London.

These agents were the metropolitan private banks, of which there were about sixty in 1832. Private banking in London was considerably older than its provincial counterpart, and some of the oldest firms had evolved from the goldsmiths' trade. Richard Hoare, goldsmith, the son of a successful horse-dealer, for instance, had established a bank in Cheapside in 1672, and in 1690 removed it to Fleet Street, where it still remains. And Andrew Drummond, a Scottish goldsmith, had set up a bank at Charing Cross in 1717, where it remained until it was taken over by the Royal Bank of Scotland in 1924. These West End banks, and others such as Coutts' in the Strand, which had also originated in a goldsmith's shop, or Herries Farquhar and Company in St James's Street, catered largely for the special needs of an aristocratic clientèle, whose rents were lodged there to be drawn on as required.

> *The aristocrat who hunts and shoots,*
> *The aristocrat who banks with Coots*

commented W. S. Gilbert in *The Gondoliers*. But the banks in the City were more numerous. In Lombard Street itself, the headquarters of London banking, there were among others the firm now known as Martin's, which claims to be the oldest bank of all, and Vere, Glyn and Hallifax, established in 1754 and still trading as Glyn, Mills and Company, while within a stone's throw there was Williams Deacon's, still in Birchin Lane after nearly two centuries, and a score of others which no longer survive.

Unlike their country counterparts, the London bankers did not issue their own notes after about 1780, and relied instead upon those of the Bank of England. The City bankers' customers were mostly merchants, lawyers and tradesmen, but much of their business was conducted on behalf of the country bankers, for whom they bought and sold government stock, accepted drafts and deposits and generally acted as providers of advice and information. Often there was a close family connection between the country bank and its London agent, as in the case of Taylor and Lloyd of Birmingham with Hanbury, Taylor, Lloyd and Bowman of Lombard Street (the original nucleus of the modern Lloyds Bank); or a London banker might himself be a partner in a provincial firm for which he acted, as in the case of Lewis Loyd, who was partner in a Manchester bank and whose London firm, Jones, Loyd and Company, acted as correspondents for twenty-eight country banks in 1819.

Thus by the opening of the nineteenth century the country was already equipped with a system of credit which operated through the Bank of England and a large number of small independent privately-owned firms. The nation-wide control of credit was still (judged by later standards, at any rate) crude and sporadic. The Bank of England could exact some degree of influence through the supply of government stocks and short-term loans, which formed an important part of the assets of both town and country banks. But the private banks did not usually hold large reserves in gold or Bank of England notes, and so the chief means of co-ordination of the activities of the country banks was exerted through the London money market. Country banks in prosperous agricultural areas of the country accumulated large deposits which they wished to invest at a profitable rate of interest, but for which they could find no outlet locally. These surplus funds were sent up to their London agents, who lent them for short terms to the banks in primarily commercial and industrial areas where the demand for credit exceeded the local supply. This system worked well in normal times, but when money was short provincial banks would look to their London agents for support, and the London agents in turn would look to the Bank of England as the holder of the only substantial reserve of gold in the whole country.[1]

The main instrument of the London money market was the bill of exchange, which at the beginning of the nineteenth century was already a device of great antiquity. The bill of exchange is a written acknowledgment of the existence of a debt, an I.O.U. recording the debtor's undertaking to pay at a specified date. A manufacturer, for instance, would use a bill to embody the settlement of the sale of £100 worth of goods. He would order the purchaser to pay £100 either on demand or at a fixed time in the future, and the purchaser would accept (i.e. acknowledge the existence of) the debt by signing the bill. But the manufacturer, or drawer of the bill, would have debts of his own (perhaps for the purchase of raw materials), and he would therefore order his customer, the acceptor, to pay the £100 not to the manufacturer, but direct to the manufacturer's creditor, and the latter, too, might use the same bill to settle a debt of his own by adding his signature. Thus the bill would pass from hand to hand in settlement of a multitude of debts, a negotiable instrument and legally binding undertaking to pay the debt, guaranteed by all parties to it – the

[1] R. S. Sayers, *Lloyds Bank in the History of English Banking*, 1957, pp. 9–11; L. S. Pressnell, *Country Banking in the Industrial Revolution*, 1956, pp. 76, 80.

drawer, the acceptor and the subsequent endorsers – sometimes over a hundred in number.

The practice as it existed in 1802 was clearly described by an eminent London banker.

> Let us imagine a farmer in the country to discharge a debt of £10 to his neighbouring grocer, by giving him a bill for that sum, drawn on his corn factor in London, for grain sold in the metropolis; and the grocer to transmit the bill, he having previously endorsed it, to a neighbouring sugar baker, in discharge of a like debt, and the sugar baker to send it, when again endorsed, to a West India merchant in an out-port, and the West India merchant to deliver it to his country banker, who also endorses it, and sends it further into circulation. The bill, in this case, will have effected five payments, exactly as if it were a £10 note payable on demand to bearer. It will, however, have circulated chiefly in consequence of the confidence placed by each receiver of it in the last endorser, his own correspondent in trade. . . . Liverpool and Manchester effect the whole of their larger mercantile payments . . . by bills at one or two months' date, drawn on London. The bills annually drawn by the banks of these towns amount to many millions.[1]

But besides this use for the settlement of debts, bills of exchange were also used to raise money, and in the nineteenth century this became their primary function. The debt which the bill represented could be sold to a financier who would buy it as an investment. But as the purchaser would lose the use of his money until the date for payment of the bill (usually not more than three months ahead for inland bills), he would charge the seller interest. This interest is known as 'discount', and its rate would fluctuate in accordance with the current state of supply and demand for credit, in times of credit shortage the discount rate being high and the sum actually received by the seller of the debt being correspondingly lower.

In the critical year 1797 the government had authorized the Bank of England to suspend cash payments for notes, and a great expansion of paper credit had ensued. During the Napoleonic wars the bankers in the busy industrial areas had required greatly increased facilities to draw loans on their London agents, but the latter had been unable to supply these needs fully, partly because they had themselves to rely upon the

[1] Quoted in King, pp. 31–2.

support of the Bank of England in times of stress, and the Bank was then refusing to accept (i.e. buy at a discount) bills with more than sixty-five days to run. To meet these demands there emerged a relatively new specialist, the bill broker, whose business was to negotiate the buying and selling of bills of exchange for the private banks.[1]

In the first decade of the nineteenth century one of the principal London bill brokers was Thomas Richardson. His career had begun as a clerk in the London banking firm of Smith and Holt, whose founder, Joseph Smith, had originally been a wool factor trading with, among others, the Gurneys, an old Quaker family of wool merchants in Norwich. John and Henry Gurney, too, had in course of time graduated into banking, and as East Anglia was a rich agricultural area with surplus capital, Smith in London frequently furnished them with bills of exchange as short-term investments, and for this service he charged the Gurneys a commission. In 1802 Richardson suggested that it would be more advantageous for the sellers rather than the buyers of bills to pay the brokers' commission, but Smith's rejected the idea and so Richardson left to set up his own business. He at once offered to supply the Gurneys with bills without charging them a commission. Smith protested that the Gurneys had been responsible for Richardson's resignation; the Gurneys denied the accusation – how, they wrote from Norwich, in true Quaker style, 'should it be possible for thee to entertain of us the opinion that we should be capable of so dishonourable a conduct as to prepare the mind of Thos. Richardson for leaving his situation with thee and adopting his present plans?' But although they were scrupulously honest, the Gurneys could not ignore such an advantageous offer as Richardson's. Gradually they transferred most of their bill work to him. His firm expanded rapidly; in 1805 he took in a partner, John Overend, and two years later John Gurney's own son, Samuel, joined the business.[2]

At the age of fourteen Samuel Gurney had been placed in the counting house of his brother-in-law, Joseph Fry, tea merchant, and London banker. At twenty-one he had joined Richardson and Overend, and had married in the following year, 1808. Through the honesty of all its dealings the firm soon became by far the biggest bill broking business of the day, with an annual turnover in 1823 of £20,000,000. Until his death in 1856 Samuel Gurney lived with his large and devoted family at his country house at West Ham, driving daily through the hideous poverty of the East End to Lombard Street, where his firm – known after 1827 as

[1] Pressnell, pp. 85, 94, 97, 99.   [2] King, pp. 17–23.

Overend, Gurney and Co. – had its famous premises at the corner of Birchin Lane. It was perhaps this daily reminder of human suffering as well as the natural goodness of a Quaker that prompted his life-long philanthropic work for the education of the poor, the relaxation of the excesses of the criminal law and the reform of prison discipline – the latter an interest in which he frequently assisted his more famous sister, Elizabeth Fry. Business of the most competitive kind never tainted him – he once refused to prosecute a forger, who had caused him considerable losses, because the penalty was death; 'We have thee under our power,' he told the cringing wretch. 'By the law we must hang thee – but we will not do that; so' – opening the private door of his office – 'be off to the Continent, and beware of ever returning.'[1]

By about 1815 the modern bill market, dealing mostly in loans of less than three months' duration, was securely established, with London as its hub. During the next half century the scale of its operations was enormously enlarged, but its function remained substantially unchanged. This was to supply and circulate short-term capital. The fixed capital assets of the new industrial England – factory buildings, machinery and all the expensive equipment required for large-scale manufacture – were largely financed by the industrialists themselves, either by ploughing back the reserves established in prosperous years, or by taking in a wealthy partner – a large landowner, perhaps, who could mortgage his estate – or by striking bravely out on their own into some new and potentially profitable field of endeavour. Until almost the end of the century, when limited liability companies first became widespread, the London money market played little direct part in the financing of industry. Its concern was with the smooth circulation of goods, not with their production, and in this purely commercial process, where liquid funds were constantly required, the City provided the channel through which the national supply and demand for short-term credit were brought together.

Because industry was still to a large extent privately owned and financed, either by individuals or by partnerships, the field of activity of the Stock Exchange in the early nineteenth century was still very restricted. The buying and selling of stocks had been carried on since the establishment of the first joint stock companies in the sixteenth century, but there were not enough companies to give rise to the formation of a regular exchange, and it was not until the establishment of the Bank of England and the permanent National Debt in the 1690s that specialist dealers in stocks began

[1] Mrs Thomas Geldart, *Memorials of Samuel Gurney*, 1857, p. 37.

to emerge. After a great many ephemeral companies had been set up during the South Sea Bubble, an Act of 1720 had forbidden the formation of companies except by royal charter or Act of Parliament. For many years, therefore, the principal activities of the Stock Exchange had been largely confined to government stock and government lotteries. In the 1790s dealings in the new canal company shares began, and soon afterwards there were water, gas and dock company stocks, but the first official price list to be published 'By Authority of the Committee of the Stock-Exchange', in 1803, was still largely concerned with the public funds.

By this time, however, these dealings in the National Debt had proliferated so greatly that the Stock Exchange itself had at last acquired a properly organized constitution. Hitherto the brokers and jobbers had met in the coffee houses of 'Change Alley, and latterly in premises in Threadneedle Street. In 1801 some thirty of them raised a capital of £20,000 in four hundred shares of £50, bought a site in Capel Court within a stone's throw of the Bank of England, and built themselves a home of their own. The new Exchange was regulated by a deed of settlement, and admission to it was restricted to candidates balloted for by an elected committee. It was opened early in 1802, with some five hundred members, a crowded noisy hall where 'over almost every bargain a glass of sherry used to be drunk', and although it has now been entirely rebuilt the home of the Stock Exchange is still in Capel Court.[1]

The National Debt consisted of a variety of stocks, of which 'Consols' (originally the 3% Consolidated Bank Annuities of 1751) were the most famous. In the eighteenth century each issue was usually raised by public subscription, generally in the spring at the time of the Budget. A small deposit was payable on allotment, and the balance by instalments over the next few months. Loans could be obtained from the Bank of England on the security of stock before all the instalments had been paid, and so there was plenty of scope for speculative dealings on the Stock Exchange. But abuses had crept in, particularly in the period between application for stocks and their allotment, and as the scale of public borrowing increased enormously between 1793 and 1815, a more reliable way of floating new stock had to be found. The government began to invite competitive tenders for loans, and so there emerged a small class of great financial

---

[1] E. Victor Morgan and W. A. Thomas, *The Stock Exchange. Its History and Functions*, 1962, pp. 19–20, 38, 62, 102; Charles Duguid, *The Story of the Stock Exchange. Its History and Position*, 1901, p. 95.

contractors who made themselves responsible for the subscription of loans of many million of pounds. They would themselves subscribe a large part of the money required for a loan, but they also obtained contributions from other sources in the City – the Bank of England, the South Sea and East India Companies, the two great insurance companies and a variety of large-scale mercantile interests; with the list for the whole sum complete the bid was then submitted, and if successful the loan was subsequently sold piecemeal at a premium. For the government the main advantage of this system was that the contractor was responsible for the entire loan, even if his contributors failed in their sub-contracts. For the contractor, the potential profits were enormous; and so, too, were the risks.

By these means enormous sums were raised in the City of London for the conduct of the French Revolutionary and Napoleonic wars, and the National Debt rose from £228 million in 1793 to £709 million in 1816. London bankers such as Robarts, Curtis and Company and Smith, Payne and Smith, had an important part in the loan contractors' syndicates, but the principal entrepreneurs were often of foreign extraction. The brothers Benjamin and Abraham Goldsmid were the sons of a Dutch Jew who had settled in England as a merchant in 1763. At first they had sub-contracted for government loans, then they had been the principal contractors in 1804 and 1805, but in the end both of them had been driven to suicide, Benjamin, who owned a fine house at Roehampton, in 1808, and Abraham two years later, when he had been unable to meet his liabilities through a fall in market prices.

In the same year, 1810, had died Sir Francis Baring, founder of the famous house of Baring Brothers, and himself the grandson of a Lutheran pastor in Bremen. Francis Baring had been born in Devonshire, where his father had settled as a cloth merchant, and early in life had come to London to establish an import and export business which later developed into a great merchant bank. He had built up commercial connections all over Europe and through his son, Alexander, who had been sent in pursuit of business to America (where he had married the daughter of a wealthy senator), the firm had been involved in the Louisiana Purchase in 1802–4. At home the Barings were involved in several government loans and at the time of his death Sir Francis was described as 'the first merchant in Europe'.[1]

[1] Morgan and Thomas, pp. 44–9; L. H. Jenks, *The Migration of British Capital to 1875*, 1938 edn, p. 19.

After 1810 the City was open for the establishment of the greatest mercantile dynasty, that of the Rothschilds. Nathan Meyer Rothschild was one of the five sons of a Frankfurt banker who had been agent to the Landgrave of Hesse Cassel and had lent large sums to the Danish government. All of his sons except the eldest had been sent abroad to establish branches of the family business in Vienna, Paris, Naples and London, and the unity of this cosmopolitan family was subsequently maintained by frequent intermarriage. Nathan Rothschild had come to Manchester in 1797 to buy cotton goods for Germany, had become a naturalized British subject in 1804, and shortly afterwards had settled as a general merchant and financial contractor in New Court, St Swithin's Lane, where the business remained for over a century. Through his purchase of gold imported from Calcutta by the East India Company he had come to the notice of the government, which urgently needed bullion for the payment of subsidies to its European allies, and he had become responsible for the whole of this branch of Treasury business, as well as for the transmission of funds to Wellington's armies in Spain. To get quick and reliable news he and his family had their own couriers on the Continent, and their own pigeon post. It was one of Nathan Rothschild's agents, waiting at Ostend, who had brought the first news of the result of the Battle of Waterloo to London, several hours before the government had knowledge of it.

With the return of peace government borrowing declined very greatly, and indeed was not resumed on such a scale until the war of 1914–18. But its effects remained. It had diversified the social structure of the nation by greatly increasing the number of people able to live on small independent incomes derived through the great loan contractors from a holding in the public funds – a point of particular significance for London, where many of these people lived. And in a wider context, the war-time exigencies which had been made upon it showed to the world at large that the City of London had no rival in the organization of resources for the movement of money and goods.

After the war, therefore, foreign governments began to resort to the City for their loans. Barings organized the payment of reparations by France, while Rothschilds floated loans for Prussia and Russia (1818–21). Then came half-a-dozen of the new South American republics, and Greece. Between 1822 and 1825 some twenty loans for foreign states, totalling a nominal figure of about £40 million, were issued in London, as well as numerous others for joint stock companies operating abroad. This boom in investment overseas was matched at home by a wave of reckless company promotion, all speculation being considered safe now that the Bank of England, by resuming cash payments for notes in 1821, had made Britain the only gold-standard country in the world. In 1824–5 prospectuses for 624 companies were issued, including some for such unconvincing projects as the drainage of the Red Sea for the recovery of the treasure abandoned there by the Jews during their precipitate departure from Egypt. In circumstances such as these confidence was bound to evaporate eventually, and the collapse came in 1825 when the Bank of England began to refuse to discount bills of exchange. Pole, Thornton and Company, London bankers who managed the accounts of forty-four provincial banks, were unable to meet their liabilities; within two years eighty commissions in bankruptcy were issued against country banks, and in 1827 only 127 of the 624 companies so enthusiastically projected a year or two earlier were still in existence.[1]

One of the few City men to emerge from the crisis of 1825 with an enhanced reputation was Henry Thornton, the junior partner in Pole, Thornton and Company. He was then a young bachelor living with his sisters at Battersea Rise. His father, a close friend of William Wilberforce and a prominent member of the Clapham Sect, had died in 1815, and young Henry had only been admitted to the partnership a few months before the crisis. A series of letters which his sister Marianne wrote to Hannah More describes Thornton's lonely efforts to save the firm, and also the workings of the City in moments of stress. Young Thornton had found that his four partners, all of whom were either absent or incompetent at the time of the emergency, had imprudently allowed their cash reserves to fall to a dangerously low level, trusting that the firm's hitherto unshakeable credit, backed by the great landed wealth of the sleeping partner, Sir Peter Pole, would enable them to borrow whenever they pleased. But on Saturday, at the height of the crisis, there had been a run on the bank – 'everybody came in to take out their balance, no one brought any in'. All attempts to borrow emergency funds failed, and at four o'clock, an hour before closing time, Thornton had 'ordered the balance for the day to be struck, and found that during the next hour they would have to pay thirty-three thousand, and they should receive only twelve thousand. This was certain destruction, and he walked out, resolved to try one last resource.'

His last resort was John Smith, partner in a rival banking firm, to whom Thornton gave his word that his house was solvent but unable to get at its

[1] Morgan and Thomas, pp. 80–3; King, pp. 35–6.

resources at short notice. With this assurance Smith had promised to lend whatever was available to see him through the next hour and had returned with Thornton

> to watch the event. Two people had chanced to pay *in* some money whilst Henry had been absent, this, with what he had borrowed [from Smith] exactly met the demand upon them – but never, he says, shall he forget watching the clock to see when five would strike, and end their immediate terror – or whether any one would come in for any more payments. The clock did strike at last, and they were safe for the moment, but as Henry heard the door locked, and the shutters put up, he felt they would not open again at that dear House, which every association led him to love so dearly.

> John Smith had been so struck by Henry Thornton's calmness that he resolved to ask the Bank of England for a further loan to save the tottering firm – an unheard-of request in those days. At eight o'clock the next morning, Sunday, he and Thornton met the Directors of the Bank and explained that the firm was not only sound but still 'worth a good deal of money'. ' "Well then," said the Governor and Deputy Governor of the Bank, "you shall have four hundred thousand pounds by eight to-morrow morning, which will I think float you." ' And at six o'clock on the Monday young Thornton had driven off in the dark from Battersea in his gig to meet the Governor and Deputy Governor, 'who for the sake of secrecy had no clerks there, and they began counting out the Bills for him. "I hope this won't overset you my young man," said one of them, "to see the Governor and Deputy Governor of the Bank acting as your two clerks." '

> But a week later, despite this august support, 'there was another tremendous crash among the Country Banks', and Thornton had decided to stop payment, for 'if he had borrowed more money it would have only been to lend to Country Banks, who might all have stopped tomorrow'. This was the end for Pole, Thornton and Company, but Henry Thornton was now so widely respected that he soon afterwards entered the partnership of Williams, Deacon and Company in Birchin Lane, where (as mentioned previously) the firm still exists to this day.[1]

The failure of so many banks during the crisis of 1825 revealed the dangerous instability of a banking system based on small privately-owned

[1] 'Letters from a Young Lady', in *Papers in English Monetary History*, ed. T. S. Ashton and R. S. Sayers, 1953, pp. 96–108.

local firms. 'Any petty tradesman, any grocer or cheesemonger, however destitute of property, might set up a bank in any place,' declared the Prime Minister, Lord Liverpool, and within a few months, therefore, an Act was passed authorizing the establishment of joint stock banks outside a radius of sixty-five miles of London, provided that they had no office in the metropolis. In 1833 another Act made clear that joint stock banks which did not issue their own notes could be set up in London. Thus the Bank of England lost its monopoly of joint stock banking; it still remained for many years by far the largest such institution in the country, but the rapid growth of these new banks, commanding much larger resources than many of their privately-owned rivals, was an early portent of the new banking structure that was soon to emerge. By 1841 there were 115 joint stock banks in England, all but half-a-dozen of which had been set up in the provinces, where they could issue their own notes. The most important of the London companies were the London and Westminster of 1833 and the London and County of 1839. But the overall number of banking firms had already begun to decline, for the number of privately-owned banks had fallen from 554 in 1826 to 321 in 1841, many of them having amalgamated with joint stock companies.

In the main, however, banking was still localized, and the new joint stock banks had to attract customers. They therefore offered good rates of interest to depositors, but this compelled them to make the utmost use of the money so obtained. They kept very small cash reserves and sent as much of their surplus as they dared to their London broker to purchase bills of exchange, which could always be realized at short notice if an unexpected local demand for money should arise. Thus the London bill market received a tremendous stimulus, and in 1836 Samuel Gurney stated that the discount business there had doubled in the previous five years. The age of localized joint stock banking, extending from about 1830 to about 1870, before the process of amalgamation began to produce a few giant monoliths each with its own national network of branches able to equalize within its own organization the supply and demand for credit in different parts of the country, was also the age in which the London bill market reached its peak in the distribution of domestic credit.

Meanwhile the London bankers were taking stock of their position after the crisis of 1825. Previously they had relied upon the Bank of England to re-discount their bills whenever they were pressed for cash. But at one stage of the crisis the Bank had refused to discount, and they therefore realized that in an emergency the whole credit structure of the country depended in the last resort upon the resources of the Bank, and that these might not always suffice. So after the crisis of 1825 the London banks ceased to re-discount with the Bank, and began to establish their own reserves, held partly in Bank of England notes and partly on deposit at the Bank itself. But in order to prevent their reserves from being wholly idle they also invested a proportion of them in securities available on demand. Government stocks were of course quite unsuitable for this purpose, and even bills of exchange, which might have a month or two to run, would be useless to a banker who found himself in Henry Thornton's predicament in 1825. So there arose among the London bankers the practice of depositing part of their surplus funds with the brokers, redeemable on call.

This development produced a change of great importance in the workings of the bill market, for the brokers who accepted such deposits ceased to be mere intermediaries, charging a commission for their services in the buying and selling of bills for their customers. Instead they became principals, or dealers, employing borrowed money for which they had to pay interest and which they were liable to have to repay at a moment's notice, and needing therefore a constant supply of borrowers who were willing to pay a rate of interest slightly higher than the banks expected from the dealers for their deposits.

At first only Overend and Gurney were in a large enough way of business to be able to undertake this direct dealing in bills, and even they would have been unable to do so without an opportune fall in the market rate of interest after the crisis of 1825. Five per cent was the maximum legal rate of interest chargeable under the old Usury Laws. A bill broker acting as an intermediary could take bills at 5 per cent discount, find a buyer for them at the same rate and legally charge a commission for his services; but if he acted as a principal he would receive no commission, and the law forbade him to sell at more than 5 per cent. Direct dealing in bills or any other form of money was not therefore a legal practical proposition so long as the market rate remained at the maximum; but if it fell below 5 per cent a margin would open between the rate the dealer had to pay to the depositor and the rate which he could legally charge to the borrower.

After 1825, when the London bankers began to place money on call with a few large brokers, the market rate of interest remained below 5 per cent until 1839. Direct dealing in bills therefore became possible, and in 1830 the growth of this new form of business was accelerated when bill brokers or dealers were for the first time allowed to open their own discount accounts at the Bank of England. When pressed they thus became able to apply for official accommodation, and their dependability in the eyes of the banks on whose short-term deposits they relied for their business was correspondingly enhanced. Three years later the Usury Laws, which had until recently prevented the development of bill dealing, were partially relaxed by the exemption of bills of up to three months' usance. Direct dealing in bills was to remain for some years a comparatively small part of the total business of the London money market, but its gradually growing importance after 1833 conferred upon the market the function of a shock absorber between the Bank of England and the commercial banks. When an increased demand for cash arose a London banker would no longer re-discount with the central Bank, but would call in his short loans to the bill 'brokers', or dealers, as they should now be called. The dealer would usually be able to meet such a demand by borrowing from another source, and only when the total supply of ready money failed to meet the demand was there any need to re-discount with the central Bank. In moments of real crisis this was still necessary, of course, but at all other times the bill dealers were able to iron out minor fluctuations in the national credit situation. Like the measuring scales in a laboratory the London money market was becoming a scientific instrument of great accuracy and precision; and like all such instruments it required delicate handling to avoid a smash.

The ultimate responsibility for seeing that the scales were not overloaded rested with the Bank of England. But although the Bank had long recognized the responsibilities of its special position as banker to the government and as the sole issuer of notes in London, it was still very uncertain how to achieve any degree of credit control. It regarded its own discount operations as its principal means of control, and was convinced that notes could always be safely issued against bills of exchange, provided that the bills represented genuine commercial business and not mere speculative dealings. It considered – astonishingly, in view of later developments – that the rate which it charged for discounts had no effect on the volume of business, and the Bank rate had therefore remained unaltered at 5 per cent from 1746 until 1822. It had ignored both the foreign exchanges and the price of gold.

The crisis of 1825 provided a sharp shock to this limited outlook. At one stage of the crisis, when the country was said to have been 'within twenty-four hours of barter' and the Bank was lending freely, it had had

F

to suffer the indignity of applying for assistance to the Bank of France. Thereafter it began to watch the foreign exchanges, and to aim at balancing its liabilities by gold and securities. In order to achieve a greater degree of equilibrium the Bank ceased to play an active part in the discount market, and fixed its rate for discounts well above the market rate, so that it would only become involved in times of emergency. This, the underlying theory of the Bank's policy from 1825 to 1844, marked a great advance in the development of central banking technique, but the Bank's rate for discounting, although no longer fixed permanently at 5 per cent, still remained too rigid, and its only effective weapon capable of active use in a crisis was the clumsy one of shortening the acceptable usance period of bills of exchange.[1]

This largely passive policy of the Bank was not strong enough to prevent another crisis at the end of the 1830s. The new joint stock banks indulged in reckless re-discounting, sometimes up to six or eight times the amount of their paid-up capital, and their portfolios often included bills of very doubtful value. In the field of overseas finance the crisis of 1825 had put an end temporarily to the series of foreign government loans, but in the 1830s British capital transmitted through London was finding a new outlet for investment in the development of the United States of America. Between 1830 and 1836 Anglo-American trade doubled, and capital which passed through the hands of Samuel Gurney or Barings was used to finance American banks, canals and all the expensive apparatus required for the efficient movement of goods – the essential pre-requisite for the development of large-scale industry there. With almost unlimited supplies of cheap money available in the City, the bills of 'the old highly respectable American Houses in London' were in great demand among the brokers, until in 1836 the Bank of England became alarmed at last at the size of these American credits and refused to accept them from the brokers. The brittleness of the national credit situation was revealed, and in 1839 the Bank again had to apply for support in Paris. Something more was needed from the Bank to ensure the sound control of credit; the sequel was the Bank Charter Act of 1844.[2]

The Bank Charter Act, which governed the operations of the Bank of England until well into the twentieth century, marked a new epoch in the structure of English banking. Its enactment was closely followed first by a tremendous boom in railway shares, which produced a correspondingly

[1] King, pp. 12, 36–43, 63–8, 89, 273.   [2] King, pp. 92–7; Jenks, pp. 77–8, 84.

enormous expansion in dealings on the Stock Exchange, and then by the crash of 1847. The City emerged from these four critical years, 1844–7, battered and breathless but with its command of the capital resources of the country more powerful even than before, and with the Bank of England chastened and more willing to accept its peculiar responsibilities.

After the crises of 1836–9 there had been much debate about how the Bank of England might control the excessive growth of bill credit, and two schools of thought had emerged, the 'Currency School' and the 'Banking School'. The former maintained that the problem was really one of currency control, and that if the issue of notes were precisely related to the supply of bullion, the volume of credit available would automatically adjust itself in proportion to the quantity of notes.

The leading exponent of this theory was Samuel Jones Loyd, later Lord Overstone, the formidable senior partner in the bank of Jones Loyd and Company, whom Charles Dickens is said to have used as a model for his Mr Dombey. He and his firm epitomize in miniature the progress of English banking in the nineteenth century. His father, Lewis Loyd, had been a Welsh dissenting minister in Manchester, had secretly married a Miss Jones, the daughter of 'a sort of half banker, half manufacturer' in his congregation, and in due course been taken into the firm and sent to London to establish an office in the City. There, in Lothbury in 1796, Samuel Jones Loyd had been born and later sent by his now prosperous father to Eton, Trinity College, Cambridge, and the House of Commons. Hard, logical and remorseless, and an inveterate enemy of the new joint stock banks, Samuel Jones Loyd accumulated a personal fortune of over two million pounds and built his family firm up to become the largest private banking house in the City, only for it at last to amalgamate, in 1864, with the thriving joint stock London and Westminster Bank. He lived on until 1883, largely forgotten, a lone survivor from the controversies of the 1840s.[1]

Sir Robert Peel had been converted to the Currency Theory of banking in the 1830s, and was probably much influenced by the writings of Samuel Jones Loyd, although there was never any direct connection between the two men.[2] By Peel's Bank Charter Act all provincial banks which issued

---

[1] T. E. Gregory, *The Westminster Bank Through A Century*, 1936, vol. II, pp. 158–61, 186; F. G. Hilton Price, *A Handbook of London Bankers*, 1890–1, pp. 94–6.

[2] J. K. Horsefield, 'The Origins of the Bank Charter Act, 1844', in *Papers in English Monetary History*, ed. T. S. Ashton and R. S. Sayers, 1953, p. 110; Gregory, vol. II, pp. 161–3.

their own notes, whether privately owned or of the joint stock variety, were forbidden to issue more notes than they had had in circulation at the time of the passing of the Act; if a bank of issue failed, it lost its right of issue, and if a private bank amalgamated with a joint stock, both were to lose their rights. The Bank of England itself was divided into the two departments of note issue and banking. It was authorized to create £14 million of notes against securities (known as the 'fiduciary issue'), and as many more notes as it wished against its holdings of bullion. In future it was to publish weekly accounts.

The effect of the Act of 1844, and of the Joint Stock Banks Act which was passed in the same year, was to give a new lease of life to the private banks. The intention was to confer an eventual monopoly of note issuing upon the Bank of England – this was not finally achieved until 1921, when the last country bank with rights of issue was absorbed by Lloyds – but the immediate effect was to discourage the amalgamation of joint stock and private banks, and so to prolong the still largely localized structure of the national banking system. The stringent rules imposed for the establishment of new joint stock banks temporarily put an end to such foundations – there was only one between 1846 and 1860, compared with 72 between 1826 and 1840. Banking divisions became stereotyped, and although amalgamations between non-issuing banks continued, and the existing joint stock banks could still grow by opening branch offices, the process of centralization into large concerns either based in or looking towards the City was artificially arrested for a few years – to the great advantage in the 1850s and early 60s of the London discount market, so much of whose domestic business depended upon the old localized system of banking.[1]

After the Bank Charter Act the Bank of England could look forward to the day when it would possess a monopoly of note issuing. For this reason alone the Act was therefore a vital landmark in the evolution of central banking, but in the 1840s the Act had other very different effects. It had provided the Bank with a simple rule-of-thumb for the control of note issue – above the fiduciary £14 million it could issue as many notes as it wished, provided that they were backed with bullion, the holdings of which would in turn be related to the foreign exchanges. But the corollary to this automatic regulation was the loss of the element of discretion in the Bank's control of credit; and discretionary control is an essential ingredi-

---

[1] Gregory, vol. I, p. 196; Joseph Sykes, *The Amalgamation Movement in English Banking, 1825–1924*, 1926, p. 20.

ent in the technique of central banking. In its commercial transactions the Bank suddenly became as free as any other bank to operate for the sole benefit of its shareholders; it began to compete aggressively for business, and in September 1844 it reduced its rate for discounting bills of exchange to 2½ per cent. In order to compete against the other banks and the discount dealers it was now necessary for the Bank's rate to fluctuate according to the state of the market, instead of remaining virtually stable as hitherto; and in the rate of discount which it charged for bills the Bank began to discriminate according to their individual quality. Thus although the Bank's active competition for discounts was to prove disastrous and was soon abandoned for good, this short interlude did establish the principle of the minimum variable Bank rate – the publicly announced minimum rate at which the Bank was prepared to do business for best-quality short-term bills, a rate which in times of stress could be and indeed was eventually raised to check demand. Almost by accident there had emerged one of the most powerful weapons of modern central banking technique, the variable Bank rate, a weapon which the Bank did not abandon during its retreat to a more detached position after the crisis of 1847.

Competition from the Bank of England did not adversely affect the discount houses already in the business. As the structure of the national banking system remained to a large extent localized, it was still their function to equalize the supply and demand for short-term money between different parts of the country, and in the late 1830s they had benefited greatly from the commercial banks' increasing fondness for lending money at call. This practice had encouraged the growth of dealing in bills, as opposed to acting as brokers, and by the 1840s there were three great houses besides Overend, Gurney – Bruce, Buxton and Company, Sanderson and Company, and Alexander and Company, the last of which survives, to this day, still in Lombard Street. But in the 1840s Overend, Gurney's business was bigger than that of the other three put together, and under Samuel Gurney's management the firm was already approaching the position from which it could, in the words later used by *The Times*, 'rightly claim to be the greatest instrument of credit in the kingdom'.[1]

The Bank's entry into the market coincided with a dangerous proliferation of railway building schemes. Much of the capital for the early railways had been subscribed in the provinces, with support from loans in the City – £20,000, for instance, from Richardson and Overend to the

[1] R. S. Sayers, *Central Banking after Bagehot*, 1957, p. 1; King, pp. 103-20.

Stockton and Darlington in the 1820s. But now that these early railway companies were beginning to pay good dividends, the Stock Exchange took an interest. 'A solicitor or two, a civil engineer, a Parliamentary agent, possibly a contractor, a map of England, a pair of compasses, a pencil, and a ruler, were all that were requisite to commence the formation of a railway company,' a stockbroker recalled. Towards the end of November 1845 – the deadline for the deposit of plans for the ensuing parliamentary session – draughtsmen and printers were remaining 'at work night after night, snatching a hasty repose for a couple of hours on lockers, benches or the floor'. One company brought over four hundred lithographers from Belgium, and the Railway Department of the Board of Trade engaged a large establishment of extra clerks to cope with the rush. On the last night, a Sunday, all went well until eleven o'clock, but thereafter the staff could not keep pace. At midnight precisely the doors were shut, but a quarter of an hour afterwards a late arrival refused to be denied and had to be forcibly ejected. Outside the Stock Exchange and the offices of the embryo railway companies dealings went on long after normal hours, many of them of a very dubious nature, for in those days no money deposit was required from an applicant for shares. 'Hundreds of men both in London and the provinces applied, many without the remotest idea of ever paying the deposit to the bankers that was asked for in the letter of allotment, and without the slightest means of doing so.' By the end of 1845 Parliament had authorized the raising of no less than £60,000,000 of new railway capital.[1]

Throughout the whole of 1845 and 1846 the Bank of England's rate for discounting was actually *below* the market rate. The Bank Charter Act of 1844 had imposed stringent rules for the issue of notes, and neither the Bank nor the government was expecting an over-expansion of trade. But in 1847 funds began to be drawn away abroad, calls for the payment of railway shares so enthusiastically subscribed for a few months earlier became heavy, and a bad harvest (plus the failure of the Irish potato crop) demanded large-scale imports. At last in April 1847 the Bank reversed its policy of cheap money, and raised its minimum rate to 5 per cent; even this was only available for bills with a few days to run. In the summer there were numerous mercantile failures, 'beyond all precedent in the commercial history of the country', and soon afterwards the discount houses of Sanderson's and Bruce's both stopped payment, to be quickly followed by several large provincial banks. At the Stock Exchange, 'the sound of the

[1] Duguid, pp. 148–50; *Annual Register*, 1845.

hammer declaring defaulters was heard with disastrous frequency day after day,' and in those days before limited liability, when every shareholder could be called upon for his proportion of the total liabilities of a company, 'many innocent men liable for calls had to fly the country, as if they had committed some crime, and to live abroad for many years upon what remnants of their property they could manage to save from the general wreck.'[1]

The Bank of England now became virtually the only source for accommodation, and although the minimum rate for discounting had been $5\frac{1}{2}$ per cent since August 1847, almost all business was in fact transacted at far higher rates – in October even Overend, Gurney were charged 9 per cent for short-term bills. But still the Bank's reserves continued to fall, and on Friday 22 October a deputation of City bankers and merchants, of whom Samuel Gurney was one, called upon the Chancellor of the Exchequer to entreat him to suspend the restriction imposed by the Bank Charter Act upon the Bank's issue of notes. On the Monday, 25 October, the Treasury's answer was delivered to the Bank. It advised the directors to continue to discount 'upon approved security', but to raise the rate of interest to 8 per cent; and if this course should lead to infringement of the Act, 'her Majesty's Government will propose to Parliament, on its meeting, a bill of indemnity'.

Thus the Bank Charter Act had been suspended within three and a half years of its enactment. The effect of this shock to the commercial life of the nation was sharp and surprisingly short. From September to November 1847 great mercantile houses in the City had been falling like autumn leaves, including four in which the Governor of the Bank of England himself and three of his co-directors at the Bank were partners, but immediately after the suspension became known 'there was at once a great and instantaneous restoration of confidence', and by the end of the year the Bank's rate was back to 5 per cent. But the Bank itself had learnt a bitter lesson from the crisis which its own indiscreet behaviour from 1844 to 1847 had done so much to bring about. Never again, except in times of emergency, did it revert to competing in the discount market: it abandoned the idea that it was as free to act as any other joint stock bank, and for discounting it began to charge a minimum rate well above the market rate. Consequently its bill portfolio fell from the peak of £12,000,000 in October 1847 to £3,000,000 in 1849, and thereafter it settled at around £6,000,000 in the 1850s. In normal times the Bank's rate now stood above the market rate, but when money was short and there were increasing

[1] Duguid, pp. 154–5; King, pp. 137–45.

applications to the Bank, its rate was sometimes below the outside rate. It almost seemed, in fact, as if the Bank had reverted to its old practices before the Act of 1844. But during the three disastrous ensuing years the Bank had evolved a new device to enable it to compete against its rivals – the principle of the minimum variable rate – and now that it had withdrawn from an active share in discounting it could and did employ this device to maintain contact with and regulate dealings in the short-term money market. The Bank rate was no longer a fixed star in the City firmament, as it had been before 1844. Slowly, and perhaps largely unintentionally, the Bank was learning the techniques of modern central banking, which would enable it to become the regulator of a market rapidly growing in size, power and delicacy.[1]

The management of this great engine, the London money market, was in the hands of a comparatively small number of able, honest and industrious men. At the summit of financial power still presided the great merchant banking dynasties of Baring and Rothschild, both originally of foreign extraction. The second and third generations of the Barings, sons and grandsons of Sir Francis, collected two peerages and a chancellorship of the exchequer, but even so they were overshadowed by the Rothschilds. The Rothschilds had no peerage yet – apart from the Austrian barony which enabled Lionel Nathan, the eldest son of Nathan Meyer, founder of the English branch of the business, to style himself Baron Lionel de Rothschild – and they produced no chancellor of the exchequer either, for as Jews they were still precluded from the House of Commons. But in their inexorable success in business the Rothschilds had no rivals; there were several great town houses in Piccadilly, and around Tring and the Vale of Aylesbury, their country headquarters, they owned half-a-dozen mansions and 30,000 acres of land as well as a suburban house at Gunnersbury. When Baron Lionel died in 1879 his personal estate was valued at some £2,700,000, and he had even contrived at last to become a Member of Parliament, in the Whig interest, for the City of London, for which he was repeatedly elected from 1847 onwards, although his refusal to take the oath 'upon the true faith of a Christian' prevented his taking his seat until 1858 – a long campaign on behalf of his co-religionists which earned him the unusual sobriquet of the King of the Jews. He remained in the Commons for almost sixteen years, but never once made a speech there; his power lay elsewhere.[2]

[1] King, pp. 141–8, 157, 163–6; *Annual Register*, 1847.
[2] Cecil Roth, *The Magnificent Rothschilds*, 1939, *passim.*

Next in the City's hierarchy of power came the old private banking families, such as the Glyns or the Hoares. In these firms the partners all shared one large room, comfortably furnished in the manner of the smoking-room of a West End club, and warmed by a blazing open fire. Here each partner had his desk, and in these well-appointed surroundings they discussed the business of the day. George Carr Glyn, the third generation of bankers in his family, and the owner of a large house off Belgrave Square, exemplifies the mid-nineteenth-century private banker. He became a partner in 1819 at the age of only twenty-two, and remained in Lombard Street until his death more than fifty years later, in 1873. He too became a taciturn backbench Whig M.P., but in the City he was an active promoter of the building of the St Katharine Docks, and later became chairman of the London and Birmingham Railway, from whose workshops in Buckinghamshire he ultimately took his title of Baron Wolverton. Personal relationships through his wife's family probably occasioned his participation in both these great ventures, a fact which reflects the underlying weakness of the private banks – their reliance upon personal connections, and in particular their dependence upon the existence of heirs of sufficient capacity to carry on the business. The Rothschilds were able to manage this unpredictable problem as successfully as every other aspect of their affairs – perhaps because they had so often married their Continental cousins, who were well aware of their responsibilities in the matter – but George Carr Glyn, although he had taken the precaution of making himself the father of nine sons, was less fortunate. None of the nine devoted himself primarily to the bank, and rejuvenation came, therefore, in 1864, through amalgamation with another old private firm, Curries and Company of Cornhill. The Hoares, too, of Fleet Street, were in much the same situation. Here, in the middle of the nineteenth century, there were only two partners, Peter Hoare, with a country estate in Devonshire, and his cousin Henry Hoare, whose estate was in Kent. They were both deeply religious, but Peter Hoare was High Church while Henry was Low, and as they 'took it in turns to spend six months on end at the Bank and were never in Fleet Street together for more than a few hours at a time' they seldom met except for the discussion of essential business.[1]

Except at the very summit itself, power in the City was in fact beginning to pass to the new men of the joint stock banks – to salaried professional officers like James William Gilbart, first general manager of the London

[1] Roger Fulford, *Glyn's 1753–1953. Six Generations in Lombard Street*, 1953, *passim*; *Hoare's Bank. A Record 1672–1955*, 1955, p. 52.

and Westminster Bank. During his twenty-six years in this post (1833 to 1859) he built the new company up from nothing to the largest of the new London joint stock banks, with half-a-dozen branches and an impressive headquarters in Lothbury opposite the Bank of England. He gave evidence before innumerable parliamentary committees, he wrote several treatises on banking, he was elected a member of the new Statistical Society of London and a Fellow of the Royal Society, and in his will he endowed an annual lecture on banking. But although he lived frugally and never married, he left only some £40,000. 'The appointment to the office of bank manager did not,' as he himself complained, 'raise him to the same social position as a [private] banker', and the public 'considered him as holding an office analogous to that of chief clerk in a private bank'. Gilbart was an outstanding man in the first generation of the new profession of bank manager; he had many difficulties to contend with in his dealings with his board of directors, including that of his own salary, £1,500 per annum, which he considered to be too low, and he did not live long enough to see his profession achieve its respected modern position; but his career showed in which direction banking power was beginning to move in the City.[1]

Beneath the great men at the top of the City pyramid toiled an ever growing multitude of clerks, who for a wage of about £80 to £120 a year laboured daily from 9 or 9.30 in the morning until 6 or 7 or later in the evening. Until well after the middle of the nineteenth century there were no Saturday half-holidays, no old-age pensions, and if the bank failed the staff would find themselves in the street, some of them perhaps too old to find another job. Yet despite the long monotonous hours and the shabby gas-lit buildings in which they usually worked, clerkships in the City were always keenly sought after, particularly in the older private banks, where there were often valuable additional perquisites. At Hoare's the junior clerks lived in the house in Fleet Street, though their rooms on the top floor were quite shut off from those of the family. At the quarter days they were awakened by the old watchman at 6.30, and at 7 their names were called over downstairs by the partner on duty. 'Discipline was very strict,' one of them later recalled, 'and you were kept hard at work the whole day because there was a certain amount to be done and it had to be completed by the junior Clerks before dinner time.' This was at 5 o'clock, when the doors of the bank were closed to the public, and dinner 'of a very substantial character' was served for the whole staff except for the two duty clerks who were still working downstairs on the balance for the day.

[1] Gregory, vol. II, pp. 205–7.

The senior clerk took the chair, and two of the porters acted as waiters; there was an elaborate ritual of toasts, for four bottles of wine were always provided, 'and if the Balance was agreed before the dinner was over one of the Porters from downstairs was sent up to make the announcement, "Gentlemen, the Balance is right," and always received from the Chairman a glass of wine for his pains.' But if the balance was wrong the clerks returned to their labours. Many of them remained in the service of the same firm for the whole of their working life – often over fifty years, for retirement without a pension was impossible – and by their industry and loyalty helped to build up the supremacy of the City of London in the nineteenth-century financial world.[1]

This supremacy was never more apparent than in the 1850s, when all the multifarious activities of the City were increasing by leaps and bounds. The last vestiges of protectionism had been discarded, and industry, commerce, agriculture and shipping were all enjoying the benefits of their new freedom. Internally the penny postage, the electric telegraph and the completion of many railway-building projects were making their influence felt, and all these developments were balanced by the news of the discovery of gold in California (1849) and in Australia (1851), first supplies of which quickly began to arrive in London. Money was cheap again – in April 1851 the Bank rate fell to the unheard-of level of 2 per cent – and after the boom in domestic railway shares in the 1840s there was a renewed flow of British overseas investment, to French railways, Italian railways, railways everywhere in Europe, to public utilities and mines, all canalized through the City of London, often with the help of the Rothschilds and the Barings. At the Stock Exchange the establishment of several new exchanges in the provinces in no way diminished London's predominance, and the growth of business in Capel Court was so great that a new house more than twice the size of the original one had to be built in 1853–4. Everybody was an investor, or at any rate everybody who had any spare cash, and this now included, according to a report prepared for the House of Commons, such unexpected people as cotton spinners, cooks and relieving officers, butchers, coachmen and beer-sellers, mail-guards, butlers and even domestic servants.[2]

This tremendous economic expansion was matched by a corresponding

[1] Fulford, pp. 166–72; *Hoare's Bank*, pp. 55–61.
[2] Jenks, pp. 164–73; *Annual Register*, 1846.

expansion of banking activity. In prosperous agricultural districts it was said in 1858 that 'almost every farmer, even those only paying £50 per annum rent, now keeps deposits with bankers', and deposits at the London joint stock banks rose from £8,850,000 in 1847 to £43,100,000 in 1857. With this growth of deposit banking the modern cheque was gradually superseding the freely circulating bill passed from one endorser to another as the normal means of payment of debts. Instead of discounting a customer's bill of exchange, bankers were making advances on security or personal credit, against which cheques could be drawn, and the admission of the joint stock banks to the London Clearing House in 1854 was a very important landmark in this process. The Clearing House derived from the seventeenth-century goldsmiths' practice of keeping running accounts with each other for the easy transfer of money; later the London bankers had performed these operations in a public house, and then in a rented house in Lombard Street. Here each of the thirty-two London private banks which were members of the Clearing House in 1827 had their own pigeon-hole, into which clerks from every other bank dropped bills and cheques payable by the owner of each pigeon-hole. At the end of the day all the balances were added up and outstanding amounts were paid, probably in Bank of England notes. But all the member firms were private banks, and they had consistently refused to admit their joint stock rivals. By 1854 the inevitable could no longer be resisted, and the London and Westminster, the London Joint Stock, the Union Bank of London, the London and County, and the Commercial of London were all reluctantly granted membership. The Clearing House itself, now in Abchurch Lane, was greatly enlarged at about the same time.[1]

The growth of payment by cheque meant that a bank's possession of the right to issue its own notes declined in importance, while the value of a London office increased. In 1866 the National Provincial Bank, which had hitherto operated exclusively outside London and so possessed a joint stock bank's right to issue notes, decided to forgo the profits on its provincial issue of nearly half a million pounds-worth of notes in order to acquire the greater advantage of a London office. Joint stock banks were, in fact, forging ahead, and by 1867 the number in membership of the Clearing House had risen to eleven while private banks in membership had declined to thirteen. The restrictions placed upon joint stock banks by the Act of 1844 were repealed in 1857, and an Act of 1862 for the

[1] J. H. Clapham, *An Economic History of Modern Britain*, vol. I, 1926, pp. 283–4; vol. II, 1932, pp. 335–6; Gregory, vol. I, pp. 167–74.

consolidation of joint stock law had granted limited liability on bank shares. Public opinion was moving in favour of joint stock banking, and the huge companies of modern times were emerging. Between 1849 and 1865, for example, the deposits at the London and Westminster rose from £3·7 millions to almost £20 millions, and in the four years 1861–4 this bank absorbed the Commercial Bank of London, the London and Middlesex Bank and Jones Loyd and Company. The disappearance of the latter, the private bank which had for so long been associated with Samuel Jones Loyd, Lord Overstone, was regarded as a portent. 'Private banking has now ceased to be of any importance,' said a contemporary, 'and the amalgamation of the still existing houses with great Joint Stock banks has become a mere question of time.'[1]

The expansion of trade and of joint stock banking in the 1850s had important repercussions in the discount market. In their competition for custom the joint stock banks offered ever higher rates of interest to depositors, and this money was loaned at call in ever larger amounts to the London money market. Here the brokers still retained their function of providing the channel through which the spare capital of one part of the country found its way to other parts of the country where it was required, but the growth of the joint stock banks' call loan practice had compelled them to act increasingly as money dealers on their own behalf, as well as brokers acting on behalf of clients. In general the discount houses paid interest at only one per cent under the prevailing Bank rate for money from the joint stock banks, and the margin of profit on their money dealings was therefore extremely small in relation to the total sums involved. So they were unable to establish reserves of their own. 'They could not afford to pay interest for money and not to use it,' said David Barclay Chapman, the senior partner at Overend, Gurney after the death of Samuel Gurney in 1856; 'It is the nature of the business [of the money-dealing houses in Lombard Street] to bring into action and useful employment the banking money of the country; it is their business to use it.'[2]

In normal times the discount houses' lack of substantial reserves did not appear to matter greatly; when they found themselves pressed they could apply to the Bank of England for accommodation. But if there should be any general abuse of bill credit facilities the situation could quickly become extremely dangerous, for the commercial banks relied on the Bank of England too – 'You always come back to the Bank of England at

[1] Sykes, pp. 31–8; Gregory, vol. I, pp. 277–8, 293.
[2] King, pp. 176, 183, 245–6.

last,' remarked Walter Bagehot. And the position of the Bank itself in relation to the London money market was no longer one of absolute supremacy. Its reserves in the mid-1850s were no greater than they had been a decade earlier, and its deposits, although still greater than those of any other single bank, amounted to less than one-fifth of the total of the other London banks. Its potential responsibilities in times of crisis were growing with the general expansion of financial activity in the 1850s, but its immediate day-to-day responsibilities as the central bank of reserve precluded it from taking its full share in the profits of this general expansion, and there was therefore little corresponding growth in its resources. Hitherto it had controlled the market through its overwhelmingly superior strength; now it was beginning to have to exert this influence over an increasingly complex mechanism which was rapidly outstripping the Bank's own resources.

The difficulty of this task was revealed by the world-wide crisis of 1857, which may be regarded as the first crisis of external origin to hit the City of London. There the effect of several years of over-trading in credit facilities had been repeatedly postponed by timely deliveries of gold from Australia – 'We have looked to the arrival of those steamers from Australia,' said Chapman, 'as much almost as to anything else, to know whether we were safe in going on with our business' – but in the autumn of 1857 the break came at last. News of the Indian Mutiny, high discount rates in Europe and above all the crash of numerous banks in America forced the Bank rate up to 8 per cent and produced numerous mercantile failures. Short-term loans were called in on an enormous scale, and by 9 November, when the rate was raised to 10 per cent, the Bank's reserves had fallen to £2,834,000. On the next day it lent over one million pounds, and on 12 November it obtained the government's permission to suspend the Act of 1844. Thereafter the panic subsided quickly, but only after the Bank had issued an excess of nearly a million pounds beyond the normal limit.

During the crisis the Bank had borne almost the entire market demand for discounts, and on the day of the suspension of the Act it had lent no less than £700,000 to a single firm – Gurney's. The directors of the Bank were determined never to get into such a situation again, and in March 1858 they debarred the bill brokers and discount houses from the right to take bills to the Bank for discount. The Bank would certainly have been wiser if it had attempted to control abuse of credit by exercising more severe discrimination in its acceptance of bills according to their quality. The arbitrary decision to restrict the total quantity of credit facilities would be extremely difficult to enforce in moments of crisis when the existence of many great firms would be endangered by the lack of such facilities on any terms, and there was much ill-feeling in the City towards the Bank's new policy of keeping strong. In 1860 Overend, Gurney's, no longer the tower of strength which it had been for so long in the days of Samuel Gurney, allowed itself to be provoked into foolish retaliation by a minor decision of the Bank; on one day it withdrew £1,650,000 from its account at the Bank, all in £1,000 notes. Sensation ensued, and the Bank raised its rate by half a point, but the notes were returned within a few days.

The 1860s were a dangerous time for the indulgence of such mutual recrimination, for a tremendous surge in the number of commercial companies of all kinds was proceeding. Successive changes of law made between 1855 and 1862 had extended the right of limited liability to any group of seven or more persons who wished to form a limited company, and the formalities of incorporation were reduced to the subscription of a memorandum of association to be registered at the Board of Trade.

> *Some seven men form an Association*
> *(If possible, all Peers and Baronets)*
> *They start off with a public declaration*
> *To what extent they mean to pay their debts.*
> *That's called their Capital.*

In 1863 alone 689 new companies were registered, to the great benefit of the dealers in the Stock Exchange, but few of them were as yet concerned with industrial projects, and it was chiefly in the City that the uses and abuses of limited liability were first explored.

There the success of joint stock banking, the statutory authorization of limited liability as a matter of right, and the Bank's new rule debarring the privately-owned discount houses such as Overend, Gurney from re-discounting at the Bank had all combined to suggest that bill dealing would be a profitable field for limited liability discount *companies*. The first such companies, the National Discount Company Limited and the London Discount Company Limited, were established in 1856, each with a capital of £1,000,000. They both survived the crisis of 1857, and their success prompted less reliable flotations. In 1859 there appeared Albert Gottheimer, wine merchant, a smart young operator well able to exploit the opportunities for unscrupulous profits provided by the new Limited

Liability Acts. He established the Mercantile Discount Company Limited, with a capital of only £200,000, dressed up nevertheless with the promise of a dividend of at least 10 per cent in the first year. This promise was in fact kept in the summer of 1860, but a temporary crisis in the leather trade had revealed the precarious business of the new discount companies, and in November the London Discount Company realized that the risks were too great and went into voluntary liquidation. This honourable decision caused considerable surprise, for the company's net profits in four years' business were £60,000, and in the ensuing discussion the most dishonourable winding up of Gottheimer's Mercantile Company evoked little comment. The directors said they hoped to pay back £15 of every £25 paid-up share, while Gottheimer himself went away with substantial compensation for the cancellation of his contract. Soon he was to return to repeat this cycle of fraud on a larger and more disastrous scale.[1]

By the mid-1860s the London money market had achieved the pre-eminence which Bagehot described as 'by far the greatest combination of economical power and economical delicacy that the world has ever seen'. The total deposits in London banks were three times as great as the City's nearest rival, New York, and nearly ten times as great as those of Paris, and through the machinery of the Lombard Street market this colossal wealth could be lent in sums which it was still impossible to obtain elsewhere. To the long succession of earlier foreign investments there was now added investment in the Victorian Empire – railways in Canada, public works in Australia, the Cape and the West Indies, all chiefly in the 1850s, and after the Mutiny of 1857, railways in India, which in the ten years 1858 to 1867 absorbed over £61,000,000 of British capital.[2] London was becoming more and more the resort of merchant banking houses of foreign origin – George Peabody, for instance, from Baltimore in 1838 (later to become J. B. Morgan and Company, and still surviving in the City as Morgan Grenfell and Company Limited), Hambros from Copenhagen about 1848, and Speyers from New York in 1862 – all dealing in international trade and finance and thereby extending still further the foreign ramifications of the City. By the mid-1860s the idea that any undertaking anywhere which was likely to pay could perish through want of money had, indeed, entirely disappeared – this perhaps was the central achievement of the London money market in the nineteenth century.

[1] King, pp. 191–205, 213–29, 245–6.
[2] Walter Bagehot, *Lombard Street*, 1931 edn, pp. 3–6; Jenks, pp. 201–6, 219.

The safe operation of this unique instrument depended, of course, upon the honesty of the men of the City, and upon their capacity to detect and reject undertakings which would *not* pay. The lack of both these qualities among a mere handful of prominent men was to reveal in 1866 to a large number of innocent and trustful people just how precarious was the balance between prosperity and ruin.

In the early 1860s there was a speculative bubble in the flotation of limited liability companies. New banks and discount companies were established, and then credit companies for dangerously vague and all-embracing purposes. It was in this latter field that Albert Gottheimer reappeared in 1863. In order to attract funds from trustful small investors – clergymen and widows were apparently particularly susceptible to the blandishments of his prospectuses – or perhaps in order to disassociate himself from his previous activities, he changed his name to the supposedly more trustworthy one of Grant, to which he added in due course a touch of social distinction by adding the prefix 'Baron', and in 1865 the still widely respected suffix of M.P. (for Kidderminster). With his usual dexterity he floated a company called the Credit Foncier and Mobilier of England in imitation of similar concerns which had burgeoned in France some years earlier, while a former colleague of his, H. J. Barker, became the manager of another new all-or-any-purpose finance company. Barker was a friend of D. W. Chapman, the partner in Overend, Gurney chiefly responsible for the examination of securities, and it was Barker who first introduced dubious business to this august firm. Largely through the negligence of Chapman, an extravagant and easily flattered man entirely unsuited for the unremitting attention to business which his position in the firm demanded, Gurney's had by 1863 become inextricably involved in the financing (and even the management) of a variety of fixed-asset businesses, of which a fleet of steamships proved the biggest loss-earners, all based on the normal slippery short-term loans of the money market. With the enthusiastic support of promoters like Grant and Barker 'they covered the seas with their ships, ploughed up the land with their iron roads', and despite annual profits of £200,000 on the usual discount business of the house, Gurney's were by 1864 incurring a net loss of about £500,000 a year.[1]

Belatedly the partners attempted to save their house by separating the still profitable discounting business from the enormous liabilities which their recent extraneous activities had accumulated. In order to pay off

[1] King, pp. 320–2, 246–51.

G

these commitments the firm was converted into a limited liability company with a capital of £5,000,000, and by a private deed the partners guaranteed the new company against the previous losses. The news, made public in July 1865, that Overend, Gurney and Company – the 'Corner House' at the junction of Birchin Lane and Lombard Street, whose very name had for so long been spoken of with a 'curious solemnity, almost under the breath', and whose only modern counterpart for quality and reliability was perhaps until recently provided by Rolls-Royce – that this great house was to descend into the common ruck of limited liability, caused a tremendous sensation. But there was a rush for the shares, for the recent losses were as yet unknown, and no one 'would ever believe a word against them, say what you might'; and the shares were offered on the attractive terms of £50 each, of which only £15 was to be paid at first call. By October they had risen to a premium of almost 100 per cent.

But it was all too late. The partners' losses proved to be much greater than they had expected – some £5,000,000 altogether – and in January 1866 they were compelled to start realizing their own private assets, which included the sale of their estates. Rumours began to circulate, the shares fell back almost to par, the Bank rate was increased. The default of Watson, Overend and Company, a firm of railway contractors which in fact had no personal connection with Gurney's, added to the uncertainty. In the course of two months deposits of some £2,500,000 were withdrawn, the shares fell to a discount, and in March it was being said that 'company winding-up seems likely to become one of our national institutions'. The directors considered the possibility of calling up more of their shareholders' subscriptions – only £15 of each £50 share had as yet been paid – but this would merely have produced more doubt and more demands on the house. So as a last resort they applied to the Bank of England, and the Bank, after examining the books, refused to help.[1] The time for the final reckoning had come, and on Thursday, 10 May 1866, at 'about half-past three o'clock in the afternoon the great house at the "corner", of wider than European fame, shut its doors, and made confession of insolvency'.

The effect of the fall of Overend, Gurney and Company was like 'the shock of an earthquake. It is impossible to describe the terror and anxiety which took possession of men's minds for the remainder of that and the whole of the succeeding day. No man felt safe.' There was a tremendous run on the banks, and Lombard Street was invaded by crowds of struggling and half-frantic creditors. At about noon on the next day, Friday, 'the

[1] King, pp. 238–42, 253; Bagehot, pp. 259–60.

tumult became a rout. The doors of the most respectable Banking Houses were besieged ... and throngs heaving and tumbling about Lombard-street made that narrow thoroughfare impassable.'[1] In the evening Gladstone, the Chancellor of the Exchequer, authorized the suspension of the Bank Charter Act – the third such occasion since the passing of the Act in 1844 – but before the panic gradually subsided ten banks and dozens of mercantile and other houses of varying importance, including the great railway building firm of Peto and Betts, were dragged to ruin by their connections with Overend, Gurney and Company.

Within a few weeks of the crash the creditors of Gurney's, to whom debts of over £5,000,000 were due, were demanding that the shareholders should meet these gigantic debts by the call-up of the £35 as yet still unpaid on each of their £50 shares. But the shareholders maintained that when they had purchased their shares in 1865 they had not been informed of the enormous commitments of the old firm, and that they were therefore not liable for them. The question hinged upon whether the directors had acted fraudulently at the time of the formation of the limited liability company, and in 1869 they were all tried for conspiracy. The real culprits – D. W. Chapman, whose irresponsible negligence had led to his exclusion from the firm in 1865, and his cronies of the underworld of sham paper finance, such as Barker and Grant – never even took their place in the dock. But the directors had stood their ground and honestly attempted to put their house in order. At the trial their counsel said that 'every shilling's worth of their property has been sold and realized for creditors; and but for the kindness of friends they might now be in actual destitution'. They were all acquitted, and the shareholders therefore had to pay up. There were three calls between 1866 and 1869 for the payment of the balance on each of their £50 shares, and in the end, despite their agonized protests that 'if the creditors knew how many homes have been broken up and how many well-to-do people ruined by the calls that have already been made, they would forbear to press for immediate payment', the shareholders had to pay £40 on each share. The final liquidation of the affairs of Overend, Gurney and Company was not completed until 1893, when the shareholders received the last instalment of a total return of £7 18s. 2d. per share.[2] By this time Grant, too, had suffered through his

[1] *The Bankers' Magazine*, vol. xxvi, 1866, p. 639; *The Illustrated London News*, 19 May 1866; *The Times*, 12 May 1866.

[2] *The Bankers' Magazine*, vol. xxvii, 1867, p. 1072; vol. xxx, supplement to January issue, p. 53; King, p. 254.

frequent attendance at the bankruptcy courts to which his earlier activities had brought so many other people, and even the memory of the Gurneys' former financial pre-eminence had been largely forgotten. Earlham Hall, for so long the family's home outside Norwich, is now occupied by the new University of East Anglia.

The crisis of 1866 was a purely British affair. It was also the last of the classic nineteenth-century upheavals in the money market – the Bank rate did not again reach 10 per cent, nor was the Bank Charter Act again suspended, until 1914. During this half century the resources of the Bank of England continued to decline in relation to those of the joint stock banks, and the continuing decline of the old private banks was gradually producing the modern banking structure, dominated by a few giant joint stock banks with branches all over the country. This in its turn caused a decline in the circulation of the inland bills of exchange which had earlier contributed so much to the achievement of London's supremacy in the money market; the multi-branch joint stock banks were able to equalize the supply and demand for short-term money in different parts of the country from the resources of their own organizations, and they even began to grant loans direct to their customers instead of using bills. But side by side with these domestic changes commerce and finance as a whole were becoming more and more international in structure, and in the renewed foreign loans boom of the late 1860s and early 1870s London obtained a very large share of the business. In 1870, for instance, J. S. Morgan undertook the risk of lending £10,000,000 to the French provisional government at Tours, and subsequently the payment of the French indemnity to Germany was largely financed through bills drawn on London. The ramifications of international dealings were in fact becoming ever more complex, and with this increasing complexity there came, too, at last, a realization of the common interests which united the different elements of the London money market in times of crisis; and so when Barings were in difficulties in 1890 the London banks successfully co-operated under the leadership of the Bank of England to avert a repetition of the events of 1866 – the most striking example of the moral ascendancy which the Bank, despite the loss of its old preponderant strength, had with such difficulty achieved by the end of the nineteenth century.[1]

The crisis of 1866, with the sudden virulence of its impact on the fortunes of so many hitherto unsuspecting people, was also a portent of

[1] King, pp. 266–8, 273, 283.

the increasingly precarious position of the whole nation in the later years of the nineteenth century. In 1815 England had still measured her wealth largely in the land and its products, and except in years of bad harvests her food had still been grown at home. By the 1870s the population had more than doubled, and to feed these new teeming millions more and more food was being bought abroad. Exports to pay for these purchases, and for the purchase of raw materials, were therefore becoming the life-blood of the nation, but it was just at this moment, in the late 1870s, that British exports of manufactured goods began to encounter much stiffer native competition than hitherto, notably in the United States and Germany. A new commercial and industrial world was emerging, in which Britain no longer had a lead over all other nations. Now she had to face foreign competitors whom she had herself often helped to establish by loans and by the export of men and machinery, whose success must endanger British exports, yet whose failure too might have adverse effects upon Britain's finances.

The financial men of the City of London had played a central part in the creation of this new Britain which had at first led the world and which was now beginning to have to pay the first of many instalments towards the price of maintaining her precariously balanced urban and industrial way of life. Their rôle had been neither creative nor deliberate; they had not provided much money for industry, and they had seldom given much thought to the long-term consequences of their acts. They had been, and were to continue to be, the indispensable intermediaries who provided the financial mechanisms for the efficient circulation of both money and goods, and without which the industrialists would have been unable to buy their raw materials or pay their employees or sell their products. From the 1840s they had, too, channelled the resources necessary for the building of the railways without which the needs of the great new towns could not have been supplied. It is indeed hard to conceive the existence of this new Britain without the existence of the London money market – the new Britain in which two Reform Acts and the repeal of the Corn Laws had tilted the balance of political power decisively away from the old landed aristocracy towards the new urbanized social structure of which London itself, ever growing in size and numbers, provided the most striking example.

And it is certainly impossible to conceive London as it was in 1870 without this hidden source of wealth. How difficult it is, said one perceptive observer in 1869, 'to give a rational explanation of the existence

and growth of this enormous metropolis. We find many thousands here
who live by supplying one another's wants; and the question arises,
whence comes the original means by which such a state of things is
rendered possible? What, in fact, is the primary fund of which these
persons manage to secure a share?' London, he continued, was 'in effect
the shop not only of the greater part of England south of the Trent, but
of a great portion of the civilized world, and we perceive that the sums
expended here in retail purchases and in the employment of tradesmen
must be enormous'. To the armies of tradesmen must be added those
Londoners employed by the government or in 'the various manufactures
of particular districts', and those actually engaged in foreign commerce.
But all the wealth created by these various categories of people could still
not account for the existence of this prodigious place, and there therefore
remained one other source to explain it – 'the large share the inhabitants of
London possess in the profits of commercial operations carried on at a
distance. . . . Capital belonging to residents in London is lent to every
Government, and engaged in almost every enterprise throughout the
world. All these facts require to be contemplated, before the great fact
of the existence and continued growth of such a city can be felt to be
natural.'[1]

[1] T. A. Walton, 'On the Classification of the People by Occupations', *Journal of the Statistical Society of London*, vol. XXXII, 1869, p. 284.

3

The Growth of
London before the
Railways

ON THE morning of 8 January 1822 William Cobbett set out from
his house near Kensington to ride to Lewes, the county town of
Sussex, a distance of some fifty miles. His journey took him
through the southern outskirts of London, across Kennington Common,
past the clusters of new houses at Stockwell and the stucco villas which
lined one side of the long slope up Brixton Hill. For him the district
between 'London and Croydon is as ugly a bit of country as any in
England', and London itself was nothing but a great festering sore,
an 'infernal Wen', a 'smoking and stinking WEN', perpetually sucking
into itself the strength and goodness of the rest of the nation. Even
Croydon, then a small market town, had 'swelled out into a Wen',
he noted with disgust, and in the evening he sat down to describe the
repulsive features of this first quasi-urban stage of his journey to
Lewes.

From Saint George's Fields [in Southwark], which are now covered
with houses, we go towards Croydon, between rows of houses, nearly
half the way, and the whole way is nine miles. There are, erected
within these four years, two entire miles of stock-jobbers' houses on
this one road, and the work goes on with accelerated force! . . . What
an at once horrible and ridiculous thing this country would become, if
this thing could go on only for a few years! And [he continued, as
his furious indignation mounted] these rows of new houses, added to

the Wen, are proofs of growing prosperity, are they? These make part of the increased capital of the country, do they? But, how is this Wen to be *dispersed*? I know not whether it be to be done by knife or by caustic; but, dispersed it must be![1]

If William Cobbett had studied the figures in the census taken in the previous year, 1821, he would have seen that during the last decade alone the population of London had increased by over 21 per cent, and that it now stood at 1,378,947, or slightly more than 10 per cent of all the people of England and Wales. If he had been a young man in 1822 instead of being aged about sixty he might have lived to see his worst fears far surpassed – to see the population of his home parish of Kensington, for instance, increase more than eight-fold, from 14,000 in 1821 to 120,000 in 1871, and to see London as a whole grow inexorably at never less than 16 per cent per decade until in 1871 its population numbered 3,254,260, or 14·4 per cent of that of the whole of England and Wales.

But despite this continuous overall growth of population, the physical evolution of nineteenth-century London proceeded along a very irregular path, for the supply of land and capital and the activity of the builders and their customers were all closely related to the general financial and economic situation of the whole country, which (as we have already seen) fluctuated very greatly. And from about 1830 onwards the pace and even the general direction of London's progress was transformed by new means of movement – the horse bus, the railway, the underground railway, the tram and at the very end of the century, the tube. London exploded with the irresistible force of a nuclear reaction, and within two generations had dissipated itself in a galaxy of suburbs which surrounded the fragments of the ancient nucleus, hitherto compact and complete.

The structure of the ownership of the land on which these suburbs were built forms a bafflingly complex and constantly changing pattern. At the close of the middle ages much of the land around the ancient walled City of London had belonged to the Church. The Canons of St Paul's Cathedral, for instance, held the whole of the parish of St Pancras, the Archbishop of Canterbury and the Prior and Convent of Christ Church, Canterbury, between them held most of Lambeth, while the Bishops of

[1] William Cobbett, *Rural Rides*, ed. G. D. H. and Margaret Cole, vol. I, 1930, p. 60.

6 Westminster Bridge and the burning of the Houses of Parliament, 1834

7 The new Westminster Bridge and the new Houses of Parliament, 1872

(*over leaf*) 8 London in 1833

9 Cremorne Gardens, 1864

10 A summer day in Hyde Park, 1858

London and Winchester had large holdings in Paddington and Southwark respectively. None of these estates was lost by the Church during the Reformation, but the lands owned by Westminster Abbey passed to the Crown, whose properties in the West End around St James's were greatly enlarged. Large tracts of these confiscated church lands were soon sold to private lay owners, and here the ancient manorial courts fell into disuse. Where ecclesiastical ownership survived, the manor courts tended to survive too, as in Stoke Newington, Lambeth and Vauxhall, and even in the nineteenth century much building development in these areas was based on the ancient copyhold system of land tenure which these exiguous courts still administered. Despite frequent depletions the Church was still the largest single owner of land in London in the nineteenth century, and after the incorporation of the Ecclesiastical Commissioners in 1836 the management of all its scattered holdings was gradually united under one authority. So too were those of the Crown, under the Commissioners of Woods and Forests, augmented by more recent purchases, notably of land around Kensington Palace and in Millbank.

In the nineteenth century there were numerous other corporate owners of land besides the Church and the Crown. Many of them were charitable in origin and of great antiquity, and the size of their estates varied very greatly. First there was the Duchy of Cornwall, which had been established by Edward III for the maintenance of the heir apparent to the realm, and which in London still administers a large estate in Kennington. At the other extremity in point of size were numerous small estates like that of Thomas Seckford. In 1587 he had bequeathed lands in Finsbury for the benefit of the inmates of the almshouses which he had established at Woodbridge in Suffolk, and Woodbridge Street still commemorates this benefaction. A few years later Henry Smith, a wealthy City Alderman, had directed his executors to use part of his estate for the relief of his 'poorest kindred' and for the ransom of Englishmen captured and enslaved by Turkish pirates in the Mediterranean. After his death in 1628 his trustees bought 84 acres of land in Kensington and Chelsea; about a century later the Turkish depredations ceased, and when in the fullness of time Onslow Square and Pelham Crescent were built, Smith's grateful kindred ceased to be poor and the trustees had to find another outlet for their embarrassing wealth. In Islington, to take another example at random, there was (and still is) the estate of the Corporation of the Sons of the Clergy, which the sons of dispossessed clergymen established in the mid-seventeenth century for the relief of their suffering parents. And

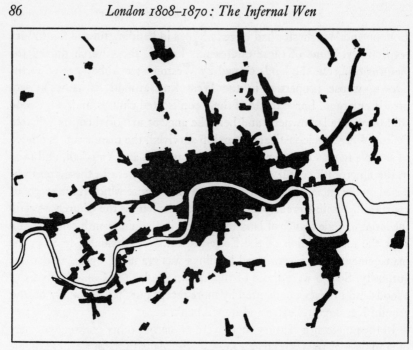

5 London at the end of the eighteenth century

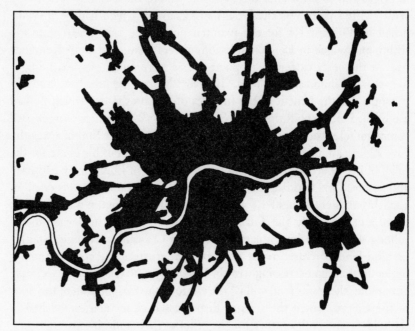

6 London in the 1830s

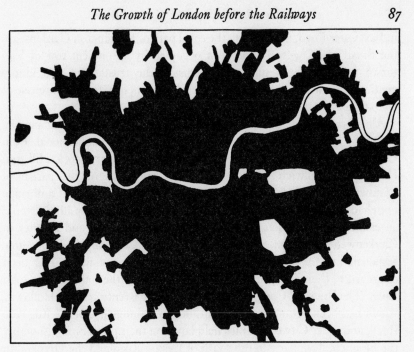

7 London in the 1870s

in Bayswater Road, overlooking the royal park of Kensington Gardens, are the Bread and Cheese Lands, now occupied by an opulent row of Victorian mansions built under the aegis of the trustees of two kindly gentlewomen who had bequeathed their little property for the purchase of victuals for the parish poor.[1]

All these estates had been established for the benefit of specific people, but there were others for more varied purposes, often educational. Eton College owned extensive lands at Primrose Hill, Haverstock Hill and Hampstead, Dulwich College had about one-third of the parish of Camberwell, Christ Church, Oxford and St John's College, Cambridge both had lands in Kentish Town, and the Brewers' Company administered an estate near St Pancras Station for Aldenham School and another in Clerkenwell for Owen School. The Mercers' Company had the same responsibility for a large scattered estate in Stepney which had been conveyed to them in 1509 for St Paul's School by the founder, Dr John Colet. The Brewers' Company also owned some twenty acres in Holloway which had been bequeathed to them for the maintenance of the Edgware Road, and other City companies held lands on their own account, notably the Skinners' Company to the south of Euston Road and the Drapers' in Islington. South of the river there were the City Corporation's Bridge House estate in Walworth, for the maintenance of London Bridge, and the Trinity House lands in Newington, for the relief of decayed seamen.

All these and many other corporate estates are easy to identify because they tended to survive for much longer periods of time than did estates in private ownership. Many of them survive to this day – indeed, parts of Lambeth still belong to the Church after nearly eight centuries – and because trustees and executors and City Companies all keep written records, the history of corporate estates can often be studied in some detail. But the greater part of the land upon which the suburbs of nineteenth-century London were built belonged to private individuals, and the history of these estates is far more complicated, and the evidence for its study far more elusive.

Speculation in land on the outskirts of London dates back to at least the middle of the sixteenth century, when the Earl of Bedford's example

[1] For much of the information contained in this and the next paragraph I am indebted to the research of Miss A. F. Riches of the Historic Buildings Division of the Greater London Council, and to Mr W. A. Eden, formerly Surveyor of Historic Buildings, for permission to use this material.

in purchasing Covent Garden was soon followed by the Earls of Salisbury (Cranbourn Street area) and Leicester (Leicester Square). The social differentiation of suburban London into the fashionable West End, with the royal palaces of Whitehall, Westminster, St James's and later Kensington, and the commercial and mercantile East End, with the port and the heavy industries, was already under way, and it was therefore natural that the landed gentry and aristocracy should tend to buy land on the western outskirts, rather than to the east of the City or in the still isolated districts south of the river. In west London some of the estates which were developed for building in the late eighteenth or nineteenth centuries were very large indeed – the Duke of Bedford's in Bloomsbury, the Earl of Southampton's in St Pancras, the Eyre and Portman in St Marylebone, Lord Grosvenor's in Belgravia and Pimlico, or the Holland, Edwardes and Ladbroke in Kensington. In the inner districts of east London the City Corporation and the City Livery Companies owned a number of mostly small estates, but the pattern of private land ownership there was in general more fragmented. There was no substantial counterpart in the east to the ring of great private aristocratic empires in the west, nor was there in south London either, although there the corporate estates of the Church, the Duchy of Cornwall and Dulwich College achieved a corresponding preponderance in Lambeth and part of Camberwell.

The parish of Kensington, on the western outskirts of London, illustrates the extent to which a handful of landlords sometimes dominated the pattern of estate ownership. The survey which was made in 1843 for purposes of tithe redemption covered 1,560 acres, or 71 per cent of all the land in the parish, most of the rest consisting of roads, land already developed or undeveloped land exempt from tithe. It shows that within this area there were only ten estates with more than 25 acres each, and of these ten four contained over 150 acres each, the largest being that of Lady Holland with 200 acres. Three of these four very large estates belonged to titled owners; between them these ten chief proprietors owned no less than 78·9 per cent or nearly four-fifths of all the titheable land. And even in Islington, which was just outside the eastern end of the belt of great aristocratic domains, the twenty-three chief proprietors owned 72 per cent of all titheable land.

Despite this preponderance of a small number of landowners there was never a shortage of building land in the outskirts of nineteenth-century London. Building was regarded as a profitable if risky undertaking, even

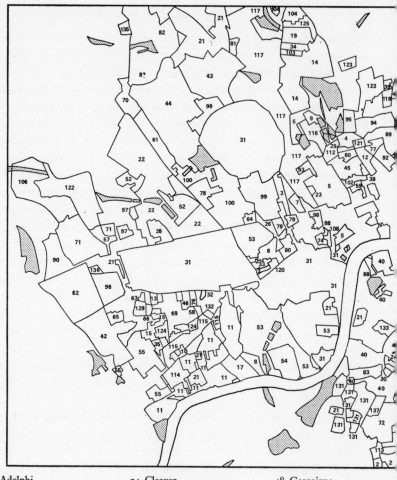

1 Adelphi	24 Cleaver	48 Gascoigne
2 Angell	25 Clothworkers' Company	49 Gibson
3 Audley	(Packington)	50 Girdlers' Company
4 Battle Bridge	26 Conduit Mead	51 Graham
5 Bedford, Duke of	27 Corporation of London	52 Grand Junction Canal
6 Berkeley (Samuel)	Bridge House	Company (formerly
7 Berners	28 Craven	Bishop of London's)
8 Brett	29 Cromer-Lucas	53 Grosvenor (Duke of
9 Brewers' Company	30 Crooke	Westminster)
10 Brompton Hospital	31 Crown	54 Grosvenor (Duke of
11 Cadogan	32 Cubitt (Kensington)	Westminster) – Cubitt
12 Calthorpe	33 Curzon	55 Gunter
13 Camden Charities	34 Dartmouth, Lord	56 Haberdashers' Company
14 Camden, Earl of	35 Day	57 Hall
15 Campbell-Cole	36 De Beauvoir	58 Harlar
16 Charterhouse	37 De Crespigny	59 Harpur Trust (Bedford
17 Chelsea Hospital	38 Doughty	Charity)
18 Choumat	39 Drapers' Company	60 Harrison
19 Christ Church College,	40 Duchy of Cornwall	61 Harrow School
Oxford	41 East	62 Holland (Ilchester)
20 Christie	42 Edwards (Lord	63 Hoof
21 Church Commissioners	Kensington)	64 Hope
(various estates)	43 Eton College	65 Hutchins
22 Church Commissioners	44 Eyre	66 Inderwick
(former Bishop of	45 Foundling Hospital	67 Ironmongers
London's)	46 Freake	68 Jesus College,
23 City Lands	47 French School	Oxford

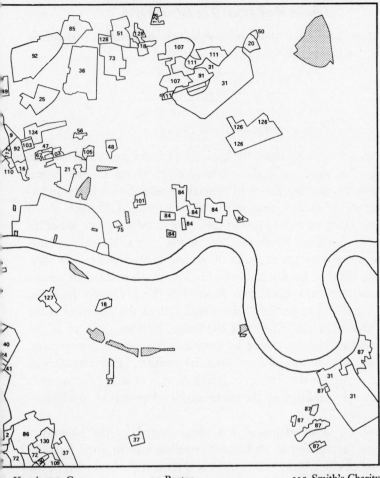

though agricultural land commanded relatively high rents, particularly
if used for market gardening.

> *The richest crop for any field*
> *Is a crop of bricks for it to yield.*
> *The richest crop that it can grow,*
> *Is a crop of houses in a row.*[1]

Landowners seldom undertook the business of development themselves.
In practice they either sold their ground outright for a lump capital
sum – a method sometimes favoured by small owners who could not undertake the expense of estate management – or they retained the freehold and
granted leases long enough to permit the lessee to make a profit out of his
investment in building. By this second means they could enlarge their
immediate income by the creation of ground rents arising from their
building leases; they need not necessarily involve themselves in a large
capital outlay, and they could look forward to the day when the leases
would expire and they or their heirs would inherit the reversion of the
buildings erected at the expense of the lessee. Because so much of the
land around London was owned by families concerned to preserve and
enhance their long-term social and financial position, or by corporations
equally concerned for the future, the leasehold system was by far the most
common means employed in the suburban development of nineteenth-
century London.

The business of development was often started by the landowner
promoting a private Act of Parliament enabling him to grant building
leases for up to ninety-nine years – the usual term at the beginning of the
nineteenth century. He would employ a surveyor to draw up a plan for the
layout of all or part of his estate, and he might then start to build roads
and sewers at his own expense. When individual plots or blocks of plots
were offered for building the prospective lessee would sign a building
agreement with the landlord in which he undertook to build a specified
number of houses of a stipulated size, quality and cost, and sometimes in
accordance with elevational designs prepared by the estate surveyor, while
the landlord covenanted that after the completion of each house he would
grant a building lease for a specified term and ground rent. These leases
were in practice usually granted not to the builder but to his nominee –
sometimes the first occupant of the new house, or more usually to some-

[1] Quoted in H. J. Dyos, *Victorian Suburb. A Study of the Growth of Camberwell*,
1961, p. 87.

one wanting a safe investment in bricks and mortar, to whom the builder sold his right to be granted a lease. The builder thus (in theory at least) received a capital sum from which he recovered his outlay in building plus, he hoped, a substantial profit, and was free to move on to similar work elsewhere, leaving landlord and tenant to their own devices for the remainder of the lease.

In practice there were infinite variations in the processes of development. The building of streets and houses upon a single estate might be spread over several decades, periods of feverish activity in boom years alternating with periods of complete stagnation when rows of empty or half-finished houses proclaimed bankruptcies and unemployment. As the urban frontier advanced and land became 'ripe' for building, land ownership tended to become more fragmented. Parts of a single privately-owned estate might be sold or leased for 999 years; the speculators in rising land values moved in, and the distinction between landlord and builder became blurred. Landowners, or speculators, as they might at this stage be often more appropriately called, frequently built houses on their own account, while builders became landowners. The providers of capital might also become actively involved, either by design or by force of circumstance. Functions coalesced or overlapped, and there was scope for everyone, from clergymen or elderly spinsters to petty tradesmen and hardened men of affairs, to participate in some way or other in the hurly-burly of suburban development.

Nevertheless there were some advantages in the leasehold system, at least theoretically. The landlord, who was concerned for the distant future as well as the immediate present, had a financial incentive to provide a good layout, with his proposed streets properly integrated into that of the surrounding estates. In the building agreement he could protect both his own interest and that of his future tenants by including detailed stipulations to ensure high quality in both design and building, and he could prevent the deterioration of his estate by prohibiting the practice of obnoxious trades. The builder had no large outlay in the purchase of an expensive freehold interest, so he could operate rapidly on relatively little capital, thereby increasing the total supply of houses and keeping rents down. Throughout the whole period of the ground lease there was some degree of overall supervision of an estate, and when the leases began to expire the undivided ownership of the freehold would permit planned redevelopment.

But there were also a number of disadvantages, including even the ease

H

with which a man with little or no capital could engage in speculative building. Almost all houses built by speculators were financed on credit of one kind or another. A speculative builder, according to Thomas Burton, himself a builder who only worked under contract, was 'a man that builds a house for the express purpose of selling or borrowing a sum of money upon it, and parting with his lease at an advanced ground-rent'. The procedure was to 'take a piece of ground; get materials for your buildings on credit; borrow money upon mortgage; get a tenant in at an excessive rent'. When groups of building craftsmen in different trades worked together in a single speculation it was not uncommon for one member of the partnership to end in debt to another, but to be incapable of paying in money. He could only pay by more building, and so the whole process, known as 'working blood for blood', would begin again, and lead in due course to numerous bankruptcies and rows of half-finished or empty houses. In 1833, for instance, houses were still being built in Hackney Road when others already stood empty and untenanted in the adjoining street. Under the leasehold system it was in fact easier for a man to start speculating than to stop, and the result was excessive building followed by a slump.[1]

Another disadvantage was the absence, except in parts of East London, of new building specifically for the working class, for most early nine-teenth-century landlords, being anxious for the maintenance of the value of their property, intended that their estates should be occupied by the upper or the middle classes. But at that time few landlords or their agents could exercise sufficiently close supervision to prevent unscrupulous builders from ignoring the provisions of the articles of agreement. Not all builders were dishonest, but the leasehold system produced shoddy and outwardly pretentious as well as good building, and when the landlords failed or found it in practice impossible to enforce covenants for repairs and maintenance or to prevent unauthorized building in gardens and back yards, many houses intended for the 'respectable' classes often degenerated into slums within a decade or two of their erection. Once this process had begun it was almost impossible to reverse it. Decaying houses intended for occupation by a single family, with cellars, large rooms and an inadequate water supply, were invaded by half-a-dozen or more families, for whom they provided utterly unsuitable accommodation. The ground landlord did not gain, for another disadvantage of the leasehold system

[1] P.P., 1833 (690), vol. vi, *Report and Minutes of Evidence from the Select Committee on Manufactures, Commerce and Shipping*, pp. 105–15.

was the multiplicity of leasehold interests which it often established – from the freeholder to the builder's nominee, from the nominee to the occupant, and then later from a lodging-house keeper, perhaps, to a 'house farmer' whose sole aim was to squeeze in as many weekly tenants as he could. In conditions of this kind the covenants contained in the ground lease became unenforceable, and the regeneration of the property had often to wait through long years of human misery until the original term expired.

There was also some public control of building, but it was not aimed at the prevention of social evils of this kind. The main objects of the London Building Act of 1774, which remained in force until 1844, were the prevention of fire, the restriction of encroachments on streets and the control of dangerous structures. There were rules for the thickness of walls and types of materials to be used, and professionally qualified district surveyors were to be appointed to see that the Act was observed. But there was no regulation of the width of new streets, or of the height, lighting or ventilation of rooms. Dark narrow courts could still be built, sometimes with no open space at the rear, and underground rooms were still common. The Act only applied to the Cities of London and Westminster and a number of adjacent parishes. Outside this area there was no public control of any kind, and even within it supervision of building can hardly have been strict, for in 1839 there were only thirty-three district surveyors at work.[1]

The success or failure of early nineteenth-century owners in providing and maintaining reasonable standards of housing on their estates depended in large measure on the vigour of their own efforts. Wealthy landlords like the Duke of Bedford in Bloomsbury or Lord Grosvenor in Belgravia could employ their own permanent staff to supervise both builders and tenants, and they were therefore more likely to be able to prevent creeping deterioration than an owner of only a few acres, or than an owner like the Marquess of Northampton, whose neglect of his extensive property in Clerkenwell, much of it laid out between 1815 and 1818, reaped its inevitable crop of slum tenements in later years.[2] But there were also extraneous factors in the equation. The geographical position of an estate

---

[1] C. C. Knowles, 'A History of the Regulation of Building in London and of District Surveyors 1189–1954', 1955, pp. 54, 61–4, 69, 76 (typescript in Members' Library, County Hall).

[2] Donald J. Olsen, *Town Planning in London, the eighteenth and nineteenth centuries*, Yale University Press, 1964, pp. 102–3.

and the persistent westward movement of the upper classes for instance, made the task of a landowner very much easier in Kensington than in Hackney. A badly managed adjacent estate could exert a fatally adverse influence, and after the 1830s the sudden arrival of a railway company might cut across a homogeneous street pattern and spawn little restricted enclaves where nobody chose to live and where the vacuum could only be filled by the very poor, who had no choice. And then too there was the most unstable factor of all – the builders.

At the beginning of the nineteenth century the London builders had not been greatly affected by the Industrial Revolution, and the organization of their trades still included almost every stage of industrial development. At the bottom of the scale there were the general labourers, many of whom were of Irish extraction, and the apprentices and journeymen. Next there were the traditional small master craftsmen – bricklayers, carpenters, joiners, masons, painters or glaziers – who employed a few labourers and journeymen and confined themselves to work in their own trade. Above them were the masters who would contract for or speculate in the erection of complete buildings, but who would only employ work-men in their own trade and sub-contracted with other masters for the rest of the work. Most of the fabric of Georgian London had been built by these means, much of it without the help of architects, but in the second half of the eighteenth century another type had emerged, the under-taker who was often not a craftsman at all but who erected complete buildings and made his own contracts with the master craftsmen of each trade.

In the decade after the close of the French wars in 1815 there was an almost unbroken boom in building, and the volume of work in London increased vastly. Much of this work was routine house-building of the kind which Cobbett denounced, but it also included an unprecedentedly large number of contracts for buildings of great size and cost – barracks, churches, docks, bridges and theatres – where the customer was either the government itself, or a public commission backed by the govern-ment, or a joint stock company. In order to meet this new and more sustained demand it now became possible for a large-scale building undertaker to go one step further and employ his own workmen in all trades on a semi-permanent basis. Customers, too, began to think that competitive tendering was the most economical method of building, and so gradually there emerged the modern building contractor, moving from one great job to another with his own staff of clerks, foremen and artificers.[1]

Alexander Copland was the prototype of these new men, but his working life was relatively short and the organization which he built up did not achieve the permanency of that subsequently created by Thomas Cubitt. Copland had been trained in the Royal Academy Schools and in his father's building business, but he had soon struck out on his own in the erection of barracks (including the still surviving guard house in Hyde Park) and military hospitals. His contracts for the government, scattered over many parts of the country, exceeded one million pounds, he had his own wharf in London and at one time he employed some seven hundred men. During the short-lived Peace of Amiens (1802–3) he built Albany Chambers off Piccadilly as a speculation, and in 1808–9 he was the principal contractor for the rebuilding of Covent Garden Theatre to the designs of Robert Smirke, to whom he was related. Two years later his partner Henry Rowles was the sole contractor for the rebuilding of Drury Lane Theatre, and in the 1820s he himself was engaged in building St Katharine's Docks. He died in 1834, on the eve of the railway age which so vastly enlarged the field of operations of many men of his capacity.[2]

Thomas Cubitt's career was much longer, and nearly all of his work was done in London, where the demand was both sufficiently great and continuous to support a permanent establishment. He entered the industry at the bottom as a journeyman, but in about 1809 he set up on his own as a master carpenter. In 1815 he contracted to build the London Institution in Finsbury Circus subject to a penalty clause for completion by a certain date, and in accordance with the usual practice he began to sub-contract with other masters for the bricklayers' and masons' work. But he 'was determined not to be left at the mercy of this complicated and inefficient system', and he therefore bought a site in Gray's Inn Road, erected his own workshops, 'purchased horses, carts and material, and engaged . . . gangs of carpenters, smiths, glaziers, bricklayers and other workers'.[3] So

---

[1] E. W. Cooney, 'The Origins of the Victorian Master Builders', *Economic History Review*, Second Series, vol. 8, 1955–6, pp. 167–76; M. H. Port, 'The Office of Works and Building Contracts in Early Nineteenth Century England', *Economic History Review*, Second Series, vol. 20, 1967, pp. 94–110.

[2] Cooney, p. 170; *Survey of London*, vol. xxxii, 1963, pp. 372–6; H. M. Colvin, *A Biographical Dictionary of English Architects, 1660–1840*, 1954; private information kindly supplied by Mr P. A. Bezodis.

[3] Sir Stephen Tallents, *Man and Boy*, 1943, p. 30; Colvin.

emerged the first recognizably modern large-scale building firm, employing men from all the old separate trades on a continuous wage basis.

To maintain this expensive establishment he needed an uninterrupted sequence of work, and during the next quarter of a century Cubitt became the greatest house-building speculator in London. He began on the Calthorpe estate near his workshops in Gray's Inn Road, and at Highbury Park, Islington (where he had his own brickfields), but in 1821 he contracted with the Duke of Bedford to build the south side of Tavistock Square, Bloomsbury. In the course of the next three years he took all the remaining ground on the Bedford estate south of Euston Road, and after laying out sewers and roads, began to build houses in Woburn Place, Endsleigh Street and Gordon Square, many of them to the designs of one of his brothers, Lewis Cubitt. Simultaneously he began to build on an even larger scale on Lord Grosvenor's estate in Belgravia, where he was responsible for half of Belgrave Square, the northern side of Eaton Square, and later for much of Pimlico. He continued to work in this area, nicknamed 'Cubittopolis', until his death in 1855. In 1827 he dissolved his early partnership with his other brother, William, who retained the workshops in Gray's Inn Road while Thomas established a new depot at Thames Bank, Pimlico, near the scene of his principal later works. By 1828 William Cubitt was employing about seven hundred men and Thomas about one thousand.[1]

The Cubitts' scale of building in London was unique at this time, although it was soon to become common among the railway contractors. But there were a few other builders with their own regular labour force and their own yards and workshops, often near the river or a canal – Thomas Burton, for instance, who between 1825 and 1832 employed an average of 170 men, mostly for repairs and alterations in the City and West End, or Bennett and Hunt of Horseferry Road, who built the Athenaeum and the Carlton club-houses in Pall Mall, or Lee and Sons of Chiswell Street, Moorgate, who built the Travellers'. Firms of this kind did not often survive for long after the departure of the original founders, company formation being still almost unknown in the building industry, but by the 1850s they had become so numerous that all the big London jobs were in their hands, and their members had had their own trade

[1] Colvin; Olsen, p. 59; Cooney, p. 172; P.P., 1828, vol. iv, *Report and Minutes oj Evidence of Select Committee on the Office of Works and Public Buildings*, p. 405; Hermione Hobhouse, 'The Building of Belgravia', *Country Life*, 8 and 22 May 1969, pp. 1154–7, 1312–14.

organization since 1839, the London Master Builders' Association. One firm, C. and T. Lucas, even had workshops at faraway Lowestoft, where much of the joinery which still exists at the Royal Opera House, Covent Garden, was made in 1857 before being transported, probably by sea, to London for assembly.[1]

One of the first great contractors to move over from building to the limitless field of railway construction was Sir Samuel Morton Peto (1809–89). He had been apprenticed to his uncle, Henry Peto, a builder in the City from whom he learned how to lay eight hundred bricks a day. After Henry Peto's death in 1830 his two nephews, Samuel Peto and Thomas Grissell, formed the great partnership whose contracts included the building of Hungerford Market, the Reform, Conservative, and Oxford and Cambridge club-houses, the Lyceum, St James's and Olympic theatres, the Nelson column in Trafalgar Square and the major part of the new Houses of Parliament. In 1846 the partnership was dissolved; Grissell retained the building contracts while Peto went over to large-scale railway building in partnership with E. L. Betts. Peto had already built a section of the Great Western Railway line on the outskirts of London, and now he ranged all over England and later, in conjunction with Thomas Brassey, as far afield as Canada and Australia. He sat as a liberal member for many years in the parliament house which he had previously con-tracted to build, and his career was only ended when Peto and Betts had to suspend payment after the crash of Overend and Gurney in 1866.

Contract building on the scale undertaken in London by firms like Grissell and Peto produced a new figure in the building world – the quantity surveyor. Pricing by measuring the completed building was giving way to precise advance measurement before construction began, and this method was employed by the builders of several of the Pall Mall club-houses, the leading practitioner being Henry Arthur Hunt, son of the Hunt of the building firm of Bennett and Hunt. The new profession came into its own in 1837 when Hunt was employed to take out the bills of quantity for Barry's designs for the new Houses of Parliament, the final cost of which eventually exceeded £1½ million, and thereafter it became normal practice to use a quantity surveyor for all large building contracts.[2]

---

[1] *Survey of London*, vol. xxix, 1960, pp. 355, 390, 403; vol. xxv, 1970, p. 82; J. H. Clapham, *An Economic History of Modern Britain*, vol. I, 1962, p. 165; vol. II, 1932, p. 146; R. W. Postgate, *The Builders' History*, 1923, p. 197.

[2] F. M. L. Thompson, *Chartered Surveyors. The Growth of a Profession*, 1968, pp. 85–93.

GEORGE M. SMILEY MEMORIAL LIBRARY
CENTRAL METHODIST COLLEGE
FAYETTE, MISSOURI 65248

But firms large enough to undertake jobs of this scale were exceptional. The London building industry as a whole remained extremely conservative in its structure, and apart from the introduction of cast iron the technical innovations which occurred before about 1850 were not widely used until the closing years of the century.[1] The census of 1851 shows that only fifty-seven London 'builders' (i.e. general contractors) employed fifty or more men, and only nine of these fifty-seven had over two hundred employees. There were altogether 739 self-styled 'builders', many of them with fewer than ten men apiece, and as a class of employers they were still far outnumbered by the master carpenters and joiners. The master craftsmen of a single trade still predominated in the London building industry as a whole, most of them employing only about half-a-dozen men, and confining their work to a comparatively small area around their place of business. When the Bishop of London rebuilt his house in aristocratic St James's Square in 1819–22 his architect, S. P. Cockerell, employed seven different master craftsmen, of whom at least four were local men, and at about the same time the Bishop's neighbour, the Earl of Bristol, was content to employ a carpenter from round the corner to take charge of the lavish rebuilding of his house.[2]

The large-scale building contractors were, in fact, few in number, and with the notable exceptions of Thomas Cubitt and James Burton (who in the early years of the nineteenth century built some 900 houses on the Foundling and Bedford estates in Bloomsbury) they seldom engaged in speculative building in the suburbs. In this field small local firms continued to enjoy an overwhelming preponderance. Recent research by Dr Dyos on the monthly returns of the District Surveyors shows that of the 1,102 firms engaged in building houses in London in 1872, 827 had only six or fewer houses under construction, 127 had between seven and twelve houses, 81 had between thirteen and twenty-four, and only twenty-four firms in all London were building twenty-five or more houses in that year. Expressed differently this means that over 83 per cent of all the houses then under construction were built by firms with not more than twenty-four houses on their books at that time, and that 75 per cent of all firms built six houses or less. And Dr Dyos goes on to say that this state of affairs had existed for some time, for between the 1840s and the 1870s

---

[1] Marian Bowley, *Innovations in Building Materials*, 1960, p. 53.
[2] *Survey of London*, vol. xxix, 1960, pp. 105, 203.

'there was virtually no change in the overall structure of the London housing industry'.[1]

These conclusions are supported by more detailed studies of the pattern of speculative building in different districts. In North Kensington in 1845, 137 houses were built by 31 firms, of which 2 were responsible for 26 and 28 each, while none of the other 29 firms had more than 11 houses each. In 1871 the pattern had not greatly altered; 327 houses were built by 59 builders, the largest firm having only 21 houses and only 8 having more than 10 each.[2] On the ninety-acre estate of the Mercers' Company in Stepney, where some 1,100 houses were built between 1811 and about 1850, one builder, William Dempsey, built some 570 houses, but only two others reached a three-figure output during the whole period of over thirty years. On the other side of the river, in Lambeth, and doubtless in many other districts too, we are told that house-builders seldom ventured more than a mile from their yards or engaged to build more than ten houses at a time, while in Camberwell during the three prosperous years 1850–2 none built more than thirty houses.[3]

In 1851 there were over 66,500 people engaged in building in London. Building was, in fact, London's biggest single industry, and during the previous decade alone over 43,000 new houses had been built there.[4] The primary requirements – land and materials – were both costly, and the questions therefore arise, what were the profits for the landlords, and what were the sources for the gigantic sums of capital needed to keep the builders busy?

Neither question can be answered with any precision, but the very great variations in the scale of building provide some clues. The supply and demand for housing were constantly affected by the general credit situation of the country, and in particular by the price of food, the price of imported timber and (in the first half of the century) the current yield on Consols. When the rate of interest on Consols reached about 4 per cent, the rate for building loans, always a little higher, would reach 5 per cent or above. But under the Usury Laws interest above 5 per cent was forbidden,

[1] H. J. Dyos, 'The Speculative Builders and Developers of Victorian London', *Victorian Studies*, vol. xi, Supplement, 1968, pp. 641–90.

[2] Greater London Record Office, District Surveyors' Returns.

[3] Jean M. Imray, 'The Mercers' Company and East London, 1750–1850', *East London Papers*, vol. 9, 1966, pp. 3–25; Dyos, *Victorian Suburb*, p. 125; *Survey of London*, vol. xxvi, p. 11.

[4] *Census of Population*, 1851, vol. I, p. 9; R. Price-Williams, 'The Population of London, 1801–81', *Journal of the Statistical Society*, vol. xlviii, 1885, pp. 412–13.

and so when the margin of interest between Consols and the more risky private loans became narrow the supply of capital for building collapsed. After the return of peace in 1815 the yield on Consols fell, there was an acute shortage of housing, the 222,000 families of Middlesex being crammed into only 130,000 houses, and in 1817 there began a steady increase in the scale of building. This culminated in the tremendous boom of the early 1820s, which reached its peak and its end in 1825, when the great financial crisis was followed by almost a collapse of private building in London. House building did not begin to recover until about 1836, when the excessive supply created in the early 1820s was at last exhausted, but even in 1840 the number of bricks produced in London was less than half the production of 1825, and many of those produced in 1840 were no doubt used for railway construction as well as for houses. In the 1840s the level of building continued to increase, particularly that of house building, until the financial crisis of 1847; and between 1856 and 1868 there was another broad upward movement.

The profits which a landowner might make when he began to develop his estate must therefore have depended greatly on the timing of his decision. If he were wise enough, or more probably lucky enough, to start at the beginning of an upward curve in the building cycle he might expect to dispose of his land to the builders without difficulty, and within two or three years the income which he would receive from the ground rents of his building leases would be far greater than it had been when the land was being used for agriculture. But if he had started in say 1823 or 1824, and laid out some of his own money in the building of roads and sewers, he might well have found himself stuck for years with rows of half-finished houses and a fistful of leases to bankrupt builders. Landowners with liquid capital resources of their own, such as the Duke of Bedford or the Governors of the Foundling Hospital estate, both with lands in Bloomsbury, could counteract the effects of a building depression by extending the initial period of usually one or two years in which building lessees only had to pay a nominal or peppercorn rent. Some landowners made loans to their builders, and when a building project was finished it was common practice for landowners to buy some of the improved ground rents which development had created – i.e. the difference between the ground rent stipulated in a building agreement and the rent which the builder could get for the house or houses he had built, usually assessed at about twenty years' purchase. In the crisis year of 1847, for instance, when building on his Figs' Mead land to the north of Euston Road was in full swing, the Duke of Bedford spent over £12,000 on the purchase of improved ground rents, and the pace of development was hardly affected.[1]

The greater capital resources available on many of the larger estates was indeed one reason why building development often proceeded more smoothly there than on smaller holdings, but in all estate developments large amounts of capital were needed. Banks were probably not an important source, although the London and Westminster and the London and County joint stock banks did lend direct to developers on mortgage, and in 1854 the Commercial Bank of London was lending to the Temperance Permanent Building Society.[2] Insurance companies were a more important source. Thomas Cubitt had borrowed £20,000 from the Sun Insurance Office in the 1820s, as well as an unspecified sum, during his operations in Belgravia, from the Guardian Assurance. The insurance companies were selective with their loans, however, and in general only made advances to builders of substance. The scale of their lending was evidently rising in the 1840s and 1850s, and in the single year 1865 the London Assurance lent £113,000 to speculative builders. One company, the British Empire Mutual Life Assurance Company, even entered the building development business on its own account and bought an estate in Camberwell, with apparently not very successful results.[3]

Building societies were not numerous in London until the 1840s. At first they were of the terminating variety, members subscribing regularly to a capital fund from which they borrowed in turn the capital needed to build or buy a house; when the whole operation had been completed the society came to an end. Permanent societies, in which the lenders or investors and the borrowers for the purchase of houses formed two quite distinct groups, soon superseded the terminating type, the first of them, the Metropolitan Equitable Investment Association, being formed in 1845. Between 1843 and 1853 357 terminating and 34 permanent building societies were formed in London. Lending for the purchase of houses was their main business, most of the advances being for less than £300 each. Some societies also lent direct to speculative builders, which sometimes

---

[1] J. Parry Lewis, *Building Cycles and Britain's Growth*, 1965, pp. 13, 27–8, 70, 101; A. K. Cairncross and B. Weber, 'Fluctuations in Building in Great Britain, 1785–1849', *Economic History Review, Second Series*, vol. 9, 1956, pp. 283–91; R. C. O. Matthews, *A Study in Trade-Cycle History*, 1954, p. 117; Olsen, pp. 36, 71, 82–3.

[2] Dyos, 'Speculative Builders', p. 665; Seymour J. Price, *From Queen to Queen. The Centenary Story of the Temperance Permanent Building Society 1854–1954*, 1954, p. 18.

[3] Hobhouse, pp. 1154–7; Dyos, 'Speculative Builders', p. 668, quoting material supplied by Dr D. A. Reeder; Dyos, *Victorian Suburb*, p. 119.

resulted in the societies themselves becoming involved in the business of speculation. By the 1860s, it has tentatively been estimated, one house in every seven or eight built throughout the whole country was financed by the building societies.[1]

A large proportion of the capital used in suburban development was, however, probably raised locally and/or privately. Profits from one successful speculation were re-invested in another venture, while the mostly middle-class migrants who came to the new suburbs invested at least some of their savings there by the purchase of houses. In the days before the railways the range of investments offered on the Stock Exchange was extremely limited, and even after the railway companies had greatly widened the field industrial stocks were still almost unknown until the 1870s. Foreign loans absorbed a large proportion of the total national supply of capital, but much of what was left went into bricks and mortar. The channel by which it arrived there was usually the lawyer's office.

In 1841 the number of people of independent means living in London was 66·6 per cent above the national average. Ten years later there were well over 33,000 people 'of Rank or Property' not engaged in any occupation,[2] and the census enumerators' books for middle-class districts frequently describe householders, both male and female, with no regular form of employment as 'owners of houses and property'. These, evidently, were the people, living both in London and the provinces, who supplied substantial quantities of capital for suburban development. Many of them were women. In those days the unmarried daughters of well-to-do middle-class parents were not expected or trained to support themselves, and financial provision for them forms an important part of many Victorian wills. When they inherited these legacies the family lawyer advised them on how to invest, and innumerable London title deeds testify to the favour with which spinsters or widows regarded house property – safe, solid mortgages at 5 per cent for those who had to be thrifty, or perhaps some improved ground rents for those more wealthy.

The lawyers, of course, were delighted, for this kind of investment provided them with plenty of work. Often they themselves became actively involved in the business of suburban speculation, for they were well

---

[1] E. J. Cleary, *The Building Society Movement*, 1965, pp. 45–8, 73, 289; Seymour J. Price, *Building Societies. Their Origin and History*, 1958, pp. 122, 208.

[2] Joseph Fletcher, 'Moral and Educational Statistics of England and Wales', *Journal of the Statistical Society*, vol. XII, 1849, p. 259; *Census of Population*, 1851, vol. I, p. 9.

informed and, through the advice which they tendered to their clients, well placed to direct the investment of large sums of money. The whole system of this lawyer's paradise was aptly described by the celebrated architect John Nash.

> The artificial causes of the extension of the town are the specula-
> tions of Builders, encouraged and promoted by Merchants dealing
> in the materials of building; and Attorneys with monied clients,
> facilitating, and indeed putting in motion, the whole system; by
> disposing of improved ground-rents, and by numerous other devices,
> by which their clients make an advantageous use of their money; and
> the attorneys create to themselves a lucrative business from the
> agreements, leases, mortgages, bonds, and other instruments of law,
> which become necessary, throughout such complicated and intricate
> transactions.[1]

Not all building was of the private speculative variety. A sizeable proportion of the industry's output was financed by the government out of taxes or from public funds raised in the City, and this was particularly common in the case of the largest contracts – for the General Post Office or the British Museum or the new Houses of Parliament, for in-stance. Many of the churches built in the 1820s were also paid for out of money voted by Parliament. And joint stock companies sometimes raised capital by public subscription for expensive projects such as the building of Drury Lane Theatre or several of the new bridges across the river.

During the first third of the nineteenth century London was spreading steadily, both outwards and by accretion round existing villages and other small settlements. To the north there was extensive building in Blooms-bury, notably on the estates of the Duke of Bedford and the Foundling Hospital, and in Islington and St Pancras. Most of this work was on traditional Georgian lines, the streets being lined with almost uniform brick-fronted houses and the 'squares' becoming ever longer and narrower. Much the same was happening a mile or two farther west on the Portman estate along the east side of Edgware Road, but in between lay the Crown estate of Marylebone Park where John Nash was laying out his artificial lake and his great stucco-fronted terraces (described on page 113). North of the park, on the rising ground at St John's Wood, a new form of develop-ment was proceeding in the 1820s on the Eyre estate. Here for the first

---

[1] Quoted in John Summerson, *John Nash, Architect to King George IV*, 1935, p. 110.

time in London the terrace was discarded in favour of the detached or semi-detached house – an innovation soon to be copied elsewhere, and to have widespread influence on the nineteenth-century suburban scene.

In east London land values were lower, the world of fashion and wealth was far away, and the new building in Bethnal Green, Whitechapel and Stepney was unpretentious and unremarkable. This was the industrial and mercantile side of London, where the ground landlords' control of development was usually less effective than in the more prosperous residential districts to the west. The marshy meandering southward course of the River Lea formed a barrier to more distant expansion and even as late as the 1840s Stratford was still not joined to the City by a continuous line of building.[1]

But the areas of most rapid growth were in the west and the south. To the west there were no physical barriers and in Paddington the population increased from less than 2,000 in 1801 to over 25,000 in 1841. Paddington, through the extension of the Grand Junction Canal in 1795, had for a short while become an inland port, and in 1831 half the male population of the parish was engaged in retail trades and small businesses. But the westward pull of fashion was also making itself felt there, and on the Bishop of London's estate at Tyburnia S. P. Cockerell's plans for a spacious sequence of squares, crescents and terraces were by the 1830s beginning to attract the professional and more wealthy commercial classes.[2] Farther south the rebuilding of Buckingham House as the principal royal palace had suddenly made Lord Grosvenor's desolate marshy ground to the west desirable for building development, and when Thomas Cubitt began in 1825 to raise the level of the land by using the spoil from St Katharine's Docks, then in course of construction near the Tower of London, the success of his gigantic speculation in Belgravia was assured. Hans Town, built in the 1780s by Henry Holland and hitherto standing almost isolated in open country, at last became a part of London, and soon terraces and squares were sprouting up in nearby Brompton and South Kensington – Brompton and Alexander Squares in the 1820s, followed by Pelham Crescent on the estate of Henry Smith's trustees in the 1830s, and Thurlow and Onslow Squares in the 1840s – many of them designed by George Basevi, the architect of Belgrave Square. And even in faraway North

---

[1] W. Ashworth, 'Types of Social and Economic Development in Suburban Essex', in *London Aspects of Change*, ed. Ruth Glass, 1964, pp. 62–87.

[2] D. A Reeder, 'A Theatre of Suburbs; Some Patterns of Development in West London, 1801–1911', in *The Study of Urban History*, ed. H. J. Dyos, 1968, pp. 262–3.

Kensington James Ladbroke was busying himself as early as the 1820s with plans and an Act of Parliament for the layout of the great estate whose church, square, crescents and communal gardens were in due course to provide one of the last examples of London's great tradition of residential development, inaugurated two centuries earlier in the Inns of Court and Covent Garden, and tracing its pedigree through Bloomsbury and the West End to this distant Victorian outpost in Notting Hill.[1]

Until the early nineteenth century the Thames had barred London's southward growth, but between 1816 and 1819 three new bridges were built at Vauxhall, Waterloo and Southwark, plus a network of new turnpike roads extending out to Kennington, Newington Butts and Camberwell. In the 1820s the population of both Lambeth and Camberwell increased by over 50 per cent, most of the new houses being built in terraces – the poor relations of those going up in Kensington – or in pairs in the flat plains of Stockwell, Brixton and Peckham. But farther out, on the rising ground at Denmark Hill, Tulse Hill and Brixton Hill there were large detached villas set in spacious gardens, and in these quasi-rural surroundings prosperous merchants and professional men were finding a refuge from the noise and dirt and constriction of the City and the inner suburbs.

The history of John Ruskin's family illustrates this early phase of the nineteenth-century flight to the new outer suburbs. Until 1823 John Ruskin's father, a wine merchant, lived in a terrace house in Hunter Street near Brunswick Square, St Pancras; his office was in Billiter Street in the City, and every summer the family moved for a few weeks to lodgings in Hampstead or Dulwich. In 1823 he took a three-storey semi-detached house at Herne Hill, the previous occupant of which had been a linen draper in Cheapside. He continued to attend his office daily, returning to dine at Herne Hill at half-past four. Of their neighbours the family saw almost nothing. 'They were for the most part well-to-do London tradesmen of the better class' and often had 'great cortège of footmen and glitter of plate, expensive pleasure grounds, costly hot-houses, and carriages driven by coachmen in wigs.' By 1842 Ruskin's father could afford to take a larger and detached house at Denmark Hill, where he lived until his death in 1864. John Ruskin's loving descriptions of Herne

[1] Ashley Barker, 'Nineteenth Century Estate Development in South Kensington', *Annual Report of the Kensington Society*, 1967, and 'The Nineteenth Century Development of Notting Hill', in unpublished proceedings of the Kensington Society Conference on Town Planning and Housing in North Kensington, 9 October 1965.

Hill in his childhood go far to explain the attractions of such suburban sites.

> The view from the ridge on both sides was, before railroads came, entirely lovely: westward at evening, almost sublime, over softly wreathing distances of domestic wood; Thames herself not visible, nor any fields except immediately beneath; but the tops of twenty square miles of politely inhabited groves. On the other side, east and south, the Norwood hills, partly rough with furze, partly wooded with birch and oak, partly in pure green bramble copse, and rather steep pasture, rose with the promise of all the rustic loveliness of Surrey and Kent in them, and with so much of space and height in their sweep, as gave them some fellowship with hills of true hill-districts.[1]

Such was life in what might have been called the stock-jobber belt, an area which according to William Cobbett extended a great deal farther south than Herne Hill.

> The town of Brighton, in Sussex, 50 miles from the Wen, is on the sea-side, [he noted in 1823] and is thought by the stock-jobbers, to afford a salubrious air. It is so situated that a coach, which leaves it not very early in the morning, reaches London by noon; and, starting to go back in two hours and a half afterwards, reaches Brighton not very late at night. Great parcels of stock-jobbers stay at Brighton with the women and children. They skip backward and forward on the coaches, and actually carry on stock-jobbing in 'Change Alley, though they reside at Brighton.[2]

At this time there were only twenty coaches running daily between London and Brighton, so this skipping backward and forward must have been very small in scale. But in 1825 some 600 short-stage coaches were working from the City and Westminster, and they made some 1,800 journeys daily, chiefly to such suburban districts as Paddington, Camberwell and Clapham. Road-communications were becoming of vital importance to the capital and in the early nineteenth century a number of new turnpike roads were built. North of the Thames there were New North Road (1812), Archway Road (1813) and Caledonian Road (1826), followed by Finchley Road (1826–35) and the route from Marylebone to

---

[1] Quoted in *Survey of London*, vol. xxvi, 1956, pp. 10–11.
[2] Cobbett, vol. I, p. 148.

Tottenham now known as Albany Street–Parkway–Camden Road–Seven Sisters Road; while to the south there was the complex network radiating out from St George's Circus, Southwark, to the new bridges leading to Westminster and the City. In 1826 the fourteen turnpike trusts in the vicinity of London to the north of the Thames were amalgamated under one body of commissioners appointed by the government; but in south London fifteen separate bodies were still administering the principal roads there in 1831, and the joint stock company owners of the nine major road bridges across the river between Hammersmith and Waterloo continued to levy tolls until they were finally bought out by the Metropolitan Board of Works in 1877–80.[1]

Thus before a single line of railway had been built in London several of the most deep-seated problems of later suburban life already existed. The well-to-do were beginning to forsake their now ageing and constricted houses in the central areas for the greater space and privacy which they could afford to buy on the outskirts. This process was to continue over and over again – in 1871, for instance, John Ruskin gave up his house at Denmark Hill, now hemmed in by more recent building – and indeed it still continues to this day. Each outward migration left behind it an area already in decline, which was quickly filled by the less prosperous or the poor. In the sixteenth and seventeenth centuries the slums had been on the outskirts of the town, but now they were to be in the centre, and the constant leap-frogging of those who could afford to choose where they lived over those who could not greatly aggravated the physical separation of one social class from another. It also created the modern problem of the journey to work, the handful of Brighton stock-jobbers who travelled by coach being the precursors of the thousands of modern railway commuters. The pattern of megalopolis was beginning to emerge.

While suburban London was thus proceeding on its outward march, two internal transformations were also going forward – the building of the London docks and the formation of Regent Street and Regent's Park. These were the first important improvements to be made to the fabric of

[1] T. C. Barker and Michael Robbins, *A History of London Transport*, vol. I, 1963, pp. 4–5; H. J. Dyos, 'The Growth of a Pre-Victorian Suburb: South London, 1580–1836', *Town Planning Review*, vol. xxv, 1954, pp. 59–78; Peter Hall, 'The Development of Communications', in *Greater London*, ed. J. T. Coppock and Hugh C. Prince, 1964, p. 56; T. F. Reddaway, 'London in the Nineteenth Century: the freeing of the Bridges, 1800–1880', *The Twentieth Century*, vol. 151, 1952, pp. 163–77.

I

London since the Great Fire in 1666 and they provide an apt reminder that London has the rare distinction among the great cities of the world of being both a major port and a capital seat. The docks were the work of the merchants and financiers of the City, while the adornment of the West End was initiated by the Crown – or rather, the Prince Regent.

During the course of the eighteenth century the trade of the Port of London trebled in value and in the number and tonnage of ships. But the legal quays, licensed for the clearance of imports and all situated on the north side of the river between London Bridge and the Tower, had not been enlarged since 1666, and almost the only eighteenth-century improvement had been the establishment of sufferance wharves, mostly on the south side of the river, with limited rights for the discharge of certain goods brought there in barges. Most vessels therefore had to load and unload at moorings in the stream, and the Pool of London – the stretch of river below the bridge – had become crammed with hundreds of lighters, barges and hoys, colliers bringing sea-coal from Tyneside, and finally the great ocean-going ships whose ever growing size was progressively constricting them to the narrow channels with the deepest water. Congestion was particularly acute between July and October, when the prevailing winds brought the great West Indiamen with their rich cargoes of sugar, rum, cocoa, coffee and indigo. Over 100,000 hogsheads of sugar might arrive in a single season, but there was only enough space in the warehouses for a third of this quantity, and loss of goods by theft throughout the port was estimated to exceed half a million pounds a year.

When war broke out with France in 1793 the very existence of the nation depended on its foreign trade. The negligence and inefficiency of the City Corporation, which was responsible for the administration of the port, could no longer be tolerated, and in September the principal West India merchants set up a committee to consider how to improve conditions. William Vaughan, a naval architect and a director of the Royal Exchange Assurance, advocated the building of a series of enclosed tide-free docks between the Tower and the Isle of Dogs and early in 1796 a powerful group of users of the port decided to apply to Parliament for power to build a wet dock at Wapping.

The Corporation at once objected, of course, but the evidence in favour of wet docks was so overwhelming that the City Fathers felt obliged to sponsor a rival scheme, for building at the north end of the Isle of Dogs. This proposal had two great advantages – the land was cheaper, the Isle of Dogs being still used for the pasture of cattle, and access from the east would be much easier for large ships than at Wapping, farther up the river. Many of the West India merchants had changed their minds and given their support to the City's scheme, and so in 1799 Parliament decided in its favour.

The Act of 1799 established the West India Dock Company with power to raise capital and enclose nearly three hundred acres of land in the Isle of Dogs between Limehouse and Blackwall. The company was to build two parallel wet docks, each half a mile long and entered from the river by basins and locks at either end. There was to be enough quayside accommodation for six hundred ships, whose cargoes were to be discharged into huge ranges of warehouses, and both docks and warehouses were to be surrounded by a wall twenty feet in height. To guarantee a return on this enormous capital outlay the company was granted the right for twenty-one years to compel all ships with cargoes of West Indian produce to unload within the new docks and pay the company's charges.

The West India Import Dock was opened in August 1802, and in the following year the Warehousing Act allowed importers of West Indian produce to store their goods in the warehouses there without payment of duty until actually sold. This Act marks the establishment of the modern system of warehousing in bond – so-called from the bond which merchants had to give for the privilege of duty-free storage, and guaranteed by the joint locks of the Crown and the owner of the goods – which has proved of immense value in the development of London's entrepôt trade.[1]

The building of the West India Dock was only the first of a long series of such projects, gigantic in both scale and cost. In 1800 the London Dock Company was established to build in Wapping, and in 1803 the East India at Blackwall, both on the north side of the river, while on the south side four companies were set up by 1811 to build between the Pool and Limehouse Reach, primarily for the timber trade. Within little more than a decade Parliament authorized the investment of nearly five and a half million pounds in the building of docks, and in 1810 it was estimated that the cost of unloading and warehousing had decreased by 18 per cent since the improvements had been commenced. For perhaps the only time in its history the Port of London became one of the sights which both native and foreign visitors most wished to see.[2]

---

[1] James Bird, *The Geography of the Port of London*, 1957, pp. 85, 127–8.

[2] Arthur Bryant, *Liquid History*, 1960, p. 24; W. M. Stern, 'The First London Dock Boom and the Growth of the West India Docks', *Economica*, vol. xix, 1952, pp. 59–77.

More new docks were built in later years, notably the St Katharine, Tower of London, designed by Thomas Telford and constructed in part by Alexander Copland in 1825–8, and the Victoria Dock below Blackwall, which was opened in 1855 and was the first in the port with a main line railway connection. There was fierce competition for custom among the various companies, all of which also had to contend with the competition from lighters and barges in the loading and unloading of sea-going ships. Parliament insisted that these river craft should be exempt from dock charges, a privilege which naturally encouraged the unloading of cargoes into barges outside the docks, and often the conveyance of such goods direct to riverside wharves outside the dock companies' authority. With the union of the West and East India Dock Companies in 1838 a long process of amalgamation began. This ultimately resulted in the establishment of five separate dock systems, all of which were taken over by the Port of London Authority, an independent public trust established in 1909. By this time the City Corporation had lost almost all its powers over the river, many of them to the Thames Conservancy, which had managed the port from 1857 until 1909. By this time, too, the paramountcy of the Port of London had long been recognized, for as early as 1833 a partner in the great City firm of Baring Brothers had stated that he could 'see no port in the world to be compared with it as a centre upon which commerce must turn'.[1]

While the new docks appropriate to the needs of the greatest port in the world were being built in east London, something quite different was proceeding at the other end of the town. There, by a series of fortunate chance events, the West End was being transmogrified by the only great piece of town planning ever to be executed in London. These 'metropolitan improvements' extended from Regent's Park in the north to St James's Park in the south, and included a canal, two barracks and a great new thoroughfare cut through the existing fabric of narrow crowded streets. To the west of St James's Park a new royal palace arose, while to the east there was a great new *place* – Trafalgar Square – and a reconstruction of the neighbouring parts of the Strand.[2]

The one thing that was not an accident in all these exhilarating events

[1] Bird, pp. 73–4, 101; Bryant, p. 30; Sir Joseph G. Broodbank, *History of the Port of London*, vol. I, 1921, p. 183; P.P., 1833 (690), vol. VI, *S.C. on Manufactures, Commerce and Shipping*, p. 67.

[2] For the rest of this chapter see John Summerson, *Georgian London*, Pelican edn, 1962, and John Summerson, *John Nash, Architect to King George IV*, 1935, *passim*.

was that they took place either on land which already belonged to the Crown or on land which was bought by the Crown in order to permit their realization. London's chaotic local administration in the early nineteenth century was not remotely capable of executing such immense schemes, and the Crown's assumption of responsibility for them, and retention of responsibility for the lesser metropolitan street improvements which continued for many years after the death of the original sponsor, George IV, in 1830, indirectly postponed still further the day when London was finally granted its own municipal authority.

The first accident was the complicated character of the Prince Regent himself, who so fortunately combined the enthusiastic pursuit of women with an equally enthusiastic patronage of the arts. It was fortunate too that he became Regent in the same year, 1811, as Marylebone Park reverted to the Crown at the expiry of a long lease. Finally, there already existed a close personal liaison between the Prince Regent and his favourite architect, John Nash, who occupied the post of architect in the Office of Woods and Forests, the department responsible for the administration of the Crown lands. The nature of this liaison is shrouded in secrecy, but it seems at least likely that Nash's wife had been the Prince's mistress and had borne him several children.

Most of the Crown lands in west London had been acquired by Henry VIII, and until 1760 had been the private property of successive sovereigns. George III, however, had surrendered the ancient royal estates in exchange for a fixed civil list voted by Parliament out of public money, and in 1786 their administration had been entrusted to a statutory body from which there ultimately emerged the Commissioners of Woods, Forests and Land Revenues. The opportunity for improvements which the reversion of Marylebone Park in 1811 would create had been foreseen for some years, and in 1810 the government's own architects, of whom Nash was one, had been instructed to prepare plans. In the following year the Prince of Wales became the Prince Regent and Nash's designs were selected by the Commissioners of Woods and Forests.

Marylebone Park was farther north than the fashionable residential areas of the West End, and the problem was therefore how to lure the nobility and gentry to live beyond the New (now Marylebone) Road, hitherto the outermost boundary of acceptable domicile. The park itself, as ultimately laid out by Nash, became an aristocratic 'garden city' with eight large villas set among groves of new plantations with a large and artfully contrived lake not far away, all surrounded on three sides by long blocks of stucco-fronted terrace houses. This was a building speculation, though conceived in novel terms of design, and to get suitably wealthy customers for it a new street was provided to link this northern outpost with St James's and the West End. In his first designs Nash had disguised the crossing of the Marylebone Road by a gigantic circus with a church in the middle of it, but only the southern half (now Park Crescent) was actually built, the lessee having become bankrupt. Even this truncated version, leading on to Park Square, was impressive enough for its purpose, and the houses in and around the Regent's new park were soon finding tenants.

At its southern end the Regent's new street began, appropriately, in front of his town residence, Carlton House. Its northward course, at first suitably straight and formal, and then varied by a circus, the great curving Quadrant section, the delicate bend leading up to Oxford Street, another circus and the final twist into Portland Place, the Duke of Portland's great wide street which debouched into the park, are all so ingeniously managed that they conceal the fact that the route was largely determined by the ownership of the land which the street traversed. After an Act of 1813 had authorized the Commissioners of Woods and Forests to build the street the Treasury still maintained tight control over expenditure; to buy land – freeholds, leaseholds and the goodwill of innumerable businesses – was very costly, and it was therefore necessary to keep purchases to a minimum. The Crown already owned all of the land required to the south of Piccadilly, and a substantial block to the northwest of Piccadilly Circus as well. But it did not own the land due north of the Circus, and so it was cheaper to swing the line around through Crown property than to follow a more direct route. Virtually no purchases were needed south of Vigo Street (at the north end of the Quadrant), and from there almost to Oxford Street the line followed the course of Swallow Street, an old narrow road now to be greatly widened, part of whose eastern frontage also already belonged to the Crown. Only in the northern stretch, between Conduit Street and the south end of Portland Place, were extensive purchases necessary. Nash's route was therefore a cheap route. And it had another advantage too. Throughout most of its course between Piccadilly and Oxford Street it followed the frontier, hitherto insecurely guarded by Swallow Street, between the tortuous purlieus of Soho on the east and the more spacious and well-to-do streets of the Burlington estate and Hanover Square on the west. By restricting access to the new street from the east to a minimum – and it was originally much more restricted than it is today – Nash's route succeeded, to borrow Sir John Summerson's phrase, in 'damming up Soho' – an idea entirely consistent with the notions of town planning prevalent at that time.

Most of Regent Street was built between 1817 and 1823. Sites were let on long leases to building speculators, of whom James Burton, father of the architect Decimus Burton, was one of the most ambitious. Nash himself supplied some of the designs, and when nobody else would do it he even undertook the building of the whole of the Quadrant himself. Three churches and a gigantic new sewer were built, as well as shops, chambers and houses, while in the park the Grand Junction Canal, then in course of extension from Paddington to the Docks, was made to skirt around the estate and provide it with a suitably picturesque northern boundary. East of the park there were a market, a barracks and a couple of 'model villages' – Park Villages, East and West. With extraordinary speed the whole gigantic enterprise took shape, and when building operations were at their height George III died and was succeeded by the Prince Regent.

George IV, after celebrating his coronation with unprecedented splendour and extravagance, decided that Carlton House was no fit place for a king. 'Metropolitan improvements' received a new impetus. Tumbledown Buckingham House was rebuilt at vast expense and became Buckingham Palace, the straight formal canal in St James's Park was cunningly converted into what is still the most beautiful stretch of artificial water in London, and Carlton House was demolished. Carlton House Terrace arose on its site, a triumphal arch and screen at Hyde Park Corner (by Decimus Burton) provided a suitably impressive western approach to the palace, and the royal quarter of London assumed, to a large extent, its familiar modern aspect – with Nash still in command.

But this extraordinary old man, now well over seventy years of age, was still prolific in new ideas, and his relationship with the King provided him with the opportunity to carry many of them out. Pall Mall was extended eastward to open out into a great new square at the upper end of Whitehall. The National Gallery, by William Wilkins, built to house the nation's new collection of pictures, dominates, or rather amiably presides over Trafalgar Square, the eastern approaches to which were also tidied up along the Strand. And there were more plans for another Regent Street to link Trafalgar Square with Bloomsbury, where the British Museum was being rebuilt and Thomas Cubitt was busy laying out new streets and squares on the Duke of Bedford's estate.

The success and momentum of this unique phase in the architectural history of London depended very largely upon the mysterious connection between Nash and the King; and so when the King died – ten years younger than his still proliferous architect – the whole enterprise collapsed. Nash was dismissed for his mismanagement at Buckingham Palace, and died in 1835. By this time the national attention had turned to other more momentous events. The Commissioners of Woods and Forests made a number of worthy street improvements – notably New Oxford Street, Victoria Street and Commercial Street – some of them under the direction of Nash's own step-son, James Pennethorne, and they presided over the building of more club-houses along the south side of Pall Mall – a scheme previously begun by Nash with the United Service Club and the Athenaeum facing one another across Waterloo Place, and now continued with the Travellers', the Reform, the Oxford and Cambridge and finally the Carlton. But the great days were over. Great they had undoubtedly been, for by 1830 Nash and his sovereign had provided a large part of the West End with a new and beautiful setting – a setting worthy of a great capital city.

Four years later, on the night of 16 October 1834, the Houses of Parliament were destroyed by fire. Most of the great sprawling labyrinthine accretion of centuries perished in a splendid blaze visible for miles around, and when the rebuilding began a style entirely alien to the spirit of Nash and his metropolitan improvements was adopted. It was a symbolic event in the history of both the nation and the capital. Here in this ramshackle old building the political life of the nation had recently been directed on to a new course by the struggle for the Reform Bill, and here too, in May 1833, there had passed another Act, equally momentous for the future of the capital – 'An Act for making a Railway from London to Birmingham.'

4

The Transport
Revolution

STEAM RAILWAYS were the arteries of Victorian England's economic power. Without them the infinitely intricate tissues of nineteenth-century urban society and the commerce and industry which they generated would have assumed a very different pattern, and if the ghost of William Wordsworth had returned to Westminster Bridge around 1870 he would have found that without the railways the view would still have been substantially the same as on his previous visit in 1802. The transport revolution was indeed the paramount economic event of the age.

The London and Birmingham railway, built in five years (1833–8) by an army of 20,000 labourers, was probably then the largest public work ever to be undertaken in the whole history of man, with the possible exception of the Great Wall of China. Railway constructions of this kind demanded coal, timber, iron and bricks on an unprecedentedly large scale, demands which could only be met by a corresponding revolution in production. The iron-masters used steam-powered machines to make the one and a half million tons of iron required by the railways in the five years 1846 to 1850[1]; their great new smoking foundries and workshops drew thousands of men away from the country into the towns, and meanwhile the railways, and later the steamships, were equipping themselves to bring in food and take away all the multifarious manufactures of the new urban industrialized society into which the application of steam power to the movement of men and goods was carrying the nation at express speed.

But cheap fast transport extended its influence far beyond mere matters of physical movement. The sheer scale of its equipment stimulated new

[1] Michael Robbins, *The Railway Age*, 1962, p. 31.

methods of financial organization, new skills in management and new techniques of civil engineering, all on a correspondingly vast new scale. Five and a half million pounds of capital were raised for the building of the London and Birmingham railway; Sir Samuel Morton Peto, one of the leading railway building contractors, had 14,000 men on his pay-roll, and the mile-long tunnel at Watford on the London and Birmingham was then the longest railway tunnel in the world. Feats of this nature were made possible by a new efficiency in the concentration of power, and this in turn imposed new mass disciplines of time and procedure. In the great nineteenth-century migration to the towns the ancient ties of family and place were loosened or destroyed, and there arose instead the unfamiliar regulated precision of urban life.

This tremendous social upheaval was not the result of state policy. On the contrary, the railways striding across the country became the outward symbol of the new dominance of the men of commerce and industry over the old landed interests which had hitherto ruled supreme. The early railway age was also the age of *laissez-faire*, and Parliament made no attempt to impose a planned network of lines, as happened in Belgium. Parliament itself was invaded by the railway interest, and by 1867 there were 148 railway directors in the House of Commons,[1] the precursors of the powerful twentieth-century business element there. But despite the largely passive attitude of Parliament towards the railways, the force and scope of their impact on the life of the nation soon required public regulation, over fares and safety, over problems of monopoly and competition, over rival companies' projected incursions into central London, and over the rehousing of the poor displaced by the building of new lines. The relations of the railways with the State, culminating at last in 1947 in the Act of nationalization, provide indeed the most striking example of the inexorable expansion of the activities of the State during the past century or more.[2]

So, too, the impact of the railways affected the relationship between London and the rest of the nation. In the age of *laissez-faire* the position of London as the capital city was less important than it had previously been or than it was to become once again in more recent times, and the rise of the great industrial towns of the north, to whose growth the

[1] Philip S. Bagwell, 'The Railway Interest: Its Organization and Influence 1839–1914', *Journal of Transport History*, vol. vii, 1965, pp. 65–86.

[2] See H. J. Dyos and D. H. Aldcroft, *British Transport: an economic survey from the seventeenth century to the twentieth*, 1969, *passim*.

railways contributed so powerfully, likewise reduced the relative stature of London. But within the south-eastern part of the country the building of the railways had the opposite effect. There were no great regional centres comparable in importance with Birmingham or Manchester or Leeds, or even with great ancient cities like Bristol or Norwich. The railways radiated out from London to a ring of towns along the south coast and into the wide open spaces of East Anglia, extending the ascendancy of the capital throughout the whole area (an ascendancy subsequently to be greatly emphasized by the introduction of frequent electric train services to and from the great central hub).

In London itself the railways jolted the existing social and economic structure into a new pattern, as indeed they did in greater or lesser degree in every great town throughout the country. In the City itself and its immediate environs the resident population dispersed itself outwards to the less cramped surroundings of the new suburbs. The centre became the area where Londoners worked, in shops, warehouses, offices, banks and a few specialized manufacturing industries, but where few except the poor, dependent on casual employment and unable to pay to travel to work, still lived, often in conditions of the utmost squalor and degradation. With the advent of workmen's cheap fares on the railways after 1864 the more prosperous sections of the working classes could afford to move outwards too, and very gradually the separation of work and home assumed its huge modern proportions and made it perhaps the greatest of all twentieth-century problems of town planning. The Victorian transport revolution put an end for ever to the closely-knit homogeneous city life of earlier days, and its influence still affects the social pattern of mid-twentieth-century London.

We have previously seen that the separation of work and home had already begun on a very small scale – small in terms of both the numbers of people involved and of the distance which they usually travelled – before the building of the first railways in London. Most of these early commuters depended on the time-honoured power of the horse, but a few years before the beginning of the railway age in London the efficiency of horse traction for short-distance travel was much improved by long-overdue changes in the law and by the introduction of a new type of vehicle, the omnibus. Although they used the most expensive form of locomotive power, horse-drawn vehicles in London thus proved able to withstand the competition of the railways throughout the rest of the nineteenth century, and even to retain the ascendancy in the short-distance haulage of passenger traffic until they were finally superseded by the twentieth-century Juggernaut, the motor.

At the beginning of the nineteenth century travellers to work from the suburbs such as Henry Thornton the banker, living in Clapham, journeyed in their own private carriages, but some of them may have used the short-stage coaches which in the 1820s were plying in considerable numbers between the City or the West End and the surrounding villages and suburbs within a radius of about five miles. It has been calculated that in 1825 there were some six hundred such coaches, making about 1,800 daily journeys. But fares were high – 1*s*. 6*d*. to 2*s*. single from Paddington, for instance – the proprietors had to pay a substantial tax based on the seating capacity of each vehicle and the mileage which it travelled, and they were forbidden by law to pick up or set down passengers along the inner parts of their routes between their City or West End termini and 'the stones' end', the edge of the area of paved streets. Within this paved area the licensed hackney coach proprietors still enjoyed an ancient monopoly of plying for hire. They were much less heavily taxed than the owners of the short-stage coaches, and many of their 1,250-odd vehicles were dirty and ramshackle.[1]

So long as the hackney coach monopoly existed the short-stage coach proprietors could not compete for passengers within the paved area, and the level of their fares, artificially raised by high taxation, prevented any great increase in the volume of their business. But towards the end of the 1820s the hackney coach monopoly was being widely attacked, John Nash's West End street works had greatly improved traffic conditions and a number of the old turnpike roads north of the river had been freed from tolls. It was at this moment that George Shillibeer, a young coach builder and livery stable keeper in Bloomsbury, realized that the new type of public vehicle recently introduced in Paris, where he had business connections, might also be profitably used in parts of London, despite the hackney monopoly. On 4 July 1829 he began to ply with his first two omnibuses on the route from Paddington Green to the Bank of England in the City.[2]

Shillibeer's omnibuses were long trunk-shaped vehicles drawn by three horses; inside there were two parallel benches on which twenty passengers

---

[1] T. C. Barker and Michael Robbins, *A History of London Transport*, vol. I, *The Nineteenth Century* 1963, pp. 4–7. I am very heavily indebted to this masterly study for much of the information in this chapter.

[2] Barker and Robbins, pp. 13, 18–20.

sat facing each other. Their seating capacity was therefore much greater than that of the short-stage coaches (four or six passengers inside and up to seven outside), the fare of 1s. was lower, and nobody had to travel outside. But unless the omnibuses carried a full complement of passengers these advantages would be cancelled out by the complicated incidence of taxation. Shillibeer aimed to fill his omnibuses by a succession of short-distance passengers, and this, probably, was why he chose to ply between Paddington and the Bank, where much of the route along the New Road (now Marylebone, Euston and Pentonville Roads) lay outside the paved area, and where he was therefore free to pick up and put down.

The omnibus was an immediate success – too successful, indeed, for Shillibeer soon faced fierce competition from a number of imitators. This and his heavy tax liability proved too much for him, and in March 1831 he was declared bankrupt. Six months later an Act for the abolition of the antiquated hackney coach monopoly passed through Parliament, and the way was opened for Shillibeer's rivals to exploit the commercial possibilities of short-distance travel everywhere in London.[1]

By 1834 there were 376 licensed omnibuses operating in London and five years later there were 620. They plied along all the principal roads leading out of London, but much the heaviest traffic was to Paddington (along both the New Road and Oxford Street), with the routes to Kensington and Hammersmith, to Blackwall, Greenwich, Camberwell and Kennington also yielding substantial business. The fare for intermediate journeys was sixpence and to the outer areas one shilling, the money being collected by the conductor, who stood on a step at the back and touted for passengers. The services began at about eight o'clock in the morning, and during the next two hours the omnibuses and the now less numerous short-stage coaches arrived in the City and the West End, bearing, according to an account written in 1837:

the merchant to his business, the clerk to his bank or counting-house, the subordinate official functionaries to the Post Office, Somerset House, the Excise, or the Mint, the Custom House or Whitehall. An immense number of individuals, whose incomes vary from £150 to £400 or £600 and whose business does not require their presence till nine or ten in the mornings, and who can leave it at five or six in the

---

[1] Barker and Robbins, pp. 14, 20-3.

evenings; persons with limited independent means of living, such as legacies or life-rents, or small amounts of property; literary individuals; merchants and traders small and great; all, in fact, who can endeavour to live some little distance from London[1]

were using the new omnibuses.

To keep a single omnibus in service needed from six to twelve horses, each of which in its working life of about four years cost fifteen shillings per week to feed. The running costs of the business, which also included the wages of the drivers and conductors, were very high in relation to the capital costs – only £100 for each vehicle and £20 for each horse. Omnibus management in its early days therefore proved to be a natural field for the small entrepreneur, and in the 1830s most of the operators owned fewer than ten vehicles apiece. Competition continued to be intense – so intense that on some routes rival owners were soon forming associations to regulate it – and after the rate of taxation had been reduced and the seating capacity had been increased by the introduction of knifeboard roof seats in the 1840s, substantial reductions in fares followed. In 1847 it was possible to travel from Charing Cross to Camden Town for only one penny, and threepenny fares were common. By 1850 the number of omnibuses had doubled during the previous eleven years, and the existence of these 1,300-odd vehicles showed that in mid-nineteenth-century London horse-drawn transport was complementary to, rather than in competition with,[2] the railways.

The first application of steam power to the transport of passengers in London took place on the river. Regular steamboat services began in 1815, more than twenty years before the opening of the first railway, mostly to the downstream suburbs such as Greenwich and Woolwich, but some boats went much farther, to Gravesend, Margate and Ramsgate, as well as upstream to Chelsea and Richmond. In the early 1830s boats plied to and from Greenwich every half hour in winter and every quarter of an hour in summer, sometimes achieving the unheard-of speed of fifteen miles an hour, the fares being similar to those of the omnibuses for comparable distances. Season tickets were offered at very cheap rates, and in 1837 a frequent service between London Bridge and Westminster Bridge

[1] Barker and Robbins, pp. 26, 31–7; quotation from *The Penny Magazine*, as cited in Barker and Robbins, p. 36.
[2] Barker and Robbins, pp. 35, 39, 59–61 and Appendix 2.

for only fourpence was begun. In the 1840s, the heyday of regular passenger transport by water in London, fares were temporarily reduced by competition. But there was always the winter to contend with – in January 1838 the Thames was blocked by ice; accidents were common, the explosion of the *Cricket* off London Bridge in 1847 being only one of a number of such incidents, and sometimes there were other unforeseeable perils too, such as the alarming presence of a two-ton whale, sixteen feet in length, off Deptford in 1842. Gradually summer excursion traffic became the main business of the river, and on one day at Whitsun in 1844, 40,000 passengers landed at Greenwich pier. In the 1850s the railways reached many of the steamboats' hitherto busy ports of call, and in the 1860s the underground was built immediately alongside the Thames at Westminster, beneath the new Victoria Embankment. Regular travel by river ceased to be competitive, and apart from pleasure traffic the short career of the London steamboat was over.[1]

The first steam-powered railway in London, the London and Greenwich, was opened as far as Deptford on Wednesday 14 December 1836 – eleven years after the Stockton and Darlington and six years after the Liverpool and Manchester. In 1803 London had enjoyed the distinction of being the scene of the world's first public railway, the Surrey Iron Railway from Wandsworth to Croydon, where the wagons were drawn by horses in much the same way as on the early mineral lines in County Durham.[2] But in later years London had lost the lead to the more energetic entrepreneurs of the north, and it was not until 1833 that 'Several Owners and Occupants of estates, lands and houses' between Southwark and Greenwich, and a number of 'Merchants, Bankers and others interested in the same' presented a petition to Parliament for powers to build the new railway. Eighteen counter-petitions were presented, from local landowners, riverside wharfingers and watermen, short-stage coach proprietors and carriers, from the vestries, the turnpike trustees, the commissioners of sewers and even from the City Corporation itself as governors of St Thomas's Hospital – a formidable array of opposing forces. The House of Commons hesitated, but at last the Bill passed – 198 clauses, occupying over a hundred pages of print – and became law in May 1833.[3]

[1] *Annual Register*, 1838, 1842, 1844, 1847, 1848; Barker and Robbins, pp. 40–3, 165.
[2] H. P. White, *A Regional History of the Railways of Great Britain*, vol. II, *Southern England*, 1961, p. 15.
[3] *Journals of the House of Commons*; 3 William 14, c.46, local and personal.

The Act recited that

the making a Railway, commencing at or near the South End of London Bridge . . . to or near to the Town of Greenwich in the County of Kent, with proper Works connected therewith, for the Carriage of Passengers and Cattle, and also of divers Articles, Matters, and Things, will prove of great public Advantage, by opening an additional, cheap, certain, and expeditious Communication between the Metropolis and the Towns of Greenwich and Deptford and the adjacent Districts.

It established 'The London and Greenwich Railway Company' as a body corporate, thirty-two or more subscribers having already contributed £350,000 to its funds, and conferred powers to buy lands, compulsorily if necessary, build the railway and provide a service along it. The cost of building the line was estimated at £400,000, which was to be raised by 20,000 shares, each of £20. Building was not to start until the whole sum had been subscribed, and if the costs exceeded the company's expectations, a further £133,333 could be raised by the mortgage of the company's property. There was a scale of maximum tolls to be levied – 9d. for each person for any distance – and anyone wishing to operate his own engine on the line could do so subject to the approval of its mechanical efficiency by the company's engineer. No engine was to burn coal; only coke or charcoal or such other fuel as 'shall not cause or emit any Smoke' were to be permitted.

The chairman of the new company was Abel Rouse Dottin,[1] a sixty-four-year-old gentleman with a family fortune evidently made in Barbados, who had recently lost his seat as Tory M.P. for Southampton, although he regained it in 1835. His eight co-directors included Sir William Beatty, the surgeon who had attended Nelson after his mortal wound at Trafalgar and who was now physician at Greenwich Hospital; Rear-Admiral William Hall Gage, another naval veteran who had served on the *Victory*; a clergyman; and from the City John Twells, partner in the banking firm of Spooner, Attwood and Company of Gracechurch Street, and Abel Peyton Phelps, later superintendent of the West End office of the London Assurance Corporation. These oddly assorted pioneers quickly set to work. They engaged a retired colonel, George Landmann, who had fought with the Royal Engineers in the Peninsular War, to design the railway. Soon a great swathe was being cut through

[1] *The Times*, 15 December 1836.

the dismal purlieus of Southwark – through Frying Pan Alley and Foot's Folley, the Maze, Oatmeal Yard and Crucifix Lane – and scores of dilapidated tenements and workshops were crashing down in great heaps of dusty rubble.

In order to avoid a succession of level crossings the railway itself was built on an immense viaduct of 878 arches, nearly four miles long, with a road at ground level on either side, one for pedestrians who could not afford to travel on the trains and the other for access to the arches, which the company hoped – vainly – to let as dwelling-houses. Nothing like it had ever been seen before in London, and of course it all cost a great deal more than anybody had expected – nearly a million pounds in the end.[1]

When the long-awaited opening day arrived the Lord Mayor came over to grace the occasion. There were flags and banners at the London Bridge terminus, a military band was playing, and soon after half-past one five trains conveyed the three hundred guests down to Deptford at some sixteen miles an hour. Along the line 'the bells of the parish churches by which the railroad went rang merry peals. The housetops on both sides were teeming with spectators, who loudly cheered as the engines passed.' At Deptford there was a little confusion, for a number of the guests 'wished to regale themselves at some of the neighbouring inns', while the Lord Mayor was in a hurry to get back to the 'splendid déjeuné' which the company was to provide at the Bridge House Tavern in Southwark. But at last they all returned safely to the toasts and the speeches. The Lord Mayor declared that the railway would contribute 'to the happiness by promoting the wealth and the domestic comfort of that large class of the citizens of London whose villas adorned the picturesque scenes which abounded in the neighbourhood' of Deptford and Greenwich, and 'the meeting was prolonged to a late hour in the afternoon'. London's railway age had begun.[2]

The route to Deptford along the new railway was more direct than by road, and during the first fifteen months of its existence the London and Greenwich carried more than 650,000 passengers. On weekdays there was a regular service at fifteen-minute intervals from eight o'clock in the morning until ten at night, the minimum fare for a single journey in an uncovered carriage being 6*d*. In 1838 the line was extended to Greenwich, where omnibuses waited to take passengers on to Blackheath and Woolwich, but there was little or no goods traffic, and even after the growth of

[1] Edwin Course, *London Railways*, 1962, pp. 19–24.
[2] *The Times*, 15 December 1836; *Annual Register*, 1836.

K

excursion traffic to Greenwich the company could not earn an adequate return on its capital by the carriage of local passenger traffic alone. It had originally hoped to extend its line down to Dover, but after the failure of its attempt to obtain parliamentary sanction to build through Greenwich Park it began to augment its revenues by leasing its lines near London Bridge to other companies which were now trying to obtain centrally situated termini. In 1839 the London and Croydon company's lines, with William Cubitt as the engineer, joined the Greenwich at Corbett's Lane for the last mile and three-quarters of their route up to London Bridge. Two trunk lines were also being built at this time, one to Brighton and the other to Dover, and in 1841 the London and Brighton Railway, and in 1842 the South Eastern both began to run their trains into London Bridge over the lines of the Croydon and the Greenwich companies.[1]

So within six years of its opening London Bridge station had become the terminus for four busy companies. In order to cope with this tremendous growth of traffic the Greenwich company widened the London end of its viaduct and added new tracks, and in 1844 a handsome new terminus was built in the Italian *palazzo* style which was then much in vogue. But the three tenant companies had to pay heavy tolls for the use of the Greenwich's property. In 1844 the Croydon and the South Eastern rebelled and built a rival terminus of their own at Bricklayer's Arms near the Old Kent Road, thus avoiding the use of the Greenwich lines. Within a few months of the opening of this inconveniently situated new station the Greenwich company capitulated and in 1845 it granted a 999-year lease of its property to the South Eastern at a rental which provided the Greenwich shareholders with a dividend of 4½ per cent – an arrangement which continued until both companies were swallowed up by the Southern Railway in 1923. Bricklayer's Arms was hardly used again for passenger traffic, but it had served its purpose. In 1846 the Croydon and Brighton companies amalgamated to form the London, Brighton and South Coast Railway, and in 1850 a wall was built down the middle of the London Bridge terminus to separate the premises of the two large companies which now shared the station.[2]

Away to the west another company had also been active – the London and Southampton, which had its origins at a private meeting held in 1830 at the Southampton house of Abel Rouse Dottin, later to become the chairman of the London and Greenwich. The first section of its line, from its original terminus near the river at Nine Elms, Battersea, to

[1] Course, pp. 20, 28, 30; Barker, p. 45.　　　[2] Course, pp. 31, 33.

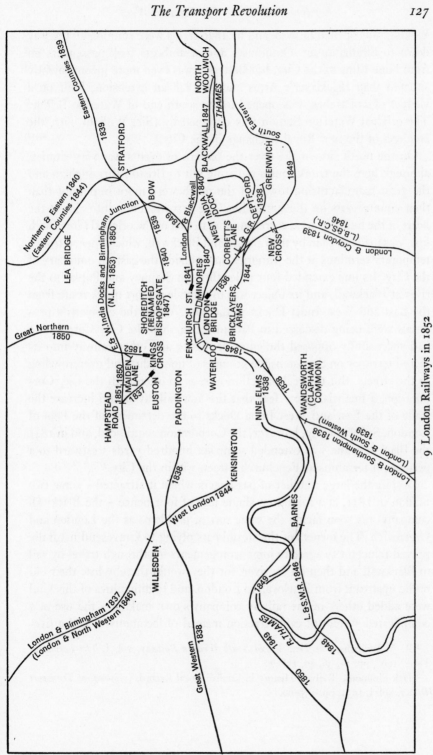

9 London Railways in 1852

Woking, was opened in 1838, and by 1840 trains were running all the way down to Southampton. Omnibuses and steamboats took passengers on from Nine Elms to the City, but Battersea was even more inconveniently situated than Bricklayer's Arms and in 1848 an extension, built on a viaduct of 235 arches, was opened to the south end of Waterloo Bridge. The original Waterloo Station was designed by (Sir) William Tite, the architect of the new Royal Exchange in the City.[1]

On the north side of the river the pattern of events was very similar, although here the trunk routes radiating out to Bristol, Birmingham and the great manufacturing towns of the north were more important than their counterparts on the south side. The first incursion into almost the heart of the built-up area, corresponding to that of the original Greenwich line, was made in 1840 by the London and Blackwall, which opened from a temporary terminus at the Minories, just outside the eastern boundary of the City. Its line extended four miles through Stepney and Poplar to the river at Blackwall, and its object was to provide a short quick route from the East and West India Docks to the City. When the company's proposals were being discussed in Parliament in 1836 the City Corporation had successfully opposed the entry of this or any other railway into its sacred territory on the ostensible grounds of noise, dirt and overcrowding in the streets. But the real objection was, as so often with the City Corporation, a financial one – fear that the new railway would increase the trade of the East and West India Docks to the detriment of the Pool of London. Subsequently, however, the Corporation acquiesced, and in 1841 the Blackwall line was extended some six hundred yards westward to a permanent terminus at Fenchurch Street, within the City.[2]

Despite the large number of passengers which it attracted – some two million in 1841, at a minimum single fare of four pence – the Blackwall company was soon facing the same sort of problems as the London and Greenwich. The owners of the steamboats plying to Gravesend naturally proved reluctant to agree to joint arrangements for through travel by rail to Blackwall and then on by river, for they would thereby lose their old traffic upstream from Blackwall to London, and to difficulties of this kind were added others of the railway company's own making – the use of a complicated system of cable traction instead of locomotives, and a five-

[1] R. A. Williams, *The London and South Western Railway*, vol. I, *The Formative Years*, 1968, pp. 11, 36, 40, 158–60.

[2] Jack Simmons, 'Railway History in English Local Records', *Journal of Transport History*, vol. i, 1954, pp. 155–69.

foot gauge for the lines instead of the standard four feet eight and a half inches.[1]

But its early arrival had given the London and Blackwall the same valuable asset as the London and Greenwich – a centrally situated terminus. During the mania of railway promotion in the mid 1840s a Royal Commission was established to consider a number of proposals for building new lines in central London, and in 1846 it concluded that no new railway should be permitted within the area of the New (now Marylebone) Road, City Road, Finsbury Square and Bishopsgate Street.[2] This decision greatly increased the value of Fenchurch Street as a terminus, and by 1850 the Blackwall company had introduced locomotives instead of cable traction, changed their tracks to the standard gauge and built a spur to Bow in the hope of connecting their lines with those of the neighbouring Eastern Counties railway there.[3]

The Eastern Counties, too, had started with a five-foot gauge (soon converted to the standard width), and had opened the first section of its line, from Romford to a temporary station east of Bethnal Green, in 1839. In the following year a permanent terminus was built farther west at Shoreditch, and by 1850 the Eastern Counties' network had reached out to Ipswich, Norwich and Cambridge, with suburban branches to Enfield and North Woolwich. Despite the advantage which access to Fenchurch Street would have for the Eastern Counties over its own badly placed terminus at Shoreditch, the company at first refused to allow a physical connection of its lines with those of the Blackwall railway at Bow. But this temporary setback did not greatly matter, for the Blackwall already had a much more powerfully ally – the great London and North Western Railway.[4]

This was the 'Premier Line', the aristocrat of the railway business. As the London and Birmingham it had obtained its first Act of Parliament in 1833, and with the young Robert Stephenson as its engineer, his great father as an occasional collaborator, and with George Carr Glyn the banker as its chairman, it had built the smooth level line which provided the first rail connection between London and the midlands and the north.

[1] Barker and Robbins, pp. 49–50.

[2] P.P., 1846, (719), vol. xvii, *Royal Commission appointed to investigate projects for establishing Railway Termini within the Metropolis*, p. 21.

[3] Course, pp. 119–20; H.P. White, *A Regional History of the Railways of Great Britain*, vol. III, *Greater London*, 1963, p. 171.

[4] White, *Greater London*, pp. 170–1.

It was concerned with long-distance traffic, particularly with the carriage of goods to the docks, and in 1831 it had accordingly attempted to obtain parliamentary powers for the southern end of its line to sweep round the outskirts of north London to the river at Blackwall. But this proposal had been rejected, and its first intended metropolitan terminus had been at Camden Town, alongside the Regent's Canal, to which freight could be unloaded for transport to the docks. By 1837, however, when the line was opened as far as Boxmoor in Hertfordshire, a southward extension to Euston Square had been authorized and built, the trains being for some years worked up the very steep gradient to Camden Town by cable.[1] During the course of the next few years Euston itself was provided with a group of buildings worthy of the whole great enterprise – a hotel and the famous 'Euston Arch', both by Philip Hardwick, and in the station itself the splendid Great Hall, where stood a statue of George Stephenson, and at the top of the staircase the Shareholders' Room, both by Hardwick's son – a group, now, alas, all demolished, which (whatever the architectural purists may say) expressed with monumental grandeur the power and confidence of the early railway age.

In 1846 the London and Birmingham became, by amalgamation with the Grand Junction and the Liverpool and Manchester companies, the London and North Western Railway. Until 1850 its line as far as Rugby provided the only direct rail link between London and the north, but in that year a powerful competitor arrived – the Great Northern. Its line from Doncaster to London had been authorized by Parliament in 1846 and opened at a temporary terminus in 1850, the extension to King's Cross (designed by Lewis Cubitt) being completed two years later.[2]

The London and North Western's answer to this challenge was the revival of its original scheme for direct access to the docks. In 1846 – the same year as the authorization of the Great Northern – the cumbrously titled East and West India Docks and Birmingham Junction Railway company was empowered to build a line from the North Western's depot at Camden Town via Bow to the docks at Millwall. The North Western provided two-thirds of the capital and two-thirds of the directors, of whom George Carr Glyn was one. Goods transport was to be the main purpose of this small but important line, but its west–east route through the northern suburbs soon attracted substantial passenger traffic as well, and in 1850 arrangements were made for its trains to run on from Bow along the London and Blackwall's line into Fenchurch Street. There was a

---

[1] Course, pp. 154–5.   [2] White, *Greater London*, p. 154.

fifteen-minute interval service all the way from Chalk Farm round to Fenchurch Street for a minimum fare of fourpence, and in the first half of 1851 over 1,750,000 passengers were carried, much to the delight of the London and Blackwall. In 1852 the East and West India Docks and Birmingham Junction Railway's route was completed with the opening of a line, for goods only, from Bow to the docks at Millwall. The company itself was mercifully renamed shortly afterwards and became the North London Railway.[1]

There was one other great company of the early years – the Great Western Railway, a lone wolf, but another aristocrat, superb in its solitary pride. Like the London and Birmingham its concern was with long-distance traffic, and it had originally planned to join the Birmingham line at Kensal Green, where the two routes are only about a quarter of a mile apart. But the Birmingham company's terms were not accepted, and all possibility of a joint terminus ended when Isambard Kingdom Brunel, the Great Western's engineer, persuaded his directors to adopt his broad-gauge track of 7 feet o$\frac{1}{4}$ inches. The Great Western proceeded on its stately course, westward to Bristol and beyond and eastward to a site near the Paddington branch of the Grand Junction Canal, where the original terminus was opened on the site of the present goods depot in 1838. The present station, a few yards farther east, was opened in 1854. It was designed by Brunel in conjunction with his friend Matthew Digby Wyatt, the architect, and since the demolition of Euston Paddington is now perhaps the finest building still surviving from the earlier phases of railway building in London. The hotel, by P. C. Hardwick, is one of the earliest buildings in England to show the influence of the French Renaissance and Baroque styles.[2]

For many years the Great Western did not trouble itself much with short-distance traffic, but at one place, Windsor, the royal country seat, where prestige was involved, it did exert itself. In 1846 a line had been built from the London and South Western at Clapham to Richmond, and two years later this was extended up the Thames Valley to Datchet, with a loop taking in Brentford. In 1849 an Act of Parliament authorized another extension to Windsor itself, only three miles from the Great Western's main line at Slough. The challenge could not be ignored; a spur must be built. Suddenly Windsor found itself beset from the north and the south

[1] Michael Robbins, *The North London Railway*, 1946, pp. 1–2; Barker and Robbins, p. 51.
[2] Course, p. 170; White, *Greater London*, p. 112.

by the two rivals, and by the end of the year it had been equipped with two separate terminal stations, never to be linked together. It was only seven years since the Queen had first travelled by train, from Slough to Paddington; the railways had arrived indeed.[1]

By the end of 1850 the framework of a national railway system had been built. Six thousand miles of line were open, and London was connected with Birmingham, the midlands and the north, with East Anglia, the principal south-coast towns from Dover to Plymouth, with Bristol and with Holyhead for Ireland.[2] Much of this prodigious undertaking had been promoted in two bursts, the first in 1836–7, when 1,500 miles of new lines had been authorized by Parliament, and the second more powerful explosion of 1844–7, when over nine thousand more miles had been sanctioned, though not all were actually built. Eleven of the Acts passed in 1836–7 had authorized new lines wholly or partly in London, while of those passed in 1844–7 twenty-five affected the capital. Within less than two decades the railways had captured the imagination of the travelling and investing public and become the symbol of Victorian power and progress.

The railways produced a tremendous acceleration in the whole tempo of human affairs. A new express chaise service, inaugurated in 1821 between London and Manchester, had attained the then remarkable average speed of eleven miles per hour. Nineteen years later a train with the directors of the Great Western Railway on board travelled from Twyford to Paddington at an average speed of fifty miles per hour. The mails were delivered more quickly, and the London newspapers were nightly dispatched far afield to the provinces. During the Chartist emergencies the speed with which troops and police could be sent from one part of the country to another greatly assisted in the preservation of order, and by 1846 the Admiralty was using the London and South Western Railway's electric telegraph for communication with Gosport. Eight of the seventeen London offices of the Electric Telegraph Company were at railway termini, and in 1851 the permanent cable laid from Dover to Calais was used to transmit via the South Eastern Railway company's wires the prices on the London Stock Exchange to the Paris Bourse and receive an answer within an hour. A year later the electric telegraph was used for the transmission of Greenwich time all over the country; ancient

---

[1] Williams, pp. 172–4; White, *Greater London*, pp. 40–1.
[2] Robbins, *The Railway Age*, pp. 28–9.

local variations could no longer be tolerated with such a precious com-
modity as time.[1]

In the long run the new precision of practice and behaviour required
and provided by the railways increased centralization, and so enhanced
the importance of London, which was the heart of the national rail network. But there were other more immediate effects, both upon the fabric
of London and upon the travelling habits of Londoners. In *Dombey and
Son*, first published in 1848, Dickens described the impact of the building
of the London and Birmingham railway at Camden Town.

The first shock of a great earthquake had, just at the period, rent the
whole neighbourhood to its centre. Traces of its course were visible
on every side. Houses were knocked down; streets broken through
and stopped; deep pits and trenches dug in the ground; enormous
heaps of earth and clay thrown up; buildings that were undermined
and shaking, propped by great beams of wood. Here, a chaos of carts,
overthrown and jumbled together, lay topsy-turvy at the bottom of a
steep, unnatural hill; there, confused treasures of iron soaked and
rusted in something that had accidentally become a pond. Everywhere
were bridges that led nowhere; thoroughfares that were wholly
impassable; Babel towers of chimneys, wanting half their height;
temporary wooden houses and enclosures, in the most unlikely situations; carcasses of ragged tenements, and fragments of unfinished
walls and arches, and piles of scaffolding, and wildernesses of bricks,
and giant forms of cranes, and tripods straddling above nothing.
There were a hundred thousand shapes and substances of incomplete-
ness, wildly mingled out of their places, upside down, burrowing in
the earth, aspiring in the earth, mouldering in the water, and unintel-
ligible as any dream. Hot springs and fiery eruptions, the usual
attendants upon earthquakes, lent their contributions of confusion to
the scene. Boiling water hissed and heaved within dilapidated walls,
whence, also, the glare and roar of flames came issuing forth; and
mounds of ashes blocked up rights of way, and wholly changed the
law and customs of the neighbourhood. In short, the yet unfinished
and unopened railroad was in progress, and, from the very core of all
this dire disorder, trailed smoothly away upon its mighty course of
civilization and improvement.

[1] *Annual Register*, 1821, 1846, 1851, 1852; E. T. MacDermot, *History of the Great
Western Railway*, vol. I, 1964 edn.

This upheaval was only one among many which took place in the outer suburbs of London in the 1830s and 40s. When the railways penetrated into the inner areas the effects were correspondingly even greater. In 1836 the homes of 2,850 people were threatened by the building of the London and Blackwall railway, while in 1845–8 the London and South Western's two-mile extension from Nine Elms to Waterloo affected 2,367 properties, and involved the demolition of about 700 houses. The railways had no obligation to make any provision for the people whose houses they destroyed, but in 1850 they had not yet made many incursions into the densely populated central districts of London, and the social problems which the railways created could still be largely ignored in Parliament. One or two thoughtful critics were already beginning to foresee that cheap train fares could enable the poor to live in suburban working-class villages and travel regularly to work in the central areas, but the realization of schemes of this kind was still far away in the future, for even the middle classes had hardly begun to exploit the possibilities of daily travel by rail.[1]

Most of the early railway promoters had expected that the haulage of goods and minerals would provide the bulk of their business, but they had soon found that a vast demand for passenger travel also existed. In 1844–5 more than three-quarters of the revenues of both the Great Western and the South Western were drawn from passenger traffic, which provided 64 per cent of the receipts of all the railways in the country. At first only first- and second-class accommodation had been provided, but a third class had soon been added – in 1839, for instance, on the London and Greenwich, with standing room only – and in 1844 Gladstone's 'Parliamentary Train' Act had required all passenger railway companies to run at least one train daily in each direction at a fare not exceeding one penny a mile, and at a speed of not less than twelve miles an hour. This was the year in which special excursion trains first attracted widespread public attention in London. On Whit Monday the London and Brighton company issued return tickets for the normal price of a single fare and put on a special train consisting of fifty-seven carriages drawn by six engines. When this remarkable equipage at last arrived at Brighton 'the passengers debouched from the terminus in an apparently endless stream' and were joined by nearly a thousand members of the Carpenters' Benevolent Society, who had chartered a train of their own. Despite the weather,

[1] H. J. Dyos, 'Railways and Housing in Victorian London', *Journal of Transport History*, vol. ii, 1955, pp. 11–21, 90–100; Williams, 1968, p. 159.

which was 'colder than for some years', between eight and nine thousand passengers went to Brighton or on to Shoreham on that day, and 70,000 to Greenwich, nearly half of them by rail.[1]

This excursion traffic provided very many people with their first opportunity for railway travel. In 1850 *The Times* commented that 'There are thousands of our readers, we are sure, who, in the last three years of their lives, have travelled more and seen more than in all their previous life taken together. Thirty years ago not one countryman in one hundred had seen the metropolis. There is now scarcely one in the same number who has not spent the day there.'[2] In the following year this new mass mobility was greatly enlarged by the Great Exhibition, a project which would have been inconceivable without the travel facilities provided by the railways. Some four million people paid one or more visits to the Exhibition, equivalent, after allowance for foreigners, to about 17 per cent of the total population of Great Britain. Cheap excursions brought thousands of visitors up to London from all over the country – twenty special trains arrived at Euston alone on a single day – and even the building of the Crystal Palace would have been impossible without the help of three leading railway engineers – Sir Morton Peto, the contractor, who guaranteed £50,000 towards the building costs, Sir William Cubitt, engineer to the Croydon and South Eastern Railway companies, who superintended the erection of the Crystal Palace, and Sir Charles Fox, the builder of many bridges, tunnels and other railway works, who actually built it, working eighteen hours a day for seven weeks to complete it by the stipulated day.[3]

But despite all this new mass travel, regular daily use of the railways to get to work remained extremely small in scale. Fares were still high for daily travel, and when season tickets were first offered there were relatively few purchasers. In 1849 there were only some 1,500 season ticket holders using Waterloo,[4] while the average length of journey of all passengers using Euston was sixty miles, which indicates that commuter traffic there was non-existent. All the early termini except Fenchurch Street and London Bridge were too far away for commuters to the City. Direct access to the docks for the carriage of freight, or indirect access by canal (Paddington, Euston) or river (Nine Elms) had dominated the thoughts of the

[1] Charles E. Lee, *Passenger Class Distinctions*, 1946, p. 12; *Annual Register*, 1844.

[2] Quoted in Robbins, *The Railway Age*, pp. 44–5.

[3] C. R. Fay, *Palace of Industry*, *1851*, 1951, pp. 73–4; Christopher Hobhouse, *1851 and the Crystal Palace*, 1950, p. 40.

[4] Williams, vol. I, p. 223.

early companies, and although several of them had subsequently succeeded in slightly advancing their termini towards the centre of London – the London and South Western's extension to Waterloo in 1848, for instance – further incursions were prevented for some years by the recommendations of the Royal Commission of 1846 on metropolitan termini.

This Commission, it will be recalled, had been established at the height of the railway mania to consider a score of proposals for new lines in London, many of them in the inner areas. A scheme to build one great central terminus for all such companies as wished to subscribe was then much in vogue, Charing Cross being the favourite site. This, of course came to nothing, but Charles Pearson, solicitor to the City Corporation, who gave evidence to the Commission, had much more far-sighted ideas. He supported a terminus at Farringdon Street, within the City, for all the railway companies north of the river, and produced plans 'for improving the habitations and increasing the comforts of persons of the middle and lower classes, by means of a Railway in connection with a suburban village'. A colony of some ten thousand houses was to be established about seven miles down the line, where the price of land was much cheaper than in the centre of London, and the clerks and 'superior order of the mechanical poor' who were to live there were to travel to and fro to work for a return fare of one penny a day. Pearson himself lived at Clapham Common, but it was 'only within the last few years' that persons of his condition of life had been

> satisfied to live out of town; we were crammed and jammed together in the City, and believed that it was essential to our convenience and to our happiness; but our habits are improved, and . . . our morals are improved. I believe there is nothing so favourable to the growth of every enlightened feeling, and so calculated to give a better tone to the habits of the lower classes of society, as that of being enabled to take them from the crowded state in which they now live.[1]

The building of working-class suburbs, which later provided a partial solution to the terrible overcrowding of parts of the central areas, was outside the Commission's terms of reference, and after hearing a great mass of other evidence it ultimately recommended that no new railway should be allowed within the area bounded by Marylebone Road, City

[1] P.P., 1846 (719), vol. xvii, *Report and Minutes of Evidence of Royal Commission on projects for establishing Railway Termini within the Metropolis*, pp. 13, 175-7.

Road, Finsbury Square and Bishopsgate Street. The rapid development of railway commuting was therefore for the moment postponed. Most people still walked to their work, often over distances of several miles each way, and of those who could afford to pay for their journey, Professor Barker has calculated that in the mid-1850s only some 6,000 to 10,000 travelled daily by rail, compared with 15,000 still using the steamboats and some 20,000 carried by the omnibuses.[1]

For short-distance travel the horse had in fact withstood the first challenge of steam. The inner area north of the river, from which the railways were excluded, had always provided the best business for the omnibus proprietors, and in 1851 the Great Exhibition brought them yet more traffic. But afterwards intensive competition was renewed and the number of vehicles in service declined. In 1855 all the omnibuses in Paris were amalgamated into one large monopoly undertaking, and shortly afterwards a French company, the Compagnie Générale des Omnibus de Londres, was formed to buy up all the London omnibuses. In the following year it managed to acquire some three-quarters of them, but this unexpected experiment did not prove successful financially and in 1859 the company was turned into an English one, the London General Omnibus Company Limited, only four of whose twelve directors were French. In 1862 the company carried over 42,000,000 passengers, but it had inherited a large debt from the French invasion and could only pay a small dividend. And so when the railways renewed their challenge in the early 1860s, the London omnibuses were busier than ever, but in some disarray.[2]

By 1850 the spate of building authorized during the mania of 1844–7 had exhausted itself, and the first pioneer stage of the railways was over. A new phase of intensive competition and amalgamations soon began. With the coming of limited liability companies the field of private investment was greatly enlarged, and the railways, whose profits in the 1850s seldom reached 4 per cent, had difficulty in raising new capital. Many of the new lines were built by new companies rather than by the existing ones; often the building contractors themselves provided a large part of the capital in exchange for the award of the contract, and were paid in the company's shares, which they hoped to sell later at a profit. This more precarious procedure led to the great boom in railway building of the early 1860s which ended in 1866, when the bankruptcy of Overend and Gurney

[1] Barker and Robbins, p. 58; P.P., *Report on Metropolitan Railway Termini*, p. 21.
[2] Barker and Robbins, pp. 61–3, 69–98.

ruined one of the greatest of the railway contractors, Sir Samuel Morton Peto.[1]

In London these new methods of railway construction were exemplified by two important lines built in the mid-1850s. After the Great Exhibition had closed, the Crystal Palace was removed to Sydenham, and in anticipation of the excursion traffic which it would stimulate a line was authorized in 1853 to run from a branch of the Brighton company at Sydenham to the South Western at Wandsworth, and then on to a terminus at the south end of the new Chelsea Bridge. The West End of London and Crystal Palace Railway was built by Thomas Brassey in association with Peto and his partner Edward Ladd Betts, Betts being the largest single subscriber, with £60,000 out of a total capital of £223,750. At the opposite end of London this same powerful partnership not only invested in and built a line from the Eastern Counties at Forest Gate to Tilbury and Southend, but they even took a twenty-one year lease of it and operated it themselves.[2]

Neither of these lines did anything to solve the mounting crisis of London's communications in the 1850s – the insufferable congestion in and around the City. During the forty years before the census of 1851 the population of the metropolitan district had doubled. In 1855 some 200,000 people entered the City daily on foot, many of them walking over from London Bridge Station, and the omnibuses made some 7,400 daily journeys through the City. In addition to this prodigious flow of passenger traffic there were hundreds of slow, cumbersome carts delivering goods to and from the railway termini, still almost all relatively far away, and until 1855 thousands of cattle were driven through the streets to Smithfield Market. Yet since the death of George IV and the eclipse of Nash in 1830 hardly any major street improvements had been made. Through govermental neglect, occasioned perhaps by fear of its potential power, London with a population of 2,362,236 in 1851, still had no overall municipal council analogous to the reformed corporations of cities like Birmingham or Manchester. Such improvements as had been made had been carried out either by the government itself – New Oxford Street (1847) and Victoria Street (1851) are cases in point – acting through the makeshift agency of the Commissioners of Woods and Forests, or by the City Corporation, which built King William Street, Princes Street and Moorgate as an ad-

---

[1] Bagwell, pp. 66–9; Harold Pollins, 'Railway Contractors and the Finance of Railway Development', *Journal of Transport History*, vol. iii, 1957, pp. 41–51, 103–10.

[2] Pollins, pp. 41–51; Course, pp. 94–5, 120–1; Arthur Helps, *Life and Labours of Mr Brassey*, 1872.

junct to the new London Bridge in the late 1820s and New Cannon Street
in the early 1850s. By 1855 congestion had reached the point that according
to Sir Joseph Paxton, the architect of the Crystal Palace, it took longer to
travel from London Bridge station to Paddington than from London Bridge
to Brighton.[1]

In 1855 a Select Committee was set up to investigate. It concluded that

> more direct lines of communication should be established, than now
> exist between the several principal points of the Metropolis

and expressed its satisfaction that the long overdue establishment of
the Metropolitan Board of Works (by then in process of creation) would
provide an opportunity for improvements to be executed by the joint
agency of the Board and the railways. The attempt made in the 1840s
to keep the railways at a distance was, indeed, no longer practicable, and
the Committee also recommended that

> the different metropolitan railway termini should be connected by
> railway with each other, with the docks, the river, and the Post-office
> [at St Martin le Grand in the City], so as to accelerate the mails,
> and take all through-traffic, not only of passengers, but in a still
> more important degree of goods off the streets.[2]

The first steps to achieve such a connection had in fact already been
taken. Charles Pearson, who in 1846 had advocated a terminus for the
north London railways at Farringdon Street, had renewed his efforts in
1851. An underground railway running beneath the Marylebone and
Euston Roads from Paddington to King's Cross and then swinging south-
east down the valley of the Fleet river would provide the Great Western,
the North Western and the Great Northern (which opened its permanent
terminus at King's Cross in 1852) with an extension to the City, and would
also sweep away the noisome tenements in the valley, whose inhabitants
could be drawn out to the new more salubrious suburbs by the offer of
cheap fares. It was an ingenious idea, but money proved hard to get. The
idea of a mainline terminus at Farringdon Street had to be abandoned, but
ultimately in 1858 the City Corporation agreed to subscribe £200,000,
which with £185,000 from the Great Western soon brought in enough
capital for building work to begin in the following year.[3]

[1] P.P., 1854–5 (415), vol.x, *Report of Select Committee on Metropolitan Communications*, pp. iii, 78, 150; Barker, pp. 65–6.

[2] P.P., *Report on Metropolitan Communications*, p. iv.

[3] Barker and Robbins, pp. 99–113.

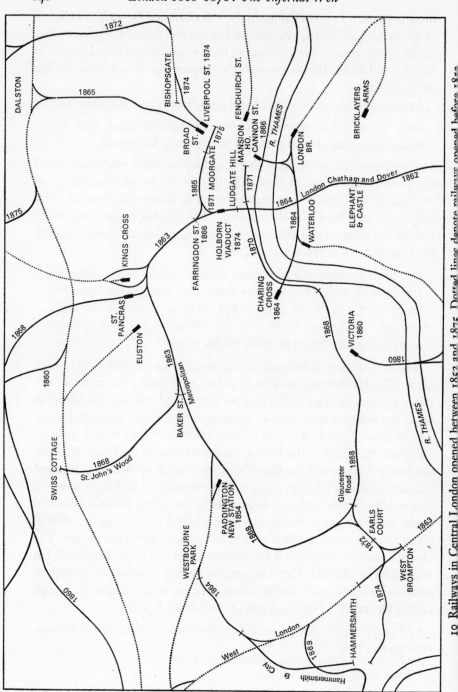

19 Railways in Central London opened between 1852 and 1875. Dotted lines denote railways opened before 1852

The Metropolitan Railway Company's line from Paddington to Far-ringdon Street was the first underground railway in the world. For most of its course it was only a few feet below ground level and much of it was therefore built on the 'cut and cover' principle. But excavation through a built-up area presented innumerable engineering problems; adjoining buildings might collapse, the brick retaining walls of the cutting itself might, and indeed sometimes did, collapse, and everywhere there were sewers and gas and water pipes to be diverted. Between Paddington and King's Cross the line ran beneath wide existing roads, but the eastern por-tion (where the contractor, John Jay, was also an important subscriber), proved far more difficult, and on one occasion in 1862 the sewer containing the River Fleet burst and flooded the excavations as far as King's Cross to a depth of ten feet. It was fortunate that the engineer (Sir) John Fowler, proved to be one of the greatest of the second generation of railway de-signers, and was later responsible for the building of another prodigy, the Forth Bridge.[1]

The Metropolitan was opened from Paddington to Farringdon Street on 10 January 1863, some three months after the death of Charles Pearson, who had worked so long for this great day. Public fears about underground travel were quickly overcome, and in 1864 some 11,800,000 passengers were carried, the trains running at ten-minute intervals in the morning and evening rush hours, and at fifteen- or twenty-minute intervals during the rest of the day. The third-class single fare was only 3*d*. The whole project proved so immediately successful that in 1864-5 the line was extended south-eastward to Moorgate Street, within almost a stone's throw of the Bank of England in the heart of the City.

The tracks of the Metropolitan were laid on both the wide and narrow gauges and at first the Great Western provided the rolling-stock. In 1864 the first feeder line was brought into service when the Hammersmith and City Railway began running trains from a terminus at Hammersmith through the rapidly growing suburbs of Shepherd's Bush and North Kensington to join the Great Western about a mile from Paddington and thence along the Metropolitan to the City. The Hammersmith line was also connected to the hitherto moribund West London line, built in 1844 from Willesden to West Kensington near the modern Olympia, and from here too trains were soon running along the Metropolitan. Farther east there were more feeders from Swiss Cottage to Baker Street, from the Great Northern's suburban lines and in 1868 from the Midland railway,

[1] Barker and Robbins, pp. 105-9, 114; C. Baker, *The Metropolitan Railway*, 1951, p. 3.

L

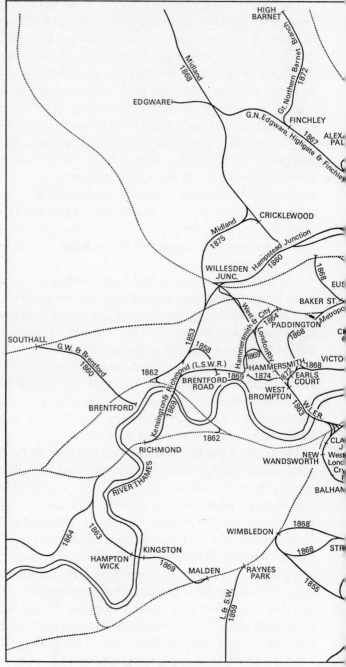

11 Railways in Outer London opened between 185

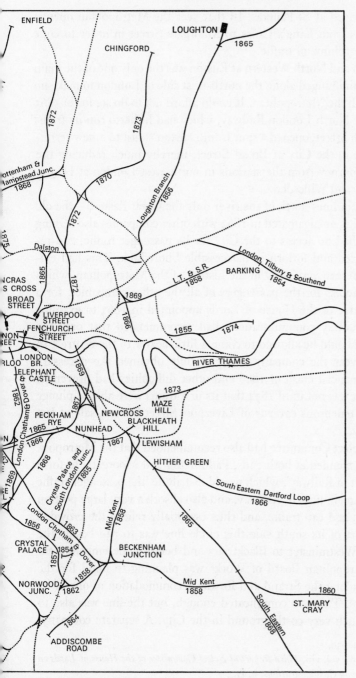

ENFIELD

LOUGHTON
1865

CHINGFORD

1872

1873

ottenham &
Hampstead Junc.
1868

1870

1872

1875

Loughton Branch
1856

Dalston

1865

1872

London, Tilbury & Southend

NCRAS
S CROSS

BROAD
STREET

L.T. & S.R.
1858

BARKING

London, Tilbury & Southend
1854

1869

1866

Liverpool
STREET
FENCHURCH
STREET

NON
REET

1855

1874

RLOO
EET

1869

RIVER THAMES

LONDON
BR.

ELEPHANT
& CASTLE

London Chatham & Dover

1862

1867

1873

MAZE
HILL

PECKHAM
RYE

1865

NEWCROSS

BLACKHEATH
HILL

NUNHEAD

N

London Chatham
1866

1868

Crystal Palace and
South London Junc.

1867

LEWISHAM

HITHER GREEN

1869

1865

South Eastern Dartford Loop
1866

Mid Kent
1858

1865

London Chatham & Dover
1863

1854

CRYSTAL
PALACE

1856

1857

1854

1858

BECKENHAM
JUNCTION

NORWOOD
JUNC.

1862

Mid Kent
1858

1860

ST. MARY
CRAY

South Eastern
1868

1864

ADDISCOMBE
ROAD

Dotted lines denote railways opened before 1852

then newly arrived at St Pancras. In that year the Metropolitan opened two new tracks from King's Cross to Moorgate Street in order to cope with this huge volume of traffic.

The London and North Western at Euston was the only one of the main lines with termini ranged along the north-west side of London to make no connection with the Metropolitan. It could afford not to do so, for in 1865 its protégé, the North London Railway, which had hitherto run its trains into Fenchurch Street, opened a spur from Dalston south to a new terminus of its own in the City at Broad Street, thereby much reducing the length of the journey from the stations in north-west London at Hampstead, Finchley and Willesden.[1]

Of all the main lines north of the river only the Great Eastern – the old Eastern Counties, amalgamated in 1862 with other companies also serving its area – still had no access to the City for its passenger traffic, and remained perplexed and forlorn in inaccessible Shoreditch. This had evidently been foreseen very early in the history of the Metropolitan, which had provided access for the passengers of all the other companies, for a Select Committee of the House of Lords appointed in 1863 to examine metropolitan railway communications had recommended that only the Great Eastern should be allowed to come a little nearer to the centre.[2] In the following year the company had gratefully obtained the necessary Act, but the financial crash of 1866 and other difficulties had prevented building, and it was not until 1874 that its first trains were able to plunge down into the tenebrous caverns of Liverpool Street Station, safe at last within the City.

This same Select Committee had also recommended that the Metropolitan should be extended at both ends, Paddington and Moorgate, to form an 'inner circuit of Railway', which would distribute 'the passenger traffic arriving by the main lines of Railway, and also absorb a very large portion of the omnibus and cab traffic, and thus essentially relieve the crowded streets'. On part of its south side this circle line was to run beside the Thames from Westminster to Blackfriars and beneath the embankment which the Metropolitan Board of Works was planning to build for the relief of traffic along the Strand and for the accommodation of one of its principal sewers. This was complicated enough, but the line was also to run through much very costly ground in the City. A separate company,

[1] Barker, pp. 120–30.
[2] P.P., 1863,(500), vol. viii, *Third Report of Select Committee of the House of Lords on Metropolitan Railway Communications*, p. iv.

the Metropolitan District, was formed to build the south side of the circle, serving the new main-line stations at Victoria, Charing Cross, Blackfriars and Cannon Street. Financial difficulties ensued, however, the chairmen of the Metropolitan and the Metropolitan District, Sir Edward Watkin and James Forbes, being already bitter rivals over railways south of the river, and it was therefore not surprising that the Inner Circle was not completed for over twenty years.[1]

In 1868 the Metropolitan extended westward from Paddington via Bayswater and Notting Hill round to Gloucester Road, where it was joined by the District's line from West Brompton. The District then took over and by way of Victoria and the new Victoria Embankment reached the station now called Mansion House in 1871. Four years later the Metropolitan, lured on by the Great Eastern's new terminus at Liverpool Street, cautiously advanced from Moorgate to Bishopsgate, and then on to Aldgate in 1876. Meantime the District extended out to Hammersmith, while Sir Edward Watkin was busy uncovering financial irregularities at the Metropolitan, of which he had recently assumed the direction. The final section of the circle, from Aldgate to the Mansion House, was the most expensive piece to build, and before it was at last completed the District had ranged far westward over less costly fields, to Ealing, Putney Bridge and Hounslow, and the Metropolitan to Willesden and Harrow via the Swiss Cottage spur. Eventually the Metropolitan Board of Works contributed £500,000 and the City Commissioners of Sewers £300,000, and the missing link was opened in 1884. Both the Metropolitan and the District also built short spurs from the neighbourhood of Aldgate to the East London Railway at Whitechapel, and thus both companies were able to run trains through Marc Isambard Brunel's tunnel under the Thames to New Cross.[2]

South of the river no underground railways were built until the coming of the electric tubes at the end of the century. This was partly because Parliament had little objection to the building of new lines above ground in the thickly populated areas there – even in 1846 the Royal Commission on railways had recommended an extension from Waterloo to London Bridge (not at once built) – and partly because the problem of communications there was quite different. There were only two main-line termini, at London Bridge and Waterloo, both situated closer to their passengers'

[1] Charles E. Lee, *The Metropolitan District Railway*, 1956, p. 13.

[2] Barker and Robbins, pp. 158–61, 209–10, 230–2; Lee, *The Metropolitan District*, pp. 12–13.

destinations in and around the City than most of their counterparts to the north of the river. Between 1850 and 1854 the volume of traffic at these two termini more than doubled,[1] and the problem was therefore the simpler one of providing more facilities for the relief of growing congestion on the railways themselves, and on the bridges. There seemed to be no reason why the railways should not be allowed to cross the river, provided that suitable sites could be found, and so between 1860 and 1866 four railway bridges were opened, leading to Victoria, Charing Cross, Farringdon Street and Cannon Street. A complex network of approach lines enabled passengers to enter either the West End or the City by rail, and within a few years south London, despite the absence of the underground, began to provide a growing volume of commuter traffic.

The first of these stations was Victoria. It provided a valuable extension for the West End of London and Crystal Palace line, whose isolated terminus at the south end of Chelsea Bridge had opened in 1858. It was built on the site of the obsolete Grosvenor canal basin, which had been mainly used for the extraction of water by the Chelsea Waterworks Company until prohibited (in the interests of purity) to continue by an Act of 1852. The site was acquired by a new company, the Victoria Station and Pimlico Railway, in which the Brighton company had a large holding. The Brighton company had also bought the West End of London and Crystal Palace in 1859, and in the following year began to run its trains into Victoria, then the only station convenient for passengers to Whitehall, Belgravia and the West End. Because it was situated in this fashionable area the previous owner of the site, the Earl of Grosvenor, laid down stringent conditions; the line was to be roofed over for some distance and the use of the station for goods traffic was forbidden, conditions which have to a large degree prevented the social decline of the surrounding property.[2]

Meanwhile, in faraway Kent, one of the most prolonged and deadly feuds in the whole history of railways had begun. The East Kent Railway Company was a contractor's affair, originally incorporated in 1853 to build a line from the South Eastern at Strood to Canterbury. Sir Charles Fox, the builder of the Crystal Palace, and his associates agreed to take nearly half the shares and pay interest on the remainder during the construction of the line, and soon Peto and Betts were also involved. In 1855 the East Kent obtained power to proceed to Dover, and three years later it was authorized to build from Strood westward to St Mary Cray, where the

---

[1] P.P., *Report on Metropolitan Communications*, p. iii.
[2] Course, pp. 95–6; Barker and Robbins, p. 141.

line was to join the Mid-Kent Railway and connect with the West End of London and Crystal Palace to reach Victoria. In 1859 the East Kent changed its name to the London, Chatham and Dover, in 1860 its trains reached Victoria and in 1861 the route to Dover was complete, twelve miles shorter than the old South Eastern's, which still passed through Redhill. Battle had been joined.[1]

In 1859 the South Eastern retaliated by obtaining power to enter the West End by an extension from London Bridge westward through Southwark and across the river to the site of Hungerford Market at Charing Cross. This entailed the displacement of St Thomas's Hospital, for which heavy compensation had to be paid, and the removal of the superstructure of the Hungerford suspension bridge for pedestrians; the brick piers were retained and still form part of the railway bridge. Charing Cross Station was opened in 1864, at the threshold of Whitehall.

In the parliamentary session of 1860 it was the turn of the London, Chatham and Dover, and it seized its opportunity with a vengeance. It obtained power for the improvement of its access to Victoria by a line from Penge through Herne Hill and Brixton to a junction with the existing line at Battersea. But the masterstroke was even more ambitious – sanction for a line due north from Herne Hill through Elephant and Castle and across the river to join the Metropolitan at Farringdon Street.

This colossal building programme, much of it through heavily built-up areas, took some years to complete. The route towards Victoria was completed in 1863, and trains reached Ludgate Hill in the following year. The junction with the Metropolitan at Farringdon Street was opened in 1866, and a separate terminus at Holborn Viaduct in 1874. The South Eastern's riposte, made in the parliamentary session of 1861, for a spur across the river from its Charing Cross extension to Cannon Street (opened in 1866), seemed feeble indeed in comparison with the metropolitan extensions of its thrusting *parvenu* neighbour, the Chatham and Dover.[2]

With four railway bridges across the river to the West End and the City a most complex network of approach lines was rapidly built through the southern suburbs in the 1860s. The Chatham and the Brighton companies co-operated to bring more trains into Victoria by building a loop line from Bermondsey through Peckham and Denmark Hill to Brixton, and the West London at Kensington was extended over the river to Clapham Junction and so on to Victoria. This enabled the Great Western to

[1] Pollins, pp. 41–51, 103–10; White, *Southern England*, pp. 39–41.

[2] White, *Greater London*, pp. 33, 36; Barker and Robbins, pp. 143–4.

use Victoria, and a second terminus alongside the existing station was built for the Great Western and the Chatham trains; the wall down the centre of the present station still marks this original division. The South Western obtained a connection with the Chatham at Battersea which enabled it to run trains from the south-western suburbs into Ludgate Hill, and on the South Eastern's approach to Charing Cross the opening of Waterloo Junction allowed passengers to Waterloo to walk across and board trains for either Charing Cross or Cannon Street. Joint arrangements of this kind were becoming increasingly common, but the enmity between the South Eastern and the Chatham and Dover continued for many years, greatly aggravated by the personal animosity between Sir Edward Watkin, chairman of the South Eastern from 1866 onwards, and James Forbes, general manager of the Chatham from 1861 and chairman from 1873. A working union was ultimately achieved in 1899.[1]

After the financial crash of 1866 the impetus of railway building was greatly reduced. The credit facilities provided by the finance companies formed in the City in the early 1860s had allowed the railway contractors to overreach themselves, and at least one authority thought that the fall of Overend, Gurney and Company had been largely due to the advances which they had made to the contractors. Overend and Gurney brought down Messrs Peto and Betts, the main contractors for the Chatham and Dover's metropolitan extensions, and thereafter the Chatham was incessantly beset with financial difficulties.[2] By 1870 the age of the contractors' lines was virtually over, and apart from the construction of the Great Central to Marylebone in the 1890s and the deeply tunnelled electric tubes, the railway network of central London had to a large extent assumed its modern shape.

Through the colossal extension of the railways in the 1860s Londoners acquired a new mobility within their rapidly expanding city, and it has been calculated that by the mid-1870s they were making some 150,000,000 to 170,000,000 rail journeys a year from one part of London to another. With the underground running alongside the river from Westminster to the City the steamboats' regular traffic declined very rapidly, and so too,

[1] White, *Southern England*, p. 42; Barker and Robbins, pp. 144–8; Philip S. Bagwell, 'The Rivalry and Working Union of the South Eastern and London, Chatham and Dover Railways', *Journal of Transport History*, vol. ii, 1955, pp. 65–79.

[2] Pollins, pp. 41–51, 103–10; R. W. Kidner, *The South Eastern and Chatham Railway*, 1963, pp. 64–5.

11 A coffee stall

12 Street scene on a Sunday morning

13 Pall Mall looking east

14 Jacob's Island, Bermondsey

15 Kensington Park Gardens, Notting Hill

16 Peabody Square Model Dwellings, Blackfriars Road

17 Crossing sweepers

18 Searching the sewers

in 1867 and 1868, when the full effect of the completion of many of the new railways was first making itself felt, did that of the omnibuses. This was the comparatively short period when the horse lost its ascendancy over the railways in the London passenger-traffic business. London was now so large that the greater speed of the railways enabled them to bring passengers in from the far-flung outer suburbs much more quickly than the omnibuses. But the omnibuses quickly recovered; they were adaptable, and they proved able to pay better dividends than the railways. They developed new routes, particularly in the West End where the railways had not penetrated, and the railways themselves, by bringing passengers into the centre, in turn stimulated the growth of this short-distance omnibus traffic. In the inner suburbs, too, the omnibus could still sometimes undercut the railways, and after 1870 the very rapid development of horse-drawn tramways presented the railways with a new and formidable competitor. Between 1869 and 1875 the London General Omnibus Company's traffic increased from 41,000,000 to over 49,000,000 passengers a year, and an average dividend of 8 per cent was paid, while the railways floundered below 5 per cent, their greatly increased traffic – perhaps three times as large as that of the omnibuses at this period – more than offset by their enormous recent capital costs.[1]

The railways had also run up a bill of social costs of incalculable dimensions. Dr H. J. Dyos, the pioneer in the study of this aspect of the history of London, has written that the 'railways had more radical consequences for the anatomy of the large mid-Victorian towns than any other single factor'. Their impact on the building fabric of London, as described by Dickens in St Pancras, has already been mentioned, but their effect on the lives of the inhabitants of the districts through which they ran was even more cataclysmic. In preparing the route of their lines through built-up areas the railway companies tried whenever possible to proceed through working-class districts, for there the price of the land would be cheaper and the landowners less likely to object. The railway surveyor would then work his way round the densely packed courts and alleys of the tenements to be demolished, offering to pay off the tenants' arrears of rent, or 'a sovereign or two to go out', or sometimes as little as eighteenpence, the rickety insanitary buildings came crashing down, and their evicted occupants were left to fend for themselves.[2]

The railways were not the only agents of this mass destruction. Some

[1] Barker and Robbins, pp. 165–6, 171–5.
[2] Dyos, 'Railways and Housing', pp. 11–21, 90–100.

1,300 houses had been cleared for the building of the first docks in 1800–5, 750 for the formation of Regent Street, 1,250 for the St Katharine Dock in 1827–8, and unnumbered others for the street improvements carried out by the City Corporation and the Commissioners of Woods and Forests in the 1830s and 1840s. Until 1853 the total number of displaced persons can only be guessed, but in that year Lord Shaftesbury persuaded the House of Lords to adopt a new standing order which required the promoters of private Bills involving the demolition of thirty or more 'labouring-class' houses in any one parish to make a return of the numbers of occupants affected. According to the probably inaccurate and conservative estimate of the 'demolition statements' which were thereafterwards made, 4,580 persons were displaced for the South Eastern Railway's extension from London Bridge to Charing Cross, 3,150 for the Chatham and Dover's metropolitan extensions, between 4,000 and 5,000 for the North London Railway's extension from Dalston to Broad Street terminus, and 4,645 for the East London Railway's line from New Cross under the Thames to Shoreditch. Almost all these works took place during the 1860s, and many other examples could be cited. In all, it has been estimated that between 1853 and 1901 some 76,000 people were involved in the railway displacements, about 70 per cent of them in the 1860s and 1870s, plus at least another 28,500 evicted for new streets and docks, making a total of well over 100,000.[1]

At first there was wide public welcome for the clearance of areas where crime, disease and overcrowding were most prevalent. The pockets of insanitary impoverishment in the central areas would be swept away and the evicted poor could go and live in the more healthy surroundings of the suburbs. But most of the poor depended on casual daily or even hourly employment; they had to live near such sources of work as were available to them, and in any case a man with an average wage of £1 a week or less could not afford a daily fare of even 6d. When they were evicted they simply moved, of necessity, into the nearest lodgings available elsewhere. The demand for cheap accommodation was thereby increased in relation to the diminished supply, rents rose, aggravated by the general rise in land values created in the central areas by the railways, and the pockets of overcrowding were merely transplanted from one place to another, more intense than ever. 'Where are they all gone, sir?', said one observer in answer to a newspaper reporter's enquiry in 1866, 'Why, some's gone down

[1] Dyos, 'Railways and Housing', pp. 13–14; H. J. Dyos, 'Some Social Costs of Railway Building in London', *Journal of Transport History*, vol. iii, 1957, pp. 23–9.

Whitechapel way; some's gone in the Dials; some's gone to Kentish Town; and some's gone to the Workus.'[1]

In the 1850s and 1860s Lord Shaftesbury and Lord Derby denounced these unwelcome social consequences of the railways, but in the prevailing climate of *laissez-faire* the railways themselves were widely and uncritically regarded as symbols and prime agents of economic progress. If they were to be required to build the same number of new houses as they demolished, they would do no good unless they were also required to receive back the old tenants, and this would be an unjustifiable invasion of landlords' rights. So nothing effective was done until 1874, when the standing orders of the House of Commons were altered to require the promoters of Bills involving displacements to provide alternative accommodation. For another decade the railway companies usually managed to evade this responsibility, and even after 1885 the alternative accommodation which they did provide was not often available at the time of demolition and was therefore used, not by those displaced, but by other families able to afford the higher rents demanded. A substantial part of the real cost of the railways in nineteenth-century London was, in fact, passed on by the companies and their unwitting shareholders to the poor.[2]

The railway companies were always reluctant house-builders – it was not their line of business. But they could be compelled to provide special cheap fares for the class which suffered most from their incursions. We have seen how as long ago as 1846 Charles Pearson had told the Royal Commission on Metropolitan Railway Termini that 'it is practicable to effect the cheap transit of a large portion of the mechanic population by means of a railroad, so as to take them at night to their dwellings, and bring them in the morning to their trade'. In 1855 he had asked the Select Committee on Metropolitan Communications 'whether it is not monstrous that commercial men should be tolerating a system where the poor are living upon ground that is worth 750 *l.* an acre per annum, when they might be transferred nightly in 20 minutes and back again to land that is to be obtained for 200 *l.* per acre'. 'The desire to get out of town is not a mere desire,' he continued, 'it is not a passion, it is a disease; the instinct of country to people who have hardly ever seen a green field comes out of them somehow.' Gradually Pearson's ideas gained acceptance, and less than two years after his death the Metropolitan became, in May 1864, the first railway in London to offer special workmen's fares. There were two

---

[1] Quoted in Dyos, 'Railways and Housing', p. 15.
[2] Dyos, 'Railways and Housing', pp. 17, 19, 96.

trains each way between Paddington and Farringdon Street, starting at 5.30 and 5.40 a.m., and the workmen could come home by any train in the day for a return fare of 3*d*.[1]

The Metropolitan introduced these trains voluntarily, but in 1860 the Chatham and Dover's Metropolitan Extensions Act, which authorized large-scale demolitions in South London, had contained, at Pearson's suggestion, a clause compelling the introduction of workmen's trains. They began to run in February 1865. There were two trains daily in each direction between Victoria and Ludgate Hill *via* Brixton, Camberwell and Walworth; the price of a weekly ticket between any two stations was 1*s*. (2*d*. a day), and in order to make certain that the trains were only used by 'artisans, mechanics, and daily labourers, both male and female', purchasers of tickets were required to give the name and address of their employer. One train left each terminus at 4.55 a.m.; they stopped at every station and arrived at the other end shortly before six o'clock. From Monday to Friday the evening trains left at 6.15 p.m., and on Saturdays at 2.30 p.m.

In 1861 the North London Railway's Act for its extension from Dalston to Broad Street contained a clause requiring one workmen's train each way for a fare of 1*d*., and in the same year the Metropolitan, by the Act for its extension from Farringdon Street to Moorgate, was also placed under a statutory obligation. Three years later it became the normal practice for Parliament to require the promoters of all new lines through the built-up areas of London to run workmen's trains. The growth of these facilities was particularly rapid along the Great Eastern's lines, where the building of Liverpool Street Station (opened in 1874) involved extensive demolitions. Other companies, with lines built before 1860 and therefore under no statutory obligation, began to introduce workmen's trains voluntarily. By 1882–3 there were 110 workmen's trains running in London, and some 25,600 workmen travelled daily on them. In the latter year the Cheap Trains Act compelled all railway companies to run workmen's trains at such times and fares as the Board of Trade might decide.[2]

The use of workmen's trains to alleviate the housing problems of the congested central areas is one of the great landmarks in the history of Victorian London. The full exploitation of this new instrument of de-

---

[1] P.P., *Report on Metropolitan Communications*, p. 158; Lee, *Passenger Class Distinctions*, p. 51.

[2] Lee, *Passenger Class Distinctions*, pp. 51–4; Barker and Robbins, p. 173; H. J. Dyos, 'Workmen's Fares in South London, 1860–1914', *Journal of Transport History*, vol. i, 1953, pp. 3–19.

liberate social engineering lies outside the scope of this book, in the 1880s and 1890s and later, when the population of Central London was falling rapidly and a ring of new predominantly working-class suburbs was springing up in such outer areas as Stoke Newington, Walthamstow, West Ham and Lewisham. By 1912 workmen's tickets represented about 40 per cent of all suburban railway journeys within six to eight miles of the centre of London.[1] The railways, and after 1870 their rivals the trams, were not, of course, the sole agents of this tremendous social upheaval. Shorter and more regular hours of work, the decline of casual employment, and the general increase in working-class prosperity all played their part too. And the whole process was only made possible by a striking growth of state intervention in matters which only a generation earlier had been considered to be the exclusive preserve of commercial enterprise.

State intervention in the affairs of the railways was, indeed, greater than might be expected. This was particularly so in London, where the lines of so many companies converged that a substantial degree of control became necessary. We have already seen that in 1846, when nineteen projects for new lines in London were put forward, a Royal Commission was established to consider the overall effects, and ultimately seventeen of the proposed lines were rejected. Again, at the second great railway crescendo in 1863–4, when rival proposals involving the demolition of a quarter of the entire area of the City were put forward, ten of the thirteen Bills were rejected, which in Dr Kellett's words, amounted to another 'noteworthy victory for the public interest'. The reports and minutes of evidence of the numerous parliamentary committees and commissions concerned with railways in London also contain abundant evidence of the attempts, however rudimentary by modern standards, to take into account the social costs of the railway companies' proposals. But Parliament failed to prevent the unnecessary duplication of termini by rival companies – Broad Street and Liverpool Street, King's Cross and St Pancras, Cannon Street and Farringdon Street are all cases in point – and for better or worse it was due to Parliament that London had remained a watershed in the national railway network, with no single great central station where all main lines converge.[2]

Apart from the underground, the railways never penetrated into the heart of either the City or the West End, although they made many

[1] Dyos, 'Workmen's Fares', p. 18.
[2] John R. Kellett, *The Impact of Railways on Victorian Cities*, 1969, pp. 10, 26, 43, 51–2, 266–7, 278.

attempts to do so. Most of these attempts were made during the 1850s and 1860s when the great railway contractors provided much of the impetus for more lines, as, for instance, did Peto and Betts in the building of the Victoria Station and Pimlico line and in the metropolitan extensions of the London, Chatham and Dover. Except in the case of the Blackfriars to Farringdon Street line these late incursions stopped on the periphery of the City and the West End at Cannon Street, Charing Cross and Victoria. The cost of even these short extensions was enormous – £4 million in the case of Cannon Street and Charing Cross – and if they had been allowed to penetrate farther the promoting companies would certainly have lost money. By the 1860s the railways themselves had become the chief agents in the transformation of land uses and the upward surge of land values in the inner districts of London. In the City they attracted storage warehouses and offices, repelled high-quality shops, and repelled or displaced private residents, while at the outer termini such as Paddington, Victoria, King's Cross and St Pancras they created zones of boarding-houses and small hotels. This was the age of the great railway hotels, of which those at Paddington and at incomparable St Pancras provide the best examples. Immediately outside the termini the railways attracted coal-yards, gas-works and industries needing their own sidings; they ruptured the existing street pattern and they created 'twilight' residential areas where housing was seldom renewed and sometimes degenerated into slums. Everywhere, but particularly in the centre, they generated more road traffic, both vehicular and pedestrian.[1]

The physical impact of the railways upon the suburbs was less pronounced than upon the central and inner areas. There, too, they cut across existing roads and streets, and sometimes competition between rival companies produced a great maze of intertwining lines, the 'tangles' at New Cross and Battersea being cases in point.

In general, however, the railways emphasized and accelerated social tendencies already either in operation or inherent in the topographical situation of a suburb, and seldom dictated the course of its development. When, for instance, a new line traversed the suburbs, a station would naturally be built at or near the centre of the existing settlement, as happened at Brixton. The area round this station subsequently became the business and shopping centre for a large surrounding residential district, but it was already on the way to assuming this function before the building of the railway, as the tithe map of 1843 clearly shows.

[1] Kellett, pp. 79, 312–24, 337–45.

Similarly the opening in 1864 of a line from Hammersmith to the Great Western main line near Paddington, where it fed on to the underground for the City, appears at first sight to have been the decisive factor in determining the modest social pretensions of suburban growth in Notting Dale around Ladbroke Grove station. But the ill-favoured situation, always isolated, at the bottom of a steep hill and with the gas works and cemetery of Kensal Green not far away to the north, would probably, even without the railway, have precluded any more aspiring development here.

And so too with workmen's cheap fares. The railway companies did not actively seek to enlarge this trade, for it was financially unremunerative in terms of the volume of traffic which it generated, and the existence of a large working-class travelling public tended to drive away the more profitable middle-class passengers. In most cases the companies (such as the Great Eastern) were compelled by Act of Parliament to provide workmen's fares, but some companies, with lines already built before 1860 and therefore with no statutory obligation, introduced them voluntarily. Dr Kellet considers, however, that with the exception of the Great Eastern's services from Liverpool Street to the area of Edmonton and Walthamstow, where an enormous expansion of working-class commuting took place towards the end of the century, there is little in the 'companies' services to suggest more than a normal response to demand pressures; a reasonably lively response in south London, a distinctly tardy one to the north-west and west'.[1]

The suburbs of the early railway age nevertheless have an ethos of their own. The Georgian terrace tradition survived far into Victorian times, often decked out, in such areas as Paddington and Kensington, with grimy stucco and debased with protruding windows and increasingly pompous columned entrance porches. But in the third quarter of the century the terrace house faced the formidable competition of the 'villa'. 'A suburb in these days, is one congerie of crude brick and mortar,' commented *The Builder* in 1848.

> It is the most melancholy thing in existence. Streets, squares, crescents, terraces, Albert villas, Victoria villas, and things of the same inviting character, stand up everywhere against the horizon, and mutely beseech us to take them. You may get a new house, of almost every conceivable pattern, and at every conceivable price down to £60 per annum. . . . We only build, now-a-days, for the gentry. If a man has a little land, or a little money, or a little speculativeness,

[1] Kellett, pp. 376–7.

or a little unemployed timber, or a number of idle workmen, he straightway buildeth a villa.[1]

Villas were the rage in many middle-class suburbs during the 1850s and 1860s. They were either detached or semi-detached, and they exhibited the uninhibited medley of 'styles' so urbanely dissected by Sir John Summerson.[2] They sprouted up in Putney, Islington, Highbury, Tulse Hill, Roupell Park, Tufnell Park, Belsize Park and many other places besides, the very word 'park', so popular at this time in the vocabulary of estate nomenclature, implying spaciousness and social decorum.

This too, at a rather lower social level, was the period when the mostly short-lived freehold land societies and the permanent building societies began to participate on a significant scale in the processes of suburban development. The original aim of freehold land societies during the Anti-Corn Law agitation of the mid-1840s was to increase the number of Liberals eligible to vote in county constituencies. The societies bought estates and sold them off to their members in small plots, each of the annual value of the forty shillings necessary to qualify for a vote. Thus the societies incidentally provided cheap plots suitable for building, and when the political results of their activities proved disappointing (the Conservatives joined in, thus cancelling the effects, and anyway purchasers' political allegiances proved unreliable) this became their main activity until changes in company law in 1856 permitted more efficient means. By 1853 44 land societies had been established in London out of a national total of 113, and the largest of them, the National Freehold Land Society, had bought thirteen estates within the metropolitan environs. At least one building society, the Temperance Permanent, bought an estate, at Stratford, and laid it out in 227 plots ranging in price from £12 to £36 each. The estate was advertised as 'distant three and three-quarter miles from the City, about five minutes' walk from Stratford Church and Forest Gate and Stratford Stations. More than twenty trains from Shoreditch and nearly forty from Stratford each day. Return tickets from Fenchurch Street to Stratford, fourpence.'[3]

[1] *The Builder*, 1848, p. 500.

[2] Sir John Summerson, 'The London Suburban Villa', *The Architectural Review*, vol. 104, 1948, pp. 63–72.

[3] E. J. Cleary, *The Building Society Movement*, 1965, pp. 51–2; Sir Harold Bellman, *Bricks and Mortar. A Study of the Building Society Movement and the Story of the Abbey National Society 1849–1949*, 1949, p. 45; Seymour J. Price, *From Queen to Queen. The Centenary Story of the Temperance Permanent Building Society, 1854–1954*, 1954, pp. 32–3.

For many of the clientèle of the land and building societies cheap access by rail to the central areas was an essential prerequisite of suburban residence. The suburbs which grew up to meet this need began to appear on a growing scale in the late 1860s, and their main history belongs to a later period. The Artizans', Labourers' and General Dwellings Company, Limited, founded in 1867, was one of the largest agents in this type of development, and by the early 1870s it was building large numbers of small houses at Lavender Hill in Battersea, and Harrow Road in Paddington, under the distinguished auspices of Lord Shaftesbury. Contemporaneously another company, the Suburban Village and General Dwellings Company, was developing a 24-acre estate between Brixton and Herne Hill, adjacent to the London, Chatham and Dover's newly opened line to the City. Here in 1868 the company was granted a 99-year lease by the Ecclesiastical Commissioners and covenanted to build roads and sewers and between 480 and 650 houses. The cheapest houses, two-storeyed and of stock brick with slated roofs, cost only £200 to build, and could be bought by instalments spread over 21 years. Builders were attracted by the promises of advances of up to 60 per cent on the cost of every house covered in, while purchasers were attracted by the cheap workmen's fares which the railway was compelled to provide. By 1872 *The Builder* reported that the estate was

> a striking instance of the new suburban neighbourhoods rising up in succession in different places around the metropolis. About the present time last year the greatest portion of the land forming the estate was occupied as market gardens, but the entire area has now been laid out in wide and spacious streets, all drained and paved, and provided with ample footpaths, and upwards of two hundred private houses and shops have already been erected and occupied, whilst a large number of new dwellings are at present in course of erection.[1]

Here, at any rate, the building of the railway was probably the decisive factor in determining the timing, pace and character of suburban growth. London had indeed become a very different place since that day in May 1833, less than forty years earlier, when Parliament, still squeezed into the ramshackle buildings long since swept away with so much else besides, had passed that now seemingly aboriginal measure, the Act for making a Railway from London to Birmingham.

[1] *Survey of London*, vol. xxvi, 1956, *Southern Lambeth*, pp. 138–9.

M

5

Industry and Commerce

IN DESCRIBING the Industrial Revolution history books written for young children usually contain a paragraph like this: 'By the end of the Georgian age, new "manufacturing" towns had sprung up near the coalmines and iron industry, mostly in the Midlands and North of England. People now worked together in large numbers, in factories, instead of at home with their families.'[1] The Industrial Revolution is presented in terms of coal, iron, steam and the dark Satanic textile mills of Yorkshire and Lancashire, while London is seldom mentioned at all. This picture often persists. London does not form part of the popularly accepted idea of the Industrial Revolution, and the fact that London was in the Victorian age the greatest manufacturing centre in the country still comes as a surprise to many people.

London's industrial primacy had existed since the earliest days of her history and still exists now. In 1801 her population was more than ten times as great as any other town in England, and of her nearest rivals – in order of size, Liverpool, Manchester, Birmingham, Bristol and Leeds – only Bristol was not a comparative newcomer among the great cities. London was in fact the only great ancient city to remain among the 'top six' throughout the nineteenth century, and for that reason alone her place in the industrialization of the nation was unique. She owed nothing directly to the recent exploitation of nearby deposits of coal or iron, but she did inherit from earlier more self-sufficient times a varied range of industries which remained for the most part structurally small in scale. London had no one predominant industry like cotton in Lancashire or cutlery in Sheffield. Despite her great size London remained, even in the

[1] R. J. Unstead, *Looking at History*, 1960 edn, p. 279.

early twentieth century, the home of small businesses, and the corollary to this was a wide diversity of industrial occupation which makes generalization extremely difficult.

The fact of London's industrial primacy is nevertheless not in doubt, thanks to the recent work of Professor P. G. Hall. In 1861 Greater London – the area of the Metropolitan Police District within a radius of fifteen miles of Charing Cross – contained some 469,000 workers engaged in manufacturing industry, or 14·9 per cent of all those so employed in the whole of England and Wales. These 469,000 workers represented nearly one-third of all employed persons in London in 1861.[1]

There was also an even greater concentration of service industries, which included building, gas and water, transport, distributive trades, banking and insurance, public administration, and professional and miscellaneous services. In Greater London in 1861 these occupied 903,000, or 24·3 per cent of all those so employed in the whole of England and Wales. These 903,000 represented over three-fifths of all employed persons in London at that date.

But despite the tremendous agglomeration of economic power which these figures express, London had another and perhaps still more important contribution to make to the advance of industrial society. Her immense population represented by far the greatest single centre of demand in the world – demand above all for food, clothing and shelter, but also demand for an infinite variety of goods ranging from luxury articles to cutlery or water-closets, all expressed on an enormous scale. Without demand, without an endless outlet for machine-made consumer goods, the factories in the children's history books could never have come into being. London's share in the creation of this demand is immeasurable in figures, but quite apart from her own manufacturing industries, it was surely great enough to earn her a place in even the simplest account of the Industrial Revolution.

Because London was such a huge centre of consumption, her imports from abroad were greater than her exports. In 1790 imports through the Port of London were valued at some £12,280,000, or 70·5 per cent of all the imports of the whole country, while exports were only £10,710,000, or 56 per cent of those of the whole country, and about half of these exports were not home-manufactured products but foreign goods transhipped in London.[2] By the end of the nineteenth century the total value of

---

[1] P. G. Hall, *The Industries of London since 1861*, 1962, p. 21.
[2] James Bird, *The Geography of the Port of London*, 1957, p. 38.

London's foreign trade was still greater than that of her nearest rival, Liverpool, but as an exporter of home-produced goods London had fallen far behind. London's industries were not, in fact, so closely concerned with foreign orders as was, for instance, the Lancashire cotton manufacture. Many of them were primarily concerned with supplying the enormous market of London itself. This was first and foremost a market for consumer goods, and so, in the words of the census report of 1831, 'fitting and finishing all the commodities requisite for the consumption and vast commerce of the metropolis' was a feature shared by many of London's principal industries.

The old-established manufactures were situated in a ring extending from Clerkenwell through St Pancras, St Marylebone, Westminster and Southwark to Stepney and the East End. In 1861 this area contained more than half of all of Greater London's workers in manufacturing industry. Some of the most important groups here were the clothes-makers, who were heavily concentrated in the West End as well as in Stepney and Bethnal Green, where they had the Spitalfields weavers as neighbours; the furniture-makers around Tottenham Court Road in the West and Curtain Road in the East; the printers in Holborn, Finsbury, the City and Southwark, and the precision workers in metal – the clock, watch and scientific instrument makers of Clerkenwell, a district described in 1858 as 'a second edition of Birmingham, in as much as its leading branches of business are purely of a metallic character'. The ramifications of Clerkenwell were indeed endless – tinplate, barometers, thermometers, engraving, light printing machinery and small delicately-made metal components of the most varied kind, all packed so closely into this small congested area that ultimately they overflowed down Hatton Garden, where the jewellers and diamond dealers congregated, to Fleet Street and even across the river to Newington Causeway where S. Smith, a firm now famous for motor-car instruments, first set up as a watchmaker.[1]

All of these trades required relatively little room for their business. For a few others, also dealing in finished goods, such as the piano-makers of Soho or the coach-builders of Long Acre, space was more important. In general, however, the more bulky trades were to be found farther out, where land was cheaper, or near the river, which provided cheap transport for heavy materials and processed goods. Their products were not luxury goods or clothing, where frequent changes of fashion required the work-

[1] Hall, pp. 28–9, 37–43, 73–7, 98; J. E. Martin, *Greater London. An Industrial Geography*, 1966, pp. 13–15.

shops to be near the centre of demand, and 'fitting and finishing' was not important for them. Often their work was noisy or smelly, and was carried on in large expensively equipped workshops employing a hundred hands or more. All this was particularly true of many of the industries on the south side of the river.

Southwark and Bermondsey were both ancient industrial centres. This was the chief centre of the leather trade, where in 1850 a third of the leather produced in the whole country was manufactured and dressed, much of it being sold in the Bermondsey Leather Market. One of the many tannery firms in Bermondsey employed over 290 men and treated 350,000 skins a year, power being supplied by two large steam engines. Hat-making here reached its greatest extent in the first half of the nineteenth century, and although much of the trade was still sub-divided among a large number of small masters, there was also at least one very large firm – Christy's of Bermondsey Street, who with some 500 employees claimed in 1841 to be the largest hat manufacturers in the world. This was one of the few south London industries dependent on fashion, and when silk and felt hats replaced 'beaver' in the second half of the nineteenth century, production here declined very considerably. But other trades impervious to fashion continued to flourish, notably vinegar-making, distilling and above all, brewing, where in 1850 Barclay, Perkins' (formerly Thrale's) Anchor Brewery employed some 430 men and had the largest output of beer of any firm in London.[1]

Farther west there was another old-established industrial centre extending southward along the little River Wandle, which entered the Thames at Wandsworth. Foreign immigrants had introduced bleaching and calico-printing there in the seventeenth century, and by 1805 the Wandle, only ten miles in length, was said to be the hardest-worked river of its size in the world. There were twelve calico-printing works, nine flour mills, five snuff mills, three bleaching grounds (one thought to be the largest in the country) and a variety of other undertakings which employed between 1,700 and 3,000 people. It was in this busy little valley that the Surrey Iron Railway, the first public railway in the world, was opened in 1803 between Wandsworth and Croydon, with a branch line from Mitcham to Hackbridge. Two years later the line was extended to Merstham, but it relied entirely on horses for the movement of traffic, and the opening of a canal from Rotherhithe to Croydon in 1809 deprived it of much of its business. Wandsworth was in any case too far away from London or the

[1] *Victoria County History of Surrey*, vol. ii, 1905, pp. 337–8, 362, 390, 397.

port to provide a suitable terminus for a railway, and with the introduction
of steam-powered machinery and new chemical processes in both bleaching and calico-printing, the Wandle's original industries declined rapidly
in the first half of the nineteenth century. But as in Southwark, others
survived, and the Wandle became an important centre for the production
of paper, paint and varnish.[1] To this day the unexpectedly dismal aspect of
parts of the Wandle catchment area, notably around Mitcham and Merton,
reveals their eighteenth- and early nineteenth-century industrial origin.

Between Southwark and the industrial concentration along the Wandle
was a large tract of flat ground where building development of a very
varied nature was rapidly proceeding in the early years of the nineteenth
century. Here the building of five new bridges and a complex network of
turnpike roads between 1750 and 1815 had opened up an area which despite its closeness to the City and Westminster had hitherto been remote
and inaccessible. Lambeth, Kennington, Vauxhall and Walworth quickly
became the resort of a wide variety of industries which needed cheap
space and cheap transport facilities.

Viewed in a national context the most important of these industries was
the group of engineering workshops which were established close to the
river in north Lambeth – so important, indeed, that they will be described
separately later on. Along the river front itself were a large number of
timber yards, of which Lett's in Prince's Meadows, to the east of Waterloo
Bridge, was the biggest. Nearby were the workshops of large-scale builders
like George Myers, who owned 'extensive steam saw-mills' there in
1850, and Grissel and Peto, the contractors for the new Houses of Parliament, who after their departure from this site were succeeded by a firm
of 'India-rubber web manufacturers'. Here, too, until 1837, upon the site
later used for the Festival of Britain Exhibition of 1951, were the kilns of
the Coade stone manufactory, whose masks and keystones still adorn the
fronts of countless Georgian London houses. Closely associated with this
was the pottery trade, which had existed in Lambeth since at least the
seventeenth century. By the nineteenth century it had concentrated along
the riverside towards Vauxhall, where several firms had large factories,
notably Doulton's, whose business benefited so greatly by the addition in
1846 of stoneware sewage pipes to their other less utilitarian products that
by 1878 they were employing about six hundred men and consuming
over ten thousand tons of coal a year.[2]

[1] *V. C.H. Surrey*, vol. ii, pp. 254–8, 261, 377, 420; Martin, p. 133.
[2] *V. C.H. Surrey*, vol. ii, pp. 250, 286–92; *Annual Register*, 1850, p. 23.

Brewing, distilling and vinegar-making were all carried on in northern Lambeth, some of the larger undertakings being the Lion brewery near Charing Cross Bridge, the distilleries of the Mawbey and Burnett families at Kennington and Vauxhall, and Beaufoy's vinegar works near Nine Elms. In 1850 more than half of all the vinegar produced in the whole country was made in Surrey, most of it in the south London suburbs. Soap- and candle-making, both then noxious trades, flourished here too, with, among others, Price's candle works, first at Vauxhall and later at Battersea. Both these ancient trades were revolutionized by the great advance in chemical knowledge in the nineteenth century, and although London did not rival Glasgow, Tyneside or south-west Lancashire as a principal centre of the new chemical industry, a number of factories were established in the suburbs. Simpson, Maule and Nicholson had a factory at Walworth for the making of aniline dyes, and Thomas Farmer, a pioneer in the use of pyrites for the manufacture of sulphuric acid, had his notoriously smelly works near Kennington Common.[1]

East of Southwark and the City the industrial scene along the water-side was dominated on both sides of the river by the requirements of the port of London. The shipbuilding yards in Deptford, Millwall and Black-wall attracted a multitude of associated trades such as anchor-, sail- and rope-making, and as steam-propelled iron vessels gradually replaced the old wooden sailing ships, a number of iron foundries were established. In one of the first of these, set up at Millwall in about 1811, 'two powerful steam-engines, one of 60, the other of 20 horse-power' were used for the manufacture of 'bar and bolt iron for the use of ship-builders and coach-makers, and iron-hoops, sheet and rod-iron for home consumption and exportation, . . . anchors and mooring-chains of any size, and all kinds of heavy forged iron-work for the navy and land-service'. Later in the century workshops of this kind turned their attention to the making of marine engines and submarine electric cables, floating docks and dredgers, while lower down the river the Thames-side metallurgical tradition was main-tained at the Royal Arsenal at Woolwich.[2]

Near to the river were to be found the food-processing industries. In Bermondsey and Rotherhithe there were a number of flour mills and bis-cuit factories, including that of Peek, Frean and Company, while on the

---

[1] *V. C. H. Surrey*, vol. ii, pp. 392–7, 404–8; L. F. Haber, *The Chemical Industry during the Nineteenth Century*, 1958, pp. 21–2, 165.

[2] Martin, p. 17; O. H. K. Spate, 'Geographical Aspects of the Industrial Evolution of London till 1850', *The Geographical Journal*, vol. 92, 1938, p. 428.

north side of the river sugar refining became heavily concentrated in White-chapel, St George's in the East and Stepney after the West India Dock Company obtained a monopoly of the landing of raw sugar. These were districts where noisome trades also tended to congregate – bone-boiling, glue-making and a variety of chemical trades – and in 1857 there were in Rotherhithe Street, for instance, 'no less than nine factories for the fabrication of patent manure; that is, nine sources of foetid gasses'.[1]

The middle years of the nineteenth century were a period of very rapid industrial expansion in the East End of London, and the old silk, clothing and furniture manufacturers acquired a host of very varied new neighbours. As in south London much of the flat ground away from the river had hitherto been neglected, but it was extremely well equipped with water transport facilities. In 1770 the Hackney Cut had by-passed the meandering River Lea above Old Ford to provide access to the Thames at Blackwall for barges coming from as far afield as Hertfordshire, and the Limehouse Cut, opened in the same year from Bow Creek to Limehouse, had provided an alternative access west of the great loop of the Isle of Dogs. The Regent's Canal, opened in 1812, provided a direct link not only with north and west London but with the great manufacturing areas of the Midlands and Lancashire, and after the building of wet docks and later of the railways, the East End quickly became a great industrial centre. Even the marshy valley of the River Lea, hitherto a barrier to eastward expansion, was used after about 1840 in its lower reaches at Bow Creek for the enlargement of the shipbuilding industry, most of the crowded water frontage of the Thames being now already occupied. And from about 1850 onwards there was a steady eastward march across the Lea into Essex, where the absence of any public control over offensive trades provided a welcome refuge for manufacturers displaced from the central districts of London by lack of space for expansion or by the stricter regulations intro-duced in 1844 by the Office of Metropolitan Buildings. By the 1870s Bow, Old Ford and Hackney Wick included jute, soap, match and India-rubber among their manufactures, rubber now being extensively used for pro-tective clothing, as well as flour mills and dyers' and confectioners' factor-ies beside the Lea canal. The modern plastics industry had its origin in a factory established in the late 1860s at Hackney Wick for the manufacture of celluloid. A large chemical works at Stratford included borax, quinine, ether, morphia and liquid ammonia among its products; while at Silver-town twelve million gallons of tar, a by-product of the gas industry, were

[1] Spate, pp. 425–6; *V. C.H. Surrey*, vol. ii, p. 260.

processed every year to make naphtha, anthracene and creosote, the last being used to impregnate one and a half million railway sleepers. The gas industry itself had made its London headquarters since 1870 at Beckton, a little farther down the river, and even the marshy isolation of the Isle of Dogs had been violated by William Cubitt, the great builder, who in the 1840s had erected Cubitt Town, soon to become the nucleus of a galaxy of timber wharves, saw-mills, brick fields, cement and iron works, as his contribution to the inexorable outward spread of industry in East London.[1]

London's industries were so numerous and varied that within the scope of this chapter only a few of the more important of them can be looked at individually. Importance can be considered either in terms of the absolute size of a particular industry in London, or in terms of the extent of its concentration in London in relation to the rest of England and Wales. The industries with the largest labour force – clothing, for instance, with 197,000 in 1861 – were important simply because of their size, and did not display any marked degree of metropolitan concentration. On the other hand the manufacture of paint, with a labour force of 2,200 in London out of a total for the whole of England and Wales of 2,700, and of rubber and tobacco, were all small industries very largely concentrated in London. Between these opposite extremes of size and concentration there were an enormous number of intermediate positions, such as those of the printers and the makers of furniture and precision instruments, each of which employed between twenty and thirty thousand hands in London in 1861 and displayed some degree of national concentration there.[2]

With such infinite variation it is perhaps easier to divide London's principal industries into two groups, which may be crudely defined as firstly the light industries which produced highly finished goods such as clothes, furniture, clocks, watches, jewellery and precision instruments, and secondly, the engineering industries, unconcerned with consumer goods, and producing tools and machinery, gas and ships. The lighter industries were in general old-established craft industries using light, often semi-processed, materials. There were therefore no heavy transport costs, and fuel costs were low too. Their long tradition of skilled labour was steadily eroded in the nineteenth century by the introduction of relatively

[1] Millicent Rose, *The East End of London*, 1951, pp. 70, 125, 145, 245; W. Ashworth, 'Types of Social and Economic Development in Suburban Essex', in *London Aspects of Change*, 1964, ed. Ruth Glass, pp. 62–4; W. Glenny Crory, *East London Industries*, 1876, pp. 25–31, 64–73; Martin, p. 139.

[2] Hall, pp. 183–4.

inexpensive machinery and the increasing use of the cheap labour of women and (particularly in the 1880s) of foreign immigrants. They combined the bespoke trade in the West End, where proximity to their market outlets was vital, and the wholesale ready-made trade east of the City, where middlemen brought goods from the producers and subsequently sold them to retailers or to the consumers. In both these branches of the trade relatively little capital was required to set up as a master, and small businesses therefore persisted, based on sweated labour and an ever increasing sub-division of the different processes of production. The heavier industries, by contrast, were either completely new, as in the case of gas, or were making increasing use of new or improved techniques, as in the case of engineering and iron shipbuilding. Their transport and fuel costs were high, and the expensive equipment which they needed required larger units of production quite different in structure from those still in use in the lighter industries.[1]

Clothing was by far the largest of these light industries, but we may perhaps look first at the allied trade of silk weaving, which in the nineteenth century, before the invention of artificial fibres, provided London's only significant contribution to the great national textile industry. It displayed many of the typical characteristics of other London light industries, but it differed from them in that by the end of the nineteenth century it was virtually dead.

Silk weaving had been carried on in Spitalfields since the middle of the seventeenth century. The trade had always been subject to violent fluctuations, and between 1765 and 1826 it was protected by a complete ban on the importation of foreign silk fabrics. Between 1773 and 1824 the wages of the Spitalfields weavers were fixed by the local magistrates under the 'Spitalfields Acts', and from about 1800 to 1826 trade prospered and expanded, despite occasional short-lived depressions. The master manufacturers bought silk from abroad, either raw or in various stages of preparation for the weavers' looms, had it thrown, twisted and dyed (usually outside London), and then put it out to the weavers, most of whom worked in their own homes in Spitalfields or Bethnal Green. Some of their houses still survive in the locality, and can easily be identified by the long attic windows of the rooms where the weavers worked.[2]

[1] Hall, pp. 113–20.

[2] J. H. Clapham, 'The Spitalfields Acts, 1773–1824', *The Economic Journal*, vol. xxvi, 1916, pp. 459–71; M. Dorothy George, *London Life in the XVIII Century*, 1925, pp. 178, 187.

Viewed in retrospect the years between 1800 and 1826 came to be regarded as the golden age of the industry in Spitalfields. Living in a closely-knit community the weavers made their own amusements; they had their own societies, devoted to history, mathematics, entomology or botany, and there were even Shakespearean readings. They were great birdfanciers and breeders of canaries, whose song enlivened their long hours of work at the looms. Many of the houses in Spitalfields had porticoes with seats at their doors, where the weavers might be seen on summer evenings enjoying their pipes.

This idyllic picture, presented in retrospect by a local resident of many years' standing, probably only described the position of the more highly skilled craftsmen, for another observer stated that he could not recollect a time 'when some in the weaving trade could not earn very large sums and others next to nothing'. Even the most skilled weaver could only maintain his prosperity by employing women and children to help him, and often these assistants were the weaver's own family. Beneath the surface, too, the structure of the industry was changing. There were new silk-weaving centres in the provinces, to which sections of the London industry began to migrate. There the prices were lower than in London, and were not ruled by the Spitalfields Acts. Some of the new London silk masters in a large way of business came from the City rather than from Spitalfields, and were wholesalers who in the prevailing climate of economic thought were becoming increasingly impatient of the established statutory control of wages. At last in 1823 they addressed a petition to Parliament. In the following year the regulations were abolished, and in 1826 the complete ban on the import of foreign-wrought silks was replaced by a customs duty of 25–40 per cent.[1]

Spitalfields proved unable to withstand this double blow. In 1838 there were still some ten thousand looms in East London, of which half were worked by men and the other half were either unemployed or were worked by women, children or apprentices. Most families owned or hired two or three looms and were engaged in the production of 'plain goods', but even the most skilful weaver could only earn about fifteen shillings a week – much the same as in the 1760s – plus another three shillings earned by his wife. From this about four shillings had to be deducted for expenses, and a child, hired at the weekly market in Bethnal Green Road, would have to be paid 1s. 2d., 2s. 2d., or 3s. 2d., the odd two pence being for the child and

[1] Clapham, pp. 459–71; George, pp. 180–8, 195; A. K. Sabin, *The Silk Weavers of Spitalfields and Bethnal Green*, 1931, pp. 14–15.

the rest for his parents. The working day was usually about twelve hours, but the sound of the looms could often be heard at two or three o'clock in the morning or on Sunday evenings – something quite unthought of in former times. The weavers themselves became physically feeble and decayed. 'The whole race of them,' it was said, 'is rapidly descending to the size of Lilliputians', and whenever cholera was prevalent they were among its first victims. Through their exhaustion, perhaps, they took no part in the Chartist agitations of the 1830s and 1840s. In Bethnal Green, to which a large part of the industry drifted in the first half of the nineteenth century, they lived in rows of cheap squalid cottages, damp, odorous and devoid of sewers. Small wonder that one weaver, when asked if he had any children, replied 'No; I had two, but they are both dead, thanks be to God!', and went on to explain to his shocked interrogator that he thanked God because he was 'relieved from the burden of maintaining them, and they, poor dear creatures, are relieved from the troubles of this mortal life'.[1]

The government attempted to help the weavers by the establishment of a school of design in Spitalfields, but it was not successful and had no influence over the industry as a whole. The last crushing blow came in 1860, when the duties on imported French wrought silks were repealed. Only a few large firms with expensive machinery could now survive, and by 1914 there were only 114 workers still employed in weaving. By 1931 there were only eleven, and the war of 1939–45 finally silenced even the last loom.[2]

The silk weavers were unusual among the London light industries in that the goods which they produced were not finished goods ready for use, but had to be further processed by other trades before reaching the final consumer. By contrast, the huge metropolitan clothing industry used partially processed materials such as silk, cloth, cotton or leather to produce finished articles ready for the purchaser. There were four principal branches of this industry – tailoring, women's dressmaking, the producduction of shirts, blouses and underwear, and the manufacture of footwear. In 1861 the 197,000 London workers in these four branches comprised nearly a quarter of all the clothing workers in the whole of England and Wales.[3]

Most of the metropolitan clothing industry was in the hands of masters

[1] George, pp. 190–1, 374; D. J. Rowe, 'Chartism and the Spitalfields Silk-weavers', *Economic History Review, Second Series,* vol. 20, 1967, pp. 482–93; P.P., 1840, vol. xxiii, *Report from Assistant Hand-Loom Weavers' Commissioners,* pp. 226–75.

[2] Sabin, p. 15; A. V. B. Gibson, 'Huguenot Weavers' Houses in Spitalfields', in *East London Papers,* vol. 1, 1958, pp. 3–14.

[3] Hall, pp. 27, 39, 184.

or manufacturers who bought the materials and employed workers to make them up, either in the masters' own workshops or in the workers' own homes. Master and worker were, however, increasingly separated by one or more middlemen. As in the silk-weaving industry, the amount of skill required varied very greatly, and so also did the earnings, which were often subject to violent fluctuations of season and fashion. Entrance to the various branches of the trade did not require a formal apprenticeship, and with ever increasing sub-division of the processes of production semi-skilled labour was constantly debasing the value of all but the most expert operatives. For a man of determination, however, the structure of the trade was still sufficiently fluid for him to be able to rise from journeyman to master, and from master to considerable prosperity, as Francis Place showed when, having learnt the declining trade of breeches-making, he changed over to tailoring, set up shop at Charing Cross, and at one time was making a net annual profit of three thousand pounds a year.[1]

All the branches of the clothing trade were strongly entrenched in their two traditional centres in the West End and the East End, but there were important variations between one branch and another. By 1861 the tailors were heavily concentrated in the streets on either side of Regent Street; on the Burlington estate (which included Savile Row and which has since become their West End headquarters) they already formed about a fifth of all the ratepayers in the area. The army clothiers were to be found around the clubs of Pall Mall, while in the East End most of the tailors were in Whitechapel, with Houndsditch the principal centre of the wholesale dealers. Women's dressmaking, numerically the largest of the four branches, was particularly strong in Bond Street, Conduit Street and around Oxford Circus, but was less concentrated in the East End. Makers of shirts and underwear were also less agglomerated, but the shoe-makers were strong in Stepney, Shoreditch and Bethnal Green as well as in the West End, and there were over four thousand of them in Southwark, conveniently close to the Bermondsey tanneries.[2]

Francis Place, writing in 1834, declared that the existence of numerous trade clubs among the tailors had raised wages during the French wars, and that the high level reached by about 1813 had subsequently been maintained. But from about 1850 onwards the productive processes of the

[1] George, pp. 210-11.

[2] Hall, *Industries of London*, pp. 41-8; P. G. Hall, 'The East London Footwear Industry. An Industrial Quarter in Decline', *East London Papers*, vol. 5, 1962, pp. 6-7; *Survey of London*, vol. xxxii, 1963, p. 454.

whole industry were revolutionized by the introduction of the treadle-operated sewing machine and the bandsaw, which was able to cut many thicknesses of material at one time. These inventions coincided with the rise of the ready-made clothing industry, whose headquarters was in Houndsditch, hitherto the centre of the old clothes trade. But the new machines did not introduce the factory system to the London clothing industry. The dealers in second-hand clothes became the new ready-made clothes makers, the machines were relatively inexpensive to buy (unlike those in the cotton industry), and with an unlimited supply of cheap labour nearby the introduction of machinery led to increasing sub-division of labour and to the perpetuation of small units of production. The skilled work, such as the cutting or in footwear the clicking, was done in the East End warehouses, often by machinery, but thereafter each process was sub-contracted out to the cheapest labour available, the middlemen or sweaters providing the link between the warehouse wholesalers and the operatives.[1]

A sweater was described in 1840 as a man who 'will fit up a room as a workshop, and will employ women and boys, perhaps a dozen, to work for him'. He provided partially made goods supplied by the wholesaler and on Saturdays he returned them and paid 'his work people at what rate he may have bargained, altogether without reference to the prices paid by the trade'. The usual daily work stint among the tailors was twelve hours or more, the workshops were almost always over-crowded and ill-ventilated, and when the gas was lit on winter evenings the temperature often reached eighty or ninety degrees. Colds, rheumatism, indigestion, headaches, giddiness, constipation, consumption, general debility and abscesses of the fingers were all common.

By the 1860s, however, four-fifths of male tailors in London worked in their own homes and either obtained work there through a sweater, which saved them valuable time, or by attending at the warehouse two or three times a week. They usually occupied only one or two rooms, and if they were engaged on slop work or government work – the cheapest forms of ready-made clothing – it was quite impossible, even when there was plenty of work to be had, for the labour of one man to maintain a family. They therefore depended on the assistance of their wives and children. Some of them, by buying their own sewing machine, managed to increase their earnings, but the spread of machinery was constantly lowering the prices paid for a particular piece of work. The price paid for making a

[1] Hall, *Industries of London*, pp. 54–9; George, pp. 163, 368.

policeman's double-breasted dress coat was two shillings and sixpence (on which the sweater's profit was sixpence), and on this work one man by himself could only earn about thirteen shillings a week. A medical officer who investigated the conditions among the London tailors in 1864 commented that 'if the operatives can only just live when the work is moderately plentiful, what must be their state of distress during . . . periods of dearth of employment!'[1]

In the same year another medical officer was investigating the conditions among the 55,000 London dressmakers and needlewomen. About 17,500 of them were employed in the dressmaking houses, mostly in the West End and the City. Here the pressure of work varied greatly according to the time of year; during the London season a working day of twelve hours or more was common, and before the 'royal drawing rooms' seventeen hours was not unknown. Many of the girls employed by the fashionable dressmaking houses lived in, were well fed, and were paid up to £25 per annum. Others, less fortunate and perhaps less skilled, lived out, and were paid from six to nine shillings a week plus tea, a wage on which it was impossible for a girl to support herself alone. But despite these conditions some girls enjoyed their vicarious connection with the *beau monde* and welcomed the excitement of the 'drawing rooms' – 'the furious haste with which the work is pushed on, the speculation as to whether it will be finished in time, and the additional refreshments provided on such occasions have, apparently, some charm for minds wearied with monotonous toil'. Not unnaturally, they ignored the long-term effect of their employment on their health and future prospects. Dressmakers 'are very much aged by the time they reach 30 or 40, being in constitution at least 10 years older than domestic servants,' reported the doctor. At thirty-five years of age they had difficulty in finding employment; they had lost their 'good taste in dress' and their fingers were no longer supple. Some tried to set up in business on their own account, others married or took service as ladies' maids, but 'too many go down in the scale, are found not to be good enough for their employment, and degenerating into poor needlewomen, drift away eastward'.

Here in the East End was the home of the slop trade, dominated by subdivision of labour, where different hands cut, fixed, sewed by machine, sewed buttonholes by hand, ironed and packed. Here too most of the

[1] P.P., 1840, vol. xxiii, *Report from Assistant Hand-Loom Weavers' Commissioners* p. 280; 1864, vol. xxviii, *Sixth Report of the Medical Officer of the Privy Council. Appendix, Sanitary Circumstances of Tailors in London*, pp. 416–30.

women were young, and even nine-year-old children were sometimes employed, 'acting as messengers'. Sometimes they earned as little as five shillings a week for a twelve-hour day and could only support themselves by taking home piecework and working at home till midnight. They only ate meat occasionally, 'replacing it by some highly flavoured substance which would enable them to swallow the staple article of their food, dry bread'.[1]

The organization of the East End footwear trade was very similar to that of the other branches of the clothing industry. It was mainly concerned with cheap shoes for women and children, most of the work was done at home for the wholesalers, and with the introduction of the domestic sewing machine the processes of production became ever more sub-divided, semi-skilled sweated labour replacing the old skilled craftsmen. By the early years of the twentieth century, however, the industry was in decline, unable to withstand the competition of the factory-made footwear which was now being produced in such provincial centres as Northampton and Leicester.[2]

Furniture-making was another light industry which shared many of the characteristics of the London clothing trade, but which also provided a number of contrasts. In 1861 nearly two-fifths of all the furniture makers in England and Wales were to be found in London, largely concentrated, like the clothing workers, in two areas, one in the West End and the other in the East End. In the west, around Tottenham Court Road, small master-manufacturers received work from the retail furniture shops such as John Maple's, which was established by 1841, and sweating soon became common. In Shoreditch and Bethnal Green, where the number of workers was much greater, the trade was based, as in the clothing industry, on the small master, the wholesale system of distribution and the sub-division of labour. The machinery used was heavier and more expensive than in the clothing trade, and even the small contractor supplied his own raw material instead of receiving it in a partly processed state from the wholesaler. But when he bought his wood from the yards near the Regent's Canal he could have it sawn and planed there by machinery before taking it home, so the result was much the same as in the clothing trade, and even the smaller number of women employed in furniture-making did not alter the fundamentally similar structure of the two industries. Little capital was needed to set up in business as a chair- or cabinet-maker or in any of

---

[1] P.P., 1864, vol. xxviii, *Sixth Report . . . Appendix, Report on the Sanitary Circumstances of Dressmakers and Needlewomen in London*, pp. 362–82.

[2] Hall, *East London Papers*, vol. 5, pp. 3–21.

the numerous other branches of the trade, and cheap labour was always available, particularly after the great Jewish immigration of the 1880s. But in the end the furniture industry diverged from both its neighbours, the slop and footwear trades, and when faced with the competition of machine-made factory goods after 1900 many of the East End masters moved out to the north-eastern suburbs where the greater space required for new methods of production was less expensive.[1]

The clothing and furniture trades were the principal fields in which sweated labour was used in Victorian London. In 1850 *The Morning Chronicle* published a series of articles exposing the system, there was a public outcry and Charles Kingsley published his famous pamphlet, *Cheap Clothes and Nasty*, soon to be followed by his novel *Alton Locke*, in which he described the conditions of the London tailors. 'What is flogging, or hanging,' he enquired, 'to the slavery, starvation, waste of life, year-long imprisonment in dungeons narrower and fouler than those of the Inquisition, which goes on among thousands of free English clothes-makers at this day?' It was now some fifty years since the State, by the Health and Morals of Apprentices Act of 1802, had made its first ineffec-tive attempt to regulate some of the conditions of labour in the cotton and woollen mills, and a series of later Factory Acts had begun to make some impression in this field. Yet within a mile of Parliament itself the hours of work of the tailors and needlewomen were longer than in the worst-regulated manufactories in the north of England, and according to Charles Kingsley even the coat on the back of one of her Majesty's ministers had been manufactured at a cheap West End showroom where the tailor who made it had had no food except a little tea during his day and a half of labour.[2] But nothing was done, nor did the investigations of the Medical Officer of the Privy Council in 1864 produce any improvement. In the 1870s the public outcry was renewed, principally through fear of the spread of in-fection from garments made in such notoriously insanitary conditions, and at last in 1888–9 a parliamentary Select Committee made a very thorough enquiry into the ever-growing ramifications of the sweating system. By this time the metropolitan local authorities were actively concerning themselves with sanitary conditions, and the Factory and Workshops Act of 1901 regulated hours of work in even the smallest workshops. But rates

[1] Hall, *Industries of London*, pp. 71–95; J. L. Oliver, 'The East London Furniture Industry', in *East London Papers*, vol. 4, 1961, pp. 88–101.

[2] Charles Kingsley, *Cheap Clothes and Nasty*, reprinted in *Alton Locke*, 1877 edn, p. lxviii; *Hansard, Third Series*, vol. 73, 1844, p. 1136 (speech of John Bright).

N

of pay remained unregulated until the Trade Boards Act of 1909 established boards with mandatory powers to fix minimum rates of wages for time workers and with similar discretionary powers for piece workers. Even these powers were restricted to certain trades, of which tailoring was the most important, and the sweating system persisted for many years, moderated, no doubt, by later more stringent legislation and by the growth of factory production, but none the less a continuing cause for shame in the industrial life of the nation.

The second great branch of industrial life in London was engineering. During the first half of the nineteenth century new techniques were rapidly displacing the ancient skills of hand and eye, and the standardized precision and speed of output of simple machinery were beginning to announce the arrival of the new industrial society. This was the great age of the engineers, when inventions, patents and scientific discoveries proliferated in one of the most powerful bursts of creative activity in the whole history of man.

Many of the engineers and men of science were of Scottish or North Country origin, but they frequently spent some time in London learning the rudiments of their skills before returning to Manchester or Glasgow. London possessed by far the greatest number of skilled craftsmen, and the watch, clock and mathematical instrument makers, the silversmiths and printers all provided natural recruits for the workshops where the new skills were being evolved. During the first half of the nineteenth century London therefore enjoyed a tremendous prestige in the field of engineering. But as the technical revolution proceeded and machinery and equipment became larger and more expensive, so proximity to the sources of coal and iron became more and more necessary. Machinery for the great Lancashire cotton industry was virtually never made in London. Old-established metropolitan engineering firms began to migrate northwards, and by the 1870s London's brief heyday was over.[1]

In the early nineteenth century many of these firms were concentrated along the South Bank of the Thames in Southwark and Lambeth. One of the first was that established by John Rennie (1761–1821), the son of a Scottish Border farmer who learned his trade with Boulton and Watt in Birmingham before setting up on his own in Holland Street near Blackfriars Road, with a house nearby in Stamford Street. He belonged to the

[1] Charles Wilson and William Reader, *Men and Machines. A History of D. Napier and Son, Engineers, Ltd 1808–1958*, 1958, pp. 4–6.

generation of engineers who made canals, docks and bridges – Southwark, Waterloo and London Bridges were all built to his designs – and after his death his second son, Sir John Rennie (1794–1874), continued in this field. His elder son, George Rennie (1791–1866), was more of a mechanic, and at the Holland Street works he made a wide variety of machinery including the first biscuit-making machine, marine engines for the Admiralty and in 1840 the *Dwarf*, the first naval vessel with screw propulsion.

But the true founder of the metropolitan school of mechanical engineers was Joseph Bramah (1748–1814), who came from Yorkshire and originally worked as a cabinet-maker before branching out on his own. The first of his many patents, taken out in 1778, was for an improved water closet which with minor modifications remained the standard model for over a century, and his beer engine, still to be seen on the bars of many public houses, was another equally long-lived device of his. But Bramah is primarily remembered for his locks, instruments of the most delicate kind which required great precision in their manufacture. At first he experienced much difficulty in making the various parts, until in about 1789 he took on a tall, strong young man from the workshops at Woolwich Arsenal. This was Henry Maudslay (1771–1831), the son of an ex-soldier employed as a storekeeper at the Arsenal. At the age of twelve young Henry had started to work there too, filling cartridges being his first job, but soon he gravitated to the smithy, where he quickly displayed an extraordinary dexterity in the manipulation of iron. He was just the man for Bramah, and for eight years they worked together, Maudslay receiving a wage of thirty shillings a week. Machine tools for making the new locks were devised, and it was during this period that Bramah patented his hydraulic press, to which Maudslay contributed the vital component of the self-tightening collar. This press provided engineers with a steady continuous pressure of practically unlimited power, later to be used by Robert Stephenson to hoist up the gigantic tubes of the Britannia Bridge across the Menai Straits, and by Isambard Kingdom Brunel for the launching of the *Great Eastern*. One of Bramah's presses is still used by the Ordnance Survey for flattening maps.

In 1797 Bramah refused Maudslay's modest request for an increase in wages and Maudslay departed to set up on his own, having previously married Bramah's housemaid. His first workshops were in Wells Street, off Oxford Street, but he soon moved to larger premises in Margaret Street nearby, where extreme accuracy and precision became the hall-mark of all his output. His work in the evolution of machinery for screw-cutting, hitherto for the most part done by hand, laid the foundations for all the subsequent advances in this basic branch of mechanical engineering, and his invention of the slide-rest for the cutting of metal led to the manufacture of machinery of all kinds in quantity, precision and at a cost which would otherwise have been impossible. The quality of the work which he exhibited in his window attracted the attention of a passer-by and led to his meeting with Marc Isambard Brunel, who had designed machinery for the manufacture of ships' blocks but had failed to find a mechanic with sufficient skill to make it. Maudslay produced a series of working models which were approved by the Admiralty in 1803, and for nearly six years he was principally engaged in making a range of forty-four machines for use at Portsmouth Dockyard, where many of them were still in use over a century later.

By this time Maudslay was employing some eighty men, and in 1810 he removed to larger premises in Westminster Bridge Road, where the street frontage of his works stood upon the site now occupied by Lambeth North tube station. Here he was able to launch out in new directions, notably marine engines, machinery for the Royal Mint, pumps, lathes, precision screws and machine tools of the most varied nature. He devised equipment for the accurate punching of holes in boiler-plates, he made the great shield which his old friend Marc Isambard Brunel needed for the Thames Tunnel, and shortly after his death his firm made the engines for the original cable haulage of trains on both the London to Blackwall railway and on the Euston to Camden Town incline of the London and Birmingham.

Maudslay's Lambeth workshops became the training centre for the next generation of mechanical engineers. He liked to recruit young men with a natural bent for engineering, and among his employees who later achieved fame and eminence were James Nasmyth (1808–90), Joseph Whitworth (1803–87) and Richard Roberts (1789–1864), all of whom went, after a spell at Maudslay's, to Manchester to establish their own works, and David Napier (1785–1873) and Joseph Clement (1779–1844), who remained in London. For James Nasmyth, later to become the inventor of the steam hammer, 'it was the summit of my ambition to get work' in one 'of the great engineering establishments of the day, at the head of which, in my fancy, as well as in reality, stood that of Henry Maudslay, of London'. Up in Edinburgh young Nasmyth set to work to make a model steam engine; he brought it up to London and called upon Maudslay. 'I could see by the expression of his cheerful, well-remembered countenance, that

I had attained my object.' He became Maudslay's 'private workman, to assist him in his little paradise of a workshop, furnished with the models of improved machinery and engineering tools of which he has been the great originator'. He and others like him learned their skills at the great slate benches with which Maudslay equipped his workshops, and on which it was his habit, on quiet Sunday mornings, to write pithy comments with a piece of chalk, either in praise or criticism of each man's work. They remembered his pleasure, even in old age, at 'having a go' himself at some intractable problem, and how 'with a few dexterous strokes, punchings of holes, and rounded notches, he would give the rough bar or block its desired form'. They remembered too, his fondness for snuff, and his delight in the musical boxes to which he was accustomed to listen as he worked at his bench. And if they did not forget their own youthful hardships, they deemed them to have been well repaid by their association with a man of such true distinction as Maudslay.

Maudslay died in 1831. The firm was continued by members of his family, and became a limited liability company in 1889. By this time it was fighting a losing battle against northern competition, and schemes for removal to the provinces were being considered when the firm finally closed its doors in 1900.[1] The great days of mechanical engineering along the South Bank were over. Joseph Clement, who after a spell with Maudslay had settled nearby at Newington Butts, was long since dead, and so too was David Napier, one of Maudslay's earliest pupils, who had ultimately set up his workshops in York Road, Lambeth, where the Festival Hall now stands. Napier was the first member of this famous Scottish family of engineers to settle in London, although his cousin, another David, established marine engineering works at Millwall in the late 1830s. At York Road two to three hundred men were employed in the production of machinery for banks, mints, arsenals and printers, much of which was sold abroad. But as at Maudslay's there was a decline in the 1870s, and the firm only survived by adopting limited liability and removing in the early years of the twentieth century to Acton, where the production of cars and aero-engines provided it with a new lease of life. In 1942 the firm was ultimately absorbed by the English Electric Group.[1]

[1] Samuel Smiles, *Industrial Biography: Iron Workers and Tool Makers*, 1863, pp. 183–235; J. Foster Petree, 'Maudslay, Sons and Field as General Engineers', *Transactions of the Newcomen Society*, vol. xv, 1934–5, pp. 39–61; J. Foster Petree, 'Henry Maudslay and the Maudslay Scholarship', *Journal of the Junior Institution of Engineers*, vol. 60, 1950, pp. 1–18.

A mile or two lower down the river from the South Bank area another of the great engineers of Maudslay's generation was engaged for nearly twenty years in a prodigious feat of engineering of great danger and difficulty. This was the building of a tunnel under the Thames from Rotherhithe to Wapping by Marc Isambard Brunel (1769–1849) and his more famous son, Isambard Kingdom Brunel (1806–59), the engineer of the Great Western Railway. As well as inventing machinery for the manufacture of ships' blocks, the elder Brunel had erected saw-mills at Battersea for the exploitation of his mechanical devices for cutting and bending timber, and had experimented with steamboats on the Thames. But his saw-mills had been largely destroyed by fire and in 1821 he was imprisoned for debt. Three years later he became the engineer of the company formed to build the tunnel; he and his son devised the great metal shield which Maudslay constructed for them, and excavations under the bed of the river began at the south end in 1825. Torrents of water frequently irrupted into the tunnel, there were panics and strikes among the workmen, and for seven years the half-finished works were abandoned. But in 1835 operations were resumed, and with the indomitable Brunels still in command the tunnel was finally completed in 1843. As a commercial speculation it proved a failure, for the carriage approaches planned by Brunel were not built and the tunnel could only be used by pedestrians. In 1865 it was sold to the East London Railway Company, and passengers travelling on the underground from Whitechapel to New Cross still pass in thousands daily through this massive monument of early Victorian engineering skill. Marc Isambard Brunel attended the opening ceremony in 1843, but he was partly paralysed and undertook little more work; only a few years later, in 1859, his son died at the premature age of fifty-three, soon after his herculean struggle to launch his mammoth steamship, the *Great Eastern*, from the stocks at Millwall.[2]

The *Great Eastern* symbolizes the history of shipbuilding on the Thames in the nineteenth century. She had been built in the yards of Messrs J. Scott Russell and Company, where the equipment included all the new wonders of the age – punching and cutting machines worked by steam, powerful travelling cranes, boilermakers' shops, saw-mills, engine-houses and the largest rolling machine in the kingdom. She was so large – 680 feet in length – that Brunel had built her broadside on to the river, but two months' effort were needed to get her afloat. In her brief life of only thirty years she proved a complete failure financially, and when she

[1] Wilson and Reader, pp. 27, 50, 154, 174.   [2] Rose, pp. 151–4.

entered the breakers' yards in 1888 the London shipbuilding industry itself was also almost dead.

During the first half of the nineteenth century the London shipbuilders
had enjoyed considerable prosperity. The yards at Limehouse, Blackwall,
Millwall and Rotherhithe were famous for the high quality of their work,
and at first the introduction of iron as a building material and of steam instead of sail merely emphasized the ascendancy of the Thames over the
provincial centres on the Clyde, the Tyne and elsewhere. London was a
great centre of engineering talent, and it was on the Thames that Francis
Pettit Smith pioneered the use of the screw propeller. In 1852–3 the
tonnage of the merchant ships launched on the Thames amounted
to over a quarter of the total output of the whole country, and the
Admiralty still ordered more than half of their outside building at London
yards.[1]

But the underlying causes of decline were already present. Only in London did the old 'gang contract' system of payment survive into the age of
large-scale industrial organization. Elsewhere the men were paid a weekly
wage, but in London they still formed themselves into gangs and bargained
with the yard-owners over the price to be paid for each job. Such a system
was quite inappropriate in an age of rapid technical change, and it was
strengthened by the powerful shipwrights' union, which immediately
after the repeal of the Combination Laws in 1824 had by means of a two-
months' strike successfully imposed its scale of prices on the yard-
owners. London shipbuilding costs, both in the construction of new vessels
and in the repair of old ones, became the highest in the country. This did
not matter greatly when the price of iron and coal remained a relatively
small item in the total cost of building a ship, but as steam-propelled iron
ships gradually replaced wooden sailing vessels, so the higher price of iron
and coal became more and more important, and ultimately the Thames-
side shipbuilding industry was killed by the lower wages and lower price
of raw materials paid by its provincial competitors.

The decline of the industry was postponed for some years by exceptional
demands for shipping. The Crimean War, the American Civil War, the
rapid increase in imports of food and the conversion of the navy from wood
and sail to iron and steam were the principal causes of this boom. New
firms were even established on the Thames, notably the Millwall Iron

[1] This account of shipbuilding is largely based on S. Pollard, 'The Decline of Shipbuilding on the Thames', *Economic History Review, Second Series*, vol. 3, 1950–1, pp.
72–89.

Works in 1859, and in the early 1860s there were some six thousand workers at the great Thames Iron Works at Canning Town. Capital was easy to come by in the City in these feverish years, and Overend, Gurney and Company were deeply involved in shipping.

When the crash came, on 10 May 1866, the London shipbuilding industry collapsed. By the end of November 27,000 shipbuilding workers were unemployed, and in 1869 a journalist described the

> mournful scene of desolation [which] greets a visitor to the once famous yards of Green, Wigram, Somes, Young...the great works and factories at Millwall, once occupied by Scott Russell, are dismantled and closed, the machinery sold, the factory tenantless, and the building yard – the birthplace of the Great Eastern – a grass-grown waste. The adjoining yards of Mare and Co., and the London Engineering Co., are in the same conditions as Scott Russell's yard. Samuda Bros. . . . are idle, and on the Isle of Dogs, where a few years ago one could count 16–20 large steamers, there are now four vessels only. . . . The prosperity of London as a shipbuilding port is at an end, and no one here looks for a revival of the business.

There was no recovery. In the years 1867–74 the tonnage of merchant ships launched on the Thames amounted to less than 3 per cent of the total output of the whole country, and apart from repair work and specialized orders for small vessels such as steam launches, little else survived of an industry almost as old as London itself.

Shipbuilding left London because in the last resort there was no overriding reason why ships should be built in London rather than elsewhere. The fortunes of the London printers in the nineteenth century show how one branch of an industry could, in response to its overriding needs, become increasingly concentrated in the capital while another branch could adapt itself to changing conditions by dispersal in the provinces.

At the beginning of the century printing was still done in substantially the same way as it had been for the previous three centuries. The compositors still stood in their shirt-sleeves before a frame containing the type, which they assembled by hand with great dexterity, while the pressmen worked in pairs, one working the roller which inked the type and the other laying on a sheet of paper and pulling the press. The industry was highly concentrated in the central areas of Westminster, Holborn, the City,

Finsbury, Shoreditch and Southwark, and some three-quarters of all London firms employed fewer than half-a-dozen men. Payment was usually by piece-rates, based after 1785 on a generally accepted scale of prices.[1]

During the nineteenth century there was a vast increase in the need for printing. The rapid spread of literacy, particularly towards the end of the century, the repeal of the taxes on advertisements in 1853 and on paper in 1861, the abolition of the newspaper stamp duty in 1855, the establishment of the penny post in 1839 and the growth of government expenditure on printing[2] all helped to raise the scale of demand to an entirely new level. The old methods of production were outmoded, and a rapid technical revolution ensued in which London led the way.

This revolution was initiated by *The Times* newspaper. At the beginning of the nineteenth century daily newspapers were still printed on wooden presses, or sometimes on the new iron Stanhope, whose output was only about 250 sheets an hour; *The Morning Post*, one of the principal London dailies, sold only about 1,250 copies a day. In 1814 John Walter, the proprietor of *The Times*, installed two steam-driven presses, each capable of producing 1,100 sheets printed on one side every hour, in which the type-bed travelled to and fro upon a belt and inking by hand was superseded by automatic rollers. This machine was invented by a German, Friedrich Koenig, and its introduction to Printing House Square marked the first step towards the modern mass-circulation newspaper. *The Times* had gained a decisive lead, and it retained it for many years. After Koenig's return to Germany two London engineers, Augustus Applegarth and Edward Cowper, set to work to exploit the steam press and in 1828 they produced an improved version capable of producing 2,000 sheets an hour, printed on both sides. This was followed twenty years later by a machine with double this output. Next came the introduction of curved stereotype plates which put an end to the need for duplicate typesetting, and finally, in 1866, the Walter Press, designed and made in Printing House Square, producing 12,000 eight-page sections every hour, printed on both sides. In 1854, within less than half a century of the hand press, and before these inventions had even been completed, *The Times* had a

[1] Hall, *Industries of London*, p. 97; Ellic Howe, *The London Compositor*, 1947, pp. 58, 60.

[2] B. W. E. Alford, 'Government Expenditure and the Growth of the Printing Industry in the Nineteenth Century', *Economic History Review, Second Series*, vol. 17, 1964-5, pp. 96-112.

circulation of 55,000 copies, while its nearest competitor, *The Morning Advertiser*, had only 6,600.[1]

This state of affairs did not last long, for by 1867 *The Daily Telegraph*, founded in 1855, had a circulation of 200,000, a figure to be dwarfed at the end of the century by *The Daily Mail*. London had, in fact, never lost its ascendancy in the newspaper branch of the printing industry. This is an essentially metropolitan business, highly concentrated in and around Fleet Street, with costly machinery and news-gathering services to maintain, and needing to be situated at the national centre of communications for the rapid daily distribution of its product all over the country. But the requirements of the other branches of the printing industry were quite different, and their history has followed a different path.[2]

The jobbing printers and the printers of books cannot be clearly distinguished from one another. In general the commercial jobbers continued to use hand presses until the middle of the nineteenth century, and the treadle machines which were thereafter introduced did not affect the small scale of their individual businesses. They could therefore afford to remain in the increasingly expensive central commercial areas where much of their work originated, often occupying ill-ventilated workshops in back streets and alleys. Even an unusually large firm like Waterlow's in Finsbury, specializing in such lines as banknotes and cheques, did not begin to move out until the twentieth century. But the book printers had different problems. Expensive machinery was needed to take advantage of the growing market for both cheaper books and for government publications, and so there emerged a few large firms, such as those of William Clowes, Eyre and Spottiswoode, and Spottiswoode and Company, highly mechanized and each employing several hundred men. By the middle of the century, however, the high costs of both space and labour were beginning to place these London firms at a disadvantage in relation to their provincial competitors, notably the Scottish printers. With the new rapidity of communication inaugurated by the railways there was no longer any overriding reason for them to remain in London, where almost all the English publishers had their offices, and a slow migration to the provinces began. Aylesbury, Beccles, Tonbridge and other towns within a hundred or so miles of London became the new home of these metropolitan migrants

---

[1] Hall, *Industries of London*, p. 105; P. M. Handover, *Printing in London from 1476 to Modern Times*, 1960, pp. 152–67.

[2] Hall, *Industries of London*, pp. 106–7.

during the second half of the century, and today hardly any high-quality book printing is done in the traditional central area of London.[1]

The history of the business founded by William Clowes in a single room in Villiers Street, Strand, in 1803, provides an illustration of this process. At first he employed only one man, but he was soon obtaining work from the government, and within four years he moved to a house nearby in Northumberland Court. There in 1823 he installed one of Applegarth and Cowper's steam presses – the first ever to be used for book production – successfully resisted the objections of his neighbour, the Duke of Northumberland, against the soot and smuts of his machine, but finally agreed to remove his steam engine on receipt of substantial compensation from the outraged Duke. He then settled in Duke (now Duchy) Street, on the South Bank, on the very site hitherto occupied by Applegarth and Cowper, and here the business stayed, handed on in ever growing size from one generation of the Clowes family to another until the whole works were destroyed by bombs in 1941. But in 1873 a branch business had been established at Beccles in Suffolk, to which most of the book printing was soon transferred. Here the firm has remained, a limited liability company since 1880, with the Clowes family of printers now in its fifth generation.[2]

The London shipbuilding industry had disintegrated, but the printers had successfully adapted themselves. In contrast with these old-established trades was a brash, pushing newcomer, the gas industry, which spread its iron tentacles all over London during the first half of the nineteenth century. Within ten years of the establishment of the first gas company nearly three hundred miles of gas mains had been laid in London, and by about 1850 there were some two thousand miles. By then few towns in England with a population of over 2,500 were still without a gasworks, and twelve million pounds had been invested in an industry whose large demands for coal and iron had in the 1820s and 1830s prepared the coal-and iron-masters to meet the far greater requirements of the railways.[3]

William Murdoch of the great Birmingham firm of Boulton and Watt is generally recognized as the originator of a practical system of lighting by coal-gas, but he did not exploit his invention, and Londoners first became aware of this revolutionary method of lighting through the activities of

[1] Hall, *Industries of London*, pp. 102–5; Alford, pp. 96–112.

[2] W. B. Clowes, *Family Business 1803–1953*, N.D., *passim*.

[3] M. E. Falkus, 'The British Gas Industry before 1850', *Economic History Review, Second Series*, vol. 20, 1967, pp. 494–508.

Frederick Albert Winsor, a volatile and unreliable German, who had acquired what knowledge he ever possessed from a French scientist, Le Bon. Winsor was a master of the arts of publicity, and in 1807 he illuminated the south side of fashionable Pall Mall, close to the Prince of Wales's house, the gas for his row of thirteen lamps being supplied from the 'carbonizing iron furnaces' in Winsor's own house nearby. The display was a success; he formed a National Light and Heat Company, from which there emerged the Gas Light and Coke Company, authorized by Act of Parliament in 1810 to raise £200,000 of capital, and incorporated by royal charter in 1812.

The new company at once sought permission to light the approaches to the Houses of Parliament, and soon it was negotiating for contracts with vestries, paving boards and the owners of public buildings such as Drury Lane Theatre. A site for the company's first gas-making plant was hastily acquired in Great Peter Street, Westminster, and when the tiny Liberty of Norton Folgate, just outside the eastern boundary of the City, wanted to use gas to light its streets, another site was bought in Curtain Road, Shoreditch, for it was then thought that the supply of gas would be a very local affair, with gasworks dotted about all over London. There were innumerable problems to solve – the design and building of the retorts and the gasometers, the purchase and delivery of coal supplies, negotiations with the innumerable public authorities responsible for the paving of the streets of London, whose often reluctant permission was needed before the gas pipes could be laid; and then the pipes themselves had to be manufactured and delivered. In these first exciting days of the new industry there was much improvization – gun-barrels were even bought in large quantities for use as service pipes to private houses, and 'barrel' is still the word used to describe small-bore gas pipes. Winsor, the founder of the Chartered Gas Light and Coke Company, was for a brief moment in his element, but he was hopelessly unbusinesslike, and when he retired to to France in 1815 to escape his creditors, his fellow directors were much relieved to be rid of him. By 1819 he had been declared bankrupt in Paris. Shortly afterwards the company granted him an annuity of £200 for life, which after his death in 1830 was paid to his widow.[1]

Between 1817 and 1825 six more companies with statutory powers were established in London, and there were also a number of smaller undertakings working under private deeds of trust. The professionals, such as

[1] Dean Chandler and A. Douglas Lacey, *The Rise of the Gas Industry in Britain*, 1949, pp. 30–46, 54–5, 68.

Samuel Clegg, engineer of the Chartered Company, moved in; explosions became less frequent, the incandescent quality of the gas was improved, there was a device for metering customers' consumption (coin in the slot meters did not appear until about 1890), and a flourishing market was developed for by-products, of which tar for the navy was at first the most important.

Between 1830 and 1836 another four companies were established, and with the Whigs in power competition became the order of the day. There was a price war, and the London pavements were frequently torn up by the acrimonious gangs of hostile rival companies. Charges were reduced from about 15s. per thousand cubic feet to 10s., and then in the 1840s there were more cuts which quickly brought gas for the lighting of private houses within the range of a much wider public. In due course many companies came to private agreements to restrict themselves to certain areas, and in 1854 five of the principal companies agreed to raise their prices. By 1857 competition was ended for good – except in the City, where one company refused all offers of peace. Three years later the Metropolis Gas Act of 1860 gave statutory authority to the companies' districting arrangements, but in return for the recognition of these local monopolies it imposed maximum charges, a limitation of dividends to 10 per cent, and an obligation to supply all consumers whose premises were within fifty yards of a main.[1]

The pioneer age of the London gas industry was now over, and within the next sixteen years the structure of the industry assumed very much the shape which it retained until it was transferred to state ownership in 1949. In the early 1860s the giant among the London companies was the Imperial, established by an Act of 1821. The original Chartered Company, with cramped works and obsolete plant, seemed doomed to decline, but when Samuel Adams Beck became the Governor in 1860 the company unexpectedly took on a new lease of life. He chartered steam collier vessels to ensure a cheap regular supply of coal from the Durham mines – one of these ships was appropriately named the *Magna Charta* – and in order to make full use of this improved supply the company decided to remove its manufacturing plant far down the river to Galleons Reach, near Barking, where coal could be unloaded direct. The building of the huge new works there began in 1868. Within a few years the inconvenient old plants at Great Peter Street, Curtain Road and elsewhere were closed, and with the vast up-to-date works at Beckton in operation the Chartered Company was

[1] Stirling Everard, *The History of the Gas Light and Coke Company, 1812–1949*, 1949, pp. 89, 100, 198–201; Falkus, pp. 494–508.

able to absorb half-a-dozen of its rivals, and at last in 1876 to amalgamate with the great Imperial. The Chartered Company now supplied almost the whole of London north of the Thames. Parts of Westminster, Chelsea and Fulham were not acquired until 1883, and the Commercial Company continued to supply part of Stepney until 1949, but elsewhere the Chartered reigned supreme, well able to exploit the new demand for gas for heating and cooking and to withstand the competition of electricity which arose in the 1880s and 1890s. Beck could retire in 1876 with his work of modernization completed and his fame perpetuated in the name which the company bestowed upon his gasworks – Beckton.[1]

Just as London's early mechanical engineers like Bramah, Maudslay and David Napier had provided a nursery for a later generation of men who subsequently achieved fame in Manchester, Glasgow and elsewhere, so too London had provided the first generation of gas engineers. London-trained men built the first gasworks at Preston, Wolverhampton and Liverpool, for instance, and in the 1820s and 1830s London iron merchants often sponsored the building of works in provincial towns and then formed companies to finance the rest of the undertaking. All these pioneers were practical men of business, but in the more secluded field of scientific experiment London also provided many of the pathfinders. Sir Humphry Davy and his still more famous assistant, Michael Faraday, both spent most of their working lives in London, and so too did William Wollaston (1766–1828), who differed from almost all his scientific contemporaries in having been educated at one of the ancient universities, Cambridge. Wollaston was the most skilful chemist and mineralogist of his day. He published fifty-six papers on pathology, physiology, optics, crystallography, astronomy, electricity, mechanics and botany, and despite his unfortunate remark in the early days of gas that 'they might as well try to light London with a slice from the moon', the infallible accuracy of his experimental work later earned him the honourable nickname of 'the Pope'.[2]

Wollaston and Davy belonged to perhaps the last generation of scientists able to avoid the advancing claims of specialization. But specialization bridged the gulf between the laboratory and the world of business and practical affairs, and opened the way for the prodigious technical advances of more recent times. In the 1850s Henry Bessemer, working at his laboratory in St Pancras, devised his process for making steel which revolutionized

[1] Everard, pp. 94, 220, 222, 235, 242, 247, 382, 411.
[2] Chandler and Lacey, p. 1; Falkus, pp. 494–508.

the commercial history of the world, while a few years later William Siemens, at his great works at Charlton near Woolwich, was inaugurating the modern conquest of time and distance through the electric telegraph cables with which he was encircling the globe. And nearby, at the Greenwich Observatory, Sir George Airy, the Astronomer Royal, was distributing Greenwich Time electrically first to Britain and then to the world, and laying the foundations whereby the Greenwich Meridian became the prime meridian whence all longitudes are measured and on which Standard Time is based. London, at least when viewed through the industrial haze from Greenwich Hill, was indeed the true hub of British nineteenth-century scientific endeavour.

To complement its enormous industrial power Greater London in 1861 also possessed almost a quarter of all the workers in the whole of England and Wales who were engaged in the provision of services of one kind or another.[1] These services were as infinitely varied as London's manufactures, and the men and women who provided them included soldiers and sailors, professional men, lodging-house keepers, hairdressers, grooms and livery-stable keepers, and the great armies of shopworkers, domestic servants and general labourers. The sum total of their labours made London's existence possible. In this brief account of their multifarious activities, pride of place must go to those engaged in the organization of food supplies, followed by those in the coal trade and those in more specialized fields such as insurance, in which London was pre-eminent.

London was fed through the agency of thousands of retailers and middlemen, who over the centuries had evolved a complicated and cumbersome mechanism of supply. The wonder is that the system worked as well as it did, for until the building of the railways rapid transport was unknown, and only in the case of milk, mostly supplied by suburban cowkeepers, was the distribution of food not dependent on ever-lengthening chains of intermediaries. The railways and the steamships shortened many of these chains. Cattle no longer had to be driven to market on the hoof through half the length of the country, and farmers in East Scotland or Cornwall would begin to grow potatoes for steam carriage by sea to London. The distance from which London could draw its food was enormously enlarged, and as the country as a whole became increasingly dependent on imported foodstuffs, so Londoners became large-scale customers for the wheat farmers of eastern Europe and Canada, for the fruit growers of

[1] Hall, *Industries of London*, p. 21.

South Africa and the cattle-ranchers of America. The commerce of food acquired a new pattern, as intricate as but more specialized than the old, in which London's wholesale markets and exchanges became the central pivot for the internal distribution of food far byond the confines of the capital itself.

In the early nineteenth century, when the Corn Laws regulating the import of foreign grain were still in operation and bread was a much more important item of food than it is now, the millers bought most of the English wheat crop direct from the farmer. They employed factors to buy far and wide, and combined their milling operations with general dealings in both corn and flour. Some of this grain ultimately passed through the Corn Exchange in Mark Lane, which had been established there in the mid-eighteenth century, and more came from the shipmasters who brought up wheat from the coastal districts of Kent and East Anglia to sell on commission at the Exchange. Barley was usually sold direct by the farmer to the local maltsters, but there was an extensive trade in oats and beans in Mark Lane, where most business was now done with samples.[1]

The price of wheat often varied very greatly from one year to another according to the size of the harvest, and large profits (and losses) were often made in speculative dealings on the Corn Exchange. There were speculative dealings, too, in foreign corn, which in times of domestic plenty could be stored in London and resold in time of dearth. Much of this imported grain came from Eastern Europe and Russia, and it was in this way that the merchants active in general trade with the Baltic became involved in the corn business. They congregated at the Baltic Coffee House in Threadneedle Street, but after the repeal of the Corn Laws in 1846 the scale of imports grew so rapidly that they moved to larger quarters at South Sea House. In the second half of the nineteenth century the Baltic Exchange became the principal centre for large-scale speculative dealings, where cargoes were often bought while still afloat, and resold, sometimes on the Corn Exchange, which became the link between the domestic and foreign branches of the corn trade. Here all grains could be sampled, bought and sent on into the country to the local merchants and millers, now beginning to accustom themselves to dealing more and more in imported produce.[2]

[1] J. H. Clapham, *An Economic History of Modern Britain*, vol. I, 1926, pp. 219, 226, 229–31; vol. II, 1932, p. 298.

[2] Clapham, vol. II, pp. 298–300; S. W. Dowling, *The Exchanges of London*, 1929, pp. 179–80.

The chief agencies for the supply and distribution of meat, fish and vegetables were the ancient markets, many of them established by royal charter either in medieval times, when the City Corporation was building up its great bastions of privilege, or in the late seventeenth century, when private individuals were willing to pay for market rights. The principal centres of the meat trade were Leadenhall Market, specializing by the beginning of the nineteenth century in poultry and hides, Newgate and Farringdon Markets for dead meat and Smithfield for live cattle, all owned by the City Corporation. With the rapid outward spread of London the volume of their business had increased enormously – annual dealings at Smithfield in 1828 amounted to 152,804 head of cattle and 1,582,530 sheep. They had become an insufferable nuisance, but the City Corporation in the 1840s was drawing a net annual income of nearly £10,000 from them (including Billingsgate) and therefore resisted all attempts at reform.[1]

Smithfield, 'that sink of cruelty, drunkenness and filth, the cattle market – where every other building was either a slaughterhouse, a gin-palace, or a pawn-broker's shop', was the principal goal of the drovers who brought their herds up to London from all over the country. To relieve the pressure there a ring of illicit markets had grown up around the metropolis, but most of the cattle for London's meat were still driven through the streets to the congested pens of Smithfield, and from there to the adjacent slaughterhouses, conducted in conditions of appalling squalor and brutality, sometimes even in cellars. And those beasts which were not brought to Smithfield were killed in similar circumstances in outlying markets, such as Newport Market near Leicester Square, or in the yards behind the shops of retail butchers all over London.

In the latter part of the 1840s Smithfield became a favourite target for the attacks of the sanitary reformers. *The Times* entered the fray, a Royal Commission was appointed and in 1850 it recommended removal. But the Corporation remained obdurate, and it was not until 1855 that the live cattle market was transferred to Copenhagen Fields, Islington. Thirteen years later the old Newgate Shambles was transferred to Smithfield, where the City Corporation equipped the huge new central dead meat market building with its own railway station. The old Farringdon Market migrated

[1] W. J. Passingham, *London's Markets*, n. d., p. 78; Joseph Fletcher, 'Statistical Account of the Markets of London', *Journal of the Statistical Society of London*, vol. X, 1847, pp. 345–60; A. B. Robertson, 'The Smithfield Cattle Market', in *East London Papers*, vol. 4, 1961, pp. 80–7.

O

here in 1892, but Leadenhall Market still survives, rebuilt in 1879–81 by a now virtuous municipality.

This transformation of London's meat marketing arrangements co-incided with the arrival of more and more meat in carcass form, already dead, and hygienically delivered by rail or steamship. Slaughterhouses required licenses, and retail butchers became mere purveyors of meat killed elsewhere. In 1876 the first cargo of refrigerated meat arrived in Smithfield from America, followed five years later by supplies from Aus-tralia and New Zealand, where great new agricultural industries were called into being by the needs of hungry urban Britain.[1]

In the fruit and vegetable trade the three principal centres of distribu-tion were the Borough Market, which was of medieval origin and had belonged since the middle of the eighteenth century to the parishioners of St Saviour's, Southwark, and Spitalfields and Covent Garden Markets, both of which had been established in the reign of Charles II and belonged to private individuals. In the inner suburbs there were also about half-a-dozen other markets where substantial quantities of fruit and vegetables were bought and sold, but by the nineteenth century they were in decline, and several of them were closed – Hungerford Market, for instance, in 1862 to make way for Charing Cross Station. Gradually Covent Garden assumed its modern supremacy under the capable management of its formidable proprietors, the Dukes of Bedford.

At the beginning of the nineteenth century there were fifteen thousand acres of market garden ground within ten miles of London. Every evening the growers loaded up their carts and around midnight they set out for Covent Garden, often accompanied by their wives. They arrived between three and five o'clock in the morning, when the dealers attended. By six or seven the growers had sold their produce, which was then distributed to the retail shops, much of it by the labour of ill-paid Irish women, who carried loads of a hundredweight to all parts of London on their heads. The fragile strawberry crop had to be carried into the market as well as out of it, and hundreds of women, many of whom had walked to London from as far afield as Shropshire and Wales for the soft fruit season, were employed in this drudgery. Like an army of moving caryatids they carried on their heads basket-loads weighing up to fifty pounds, and in the course of the three or four journeys a day which they made from farm to market they often walked thirty miles.

[1] Royston Lambert, *Sir John Simon 1816–1904 and English Social Administration*, 1963, pp. 135, 161; Clapham, vol. II, p. 304; Passingham, pp. 10–15, 78.

In 1828 the business of the market had become so lucrative that the sixth Duke of Bedford ceased to lease the collection of the tolls for a fixed rent to the highest bidder and began to manage the market himself, through his efficient estate office staff. He promoted a private Act of Parliament and erected the graceful buildings which still stand in the centre of Covent Garden Piazza. Business continued to grow, and when the Dukes' great country estates became practically insolvent during the prolonged agricultural depression which began in 1879, the enormous revenues from Covent Garden were used to subsidize them. In the 1880s the introduction of cool chambers and the increased speed of steamships brought American and Tasmanian apples, bananas, early vegetables from Madeira and the Canaries, and in the 1890s Australia, South Africa, Florida and California were all beginning to compete with France and Spain in the supply of Mediterranean commodities such as grapes, oranges and peaches. Even the establishment of railhead markets at King's Cross (for potatoes), Stratford and Somers Town did not halt the inexorable expansion of Covent Garden. Between 1860 and 1904 almost all of the buildings on three sides of the market square were rebuilt for the market by successive Dukes of Bedford, or their sites used after demolition for more cart-space, but still the congestion grew, flowing ever outward into Long Acre and St Giles's. Public demand for the complete removal of the market originated in the 1860s, and is now (1970) about to be fulfilled, more than half a century after the eleventh Duke of Bedford had in 1918 sold all his property in Covent Garden.[1]

The distribution of milk was never funnelled through markets and it therefore suffered no crisis of location like the meat and vegetable trades, nor did domestic producers face competition from abroad. In the first half of the nineteenth century London's milk was supplied either by cows kept in yards in back streets, or by the herds kept by cowkeepers in the suburbs. The town cows' milk was distributed from door to door by men, or more often women, who carried on a shoulder-yoke a pair of wooden tubs holding up to ten gallons. The suburban cowkeepers, like the Rhodes family in Islington, often owned several hundred beasts and brought their milk up by fast well-sprung carts, sometimes from farms as far afield as fifteen or even twenty miles away.

With the rapid spread of London the suburban cowkeepers retreated farther outwards. They were no longer able to distribute their milk themselves, and sold it to dealers instead. Milk brought up by the railways was

[1] *Survey of London*, vol. xxxvi, 1970, chapter vi.

also a profitable field for the dealers, but by the time it reached the consumer 'railway milk' had often deteriorated, and for some years the best-quality milk was supplied by the town dairymen. In 1865–6, however, there was a severe outbreak of rinderpest and four-fifths of the London cows died or had to be slaughtered. The wholesale dealers moved in to fill the gap, and in 1866 some seven million gallons of milk were brought to London by rail from over two hundred country stations. Big new companies built up large-scale buying and delivery organizations, and wheeled milk floats displaced the yokes and tubs used in earlier years. But somewhat unexpectedly the small cowkeepers recovered, at least partially, particularly in the poorer districts of the East End, and in 1889 there were still nearly seven hundred licensed cow-houses in the County of London.[1]

Most of the milk bought in London was probably bought for cooking, not for liquid consumption. Beer remained the most popular drink, and in contrast with milk, beer production was already big business by the beginning of the nineteenth century. Brewing in London was dominated by a dozen great firms, of which Barclay, Perkins' brewery in Southwark was in 1814 the largest, with an output of 262,000 barrels of porter. This was the brewery which had formerly belonged to Dr Johnson's friend Henry Thrale, and it was here, in 1849, that the notorious Austrian Marshal Hayman, while on a visit to the brewery, was beset by the outraged brewers and obliged to take refuge in a dustbin in an adjoining tavern until the arrival of the police. Other giants in the beer industry included such still famous names as Truman, Hanbury and Buxton in Spitalfields, Meux in Tottenham Court Road, Whitbread's in Chiswell Street, Watney's in Pimlico and Charrington's in Mile End Road. In 1836 the group of twelve big London brewers used more than two-thirds of all the malt consumed there, most of which was supplied by the maltsters situated along the Thames valley. Over half the total trade was already through 'tied houses' controlled either by loan or lease by the brewers, and the licensed victualler who brewed his own beer was already virtually extinct in London.[2]

After food and drink, London's other great life-line was heat and power. Coal had been brought to London by sea since medieval times, and by the nineteenth century metropolitan consumption amounted to about a

[1] Clapham, vol. I, pp. 227–8; vol. II, p. 303; E. H. Whetham, 'The London Milk Trade, 1860–1900', *Economic History Review, Second Series*, vol. 17, 1964–5, pp. 369–80.
[2] Peter Mathias, *The Brewing Industry in England 1700–1830*, 1959, pp. 117–38; Clapham, vol. I, pp. 68, 170; *V.C.H. Surrey*, vol. II, p. 389; *V.C.H. Middlesex*, vol. II, 1911, pp. 168–78.

quarter of the total national output. In the 1840s there were some seven hundred sailing colliers plying regularly between London and the coal-fields along the Tyne and the Wear. Each vessel carried about 220 tons of cargo and made on average ten voyages a year to bring in London's gigantic total import.

London's coal had always been taxed. There were mayor's dues and market dues and stamps and factorage fees to be paid, and some at least of these moneys were used for charitable or public purposes. The orphans of freemen of the City had for many years been maintained out of these funds, part of the cost of rebuilding St Paul's Cathedral had been met from them, and throughout much of the nineteenth century money was borrowed in advance from the proceeds of the coal tax to help pay for the building of new London Bridge, Waterloo Bridge, the Thames Embankment and some of the metropolitan street improvements made by the Commissioners of Woods and Forests in the 1840s. With so much public money involved in this large and lucrative business it was therefore inevitable that by 1800 the London coal trade should have become the object of more than seventy Acts of Parliament concerned with its regulation, and that its history during the next few decades was to be largely concerned with the removal of these restraints.[1]

At the beginning of the nineteenth century most sea-coal was brought to London as the property of the shipowner, who was a principal, not an agent. There the coal was unloaded under the supervision of the City Corporation's 'water meters', who ensured that the complicated dues were paid. The work of unloading was done by the coal whippers, usually in midstream from the colliers (of which there were sometimes over two hundred at anchor at one time), into barges which belonged to the principal metropolitan coal merchants. The coal was then ferried either to the merchants' wharves, where unloading and bagging was supervised by the 'land meters', or up-river to places almost as far as Reading. From the wharves coal found its way into the hands of lesser merchants, who distributed it in smaller quantities throughout the whole of the metropolitan area.

In the latter part of the eighteenth century the buying and selling of coal had been conducted in the Coal Exchange in Thames Street, an exclusive body which had been established in 1770 by the principal coal

---

[1] Raymond Smith, *Sea-Coal for London. History of the Coal Factors in the London Market*, 1961, pp. 131, 285; Elspet Fraser-Stephen, *Two Centuries in the London Coal Trade. The Story of Charringtons*, 1952, pp. 3, 5; Clapham, vol. I, p. 235.

factors and merchants. The Coal Exchange was analogous to the Corn Exchange in Mark Lane, but (unlike the latter) it became vested by successive Acts of Parliament of 1803–7 in the City Corporation with power to conduct a free and open market there. The intention of these Acts was evidently to free the trade from the grip of the few strong firms which dominated it, but the result was the opposite. The concentration of trade continued, and was not reversed until the labyrinth of duties was abolished and the supremacy of sea-coal itself was challenged by rail-borne coal.[1]

Up in Newcastle the coal trade was even more restrictive. There the collieries could supply far more coal than the nation required, and in order to prevent mutually damaging competition the colliery owners and lessees had formed a committee for 'the limitation of the vend'. Each collier was allocated a proportion of the total output of each class of coal, and once a year the producers of the best coal decided at what price they intended to sell during the next twelve months. The prices of inferior coals were correspondingly adjusted, and the committee met at frequent intervals to decide, according to the prevailing state of the market, how much coal to 'vend'. The committee for 'the limitation of the vend' was, indeed, in the words of Sir John Clapham, 'the most long-lived and notorious employers' combination of the early nineteenth century'.

In the rapidly changing economic conditions of the 1830s and 40s most of these constraints on the coal trade were swept away. In 1831 all customs duties on sea-coal were abolished, and the ancient City dues were consolidated at 1s. 1d. per ton, part of the proceeds of the latter being subsequently used until 1890 to pay for metropolitan street improvements. In future, too, all coals were to be sold by weight instead of by the archaic and inefficient system of measuring hitherto used. At the producing end of the trade the 'committee of the vend' was subjected to detailed parliamentary investigation, but the foundations of its restrictive practices were already being undermined by the successful exploitation of the hitherto inaccessibly deep coal seams of South Durham. The railways and the new gas industry both needed coal in vast quantities, and they needed iron too, the production of which still further enlarged the demand for coal. New coal pits opened in Yorkshire, Lancashire, Scotland and South Wales. The closed circle of the Newcastle coalmen was broken by the natural processes of economic growth, and the 'committee of the vend' was wound up in 1845.[2]

[1] Smith, pp. 85, 91, 142, 152; Clapham, vol. I, pp. 234–5, 305–6.
[2] Smith, pp. 180–1, 262, 336–7; Clapham, vol. I, p. 202; Sydney G. Checkland, *The Rise of Industrial Society in England 1815–85*, 1964, pp. 159–61.

This same year, 1845, marked the beginning of the next stage in the nineteenth-century transformation of the London coal trade. The railways began for the first time to deliver coal to London and so to challenge sea-coal's ancient monopoly. At first the quantity of this new 'inland' coal was trifling, but it grew with astonishing rapidity. The Great Northern Railway, the pioneer in this new trade, provided sidings and yards for the London merchants and at one time the company even set up as a coal dealer on its own account until debarred from doing so by law.

The nabobs of the sea-coal trade responded to this challenge with new steam screw-propelled colliers, the first of which made its maiden voyage to London in 1852. This vessel, the *John Bowes*, had a cargo capacity about double that of the average sailing vessel in the trade, and her round trip took only five days, including one for unloading, compared with the month or more required by sail. Larger steam colliers were quickly built, and soon one such vessel could do the work of at least six sailing ships. Rapid unloading became essential, and the steam-operated cranes and winders now installed in the docks began to displace the more strenuous methods hitherto practised by the coal-shippers. In 1863 a huge floating derrick, appropriately named the *Atlas*, 250 feet in length and equipped with six hydraulic cranes, was moored in the river at Bugsby's Reach by one of the principal firms of London coal merchants. It could discharge two steam colliers at once, and could handle between half and one million tons of coal a year.

But despite its rapid modernization the sea-coal trade was fighting a losing battle with inland coal, and by 1875 five million of London's eight million tons of coal came by rail and only three million by sea. The whole trade had indeed been transmuted within the space of little more than thirty years. An increasing quantity of coal was now being bought by the London merchants from the pitheads in the north, and the shipowners who also owned their cargoes and delivered them for sale in London at their own risk had been displaced by the colliery owners, coal merchants and large consumers such as the gas companies, all employing chartered vessels. A free trade had been established, and even its headquarters, the Coal Exchange in Thames Street had been rebuilt in 1847–9, to survive (until its demolition in 1963) as a monument to perhaps the greatest single distributive organization in the economic life of Victorian England.[1]

London's corn and coal trades both revolved around the exchanges which merchants had established in the latter part of the eighteenth

[1] Smith, pp. 276–7, 284–5, 291–8.

century as convenient headquarters for the transaction of their business. Over the years men engaged in other trades had felt a similar need for a common meeting ground, and the coffee houses which proliferated in the City had often supplied this need. From the informal gatherings in these convivial rooms there had gradually evolved a number of specialized exchanges which, after they had outgrown their bucolic origins, migrated to new premises and in some cases became the centre of a world-wide commercial network. The Stock Exchange itself had originated in this way. So too had the Baltic Exchange, later to become active in the corn trade, and the London Commercial Sale Rooms, established in Mincing Lane in 1811, at first for the marketing of West India rum and sugar, and later for tea and general imported produce. Garraway's coffee house had itself become a place of sale, exchange and auction for all sorts of goods, and it was here in 1821 that the first public sales of imported wool were held – an innovation which after the rapid growth of Australian and New Zealand wool production in the mid-nineteenth century led to the establishment of the Wool Exchange in Coleman Street, where for many years almost all the Australian wool clip shipped to England was sold by auction.[1]

The prototype of all these specialist exchanges was, of course, the Royal Exchange, established by Sir Thomas Gresham in the time of Queen Elizabeth, and later to become the home of the most famous of all the coffee-house exchanges – Lloyd's. This, the headquarters of marine insurance, still retains the name of the coffeeman in whose shop underwriters first began to congregate in the latter part of the seventeenth century. Subsequently they took rooms in the Royal Exchange itself, where they remained (except while it was being rebuilt after the fire of 1838) from 1773 until 1928, when they migrated first to Leadenhall Street and thence to their present home in Lime Street.

At the beginning of the nineteenth century Britain already dominated the marine insurance business of the whole world, London was supreme within Britain, and the two thousand Lloyd's underwriters had nine-tenths of the London business. During the ructions of the South Sea Bubble crisis the Bubble Act of 1720 had provided that no corporation, society or partnership other than the Royal Exchange Assurance Corporation and the London Assurance could assure ships or goods at sea. Almost all marine insurance was therefore undertaken by private individuals, most of whom frequented the 'Lloyd's' rooms at the Royal Exchange, where up-to-date

[1] Passingham, pp. 135–40, 225; Clapham, vol. II, pp. 230, 317–18.

shipping news was always available. Under a trust deed of 1811 they had provided themselves with a legally authorized committee to manage their affairs, but the responsibility for the liabilities accepted by underwriting a policy remained a matter for each individual, and the committee had no part whatever in the obligation.[1]

Fire risks provided most of the rest of the business of the London insurance market. British fire insurance dates effectively from Nicholas Barbon's 'Insurance Office for Houses', established near the Royal Exchange in 1681. In the eighteenth century half-a-dozen London companies shared most of the business, and the private underwriters took little part in it. Latterly a number of provincial companies had been formed – notably the office now known as the Norwich Union, in 1797 – and new firms in London included the Phoenix (1782), the County (1807), the Guardian, founded in 1821 by a group of London bankers, and the Alliance (1824), whose backers included Alexander Baring, Samuel Gurney and Nathan Rothschild. Most of these were unchartered joint stock companies in which only a small proportion of the full value of each share was actually paid up, thus providing a safeguard against their unlimited liability. By 1832 there were thirty-nine fire insurance companies in England and Wales, of which fifteen were in London. These fifteen had seven-elevenths of the whole business, which was dominated by the five largest London companies, the Sun, the Phoenix, the Protector, the Royal Exchange and the County.

It was in this same year that a group of these London companies formed the Fire Engine Establishment, the progenitor of the London Fire Brigade, to supplement the exiguous fire-fighting equipment maintained by the parish vestries. Hitherto each company had maintained its own establishment, but after the recent increase in the number of metropolitan companies these independent arrangements had become wasteful, and ten companies, with about two-thirds of the London business, agreed to pool their resources. At first there were fourteen engines, kept at thirteen stations, and seventy-seven firemen under the command of the superintendent, James Braidwood. The system proved extremely successful, thanks largely to Braidwood, and the establishment rose to 127 firemen and twenty stations. But after the disastrous fire of 1861 among the warehouses in Tooley Street, Bermondsey, which raged for four days and nights and in which Braidwood himself was killed, responsibility for fire-fighting was transferred to the public control of the Metropolitan Board of Works,

[1] D. E. W. Gibb, *Lloyd's of London. A Study in Individualism*, 1957, pp. 31, 51, 77–82.

and in 1866 the Fire Engine Establishment was reborn as the Metropolitan Fire Brigade.[1]

Life assurance at the beginning of the nineteenth century was still in its infancy, but was growing rapidly. For some years after its establishment in 1762 the Equitable had been virtually the sole practitioner in this field, but by 1806 there were eight Life Offices in London, and the first Income Tax Act of 1799 had already established the exemption of life-insurance premiums from liability for tax. Knowledge of the actuarial principles of life risks was still very limited, and there were many failures among the early nineteenth-century Life Offices, while others protected themselves by engaging in the more predictable area of fire insurance. But the demand was growing, and by 1839 nearly a hundred Life Offices had been formed in London, of which seventy-two still survived.

The whole business of insurance was, indeed, becoming larger, more complex and more specialized. In 1806 the Duke of Bedford began to make it a condition of all leases granted on his London estates that the tenant should insure against fire, and by the 1850s it was estimated that four-fifths of all buildings in the capital were so protected, though probably not to their full value, and in only 40 per cent of them were the contents insured too. But the business of the London companies was spreading out from the capital, where it had all originated, to the still largely uncultivated provinces, from which by 1840 the largest of them, the Sun Fire Office, was drawing 60 per cent of its home business. Most of its policyholders were still householders, shopkeepers and tradesmen, but commerce and industry were also requiring security; warehouse premiums provided over a third of its home income, and cotton mills another 9 per cent.

There was equally rapid expansion abroad. In the 1820s and 1830s several London companies appointed agents in Germany and France, and even their heavy losses after the disastrous fire which destroyed one-third of the city of Hamburg in 1842 did not prevent further rapid growth. By the 1860s there were nineteen British insurance companies operating in Hamburg alone, and agencies had been established in North and South America, South Africa and the Far East. By 1881 one-fifth of all fire insurance business in the United States was in the hands of British companies.[2]

[1] P. G. M. Dickson, *The Sun Insurance Office 1710–1960*, 1960, pp. ix, 127–8; Clapham, vol. I, pp. 286–8; Gibb, p. 79.

[2] Dickson, pp. 103, 137–40, 163–9, 221, 231–2; Clapham, vol. I, p. 293; vol. II, p. 328.

With fire insurance on this scale, and with the rapid rise of a new type of business, accident insurance (much stimulated by the growth of railway travel), the London companies' investment policies began to influence the London money market. In the early nineteenth century most of the Sun's short-term investments were in Exchequer Bills, but in the 1830s it began to lend money to brokers on the security of bills of exchange. Mortgages on landed property were regarded as safe because the value of land did not fluctuate greatly, and advances of this kind could moreover be used to bring in more business. During the 1820s, when large-scale building development was proceeding in Bloomsbury, both the Duke of Bedford and Mr Cubitt borrowed £20,000 from the Sun, and in the 1860s a Mr Tippetts obtained a large loan from this same company on the security of leasehold property in Bayswater because he was able to promise insurances of £75,000. Another company, the British Empire Mutual Life Assurance Company, even entered the building development business on its own account and bought an estate in Camberwell, with apparently not very successful results. In the 1840s and 50s the field of choice of investment was rapidly expanding; railway companies, dock companies and water companies were all needing money, and municipal authorities, preoccupied with the costly business of building sewers, were often ready to mortgage their rate revenue for a capital sum. In 1868 the Sun had an annual income of £260,401 from its home premiums. This represented about one-eighth of all the fire business in the country, which taken in aggregate, and after deduction of losses, must have provided a sizeable contribution towards the ceaseless investment needed for the economic advance of the nation. More tangibly, too, the London insurance companies set the fashion in the City for housing themselves in palatial new offices, sometimes designed by the foremost architects of the day – a fashion quickly followed by the banks and the discount houses.[1]

Meanwhile London's marine insurance business was in the doldrums. After the return of peace in 1815 there was a general decline in the volume of business, and in 1824 the monopoly hitherto enjoyed by private underwriters and the Royal Exchange Assurance and the London Assurance was abolished. New companies were formed to exploit this new field of enterprise, and by 1843 the number of subscribers to Lloyd's had fallen from 2,150 in 1815 to only 953. But during this period of decline the Committee of Lloyd's was appointing agents in all the principal ports throughout the

[1] Dickson, pp. 111, 243, 248, 304; Clapham, vol. II, p. 331; H. J. Dyos, *Victorian Suburb, A Study of the Growth of Camberwell*, 1966 edn, p. 119.

world, whose function was to deal with salvage claims and report news of shipping arrivals and departures. Lloyd's became the principal centre of the world's shipping intelligence, and when business improved again it was able to beat off the challenge of its now formidable competitors.

This revival began in the early 1840s, during the temporary exile after the destruction of the Royal Exchange by fire in 1838. *Lloyd's List* of shipping movements was produced for the first time, and the members divided into two classes, those who had the privilege of underwriting being distinguished from those who had not. In 1849 there were only 189 underwriters, but by 1854 the number had risen to 280. A corporate spirit began to evolve for the first time, and the Committee began to concern itself with the solvency of individual members. New candidates had to provide a large deposit as security before they could start underwriting, and bankruptcy was automatically followed by expulsion. By 1870 there were 402 Lloyd's underwriters, and an Act of Parliament passed in the following year made the society a legal entity with its own rules and self-governing constitution, and, most significantly of all, equipped to forbid non-members from signing Lloyd's policies. So long as Lloyd's policies could be signed by outsiders over whom the Committee had no jurisdiction, their credit remained uncertain. Now the famous mark of an anchor was stamped on every policy as a symbol of its reliability, and in this reformed condition Lloyd's advanced from marine insurance into new risks such as burglary, earthquake or hurricane, all hitherto regarded as uninsurable, and indeed into the coverage of almost any conceivable financial hazard.[1]

Yet despite this enormous growth of fire, life and marine insurance in the nineteenth century, which did so much to soften the impact of unforeseeable disaster, the needs of the vast labouring section of the community still remained neglected. The monthly or quarterly premiums demanded in the policies of the ordinary insurance companies were far beyond the resources of the weekly wage-earner, for whom the workhouse often provided the sole resort in time of trouble. Burial clubs and workmen's thrift associations existed to provide some measure of protection against sickness and death, but these Orders of Oddfellows, Foresters, Druids and Hearts of Oak had no actuarial knowledge, and many of their dearly-saved subscriptions were often dissipated in the social convivialities which were an essential element of their existence. Until the middle of the nineteenth century the poor, whose need was the greatest, derived little benefit from the great advances in insurance techniques.

[1] Gibb, pp. 82, 92–7, 109, 112–16, 131, 139–44; Clapham, vol. II, p. 327.

What was needed to fill this gap was a company or companies equipped with current actuarial experience and also able and willing to provide a nation-wide network of agents to collect weekly subscriptions from house to house. In the 1840s some progress had been made in this direction in Lancashire, the stronghold of the old friendly societies, but the birth of modern industrial life assurance can perhaps be more convincingly placed in London in 1852. In that year a deputation of working men called at the dingy office in Ludgate Hill of the Prudential Mutual Assurance, Investment and Loan Association to ask whether the association would entertain small assurances of £20 and upwards, payable by weekly instalments. During the four years since its foundation the Prudential had not enjoyed much success in ordinary insurance, and it seems to have had no particular plans for the future. The invitation was accepted, and branch offices were opened in Birmingham, Liverpool and Manchester. Expenses soared, and in 1856 a special meeting of the board of directors was held to decide whether to close the new industrial assurance department.

The board decided to continue. By the following year the annual premium income had nearly doubled, though it was still only £8,000, and 237 agencies had been established. In 1859 the Prudential took over the Liverpool-based British Industry Life Assurance Company, which brought an income of £25,000, and in 1863 an advertising campaign on the railways was mounted through W. H. Smith and Son. There was fierce competition from other companies imitating the Prudential's methods, which were even copied in America; and the inevitably high cost of door-to-door collection was often criticized. But for one penny a week a man aged twenty-five could now insure his life for seven guineas, and there was no lack of takers for terms of this kind. By 1875 the Prudential had well over two million industrial assurance policies in force. Soon afterwards it removed to its own grand new premises at Holborn Bars, designed in fiery red brick and terracotta by Alfred Waterhouse, and still the most distinctive of all the great London insurance palaces, a fitting monument to one of the mid-Victorian sources of modern working-class security.[1]

[1] Dermot Morrah, *A History of Industrial Life Assurance*, 1955, p. 18; R. W. Barnard, *A Century of Service. The Story of the Prudential 1848–1948*, 1948, *passim*.

6

Church, School and State

ON 22 July 1792 John Venn, the new Rector of Clapham, preached his first sermon in the parish church there. He was very apprehensive, for among the congregation sat the three sons of the late John Thornton, who had acquired the patronage of the living and to whose trustees Venn owed his appointment. All three Thornton brothers were Members of Parliament, and two of them were directors of the Bank of England as well. Samuel and Robert Thornton lived at Clapham in houses which they had inherited from their father. Henry Thornton, the youngest son, still a bachelor, had very recently bought the manor house at nearby Battersea Rise and invited his dear friend William Wilberforce, also a bachelor and a Member of Parliament, to live with him there. Wilberforce had accepted, and he too sat gazing critically up at the new young rector nervously discoursing in the tall three-decker pulpit.[1]

At this time Clapham was still a village, separated from London by open country. But it was only four miles from Westminster and five from the City, and wealthy merchants like John Thornton had been making their homes here in increasing numbers since the middle of the eighteenth century. John Thornton had come from a long line of Yorkshire clergymen. He had used much of his wealth in the purchase of advowsons in order to ensure continuity of the evangelical principles to which he was so devoted, and in his own parish of Clapham he had been largely responsible for the building of a new church in 1776. At the time of his death in 1790 the population of the village was about 2,700, but it almost doubled itself during the next twenty years.

[1] For this account of the Clapham Sect I am much indebted to Michael Hennell, *John Venn and the Clapham Sect*, 1958.

The Thorntons were the true founders of the Clapham Sect. It was through John Thornton's acquisition of the living there that the evangelical John Venn had been appointed to the rectory, and it was through Henry Thornton's invitation that Wilberforce came to Clapham, attracted no doubt by the twin claims of friendship and the presence of an evangelical rector. Wilberforce only lived in the parish for a few years, but although still only in his early thirties he was already the parliamentary leader in the movement for the abolition of the slave trade, and at Clapham he at once became the centre of a growing circle of like-minded friends. Henry Thornton quickly built two new houses in the extensive grounds of his own at Battersea Rise. One of these was occupied by Charles Grant, later a director of the East India Company, who engaged in the promotion of missionary and educational work in the East, and the other by Edward Eliot, the brother-in-law of William Pitt and an intimate friend of Wilberforce. Elsewhere in the parish lived James Stephen, a barrister whose early experiences of slavery in the West Indies had made him an active abolitionist, and in 1802 came Zachary Macaulay, whose early life in Jamaica had produced the same result, and John Shore, Lord Teignmouth, formerly Governor-General of India and later first president of the British and Foreign Bible Society.

These were the inner members of the Clapham Sect. They were united by their Christian faith, their philanthropic zeal and their friendship for Wilberforce. They worshipped together in the same church, they visited each other's houses, discussed and corresponded with each other, and in the world of public affairs they strove with formidable energy to put their principles into practice. Other distinguished neighbours, such as Granville Sharp and William Smith, both of them abolitionists and residents in Clapham, often joined the inner group, and there were frequent visits to or from country residents such as Hannah More and Charles Simeon. 'I am in hopes some good may come out of our Clapham system,' Henry Thornton had written as early as 1793: 'Wilberforce is a candle that should not be hid under a bushel.' And Clapham did indeed become for some twenty years or more the most influential parish in the whole country.[1]

During the eighteenth century pluralism, absenteeism and clerical ignorance and indifference had become all too prevalent in the Church of England. At Clapham, Venn's predecessor had been an absentee baronet, the Reverend Sir James Stonhouse, who had lived for some forty years at

[1] Hennell, pp. 79, 110–11, 169–77.

his country estate near Oxford. There had been a general reaction against the passion and intolerance of the seventeenth century, 'enthusiasm' was taboo, and even the celebration of the sacrament of Holy Communion had become more and more infrequent. In the words of Gladstone, the aim of the evangelical revival was to bring back 'on a large scale, and by an aggressive movement, the Cross, and all the Cross essentially implies, both into the teaching of the clergy, and into the lives as well of the clergy as of the laity'.

At Clapham Venn found that although his congregation was 'pretty large', most of its members were rich. 'They are very regular and punctual in their attendance at church, and as far as the outside of religion goes, very exemplary. But alas, here they rest, and I fear that it will be very hard to convince them that the power of religion must be felt in the heart, as well as the form of it kept up in their lives.' The poor, he found, were 'very numerous here and extremely dissolute. They have lost even the form of religion, and though their wages are very high and the benevolence of the rich great, yet many of them live in a state of extreme wretchedness by reason of their drunkenness and other vices. What can be done to reclaim them?'

What he did was to become the model for the revival of Christian life in countless parishes throughout the country. He quickly instituted a new Sunday evening service, primarily for the children of the poor, but also, he hoped, for their parents. This involved the installation of a chandelier, for lighting had not been thought necessary when the church was built in 1776, and this innovation evoked a protest meeting held at the Plough Inn. But Venn persisted. He catechized the children, he prepared them for confirmation with meticulous care, he celebrated Holy Communion every second Sunday and towards the end of his life he was preparing to build a chapel of ease which was completed in 1815, two years after his death. He visited every house in the parish, and he taught scripture in the local charity school, which was maintained by subscriptions from the rich parishioners and which was enlarged to accommodate two hundred pupils. Towards the end of his life he claimed that every child in the parish could be taught to read and write and that every family could be supplied with a bible and could find a seat in church.[1]

Towards education he displayed the characteristically severe evangelical attitude. The pupil 'may, by education, be endued with qualities friendly to the growth of Christianity. His mind may be enlightened by knowledge

[1] Hennell, pp. 12–13, 116–35.

instead of being darkened by brutish ignorance. His conscience may be awakened instead of being seared by insensibility. He may be made attentive, docile, submissive, rational; instead of being thoughtless, obstinate, intractable, void of understanding.' Attention, docility, submissiveness, reasonableness, these were the virtues which the evangelicals wished to inculcate in the poor. They themselves were rich, and they had no wish to undermine the prevailing class-structure of society. But their religious faith impelled them to work for the improvement of their less fortunate brethren. At first in Clapham they subscribed to the parish Poor Society, which enabled the poor to buy food and coal at cheap rates – a method of voluntary relief also practised in several other London parishes in the 1790s. But very soon they became dissatisfied with this indiscriminate distribution of charity, and in 1799 Venn founded the Society for Bettering the Condition of the Poor at Clapham. A committee which met regularly every month was to regulate the business of the society and the parish was divided up into eight districts, each with members allocated to it who were to be responsible for visiting the poor there. At first discovery of sickness or destitution a visitor could provide immediate financial assistance, but thereafter requests for help had to be considered by the committee. And then the rules of the society provided that:

> Before any relief is granted information should be particularly sought concerning the moral character of the applicant, particularly if he is accustomed to attend public worship; whether he sends his children to school, and trains them in the habit of industry. An account is also taken of his weekly earnings and expenses and debts; and the particular cause of his distress is to be investigated. This information will serve as a basis on which to found both the kind and quality of relief which it will be proper to administer.

The poor, in fact, were to be divided into two categories, the deserving and the undeserving. 'Bettering means more than the relief of immediate wants,' wrote Venn; 'it means to extricate him from future want, to cut off the sources of his poverty, to instil into him good principles, to elevate his mind to a state of independence, to raise him to a higher tone of character.' And he concluded with a full statement of the Victorian gospel of self-help:

> let it be the aim of this Society to say, not merely that this man was hungry and we fed him, but this man was naked and behold he

P

is clothed by his own industry; this man was a drunkard and his family in rags, behold him sober and see him decently clad. This man was idle, and poor, and miserable; now he is industrious, prosperous and happy; and above all this man was a wretched profligate and now he is moral and religious.[1]

Such were the works and ideas of John Venn during his ministry at Clapham from 1792 to 1813. It is easy to exaggerate their significance, for there were other centres of evangelicalism, of which Cambridge was the most important, but Clapham was the first and principal home of the movement, and because so many of its inhabitants were prominent in public affairs they were able to exert an influence out of all proportion to their numbers. Wilberforce is chiefly remembered for his twenty-year crusade for the abolition of the slave trade, which was finally achieved in 1807, but he also supported factory legislation, the reform of the penal code, the emancipation of the Catholics, and the abolition of the press gang and of the employment of chimney boys. The foundation of the Church Missionary Society in 1799 (originally as the Society for Missions to Africa and the East) and of the British and Foreign Bible Society in 1804 were both the work of members of the Clapham Sect. In 1802 they provided themselves with a monthly magazine, *The Christian Observer*, for the dissemination of their ideas. They supported Wilberforce in his long campaign for the reformation of manners, and were particularly opposed to duelling, bear-baiting and state lotteries. In 1823 they and their heirs – for the evangelical movement had by this time spread far beyond the confines of Clapham – established the London Anti-Slavery Society for the extinction of slavery in the West Indies, the great culminating object which was at last achieved by Act of Parliament in 1833, the year of Wilberforce's death.[2]

The evangelicals, of whom the Clapham Sect had been the original leaders, were one of the great formative influences in the moulding of Victorian England. Never in the whole history of the Church of England has any other group of Anglicans exerted so profound an effect on the life of the whole nation as they. The intensity of their religious faith and of their zeal for good works provided the foundation for Victorian morality. Their long-drawn-out struggle against inhumanity and immorality established new attitudes of mind and new modes of behaviour, and their very

[1] Hennell, pp. 137, 144–5.
[2] Ernest Marshall Howse, *Saints in Politics*, 1952, pp. 76–7, 106, 111, 154, 165.

success, particularly in the abolition of slavery, helped to engender the buoyant middle-class confidence of later years.

But with the passage of time the first inspiration inevitably lost much of its power. The original inward spiritual force degenerated into an outward code of Sabbath observance, and fervent zeal relaxed into complacency and respectability. In the field of social behaviour appearances became more important than reality, and in the second half of the nineteenth century even the fundamental truth of the Christian faith itself was questioned. Yet despite all this the evangelical code of manners survived, albeit in increasingly attenuated form. It even survived among the ever-growing number of people who had lost or never possessed religious belief, and who often involved themselves in much mental turmoil in their attempts to rid themselves of its restraints. And indeed it still survives, residually and largely unrecognized, down to the present day.

The evangelicals' moral influence was spread over a very long period of time. But in the early years of the nineteenth century their 'enthusiasm' was still regarded with widespread hostility, their clergy were seldom appointed to high office in the Church and much of their energy was devoted to causes abroad such as the abolition of slavery and the establishment of foreign missions. They were therefore not the leaders in two important developments which took place during the first quarter of the nineteenth century – the building of new schools and new churches.

The evangelicals' attitude towards education was tempered by their austere ideas for the poor. Wilberforce himself had supported Pitt's repressive legislation of the 1790s, including the Combination Acts, and after the 'Peterloo Massacre' of 1819 he voted in favour of the 'Six Acts'. They detested the democratic ideas engendered by the French Revolution as intensely as they detested slavery, and for them the first object of education was, in the words of John Venn already quoted, to endue the pupil with 'qualities friendly to the growth of Christianity'. In Clapham their teaching efforts were therefore largely concentrated on the charity school. This was one of many such schools established throughout the eighteenth century under the auspices of the Society for Promoting Christian Knowledge. Here the main emphasis was on the inculcation of industry, frugality, religious knowledge and social humility, while reading, writing and arithmetic were regarded as little more than useful means in the achievement of these objects. Until the 1780s the charity schools provided almost the only educational opportunities open to the poor, who were often debarred from the dame schools and other private schools by the cost of the fees.

These exiguous arrangements could only suffice so long as the social structure of the nation remained relatively stable. But in the latter part of the eighteenth century the Industrial Revolution and the beginning of the urban explosion presented a challenge to this antique stability, and this challenge in its turn presented the governing classes with an urgent dilemma – should the poor be educated or not? And if so, how, and by whom?

At first the demand for child labour in the new textile mills of the north provided a partial answer – there was no time for school. But on Sundays the children were at any rate sometimes free, and so, from the 1780s, there arose the Sunday schools, where the children were taught to read and to recite the catechism. Most of the pioneers of the Sunday School movement worked in the provinces, and the evangelical Hannah More's work in the Mendip Hills of Somerset, supported by Wilberforce's money, achieved widespread fame. By 1801 the Sunday schools had over 156,000 pupils in London alone, and the rapidity of their success demonstrated for the first time that universal education of some kind was possible.[1]

But the expense would be enormous – just how enormous no one yet even dreamed – and more than thirty years were to elapse before the State made its first small grant towards educational costs. Schools capable of matching the cheapness and scale of output of the new textile factories were, seemingly, the urgent educational need at the opening of the nine-teenth century; and this need was met by Joseph Lancaster and the Rever-end Andrew Bell.

In 1798 Joseph Lancaster, a twenty-year-old Quaker, opened a school for poor children in Southwark, in a room lent to him by his father, a sieve-maker. He had had some brief previous experience of teaching, but what he lacked in knowledge he made up in kindliness and sincerity. The children were taught the elements of reading, writing, arithmetic and the scriptures, the fees were low or often remitted altogether, and by 1805 there were some seven or eight hundred pupils. In order to cope with these enormous numbers he made use of the monitorial system whereby the older children instructed the younger ones in accordance with a rigid and carefully graded system. Every child, book and slate had its appointed place, there were scales of reward and punishment, and above all, Lan-caster's school was cheap. He removed to larger premises nearby in the

[1] H. C. Barnard, *A Short History of English Education*, 1947 edn, p. 11.

Borough Road, he published an account of his system entitled *Improvements in Education*, and he became famous. Distinguished visitors came to observe this new phenomenon, which in 1805 received the royal approval when the King himself said 'Lancaster, I highly approve of your system, and it is my wish that every poor child in my dominions should be taught to read the Bible.'

Orderliness and godliness were the two qualities most admired. 'I can never forget the impression which the scene made upon me,' wrote the Quaker philanthropist William Allen after a visit in 1808. 'Here I beheld a thousand children collected from the streets, where they were learning nothing but mischief, one bad boy corrupting another, all reduced to the most perfect order, and training to habits of subordination, and usefulness, and learning the great truths of the gospel from the Bible.'[1] The degree of order prevailing evidently varied considerably, for a 'monitor of order' recalled in after life that 'the babel was such that I remember one occasion trying if I should be heard singing "Black Eyed Susan". I sang and no one noticed me.' Still, sporadic order was better than none. Lancaster began to receive financial support from the nobility, and when it was objected in high places that he was not a member of the established church the King unexpectedly retorted that 'The man is a dissenter, but that has nothing to do with his plans.'

Churchmen were nevertheless alarmed at Lancaster's success, and were glad to turn to the Reverend Andrew Bell, who had served as an army chaplain in India. There he had also been superintendent of the Madras Male Orphan Asylum, and had successfully introduced a system of mutual instruction by the pupils. After his return to England he had published in 1797 an account of this experiment, and in the following year his system had been applied to the parochial school at St Botolph's, Aldgate, with some success. In the later, much-enlarged editions of his original account he borrowed many of Lancaster's ideas, and in this modified form the Bell régime was applied at the Lambeth Female Orphan Asylum, the Royal Military Asylum at Chelsea and elsewhere.

In 1805 Bell and Lancaster met on friendly terms, but in the same year Mrs Sarah Trimmer, the founder of a number of Sunday schools in Brentford, published *A Comparative View* of Lancaster's system, in which she accused him of having purloined Bell's methods; only his religious views were his own, and these were no better than those of the 'Jacobins, the Illuminati, the Philanthropinists, the sectarists and infidels'. Churchmen

[1] Frank Smith, *A History of English Elementary Education 1760–1902*, 1931, pp. 74–6.

became still more alarmed, and the unfortunate Lancaster was attacked on every side. Down at Clapham John Venn denounced him because his system 'does not embrace religious instruction'. Only the discipline could be commended. 'I approve much more highly of Dr Bell's system from which Lancaster originally obtained all his improvements.' Wilberforce and Zachary Macaulay continued to support both protagonists, as they had now become, but the early hopes engendered in the Borough Road were already fading in face of mounting religious controversy.

Lancaster himself was in personal difficulties. 'He is very conceited and has been spoiled by public favour,' observed the Rector of Clapham. In 1807 he had had to leave London in order to evade his creditors, and upon his return he had been imprisoned for a short while. Soon afterwards he and a group of friends had formed the Royal Lancasterian Society to continue his work, and in 1810 they secured the support of a committee which included Henry Brougham, Samuel Whitbread, William Wilberforce, Sir Samuel Romilly and James Mill. Lancaster was reduced to the position of salaried teaching superintendent at Borough Road. He resigned in 1814 and emigrated to America, where he died in 1838. After his resignation the society was renamed the British and Foreign School Society. In 1816 a new and much larger school was built in the Borough Road. This later became the Borough Road Training College, which remained here until its removal in 1888 to Isleworth, where it still exists, a living legacy of Lancaster's work.[1]

Meanwhile the pre-Tractarian High Church party in the Church of England had been equally active. At Hackney there lived a wealthy City wine merchant, Joshua Watson, who was one of the leading lay churchmen of his day. His brother was the incumbent of Hackney; in 1810 his brother-in-law, Henry Handley Norris, became a curate there, and later became Rector of South Hackney. They and a number of like-minded friends belonged to a dining-club known as 'Nobody's', or 'Nobody's Friends', and collectively they were often referred to as the 'Hackney Phalanx'. By 1811 several diocesan societies had been established to further the education of the poor on Andrew Bell's system, and largely through the efforts of Watson, Norris and John Bowles (another member of the 'Hackney Phalanx') a national society was now formed. In October the Archbishop of Canterbury took the chair at the inaugural meeting of the 'National

[1] Smith, pp. 78–81; Hennell, p. 136; Howse, pp. 98–9; *Survey of London*, vol. xxv, 1955, p. 70.

Society for Promoting the Education of the Poor in the Principles of the Established Church, throughout England and Wales', and a powerful committee, consisting chiefly of laymen, at once set to work. Bell himself became the society's superintendent, and in 1812 a school was opened in Baldwin's Gardens, near Gray's Inn Lane, to which adults were sent to learn the system now to be introduced all over the country.[1]

Thus two organizations, both of which still exist, had come into being, each dedicated to the education of the poor by the monitorial system. Many of the schools to which they contributed are still in use, though usually much altered and enlarged. One of them, built in 1824 under the auspices of the Rector of Lambeth, is outwardly little changed, and may be seen in Harleyford Road, Kennington, where two parallel single-storey brick ranges, one for boys and the other for girls, are united at the front by a house for the master and mistress. By 1830 the National Society could claim that it had 3,678 schools within its ambit (of which 1,083 were used only as Sunday schools) and that 346,000 children were being taught there. There was also a very large number of other Church schools not in union with the National Society.[2] Between them the National Society and the British and Foreign School Society laid the first lasting foundations of the English elementary day school.

But in terms of social costs there was a heavy price to pay for this achievement. The monitorial system was crude; the monitors themselves were ignorant and (according to the Rector of St Marylebone) they often 'acquired a very disgusting degree of self-importance'. The secretary of the National Society considered that two years' attendance at school were 'abundantly sufficient', and the very success of this easy 'education on the cheap' was subsequently the cause of long delay in the introduction of higher and therefore more expensive standards. Above all, the establishment of two rival societies marked the modern origin of the 'religious difficulty' which has for so long bedevilled English educational history.[3]

But what was the use of building schools for the inculcation of religious principles if there were no churches to assist the pupils in the practice of these principles in later life? In the latter part of the eighteenth century very few new churches had been built, and in the great new towns and suburbs which were springing up in many parts of the country there were

[1] M. H. Port, *Six Hundred New Churches*, 1961, pp. 2–4; Smith, p. 82.
[2] H. J. Burgess, *Enterprise in Education*, 1958, p. 43.
[3] Smith, pp. 83–4, 134.

vast church-less tracts where Anglican public worship was unknown. In the diocese of London alone there were eighty parishes with an average population of over 11,000 where less than half the inhabitants could be accommodated in the existing churches. In Shoreditch there were only 2,300 seats for over 43,000 parishioners. A great gulf was opening between the Church of England and a rapidly growing proportion of Englishmen, particularly of the poorer classes – a gulf which, despite all the heroic efforts to be made in the nineteenth century and after, has never yet been closed.[1]

In two wealthy London parishes the local vestries had attempted to build churches. In St Marylebone, the richest parish in the kingdom, the aristocratic Select Vestry had between 1770 and 1806 obtained four special church-building Acts of Parliament, but it was not until 1814 that these long-drawn-out labours produced their first results in the opening of the St John's Wood chapel and burial ground. Accommodation for the dead had indeed been rather more in the minds of the vestrymen than the spiritual welfare of the living. But fresh difficulties had kept cropping up. First of all there was the question of a suitable site, and then there was the interminable problem of the patronage of the new churches to be built, on which the owner, the aged Duke of Portland, refused to budge. Lastly there was the question of cost, which the vestrymen finally resolved by the promotion of another Act in 1811 authorizing the collection of a church rate not exceeding 4*d*. in the pound – an unpopular levy which, so they explained to the ratepayers, was required in order 'to give the inferior orders in the parish other regular places of divine worship, which at present is much wanting'. Action was indeed much wanting, for by this time the population of the parish had grown to some 70,000, of whom only 7,052 could be accommodated in the church and in the privately owned 'proprietary' chapels, of which there were now eight. And in the neighbouring parish of St Pancras the situation was much the same. There the Vestry had been much less dilatory and had built a very beautiful but costly new parish church out of the proceeds of a church rate. But the numerous Radicals, Dissenters and Roman Catholics living in the newly-built parts of the parish had launched fearsome attacks on the Vestry, and the building of district churches had been abandoned.[2]

By the close of the Napoleonic wars in 1815 the urgent need for a

[1] Port, pp. 5, 21.

[2] F. H. W. Sheppard, *Local Government in St Marylebone 1688–1835*, 1958, pp. 245–53.

massive programme of church-building could no longer be ignored either by churchmen or even by the government. The effect of bestowing the benefits of even the most rudimentary education upon the new urban masses might well, for them, be still open to question, but in face of the rapid spread of Dissent, of democratic ideas and economic discontent, there could be no doubt about the desirability of providing churches. But the practical difficulties were formidable, as the St Marylebone vestrymen had already discovered. What with the opposition of the Dissenters and the problems of patronage, pew-rents and the division of parishes, it was almost impossible to build a new church without the expense of a special Act of Parliament; and even then success might not be the outcome. So at last in 1818 the government stepped in and provided the established Church with a fund of one million pounds and a commission to administer its application in the provision of churches.[1]

It would, however, be wrong to attribute the establishment of the Church Building Commission solely to motives of social policy. The government required a long time to be persuaded to grant the money, and this persuasion was largely the work of the same group of High Churchmen who had founded the National Society for Promoting the Education of the Poor in 1811. Four years later Joshua Watson and his friend John Bowdler drew up a memorial to the Prime Minister, which was signed by 120 laymen. They drew his attention to 'the danger to which the constitution of this country both in church and state is exposed from the want of places of public worship, particularly for persons of the middle and lower classes'. In London alone there were fifty parishes with a total of over a million inhabitants where the existing churches were 'not capable of containing one tenth part of that multitude'. The task was too great. 'Parliament alone can do it; and we conceive it to be one of its chief duties to provide places of worship for the members of the established religion.' But nothing happened until early in 1818, when the Prince Regent announced in his speech from the throne that provision for the building of new churches was to be made; and by this time Watson and his friends, with the support of the Archbishop of Canterbury, were forming a Church Building Society analogous to the National Society of 1811. The pressure of private example and initiative had once more been successful.[2]

The Government's bill passed quickly through Parliament and soon the

[1] The following account of the Church Building Commissioners is based on the admirable study by M. H. Port, *Six Hundred New Churches*, 1961.

[2] Port, pp. 9, 13–15.

Commission was at work. Joshua Watson and a small group of his associates proved the most industrious members of this large, unwieldy body. Economy was their watchword from the start, for it was at once apparent that even a million pounds would not be enough to satisfy all needs, and £20,000 became the maximum to be spent on any one building. In London grants were made for the building of thirty-three churches, of which about two-thirds were in the 'Grecian' manner – the cheapest available – and the remainder in the 'Gothic'. Westminster got five of these thirty-three, St Marylebone and Lambeth four each, St Pancras, Newington and Chelsea two each, and fourteen other parishes one each. The three architects retained by the Office of Works, Nash, Soane and Smirke, acted as the Commission's advisers and also provided the designs for eight of these churches;[1] but church building was not their *forte* and Nash's All Souls, Langham Place, which occupied a focal point in his plans for the approach to Marylebone Park, is perhaps the most successful. Thomas Hardwick, (Sir) Charles Barry and C. R. Cockerell were among the architects of the remaining twenty-five London churches, but the financial stringency necessarily imposed by the Commissioners inhibited the designs for the whole group. The surviving churches often convey a sense of puzzled failure and disappointed hopes far removed from the pious expectations of their original progenitors.

In addition to the thirty-three churches built in London, the Commissioners also made another sixty-three grants for churches elsewhere in England, plus one in Wales. The total cost of building the thirty-three London churches amounted to some £525,000, of which the Commissioners contributed £355,252 from their million pounds, the balance being raised by private subscriptions and church rates. For this enormous expenditure 56,337 new seats were provided, of which rather more than half were subject to the payment of pew-rents for the provision of a stipend for the minister, and the remainder were free. But between 1811 and 1821 the population of London had risen by nearly a quarter of a million, and in the following decade the rate of increase was still higher. It was clear that the Commission was not even keeping pace with the problem, and by the end of 1820 its funds were nearly exhausted. In 1824, however, the government received a windfall through the unexpected repayment of a foreign loan which had previously been written off, and another half-million pounds were voted for more church building. This time there was some opposition in Parliament, but Lord Palmerston expressed the still

[1] Port, pp. 132–9.

prevailing mood when he said that 'it was the poor alone who felt the want of church accommodation', and that nothing 'could tend more to the general tranquillity and happiness of a people, than a community of sentiment, as far as it could be obtained without intolerance to any party, in matters of religious doctrine'.[1]

The half-million grant marks the opening of the second and much longer phase in the history of the Commission. The funds available were not going to be adequate, and in making grants much more emphasis was placed upon the size of the contribution to be made locally. A list of the twenty-four places most in need was drawn up, of which seven were in London, all except one in the older suburbs such as Bloomsbury and Spitalfields. Yet despite this fact, most of the London grants made during the first few years of the second parliamentary grant were for churches in the new outer suburbs, in such places as Battersea, Hammersmith and Islington, and even as far afield as Hounslow and Tottenham.

By 1830 the whole relationship of Church and State had been revolutionized by the Catholic Emancipation Act and the repeal of the Test and Corporation Acts. The Church of England could no longer be regarded as the embodiment of the religious life of the whole nation. In London the beginning of this new era coincided with the appointment of a new bishop, C. J. Blomfield, in 1828. In his first charge to the diocese of London he stated that this new situation would force the Church 'for the future to depend more entirely upon our internal resources and will be a test of their sufficiency'. There would be no more parliamentary grants.[2]

The Church Building Commission continued its labours on a much reduced scale until 1856, but by 1830 its main work was already done. For many years afterwards its achievements were decried; now it is more fashionable to defend them. The tragedy of the Commission was that it was established at a time when the Church of England was further out of touch with a large section of the people than it had ever been before or has, perhaps, ever been since. This was, indeed, the political reason for its creation. But parliaments, unaided, cannot summon up a religious revival, and there was much truth in *The British Critic*'s later reference to the 'odious vulgarity of supposing that parliamentary grants for the building of vast showy churches to hold 2,000 or 3,000 people were the legitimate and effectual way to "turn the disobedient to the wisdom of the just and make ready a people prepared for the Lord"'.[3] Most of the Commission's work

[1] Port, pp. 35, 94, 134–9.   [2] Port, pp. 96, 100, 151–9.
[3] Quoted in Basil F. L. Clarke, *Church Builders of the Nineteenth Century*, 1938, p. 25.

was done in the years immediately before the impact of the great nineteenth-century religious revival had made itself felt, before the evangelical leaven had permeated widely through the nation, before the transformation of the relationship of Church and State, and before the Tractarian movement. The Commissioners' churches – or at any rate those built before the early 1830s – had no connection with any of these events, and the plaster was hardly dry on their spacious walls before they began to look like relics of a by-gone age which could never return.

During the first three decades of the nineteenth century the Church had indeed been encountering increasingly powerful forces hostile to its ancient claims over the life of the people. Middle-class radicalism, embodied in the copious writings of Jeremy Bentham and in the ceaseless activities of Henry Brougham, Francis Place and others, was the secular counterpart of the evangelical movement. While the evangelicals were stamping their moral code on the behaviour of the nation, the Radicals were imposing their practical, utilitarian philosophy on its political, economic and social structure. They challenged the ascendancy of the aristocracy and the established Church; they demanded – and in time achieved – a complete overhaul of the entire machinery of government, and in the long run their influence proved even more pervasive and more lasting than that of the evangelicals.

This challenge was strongly felt in the field of education. The decadent grammar schools, public schools and universities, hitherto the ancient preserves of the established Church and State, were to be reformed and used for the middle classes, while the working classes were to be educated in the virtues of middle-class radicalism. For James Mill, writing in 1824, the middle class was:

the strength of the community. It contains beyond all comparison, the greatest proportions of the intelligence, industry, and wealth of the state. In it are the heads that invent, and the hands that execute; the enterprise that projects, and the capital by which these projects are carried into operation. . . . the men in fact who think for the rest of the world, and who really do the business of the world, are the men of this class. The people of the class below are the instruments with which they work; and those of the class above, though they may be called their governors, and may really sometimes seem to rule them, are much more often, more truly, and more completely under their control. In this country at least, it is this class which gives to the nation its character.

And in London there was 'an aggregate of persons of middle rank collected in one spot . . . the like to which exists in no other spot on the surface of the earth'.[1]

At first the Benthamites had hoped to spread their educational gospel through Joseph Lancaster and the still largely unsectarian Royal Lancasterian Society. Francis Place was having difficulty in the education of his nine children, and Bentham himself had offered his garden at Queen Square Place, Holborn, as a site for a model school to be conducted on a new system which he was in course of devising. Mill wrote vigorous attacks on the Church of England's National Society, while Place busied himself in 1813 with the formation of the West London Lancasterian Association, whose motto was 'Schools for All'. He accepted the monitorial system, and even proposed to extend it to secondary education. Plans were prepared for a specially designed school consisting of one huge polygonal room with nine concentric rows of desks – the educational equivalent of Bentham's 'Panopticon' prisons – and the western parts of London were divided into school districts, each with its own committee. But most of the financial support for the project came from wealthy non-conformists, and very soon Place was in disagreement with them over the rules of the parent society that only the Bible should be used for reading lessons, and that all children should be taken to a place of worship on Sundays. In 1814 he resigned, the school which the West London Lancasterian Association had hired was handed back to the British and Foreign School Society (as the Royal Lancasterian Society had now become) and in 1820 the whole project finally collapsed when Bentham withdrew his offer of his garden for a building site.[2]

By this time the Radicals had made their second, rather more successful, incursion into educational affairs, although it produced no immediate results. In 1816 their wayward parliamentary spokesman, Henry Brougham, had persuaded the House of Commons to establish a Select Committee 'to inquire into the Education of the Lower Orders in the Metropolis'. A very thorough investigation of London's schools ensued, and the committee's four reports extended to over three hundred closely

[1] Quoted in Brian Simon, *Studies in the History of Education 1780–1870*, 1960, pp. 78, 119.

[2] Graham Wallas, *The Life of Francis Place*, 1925 edn, chapter IV.

printed pages. They presented a dismal picture. There were already
twenty-seven schools in union with the National Society, and twenty-
five connected with the British and Foreign School Society, but the total
number of children taught there only amounted to some twelve thousand.
The managements of innumerable charity, Sunday and other schools
were scrutinized, and so too were those of ancient foundations like Christ's
Hospital, the Charterhouse and the Merchant Taylors'; even St Paul's and
aristocratic Westminster, which certainly did not cater for the 'Lower
Orders', did not escape. Endowments were being misappropriated,
teaching was bad. In the Bethnal Green area there were only some 1,200
children receiving instruction of any kind out of a total adult population
of 40,000, and one witness estimated that in the whole of London there
were some 122,000 children altogether untaught.[1]

But at least the problem had been uncovered, and Brougham was able
to extend his investigation to the rest of the country and to establish
Charity Commissioners to enquire into all charitable trusts. In 1820 he
introduced a Bill 'For the better education of the Poor in England and
Wales', the first attempt to establish universal compulsory elementary
education, financed partly out of local rates. It was, of course, defeated,
not only by the opposition of the Church and the Dissenters, both fearful
for their respective interests, but also because universal education was
impossible so long as the use of child labour remained largely unregulated.

After this second defeat the Radicals turned their attention to adult
and higher education. The early nineteenth century was the age of
'Institutions' – the Royal Institution, founded in Albemarle Street in
1799 for the diffusion of knowledge and the introduction of useful mechanical inventions and improvements, or the slightly later London Institution, established in Finsbury Circus for like purposes. Many working
men were avid for knowledge of all kinds, and in 1823 J. C. Robertson,
the proprietor and editor of *The Mechanics' Magazine*, heard that a
mechanics' educational institute had recently been established in Glasgow.
London, too, needed such an institute, and he and his co-editor Thomas
Hodgskin received some support from a group of working men which
held regular evening meetings at a coffee-house in Clerkenwell for reading,
discussion and music.[2] But Hodgskin sought the assistance of Francis
Place, who at once took charge. With the help of his well-to-do radical

[1] P.P., 1816, vol. iv, *Reports and Evidence of Select Committee on the Education of the
Lower Orders in the Metropolis*, pp. 29, 73, 117, 232.

[2] Simon, pp. 153–4.

friends he drew up rules and collected funds, and when the London Mechanics' Institution opened under the presidency of Dr George Birkbeck at Southampton Buildings, Chancery Lane in 1824, what had originated as a working-class project was already passing into the hands of the Radicals, the champions of the middle class.

This was the first of some seven hundred mechanics' and literary and scientific institutes to be established throughout the country during the next twenty years, about sixty of them in London. At first the lectures at the institutes were on scientific and technical subjects, and Place has recorded his complacent edification at the sight of 'from 800 to 900 clean, respectable-looking mechanics paying most marked attention' to a dissertation on chemistry. But soon history, literature and other subjects found a place, and in 1826 Brougham established the Society for the Diffusion of Useful Knowledge to provide suitable reading matter. Most institutes formed their own libraries, and in due course social evenings became a regular feature of their activities. But gradually their clientèle changed and the original working-class impetus was lost. They began to draw their main support from the prosperous skilled men who were already on the road to entering the middle classes, and after about 1860 the provision of technical education, of public libraries and day schools by the local authorities reduced the institutes' field of action. By the latter part of the nineteenth century they were in decline. They had largely fulfilled their purpose, and of those founded before 1851 only thirty-five still exist. One of these is the London Mechanics' Institution, now a constituent college of the University of London and famous under its new name, Birkbeck College.[1]

The mechanics' institutions did much to enlarge the mental horizons of those deprived of other educational opportunities. But by far the greatest and most lasting educational achievement of the Radicals was the founding of University College, the 'Godless College' in Gower Street. In the 1820s Dissenters, Catholics and Jews were all still denied entry to the two ancient universities, and the protagonists of the new college, of whom Mill, Brougham and George Grote, the historian, were the leaders, were determined that here there should be neither religious tests for entry nor religious instruction of any kind. They looked for inspiration not to Oxford and Cambridge but to the universities of Germany, to Edinburgh University, of which both Mill and Brougham were graduates, and to the

[1] Thomas Kelly, *George Birkbeck, Pioneer of Adult Education*, 1957, pp. 259, 276 313–14; Wallas, pp. 112–113; Simon, pp. 159–60.

writings of Jeremy Bentham, whose body is still reverently preserved in a glass box at University College. The teaching courses were to cover the whole field of modern knowledge. Medicine, engineering, mathematics, the sciences, political economy, law, philosophy and modern languages – all then largely or completely ignored at Oxford and Cambridge – were to be included. The fees were to be as low as possible, and the college was to be non-residential. It was indeed designed for that vast class of 'middling rich' whose educational opportunities had hitherto been so exiguous. Even the financing of the enterprise as a joint stock company expressed its practical, business-like purpose.[1]

The 'University of London', as the college was at first known, opened its doors in October 1828. From the first its professors included many of the most distinguished men of the day. In medicine, under Sir Charles Bell of Edinburgh, it quickly achieved pre-eminence; University College Hospital was opened in 1834, and it was here, in 1846, that the first major operation under an anaesthetic was performed in this country. The chemical laboratory was one of the first open to students for practical work, and one of the first university courses in engineering began here in 1833. The foundation of University College was indeed one of the most important events in the whole history of nineteenth-century London. The college provided the prototype for the 'red-brick' universities established in many provincial towns during the second half of the century, and it even had a more indirect but still powerful influence in the long-delayed re-shaping of Oxford and Cambridge.[2]

All this was not achieved without opposition. It even engendered a counterblast from the Church. In June 1828 a public meeting was held with the Duke of Wellington (then Prime Minister) in the chair and the Archbishops of Canterbury and York on the platform, at which it was resolved 'that a college for general education' should be founded. But it was to be 'an essential part of the system to imbue the minds of youth with a knowledge of the doctrines and duties of Christianity as inculcated by the United Church of England and Ireland'. This was the genesis of King's College, which was granted a royal charter and opened in 1831 on a narrow site in the Strand next to Somerset House. Its religious character inhibited some of its scientific work and in 1833 its professor of

---

[1] Simon, pp. 118–25.

[2] British Association for the Advancement of Science, *London and the Advancement of Science*, 1931, pp. 167, 265; Simon, p. 124. See also H. Hale Bellot, *University College London 1826–1926*, 1929, *passim*.

geology, Sir Charles Lyell, resigned when his chronology challenged current orthodoxy. But in 1839 its medical school followed Gower Street's example in establishing its own teaching hospital nearby – King's College Hospital, removed in 1913 to Denmark Hill – and one of its early professors, Sir Charles Wheatstone, was a pioneer in the development of the electric telegraph. In these early years there was much recrimination between the two colleges, neither of which had power to grant degrees, but in 1836 agreement was reached. The Gower Street college was renamed University College, London, and a new body, the University of London, was chartered with power to grant degrees to candidates from either University or King's Colleges or other institutions of appropriate standing. The University itself did no teaching, and was almost exclusively an examining body – the origin of the modern external degree system.[1]

Thus London achieved recognition as a seat of higher learning. It had of course always contained an enormous repository of knowledge among its inhabitants, and in their educational work in the 1820s the Radicals had had the general support of many of the 'middling rich' who were not necessarily committed to the full implications of the whole rigorous radical programme of reform. This was particularly true of the members in the lower echelons of the two ancient professions of medicine and the law. The upper strata of both professions were socially exclusive, unamenable to change, and heavily concentrated in London. The Royal College of Physicians and the four Inns of Court were small self-governing clubs of educated gentlemen whose members monopolized all the best appointments. Beneath them lurked the surgeons, the apothecaries and the attorneys, practising their still ill-defined functions all over the country, and impatient to improve both their professional and social standing. These were the men who led the way towards the emergence of the highly qualified and increasingly specialized modern professions.

Until the invention of anaesthetics surgery was a crude business to which no gentleman would be likely to be attracted. In the eighteenth century both the surgeons and the apothecaries were still organized as livery companies of the City of London, and it was only in 1745 that the surgeons had separated themselves from the barbers. In 1800 the Company of Surgeons was replaced by the Royal College of Surgeons, but its requirements for qualification were not at first strict, and the advance of its

[1] F. J. C. Hearnshaw, *Centenary History of King's College London 1828–1928*, 1929, pp. 41, 107–9; Barnard, pp. 102–3.

members' knowledge was hampered by the difficulty of legally obtaining bodies for dissection. Until an Act of 1833 permitted the use of the unclaimed bodies of paupers dying in the workhouses, surgeons were often associated in the public mind with the lucrative trade of body-snatching, and in the field of medicine it was the apothecaries who made the first great stride towards improved professional standards. The apothecaries, in the eyes of the supercilious physicians, were shopkeepers, and indeed they had until 1617 belonged to the grocers' livery company. But they also prescribed drugs and visited patients, and in 1815 they had promoted an Act of Parliament which became the model for later professional organizations. This authorized the Society of Apothecaries to examine candidates for admission and to grant licences without which no one could call himself an apothecary. The Society's examinations quickly became serious tests of knowledge, and its licences, although not granted by the State, were buttressed by their statutory origin. The Royal College of Surgeons began to tighten up its entry requirements; most candidates for medical practice began to take the examinations of both bodies, and by the 1830s M.R.C.S. and L.S.A. were becoming the letters which a doctor needed to be able to put after his name in order to set up in general practice. In 1834 a Select Committee of the House of Commons conducted an enquiry into the whole state of medical education, from which the physicians emerged with diminished reputation. But by this time a new generation of well-qualified doctors such as Thomas Southwood Smith was growing up, and they had acquired sufficient self-confidence to found their own independent organization, the British Medical Association, founded, significantly, in the provinces in 1832 as the Provincial Medical and Surgical Association. The old out-dated social distinctions between the different branches of medicine were disappearing, and with the Medical Act of 1858 there emerged the 'registered medical practitioner', qualified and subject to the exacting standards now imposed by his colleagues in his own profession.

In the legal profession the story was much the same, with the practitioners in the lower branch (i.e. the attorneys) taking the initiative in the establishment of high qualifications and standards of behaviour. The present-day Law Society dates from 1825, the first entrance examinations from 1836. At the four Inns of Court there were no qualifying examinations until 1852, and even then they remained voluntary for another twenty years. In the legal world the division between the two branches of the profession was not gradually blurred, as happened with the doctors;

it was perpetuated, largely through the conservatism of the barristers. So the attorneys went their own way, and by the second half of the nineteenth century the services to be expected of them were becoming more clearly defined as new, more specialized professions (whose functions had hitherto been often performed by the lawyers) began to emerge. There were surveyors and land agents, auctioneers, accountants and company secretaries, all beginning to form their own professional bodies, acquiring charters of incorporation and drawing up rules of admission and rules of conduct. And quite separate from the attorneys (who finally consigned their raffish past to oblivion in 1874 by changing their name by Act of Parliament to solicitors), there were the civil engineers and the mechanical engineers, each with their own institutions founded in 1818 and 1847 respectively, and the ever quarrelsome architects (1835) – all busy promoting higher levels of education and professional behaviour, and, also, their own interests and the standards of efficiency first propounded by the Benthamite utilitarians.[1]

This widespread and often unconscious acceptance of the radical ideas of the 1820s among the professional classes had not been matched, in the years after the Reform Act of 1832, by any great step forward in the provision of popular education. The middle classes had now won a large measure of power, and their interests began to diverge from those of the workers, whose claims to education now seemed less urgent. On Brougham's suggestion the government in 1833 voted £20,000 'for the erection of school houses for the education of the poorer classes' – the first state grant for education – but applications for a share of this minute sum had to be supported by either the National Society or the British and Foreign School Society. 'Ministers and men in power,' remarked Francis Place in 1833, 'with nearly the whole body of those who are rich, dread the consequences of teaching the people more than they dread the effects of their ignorance.' The Radicals relaxed their efforts, and Dr James Kay (later Sir James Kay-Shuttleworth) became the principal advocate of their earlier aims, now modified to include religious instruction.[2]

But the working classes had a long tradition of self-education of their own. This dated back to the meetings held in the early 1790s under the auspices of the London Corresponding Society. Place himself had attended

[1] W. J. Reader, *Professional Men. The Rise of the Professional Classes in Nineteenth-Century England*, 1966, *passim*.

[2] Smith, pp. 139–40; Wallas, pp. 338–9.

meetings of this kind in his youth, and during the years of repression he was certainly not the only working man who continued to educate himself by private study. After 1815 the movement revived again, with secular Sunday schools for both children and adults, and with working men's coffee-houses where both books and periodicals such as *The Mechanics' Magazine* and Cobbett's *Register* were available for customers. 'Men had better be without education than be educated by their rulers,' wrote the editors of *The Mechanics' Magazine*, 'for then education is but the mere breaking in of the steer to the yoke; the mere discipline of a hunting dog, which, by dint of severity, is made to forgo the strongest impulse of nature, and instead of devouring his prey, to hasten with it to the feet of his master.'[1]

By the early 1820s Robert Owen's educational ideas were beginning to make themselves felt in London. In 1816 he had established the first infant school in Great Britain at his factory at New Lanark in Scotland, and in 1820 his example was imitated by Samuel Wilderspin, who opened a similar school in Spitalfields. Here is his own account of his first day there:

> As soon as the mothers had left the premises I attempted to engage the attention of their offspring. I shall never forget the effect. A few, who had been previously at a dame school, sat quietly; but the rest, missing their parents, crowded about the door. One little fellow, finding he could not open it, set up a loud cry of 'Mammy! Mammy!' and in raising this *delightful* sound all the rest simultaneously joined.

> Wilderspin's wife, who had agreed to help him, could not endure these paroxysms of grief. She deserted her husband, and soon he himself was

> compelled to follow her example, leaving my unfortunate pupils in one dense mass, crying, yelling and kicking against the door!

> I will not attempt to describe my feelings; but, ruminating on what I then considered egregious folly in supposing that any two persons could manage so large a number of infants, I was struck by the sight of a cap of my wife's, adorned with coloured ribbon, lying on the table; and observing from the window a clothes-prop, it occurred that I might put the cap upon it, return to the school, and try the effect. The

[1] Simon, pp. 186, 215, 230.

confusion when I entered was tremendous; but on raising the pole surmounted by the cap all the children, to my great satisfaction, were instantly silent; and when any hapless wight seemed disposed to renew the noise, a few shakes of the prop restored tranquillity, and, perhaps, produced a laugh. The same thing, however, will not do long. The charms of this *wonderful* instrument therefore soon vanished, and there would have been a sad relapse but for the marchings, gambols and antics I found it necessary to adopt, and which, at last, brought the hour of twelve, to my greater joy than can easily be conceived.

He had learned a valuable lesson.

Revolving these circumstances, I felt that the memorable morning had not passed in vain. I had, in fact, found the clue. It was now evident that the senses of the children must be engaged; that the great secret of training them was to descend to their level and become a child, and that the error had been to expect in infancy what is only the product of after years.[1]

The Owenite ideals were indeed far removed from the orderliness and godliness being propounded in the monitorial schools of the church societies. Soon they were blossoming out into co-operative societies and embryonic socialism, and by the mid-1830s there was a Free School for 'children of the disciples of Robert Owen' in Golden Square and an infant school in Charlotte Street. The constitution of the latter required that the children should be encouraged to express their own opinions, no creed or dogma was to be imposed, and admitted facts alone were to be placed before the pupils. All the children were to be treated with equal kindness, there were to be no rewards or punishments, and both sexes were to have precisely equal opportunities. Later there were Owenite Halls of Science, one in Lambeth and another in John Street, Holborn, and Chartist Halls in Mile End Road and Skinner Lane. By the early 1840s all the heterogeneous threads of the working-class educational movement were gathering together within the Chartist movement, and Chartist institutions enjoyed a short-lived, precarious existence in many parts of London.[2]

But Chartism did not draw its main strength from the capital, and the membership of these institutions remained relatively small, although attendances at lectures, discussions and social occasions were often large.

[1] Quoted in Smith, pp. 93–5.   [2] Simon, pp. 214, 234–5, 239, 246–8.

William Lovett, the Chartist leader most devoted to education, opened a bookshop in Tottenham Court Road and spent most of his later life in educational work. When Chartism began to crumble after 1848 the pre-eminent importance of working-class education was, however, still recognized at the Chartist Convention held in London in 1851, where it was asserted in terms which foreshadowed the future as accurately as had the famous Six Points of the original People's Charter. 'As every man has the right to the means of physical life,' states the third point of the Convention's programme, 'so he has to the means of mental activity. It is as unjust to withhold aliment from the mind, as it is to deny food to the body. Education should, therefore, be national, universal, gratuitous and, to a certain extent, compulsory.'[1]

Ideals of this kind could only be achieved through the agency of the State. The government had made what was to prove to be its last grant towards the building of churches in 1824, and nine years later it had made its first grant towards the building of schools. The Church would now have to rely on its own resources for the provision of accommodation for worship, while in the educational field it was simultaneously having to face the daunting task of maintaining its existing schools and improving the standard of teaching in them. A prodigious effort was made to meet this double challenge, and it was only when the Church's attempts were acknowledged to be inadequate for the full needs of the nation that in 1870 the State at last became the senior partner in education.

Bishop Blomfield ruled the diocese of London throughout most of these Sisyphean years, from 1828 until 1856. In the 1830s and 1840s the Ecclesiastical Commissioners and the Tithe Commissioners, both established in 1836, were busily overhauling the time-honoured administration of the Church's property, and Blomfield was just the man for such times. Able, aloof and often unpopular, he was the ecclesiastical counterpart of Peel, and like Peel he was devoted to efficient management. He was convinced that in populous districts the building of a church and the installation of a minister produced a 'gradual purification of the moral atmosphere all round; the growth of decency and order; and a progressive improvement in domestic economy and the social habits of the poorer classes'. In 1835 it was calculated that despite the work of the National Society and the Church Building Commissioners, about one-third of London's one and a

[1] Simon, pp. 254–5, 275; Mark Hovell, *The Chartist Movement*, 1943 edn, pp. 68, 208–9.

half million inhabitants were still 'without any Christian instruction and without any public acknowledgment of God'. The building of yet more churches therefore became the principal aim of his life in London.[1]

In 1836 Blomfield established a fund for 'the Building and Endowment of Additional Churches in the Metropolis', and by the end of the year £106,000 had been subscribed. The Church Building Commissioners still had some money, and between 1824 – the year of the second parliamentary grant – and their termination in 1856 they made grants towards the erection of ninety-four new churches in London, almost all of which were built in variants of the Gothic style. These ninety-four churches – and there were many others to which the Commissioners did not make a grant – cost some £606,000, of which the Commissioners contributed rather more than a quarter. Bethnal Green, Islington and Westminster each received eight grants, Lambeth and Paddington seven each, and St Pancras four.[2]

In Bethnal Green ten churches were built between 1840 and 1850, largely through the efforts of William Cotton, a director of the Bank of England who was sometimes referred to as 'the lay archdeacon'. Most of the wealthy inhabitants had left the district, and when one fund collector attempted to raise sixpence a head for the first church he received the reply that 'They would give him a shilling to hang the Bishop, but not sixpence for the work.' At the laying of the first foundation-stone the official party was 'abused in the most violent language' and in the well-established Bethnal Green tradition 'an infuriated ox was driven among the school-children who were assembled to sing a hymn'. Exactly where the money came from is not quite clear, for the Church Building Commissioners' eight grants in Bethnal Green only amounted to about one-eighth of the total cost of these eight churches. Cotton himself paid for the building and endowment of the tenth, St Thomas's, and the social effect of the whole programme was proved when, at the laying of this last foundation-stone in the presence of a large and orderly concourse, a working man exclaimed – or so it is said – 'I will not believe anything they say against the Bishops again. Look at these children.'[3]

Cotton also paid for the building of St Paul's, Bow Common, where he owned an estate and was anxious to demonstrate his conviction that ground landlords had a duty for the spiritual welfare of their tenants. His

[1] P. H. Welch, 'Bishop Blomfield and Church Extension in London', *Journal oj Ecclesiastical History*, vol. 4, 1953, pp. 203–15.

[2] Welch, pp. 204–5; Port, pp. 150–7.

[3] Clarke, p. 26; Welch, p. 212; Port, pp. 150–2.

religious sincerity is beyond doubt, but a handsome new church was nevertheless an essential adjunct to the successful development of many Victorian suburban building speculations. Ground landlords often presented a site and contributed handsomely to the erection of a church on their estate – the Marquis of Westminster at St Michael's, Chester Square, for instance, or Jonah Cressingham, owner of the Tulse Hill estate, who provided both the land and two-thirds of the cost of Holy Trinity Church, Lambeth.[1] Examples of this kind could be cited again and again, and who can say whether business acumen or religious piety predominated among the motives of the donors?

Blomfield himself contributed £18,000 from his own personal fortune to the building funds, but money was far from being his only problem. There were endless difficulties about patronage and the division of existing parishes, for it was not until 1843 that the Ecclesiastical Commissioners were empowered to form new districts for spiritual purposes. After the publication of Newman's *Tract XC*, and Blomfield's condemnation of it in 1842, he was increasingly beset by uncongenial and highly controversial doctrinal disputes. Above all, there was the question of the maintenance of the clergy. In the central districts of London many incumbents of ancient churches like St Giles in the Fields suffered a severe loss of income after the closure of the old overcrowded graveyards in the early 1850s. At the new poorly endowed churches, pew-rents provided an easy solution, but often they declined rapidly, particularly in the more central districts from which the well-to-do inhabitants were removing to the new suburbs. St Michael's, Burleigh Street, off the Strand, for instance, had been built in 1832–4 with half the seats free. But within a few years all the pew-renters had gone, and the remaining endowment for the incumbent was less than £100 per annum. And even where the income from pew-rents remained stable, as it often did in the outer suburbs, it only survived to provide in later years the calamitous association between church-going and 'bourgeois' respectability.[2]

Blomfield consecrated nearly two hundred new churches, though not all of them were in London. In 1854 his Metropolitan Churches Fund was replaced by a permanent new organization, the London Diocesan Church Building Society. But in that same year there appeared a detailed census of

[1] Welch, p. 208; *Survey of London*, vol. xxvi, 1956, p. 160; *Dictionary of National Biography*, William Cotton.

[2] Clarke, p. 27; Welch, pp. 205, 209; Port, pp. 136–7; Owen Chadwick, *The Victorian Church, Part 1*, 1966, p. 333.

19 Interior of an omnibus,
1859

20 The organ in the court,
1872

21 Shillibeer's Omnibus, 1829

22 Knifeboard Omnibus, *c.* 1850

23 Omnibus driver and conductor, 1877

24 Applicants for admission to the casual ward at the workhouse, 1874

the religious practices of the entire people of England and Wales. This showed that despite all efforts the Church of England could still only provide sittings for 17·6 per cent of the whole population of London, and that of the thirty areas throughout the country most in need of more accommodation, no fewer than twenty-four were in London. In Shoreditch, which headed the list, the established Church could only provide for 8·4 per cent of the population of 109,257, and even in Bethnal Green, where so much had been recently done, there was only accommodation for 16·5 per cent of the parishioners. But what was even worse was that the total number of attendants at the morning, afternoon and evening public worship of the Church of England on Sunday, 30 March 1851 – the day on which the census had been taken – amounted to less than a quarter of the population of London, without allowing for those who had attended more than once. To the problem of providing adequate accommodation there was now added public evidence for the even more intractable problem of getting the people to come at all.[1]

In education the story was much the same – the provision and maintenance of elementary education on the scale that was now required was too much for the churches' resources. But here the State began to play an increasingly active role, beginning in 1833 (as we have already seen) with a grant of £20,000 towards the building of schools for the poor. All applications for money had to be supported by either the National Society or the British and Foreign School Society, for the great majority of parents still wished their children to receive religious education of some kind. For many years the thorniest problem was to be the form which this instruction should take when the State was providing an ever larger share of the cost.

At first the Church of England, despite her altered position in the life of the nation after the Repeal of the Test and Corporation Acts and the Emancipation of the Catholics in 1828–9, was still powerful enough to obtain for her schools seven-tenths of the annual government grants. But the teaching provided by the monitorial system was rudimentary, and in 1839 the government established a Committee of the Privy Council on Education which at once announced its intention of establishing a State Normal School for the training of teachers; and schools which had received grants were to be inspected by the Council's own officers. The proposed Normal School was quickly withdrawn in face of strong opposition from

[1] *Census of Great Britain, 1851, Religious Worship: Report by Horace Mann*, 1854, pp. cxxxix, clxxxiv, cclxxviii, ccxcvii; Clarke, pp. 27, 217.

the Church, but the inspectorate survived, though much modified to meet the objections of churchmen.

Just at this time another government inspector was enquiring into the conditions of the hand-loom weavers in Spitalfields and Bethnal Green, and in the course of his report he stated forthrightly that:

> It is of the utmost importance that the public should be disabused respecting the numbers of persons receiving education in this country. From the publicity given to the proceedings of all societies engaged in forwarding education, an impression is created that there is a general diffusion of knowledge, and that the great bulk of the population is receiving education. How untrue this is in the metropolis, the researches here detailed sufficiently show.

His researches showed that in Bethnal Green alone there were eight to ten thousand children without any daily instruction and for whom no means of instruction existed.[1] In the parishes of St John and St Margaret, Westminster, 43 per cent of all the children were still without any instruction, while in the neighbouring parishes of St George, St James and St Anne, nearly 70 per cent were educationally destitute.[2]

It was for outcast children such as these that the ragged schools which first came into being in the early 1840s were intended. The 'rude habits, filthy condition and their want of shoes and stockings' often excluded these unfortunates from admission to the denominational schools. The ragged schools, largely promoted by the evangelicals, were solely for the children of the very poor and the destitute, and their function was rehabilitation rather than education, many of their pupils passing on to the denominational schools for instruction in the three R's. In 1844 the Ragged School Union came into being under the aegis of Lord Ashley (better known by his future title of Lord Shaftesbury), who remained its chairman for thirty-nine years. By 1858 there were 128 ragged schools in Middlesex alone, with 11,632 pupils.[3]

Even those children who did get to school learned little, as the first reports of the new inspectors revealed in the early 1840s. In many of the schools of the National Society and the British and Foreign School

[1] P.P., 1840, vol. xxiii, *Report from Assistant Hand-Loom Weavers' Commissioners*, pp. 262, 275.

[2] 'Report of a Committee to enquire into the State of Education in Westminster', *Journal of the Statistical Society*, vol. I, 1839, pp. 193, 454.

[3] *Victoria County History of Middlesex*, vol. I, 1969, pp. 232–3.

Society one master was in charge of some two hundred or more boys. At St John's, Hoxton, there were 292 boys under a single master assisted by eleven monitors, of whom seven were under eleven years of age. The children's attendances were short and irregular. At one typical school two-thirds remained for only six months, and often a child going first to school aged four would attend up to eight different schools before getting his first job – a situation caused by the migratory habits of the parents, who often moved about from one part of London to another in search of work. Demand for child labour was depressing the average age for leaving school, which in East London was ten and a quarter years in 1845. Thousands of parents were 'either too indifferent, or too ignorant, or too vicious, or too little able to command their children, ever to avail themselves of such educational opportunities as existed'.[1]

This was the situation which confronted Dr James Kay when he became the first secretary of the Committee of Council on Education. He realized that no lasting improvement would ever be made without better teachers. During the course of his previous work as an assistant poor law commissioner he had already interested himself in the education of the children in the workhouses in order to enable them to support themselves when they were launched into the world. He had visited three pioneer schools devoted to the rescue of juvenile offenders – the Children's Friend Society at Hackney Wick, the Victoria Asylum at Chiswick, and Lady Noel Byron's School at Ealing Grove – and his official position with the Poor Law Board had enabled him to make experiments of his own. In London it was then the practice to farm out pauper children to privately owned institutions in the suburbs, the Guardians of the Poor paying so much per child per week. The proprietor of one of these dismal establishments at Norwood, where some eleven hundred children were boarded, was willing to innovate, and Dr Kay was able to set up workshops and hire skilled craftsmen to teach. But he also introduced a new system of pupil teachers. Promising boys were given separate instruction in the evening, and were trained to become teachers, at first in the school itself and then elsewhere when they left. It was a natural development from the monitorial system, but the special training represented a great advance. Norwood became famous; distinguished gentlemen came to observe, just as they had to Joseph Lancaster's school in the Borough Road thirty years earlier, and when Kay became secretary of the Committee of Council he had at once

[1] *Minutes of the Committee of Council on Education, 1842–3*, 1844, pp. 434–516; *1844*, vol. II, 1845, pp. 113–212; *1845*, vol. I, 1846, pp. 153–5.

suggested that a Normal Training College should be formed. More schools, so urgently required, would need qualified teachers.[1]

After the withdrawal of the proposed State Normal School Kay established a training school of his own, at his own risk, at Terrace House, Battersea – an extraordinary step for a civil servant to take. Norwood supplied the first eight students, who lived at Terrace House with Dr Kay and his mother and sister. At the model schools of the National Society and the British and Foreign School Society the training in the monitorial system had been restricted to a few weeks, but at Battersea it extended over one or more years and was designed to inspire a true sense of vocation. Within a year there were thirty-three pupils, older and more mature than the juvenile monitors, better instructed, and learning to teach at the local village schools. Battersea too became famous; the Prince Consort was among the visitors in 1842, and when the first pupils completed the course their certificates of competence were adorned with the royal arms.[2]

By this time the National Society, which had led the opposition to the establishment of a State Normal School, had at last founded its own training college – St Mark's, opened at Chelsea in 1841. Here the pupils paid an annual fee of £25 and were admitted between the ages of fourteen and seventeen. Very shortly afterwards the Society opened a similar training college for women at Whitelands, Putney, and in the provinces a number of small, precariously financed diocesan colleges also came into being. In 1843 Dr Kay found that he could no longer support his pioneer school at Battersea and handed it over to the National Society. Only one training college remained outside the Society's aegis – the Home and Colonial Society's school in Gray's Inn Road, which had been established in 1836 by the happy co-operation of evangelical churchmen and dissenters for the training of teachers for infant schools. The Wesleyan college at Westminster was not founded until 1851. Whitelands and St Mark's still exist, but Kay's school, for long known as St John's College, was amalgamated with St Mark's in the 1920s.[3]

The foundation of the first teachers' training colleges in the early 1840s was a landmark in the history of English education, but their effect in improving the standard of teaching was not widely felt for some years. Meantime they imposed another heavy burden on the Church's funds, for at first the State would only make grants towards their building costs.

[1] Frank Smith, *The Life and Work of Sir James Kay-Shuttleworth*, 1923, pp. 45–62.
[2] Smith, *Kay-Shuttleworth*, pp. 104–13.
[3] Burgess, pp. 65–6, 111, 115, 118; Smith, *Kay-Shuttleworth*, p. 121.

But in 1846 Kay-Shuttleworth persuaded the government to take the next vital step. Schools already subject to government inspection were to be recognized for the training and employment of pupil teachers, who during their five-year apprenticeship were to receive a small government stipend. At the end of their apprenticeship they could compete for Queen's Scholarships tenable at the training colleges, and when they had qualified there the government was to pay one-third of their salary for service in any inspected school. Prompted by Kay-Shuttleworth's initiative at Norwood and Battersea the Church had provided the training colleges, and here, in partnership with the State, the building of the modern teaching profession now began.

In 1849 ill-health brought about by overwork compelled Kay-Shuttleworth to retire, although he was still only forty-five years of age. During the early 1850s the Committee of Council found itself beset on one side by the Voluntaryist party among the Dissenters, who opposed state aid altogether, and on the other by the High Churchmen opposed to the management committees which the State now required for all grant-aided schools. In such discordant times successive governments were content to mark time so far as elementary education was concerned; and even in the field of scientific education, where religious dissensions were not an obstacle, the progress of the State towards active participation was slow and cautious.[1]

The Prince Consort, a foreigner, made most of the running. Before his marriage to Queen Victoria in 1840 the government had already established the Geological Survey in 1835, and in the following year it had made a grant for a Normal School of Design for the teaching of art as applied to commerce and industry, from which descends the modern Royal College of Art. In 1845 Prince Albert became the president of the new Royal College of Chemistry, a privately sponsored venture housed in Oxford Street under the direction of a distinguished foreign professor, August von Hoffmann, specially imported from Germany. By this time the Geological Survey had proved unexpectedly useful through its assistance in the selection of the best stones for the building of the new Houses of Parliament, and in 1851 it and its museum of geological specimens, plus the new Government School of Mines and Science applied to the Arts, all moved into an expensive new building in Jermyn Street. The Prince Consort performed the opening ceremony. This was the year in which the Great Exhibition had demonstrated that Britain no longer held a lead in applied science. In 1852-3 the government therefore set up a new Science

[1] Smith, *Elementary Education*, pp. 203-4, 208.

and Art Department, which was transferred to the new Department of Education in 1856. It administered public grants for the teaching of science, but the rate of progress was hardly spectacular, and meanwhile shortage of funds had compelled the Royal College of Chemistry to merge with the Jermyn Street establishment. Between 1872 and 1880 the various teaching branches housed here removed to new buildings at South Kensington, erected on land bought from the profits of the Great Exhibition. As the Royal College of Science and the Royal School of Mines they were the forebears of the modern Juggernaut of South Kensington, the Imperial College of Science and Technology. The whole complex of museums and colleges at South Kensington is, indeed, a fitting monument to the Prince Consort's work for the promotion of scientific education. But at the time of his death in 1861 only the ground-work had been done, and two years later Professor von Hoffmann, after nearly twenty years' experience of British dilatoriness, returned to his native land to build a great new chemical laboratory at the University of Bonn.[1]

Education, at least of the elementary variety, nevertheless commanded widespread public attention in the 1850s and 1860s, as the proliferation of reports and enquiries amply testifies. With the enquiries there now came a mass of statistics. One report stated that in 1851 the number of pupils attending Church of England schools in London was only 3·39 per cent of the whole metropolitan population, a proportion lower than in almost every county in England but about average when compared with the principal provincial towns. Sunday schools appear to have been weak in London, where the percentage of pupils (5·9) was lower than in any other large town except Brighton – a figure which probably reflects the large number of private London day schools, many of them of abysmal standards. The value of these and other figures is somewhat diminished, however, when the same report states on one page that in 1851 there were only 74 Ragged Schools in London for destitute children, and on another page that in 1853 there were upwards of 116 such schools. But the general trend seems to have been towards slow improvement, with the proportion of pupils in weekday schools of all kinds in London rising from about one in nine of the total population in 1851 to about one in eight by 1858 – both these figures being slightly below the national averages of one in 8·36 and 1851 and one in 7·7 in 1858.[2]

[1] *London and the Advancement of Science*, pp. 171–6; Barnard, pp. 157–9.

[2] Mann, pp. 52, 61, 72, 136; P.P., 1861, vol. xxi, *Report of the Commissioners on the State of Popular Education in England*, vol. I, pp. 573, 635 (the Newcastle Commission).

At all events the government inspector responsible for visiting the Church schools in London had no doubt that the state-supported pupil-teacher system was making progress. No one, he wrote in 1859, 'can fail to have been struck with the great and decisive results to which it has so happily contributed'. And even the lot of the pauper children was improving. Several district schools quite separate from the contaminating influence of the workhouse had been established on the lines advocated by Kay-Shuttleworth at Norwood. The girls all went into domestic service and many of the boys into shoe-making and tailoring – precarious and often over-manned trades which sometimes led recruits back to the workhouse. But the Stepney school 'always had a ship in its yard' and trained its boys for the sea. Several others were finding that a little musical instruction enabled boys to enlist in the numerous regimental bands of the army; and in the opinion of the government inspector it was, after all, appropriate that boys who had been brought up entirely at the public expense should spend their working lives in the service of that public.[1]

But all this was costing the public a great deal of money – over £800,000 in 1859 – and in 1858 a Royal Commission was set up to enquire into 'the State of Popular Education in England'. This was the famous Newcastle Commission, so named from its chairman, the Duke of Newcastle, from whose report, published in 1861 in six volumes, there emerged Robert Lowe's principle of payment by results. Lowe was the Vice-President of the new Department of Education created in 1856. By his Revised Code of 1861 many existing grants, notably those for pupil teachers' stipends, were abolished, and in their place he introduced grants based on the pupils' attendance records and their performance in examinations in reading, writing and arithmetic. This system remained in operation, with some modifications, until the 1890s, and its emphasis on examination results reduced the work of the schools to a dull mechanical grind. 'The Revised Code has constructed nothing; it has only pulled down,' wrote Kay-Shuttleworth in 1868. It had not accelerated the rate of building new schools, it had discouraged all instruction above the elements and it had disrupted the training of teachers. 'These ruins are its only monuments. It has not succeeded in being efficient, but it is not even cheap; for it wastes the public money without the results which were declared to be its main object.'[2]

[1] *Report of Committee of Council on Education, 1859–60*, 1860, pp. 18, 517–24.
[2] Quoted in Smith, *Elementary Education*, pp. 271–2.

The Revised Code only applied to Church schools, and about two-thirds of all elementary schools in London were private. These private schools flourished 'upon a deeply seated foible of the national character, the passion for the genteel or the supposed genteel. . . . A cracked piano and a couple of mouldy globes, with a brass plate on the doors inscribed with the words "Juvenile Academy" outweigh with too many parents all the merits of correct spelling and sound arithmetic.' The Church schools were at least inspected, but in the private schools there was no supervision whatever. The Newcastle Commission's London investigation reported of them that 'many are held in premises injurious to health, and quite unsuitable for school purposes', while of the teachers it was said that 'none are too old, too poor, too ignorant, too feeble, too sickly, too unqualified in any or every way, to regard themselves, and to be regarded by others, as unfit for school-keeping'. Teaching in the private schools was, in fact, 'a mere refuge for the destitute'.[1]

The Newcastle Commission did at least reveal this state of affairs, and other commissions appointed in the mid-1860s revealed the state of secondary education. The four 'public' schools of Westminster, Charterhouse, Merchant Taylors' and St Paul's, only provided for 690 boys, of whom 188 were boarders; none of them had yet moved out to the suburbs or the country.[2] Besides these there were in the whole of London only twenty-four endowed grammar schools and sixteen proprietary schools for the secondary education of boys. These forty schools contained a total of just over 6,000 pupils. With a few exceptions, of which the City of London School, founded in 1837 was the most notable, most of the endowed schools were in need of 'stringent reform'. They were badly distributed – far too many were in or near the City, beyond walking distance from the new residential suburbs – 'inadequate in buildings and accommodation, and worst of all, unsatisfactorily taught and conducted'. The most useful of them were either those few which had been established within the last thirty years, or those ancient foundations which had been most subjected to change. The proprietary schools were better distributed – none of them was in the City – and almost all of them had been established since 1830. But despite these advantages they were not notably better than the

[1] *Newcastle Commission*, vol. I, p. 93; vol. III, p. 564; Smith, *Elementary Education*, p. 303.

[2] P.P., 1864, vol. xx, *Report of Commissioners on Certain Colleges and Schools*, p. 50.

endowed schools. Their buildings were often poor and their teachers inadequate.[1]

The girls' chances of 'higher' education were even smaller, for the government enquiries of the 1860s showed that for them there were only three endowed secondary and nine proprietary schools in the whole of London. These twelve schools contained less than one thousand pupils.[2] Yet even this situation represented a great recent improvement, for most of these schools had been established within the last twenty years. Three of them later achieved widespread renown. In 1848 F. D. Maurice and a number of other teachers at King's College in the Strand had founded Queen's College in Harley Street, for both girls and mature women. In the next year Mrs Elisabeth Reid had opened her Ladies' College in Bedford Square to save women from the empty futility to which social convention then condemned so many of them. It was her conviction that 'we shall never have better Men till men have better Mothers', but this was not thought to be so self-evidently true then as perhaps it is now, and her foundation met with many vicissitudes before it achieved its fame as Bedford College for Women. And in 1850 Miss Francis Buss, one of the first pupils at Queen's College, and still only twenty-three years old, had opened her North London Collegiate School for Ladies in her father's house in Camden Street, St Pancras – a school which still survives at Canons, Edgware, where its roll-call now about equals the total metropolitan provision for girls' higher education in the 1860s.[3]

The publication of the report which had revealed the terrible deficiencies in secondary education coincided with the passing of the Reform Act of 1867, which greatly extended the parliamentary franchise. Robert Lowe, the author of the Revised Code of 1862, expressed the implications of the new situation when he said, 'I believe it will be absolutely necessary to compel our future masters to learn their letters.' Britain was lagging behind other countries, notably Prussia, in the field of education, and if the churches and private individuals were unable to meet the nation's needs, the State itself must supply the deficiency. The object of the Education Act of 1870 was, in the words of its sponsor, W. E. Forster, to

---

[1] P.P., 1867–8, vol. xxviii, *Commission on the Education given in Schools not comprised within two former Commissions*, vol. I, pp. 222, 338–40; vol. VI, p. 358; vol. IX, pp. 199–280 (the Taunton Commission).

[2] *Taunton Commission*, vol. IX, pp. 179–95, 281–303.

[3] Barnard, p. 184; Margaret J. Tuke, *A History of Bedford College for Women 1849–1937*, 1939; *The North London Collegiate School 1850–1950*, 1950.

R

'fill up the gaps'. Where deficiencies existed, school boards were to be elected with power to establish and maintain elementary schools which were to be paid for out of the rates, by government grants and by school fees. The new boards were also given the power to compel the attendance at school of all children between the ages of five and thirteen. Denominational religious instruction was to be prohibited in all the boards' own schools.

Henceforth the State, through its new agent, the school boards, was to play an increasingly dominant role in the provision of elementary education. In London the school boards found that less than half the existing schools were 'completely or partially efficient', and that 80,000 children were not attending any school and had no valid excuse for absence. Some 103,000 additional school places were thought to be required – a gross underestimate, for it was soon found that the true figure was in the region of 250,000. The situation was worst in Finsbury, Southwark, Marylebone and Tower Hamlets, and in 1871 the board was already preparing to build twenty new schools – the first instalment in its gigantic task of slowly creating a new breed of Londoner, universally literate.[1]

We must now turn back to the churches and their main work, the propagation of the Christian faith. We have already seen that the religious census taken in 1851 had revealed that less than a quarter of the total population of London attended any of the Sunday public services of the Church of England. The report had contained other shocks too, of which the unexpected strength of the Dissenters was perhaps the greatest. Even in London, where they were nothing like so strong as in Wales and north of England, the number of Protestant Dissenters present at the *most numerously attended service* in each chapel on the day of the census was only about one-third less than that of the attendants at the Church of England – 186,321 compared with 276,885.[2] The Dissenters had been much influenced by the evangelical revival, which cut across denominational boundaries; most of their civil disabilities had been removed, and in the second half of the nineteenth century – the golden age of nonconformist liberalism – they were to assert an increasingly powerful influence in the public life of the nation.

In London the Independents or Congregationalists were numerically by far the largest of the Protestant dissenting sects, with 161 places of

[1] *Final Report of the School Board for London*, 1904.   [2] Mann, p. ccc.

worship. Some of these chapels could trace their history back to the time of Cromwell, while others had once been Wesleyan, or Presbyterian, or even Anglican proprietary chapels. In 1831–2 the formation of the Congregational Union in London marked the first step towards the federation of this disparate group. Next in numerical importance in London came the Wesleyan Methodists with 154 chapels, smaller buildings, evidently, than those of the Congregationalists, for they only provided about half the number of sittings. Two-thirds of these chapels belonged to the original Wesleyan connection, but there were already twenty-one Primitive Methodist congregations as well as eleven Calvinistic Methodist groups. Equally fissiparous were the Baptists, who, apart from their condemnation of infant baptism, often differed little from the Independents. In London they had 130 congregations, of which 89 were Particular Baptists. Other denominations included the Presbyterians, with 23 places of worship, the Quakers and the Unitarians with 9 each, and 48 'Isolated Congregations' which defied classification.[1]

The census also revealed the unexpectedly small number of Roman Catholics. They, too, had been relieved of most of their civil disabilities, and the encouragement provided by the conversion of Newman and a few of his Tractarian followers, plus the arrival of thousands of Irish after the famine of 1846–7, had culminated in the much-resented Papal restoration of the English hierarchy in 1850. But the total number of Catholics who heard Mass in London was found to be only about 36,000, distributed among only thirty-five churches.

In reality the census contained no comfort for any Christian, for it showed that on Sunday, 30 March 1851, the day on which the count was taken, only 874,339 of London's population of 2,362,236 attended any form of public worship; and even this figure makes no allowance for those people who went to more than one service. Nearly two-thirds of all Londoners were not attending either church or chapel, and this brutal fact proclaimed the failure of the great evangelistic effort which had been made during the first half of the century. Most of this effort had been made on the assumption that if only enough churches were provided, the people would come to them. But the census showed that even in respectable Kensington, where churchgoers might be expected to be especially numerous, the number of attendants of all Protestant denominations barely exceeded the total number of sittings available, despite the fact that two Sunday services were held in most churches, and three in some; and in

[1] Mann, p. clxxxiv; Chadwick, pp. 400, 412.

Bethnal Green, where Bishop Blomfield had built ten churches during the 1840s, the number of Church of England attendants was substantially less than the number of sittings available. Many of the new churches can only have been half-filled at any one Sunday service. To the working class the Church of England had become identified with the State and the governing classes, while the Dissenters (including even the Wesleyans, whose national membership had increased twice as fast as the population between 1800 and 1850) drew almost all their support from the commercial middle classes and had as yet made little effort to evangelize the poor. In the great migration from the country to the town the ancient habits of religious worship had been broken. Often they were not renewed in a strange new environment, and when Henry Mayhew at about the time of the religious census asked a costermonger what St Paul's Cathedral was, he received the reply 'A church, sir, so I've heard. I never was in a church.'[1]

To the ignorance and indifference of the masses there was now to be added the incipient doubts of some of the better informed. Advances in the study of geology in the 1820s and 1830s challenged the authenticity of Genesis, German biblical criticism was beginning to filter through to more conservative England, and in 1859 Charles Darwin published his *Origin of Species*. In the 1850s there was much anxious questing about for cosmic truth, one of whose manifestations in London was a fashionable vogue for spiritualism. Orthodoxy was on the defensive, and first attempts at restatements of traditional belief, such as the *Essays and Reviews* published by seven liberal Anglicans in 1860, were apt only to excite fresh alarm. Christian belief was in disorder, and in the second half of the century the churches encountered a new and rapidly changing climate of opinion. Yet despite all this, they remained a dynamic force in the lives of the millions of people whose loyalty they still commanded. The 1850s and 1860s were a period of intense religious activity, when the churches were adapting themselves to their new situation; if they could not re-convert the bulk of the nation they could and did at least survive as oases in the great expanding desert of indifference and disbelief.

It was a sign of these new times, when religion had to be taken to the people by any means available, that Bishop Blomfield's successor, A. C. Tait, frequently preached in the open air, in omnibus yards and even in Covent Garden market. When he appealed in 1863 for one million pounds

[1] Mann, pp. clxxxiv, 3–7; K. S. Inglis, *Churches and the Working Classes in Victorian England*, 1963, pp. 4, 9–16.

(less than half of which was subscribed) his main objects were the provision of funds for the maintenance of missionary clergy, additional curates, scripture readers and mission women, while the building of new churches, to which Blomfield had devoted most of his efforts, came ninth and last in Tait's order of priorities. By this time the evils of pluralism and non-residence had been very greatly reduced, and a new generation of clergy anxious to serve in spiritually destitute areas was appearing. One of the first of these was W. W. Champneys, Rector of Whitechapel from 1837 to 1860, whose work had included the provision of ragged schools, a provident society and a refuge and an industrial home for boys as well as the more conventional building of three new churches.[1]

Few of the clergy working in the slums were as yet radically minded, but from social work of this kind it was only a short step to the Christian Socialism propounded for a short while by Frederick Denison Maurice, professor of English history and literature at King's College, London. Maurice attacked the prevailing ethos of evangelical theology, with its heavy emphasis on acceptance of the existing competitive social order. He contrasted it with the Tractarian idea of the Church as a fellowship with God, but unlike the Tractarians he went on to apply their corporate notions of the Church to the everyday life of the world around him. He and his colleagues Charles Kingsley and J. M. Ludlow founded a dozen corporate workshops in London for tailors, shoe-makers, printers and other trades; in 1850 they started their own journal, *The Christian Socialist*, and proclaimed their impending conflict on two fronts 'with the unsocial Christians and the unchristian socialists'. They quickly achieved an astonishing influence among the latter, who had never met a parson like Maurice before (because none such had ever existed), but the unsocial Christians almost equally quickly extinguished them. Maurice was evicted from his professorship, Kingsley was haled before Bishop Blomfield to explain one of his sermons, and Ludlow resigned the editorship of *The Christian Socialist*. By 1854 the movement appeared to be over, its only durable achievement being the establishment of the London Working Men's College in Red Lion Square, Holborn, with Maurice as principal.[2]

Yet in reality their influence was to be more lasting. In their revolt against the social implications of evangelicalism and against the iron laws

[1] A. C. Tait, *The Spiritual Wants of the Metropolis*, 1863; G. Kitson Clark, *The Making of Victorian England*, 1962, p. 168.
[2] Inglis, pp. 262–7; Chadwick, pp. 346–63, 548; Thomas Kelly, *A History of Adult Education in Great Britain*, 1962, pp. 183–6.

of Benthamite political economy they became the first social radicals within the nineteenth-century Church of England. They did not accept the inevitability of, or the justice of, the existing structure of society, and very gradually during the second half of the century this attitude came to be shared by a growing minority of the Anglican clergy, particularly those working in London and other large towns. The damaging association of the Church with the State and the maintenance of the *status quo* was beginning to loosen – at least a little.

In the meantime others besides the Christian Socialists were applying the ideas of the Tractarians in ways not envisaged by their Oxford originators. In 1842 Bishop Blomfield had promptly condemned *Tract XC*, but he had rashly gone on to define the rubrics and require his clergy to obey them. Candlesticks might by placed on the holy table, but the candles were only to be lit at the evening service; flowers were not to be placed there; the preacher at morning service, he thought, should wear a surplice, but a black gown in the evening, and so on. Religious thought and practice was rapidly diversifying throughout the Church of England in the 1840s and 1850s, and within the huge diocese of London every sort of clergyman and congregation was represented. Some clergy obeyed and found themselves in trouble with their congregations; others disobeyed and found themselves in trouble with the bishop. The great ritual controversy had begun.[1]

One of the first of the 'Ritualistic' churches in London was St Barnabas, Pimlico, a chapel-of-ease of St Paul's, Knightsbridge, consecrated in 1850. At the time of the 'Papal Aggression' a crowd of protestors against the ceremonial innovations there had possessed themselves of the church on Sunday after Sunday, and Blomfield had not condemned them. At St Paul's, Knightsbridge, one of the churchwardens had started a legal action against the incumbent requiring him to remove the high altar and its ornaments, and Charles Lowder, one of the young curates at St Barnabas, had given sixpence to his choir-boys to buy rotten eggs to throw at a sandwich-man employed by the churchwarden to carry placards through the parish. Blomfield had suspended Lowder, who shortly afterwards removed to St George's in the East, Limehouse.

By the late 1850s there were about a score of 'Ritualistic' churches in London, but for some years public attention was chiefly concentrated on St George's and its two mission churches, one in Wapping and the other in Wellclose Square. Small mission churches were by this time one of the new means employed by the Church in its evangelistic work, but at St

[1] Chadwick, pp. 214–16.

George's the four clergy lived by rule as a community, they wore Eucharistic vestments and there was even a small group of Sisters. Trouble began in May 1859, when for week after week St George's was 'given over to the pleasure of a howling and blaspheming mob', many of whom came by train from distant parts of London. The church was temporarily closed, and when it re-opened three hundred policemen were present to maintain order. But Lowder persisted. He remained in the parish for more than twenty years; he won widespread respect for his work during a terrible outbreak of cholera, and he became one of the first Anglican clergymen to be addressed as 'Father' – a far cry from the days of John Venn and the Clapham Sect.

In the late 1860s public attention shifted once more, to St Alban's, Holborn, a small new ecclesiastical district in a poor quarter to the east of Gray's Inn Road. Here the first priest-in-charge was Alexander Mackonochie, who had previously served with Lowder at St George's. By this time the champions of Protestant Anglicanism had formed the Church Association (in 1865), which had a special fund to fight Ritualism by legal action. In 1867 Mackonochie was subjected to the first of a series of lawsuits which lasted for sixteen years, the original charges all being concerned with his manner of celebrating Holy Communion, which included the elevation of the Sacrament, excessive kneeling during the prayer of consecration and his use of incense, the mixed chalice and altar lights. In the end the campaign to 'put down Ritualism' failed, but only after Mackonochie had resigned his living, worn out in defence of practices which are now taken for granted within a large part of the Church of England.[1]

The Ritualists' sacramental approach was not the only innovation in the 1850s and 1860s. In 1857 the evangelicals began to hold Sunday evening services at Exeter Hall in the Strand. Here the emphasis was on preaching, and large congregations attended, mostly drawn from regular worshippers elsewhere, attracted by the preacher and the novelty of the surroundings. Even Westminster Abbey and St Paul's Cathedral were opened for Sunday evening services in 1858. Yet despite these and other evangelistic experiments and the greatly intensified devotion of many of the clergy, the Church was still failing to 'get through', particularly to the labouring poor. On the one hand the barrier of class was too great, while on the other the rise of secular professions, particularly that of teaching, was attracting men who might otherwise have taken Holy Orders; and even the status of

[1] Michael Reynolds, *Martyr of Ritualism. Father Mackonochie of St. Alban's, Holborn*, 1965, pp. 36–40, 56, 64, 124; *Dictionary of National Biography*, Charles Lowder.

the clergy was beginning to decline. The religious attitudes and habits of a large section of the people had been irrevocably determined during the great urban migrations of the first half of the century, and by the 1860s it was too late to reverse them. The population continued to grow, and all the churches' efforts could do no more than keep pace with this growth.[1]

One problem which beset all the churches, except perhaps the Catholic, was the question of pew-rents. We have already seen that pew-rents were necessary for the maintenance of the clergy, and how they deterred the poor from coming to church. 'Working men, it is contended, cannot enter our religious structures without having pressed upon their notice some memento of inferiority,' said the report of 1851. 'The existence of pews and the position of the free seats, are, it is said, alone sufficient to deter them from our churches; and religion has thus come to be regarded as a purely middle-class propriety or luxury.'[2] The Wesleyans and the Congregationalists were particularly dependent on pew-rents; their chapels were usually unendowed, and those in the inner districts of London were especially hard hit by the migration of many of their supporters to the suburbs. In the Church of England St Barnabas, Pimlico, was the first new church to be opened (in 1850) with all its seats free, and St Philip's, Clerkenwell, became the first church to abandon pew-rents. An association was formed for the abolition of pew-rents, and by 1870 about one in ten of all Anglican churches in London had dispensed with them; but there was little corresponding movement among the 'free' churches, and even in the Church of England there were practical difficulties besides finance, for a curate in Stepney thought that without separation of the classes 'the dirt of the people, and the fleas that we see, would prevent many people going. . . '.[3]

Despite their reliance on pew-rents, the Nonconformists were vigorous in London in the second half of the nineteenth century. Among their members there were wealthy businessmen such as the Baptist railway contractor, Sir Samuel Morton Peto, and the Congregationalist Samuel Morley, the architect of the great hosiery business which is still today a household name throughout the country. Peto and Morley both sat in Parliament as Liberals, and both of them contributed lavishly to the building of new chapels in London. The number of Congregational chapels in

[1] Leonard W. Cowie, 'Exeter Hall', *History Today*, June 1968, pp. 390–7; Chadwick, pp. 525–6; Inglis, pp. 38, 42, 327.

[2] Mann, p. clix.

[3] Inglis, pp. 50, 52, 97, 106–7.

London rose from 161 in 1851 to 250 in 1898, and the Wesleyans' Metropolitan Chapel Building Fund helped in the building of 78 new chapels between 1861 and 1885. But the outstanding free churchman was a Baptist, Charles Spurgeon, who at the age of only nineteen was invited in 1853 to the ministry at New Park Street Chapel, Southwark, one of the leading Baptist congregations in London. His weekly sermons attracted enormous attention; five thousand of them were printed, and eventually one hundred million copies were sold. While his chapel was being enlarged he preached first at Exeter Hall and then at the Surrey Music Hall, which accommodated twelve thousand people. Then he built the Metropolitan Tabernacle at the Elephant and Castle (1859–61), and here he continued to preach his 'thoroughly Calvinistic' message, subsequently almost entirely abandoned by all denominations, until his death in 1892. He was never ordained; he received no theological training whatever, yet even Gladstone expressed 'cordial admiration, not only for his splendid powers, but still more of his devoted and unfailing character'.[1]

Alone among all the churches the Roman Catholics were not associated with the existing social order, and they alone included large numbers of the working classes among their adherents. The social pattern of English Catholicism was, indeed, the opposite of that of contemporary Nonconformity, for there were few Catholic tradespeople and shopkeepers. Catholics in general were not respectable, for most of them were Irish immigrants, heavily concentrated in the years after the famine in such districts as the rookeries of St Giles in the Fields and St Marylebone, but gradually scattering all over London. They were perhaps more likely to win over the poor than any other church, but until the closing years of the century the number of priests was so small that most of their energy was concentrated on stemming the very large leakage within their own Irish membership.[2]

None of the churches ever made any large and lasting impact on the religious attitudes of the English urban working classes. They had not lost them, for they had never had them. Almost all churchgoers conformed with the worldly, conventional codes of behaviour, and so too, increasingly, did the Nonconformists, many of whose new Gothic chapels were outwardly almost indistinguishable from Anglican churches. It was this failure to reach to the bottom of the social scale that inspired William Booth to

[1] Ernest W. Bacon, *Spurgeon, Heir of the Puritans*, 1967, pp. 22, 36, 48–53, 77, 145, 160, 165; Inglis, pp. 98, 113.

[2] Inglis, pp. 119–41.

found the Salvation Army. Originally a Wesleyan lay preacher, he soon became convinced that only the poor could save the souls of the poor, and in 1865 he launched his 'Christian Mission to the Heathen of our own Country', from which the Army later evolved. He began his crusade in a tent, in Whitechapel, he preached with a strong Midland accent and dropped his aitches, and soon his working-class converts were enjoying 'the rapture of spiritual drunkards'. By the 1880s the Salvation Army had achieved a phenomenal growth, both in England and abroad, before it, too, lost its first momentum. But its initial strident success demonstrated the inability of the other Christian bodies to break through the social barriers within which their own activities were largely confined, and Cardinal Manning regarded the Salvation Army as a judgement on this failure.[1]

Shortly before his death in 1892 Cardinal Manning, looking back over his long life, also considered that 'The public feeling of the country is not and never will be with either Anglicanism or Dissent. It is not irreligious, the leaders of the Labour Unions are religious men; but its Unionism and public action is outside of all religion.' Working men wanted to participate in political and industrial affairs in order to remove social grievances, but participation in religious affairs conferred no such opportunities. The great majority of Christians accepted the existing social order, however strong their charitable impulses and actions often were. They were so deeply imbued with the evangelical doctrines of personal salvation, with conventional codes of Victorian behaviour which evolved from these doctrines, and with Benthamite laws of political economy, that they were incapable of seeing society as it appeared to the poor – at least until it was too late. In the second half of the nineteenth century they themselves were sometimes beginning to doubt the validity of their faith. Their sense of sin was transferred from religion to social reform, and the Fabian Society and the Bloomsbury Set became the early twentieth-century counterparts of John Venn, William Wilberforce and the Clapham Sect.

[1] Inglis, pp. 175–213.

7

Public Health

IN FEBRUARY 1832 cholera broke out in London. News of this terrible disease had first reached England from India in 1818. The epidemic had spread rapidly thoughout vast areas of the East, and after a short relapse had reappeared in India in 1826. Soon it reached the remote fastnesses of Russia. By 1830 it had attacked Moscow, and in the summer of 1831 it was raging in many parts of Europe.[1]

Cholera is transmitted by swallowing the cholera *vibrio*, a tiny comma-shaped bacillus. The *vibrio* is held in the victim's intestine, and the disease spreads by entering the intestine of another person. This occurs in two ways – by direct contact, or by contamination of the water supply. In filthy overcrowded conditions of living there are frequent physical contacts with human excrement, and flies, too, can carry the bacillus from infected faeces to food. In cases of direct contact the disease attacked individual families or houses. But the cholera *vibrio* can also live for up to about fourteen days in water, and when it became water-borne it attacked whole areas with terrible violence before dying away almost as suddenly as it had come.

Localized outbreaks caused by direct contact were often swiftly followed by much larger water-borne attacks, thus suggesting many erroneous explanations for the spread of the disease. This apparent capriciousness, when an epidemic attacked first a single house or alley, then leaped away to appear now in one and then in another district, often on a much larger scale, followed at last by its inexplicable, merciful departure, all added to the terror of cholera. For terror it undoubtedly excited. It attacked with appalling suddenness, its victims sometimes dying within a couple of hours of its first onset. More usually the disease lasted for several days; violent stomach pains, vomiting and diarrhoea were

[1] Norman Longmate, *King Cholera. The Biography of a Disease*, 1966, pp. 1–6.

followed by a total collapse in which the body became cold, the pulse almost imperceptible and the skin wizened and blue. There was no effective treatment, and one in every two cases proved fatal.[1]

In the first half of the nineteenth century there were two main schools of thought about the propagation of cholera. Some doctors thought that the disease was contagious, and spread by physical contact, while others thought that it existed as an evil miasma in the atmosphere, lurking dormant in decaying animal and vegetable refuse until activated by unknown meteorological conditions. Other theories had ardent protagonists too, and so when a London physician, Dr John Snow, published a pamphlet in 1849 containing part of the true explanation, namely that the disease was spread by swallowing water contaminated by the infected excretions, his conclusions were not universally accepted. It was not until 1884 that a German doctor, Robert Koch, working in India, finally discovered the cholera bacillus and proved that the disease could only be spread by swallowing the *vibrio*.[2]

Despite their ignorance of the true means of the propagation of cholera, the contagionists and miasmatists of the first half of the nineteenth century were united on one thing – the need for cleanliness. Everybody noticed that many of the worst outbreaks of cholera took place in the filthiest urban areas, and it was therefore from the shock of the terrible visitations of 1831–2, and still more from that of 1848–9, that the Victorian sanitary movement derived much of its impetus. A sense of shock was, indeed, needed to overcome both passive inertia and active resistance to reform, for sanitary improvement could only be achieved by a large and permanent extension of governmental action at both national and local levels – a process taking place simultaneously in other fields, notably in education and the regulation of factory labour, but of which the public health movement provides the clearest and most far-reaching example.

The first outbreak of cholera in England was at Sunderland, in October 1831. Parliament was then preoccupied with the great political crisis of the Reform Bill and had little time to spare for public health. There was indeed little general interest in the subject. Many doctors, even in the eighteenth century, were aware of the dangers of bad drainage and inadequate ventilation, but public health had not yet become a matter for political agitation or political action. Francis Place, for instance, whose interests covered so many fields, barely refers to it in his voluminous

[1] S. E. Finer, *The Life and Times of Sir Edwin Chadwick*, 1952, pp. 333–4.
[2] Longmate, pp. 67, 183–4, 226.

papers, and when a select committee of the House of Commons had been appointed in 1823 to consider the metropolitan commissioners of sewers, it had collected evidence but made no recommendations. Confronted, in the summer of 1831, with cholera at Hamburg, the government established an advisory Board of Health responsible to the Privy Council, and in October the Board issued instructions recommending the establishment of district Boards, to be drawn from the local magistrates, clergy and medical practitioners. These local Boards were to segregate the sick in specially commandeered houses, and infected towns were, if possible, to be isolated by cordons of troops and police.

Within a few months the cholera spread from Sunderland to Gateshead, Newcastle, Glasgow and Edinburgh, the fatalities in Glasgow alone ultimately mounting to nearly 3,200. In London Boards of Health were set up, a period of quarantine was imposed on ships arriving from the north, and on 6 February 1832 a day of national fasting and penance was announced. Four days later cholera appeared in London, at Rotherhithe, and from there it spread along the river-side, through Southwark, Lambeth, Limehouse and Ratcliffe, before leaping with its usual unpredictability to outlying districts such as St Marylebone and Hoxton. By the autumn, when few new cases were occurring, some 5,300 Londoners had died, and during a second short attack in 1833 there were another 1,500 victims.[1]

Cholera in Rotherhithe was a great deal more alarming than cholera on distant Tyneside, and within little more than a week of its first appearance in London an Act was passed 'to prevent, as far as may be possible, by the Divine blessing, the spread of the disease'. The Act empowered the Privy Council to issue instructions for the prevention of contagion, and within a few weeks doctors were being required to notify all cases of cholera, while the local Boards of Health were peremptorily ordered to set up temporary hospitals, provide the poor with medical attendance and when necessary pay for their funerals. In July the Nuisances Removal Order conferred hitherto unheard-of powers, authorizing the local Boards to scour sewers, close cesspools, clean slaughterhouses and even to enter infected private houses to wash and fumigate them. The first rudimentary machinery of public health administration was in fact being established.[2]

But all this activity was very short-lived, for the Act was only to remain in force for a limited period. Through doctors' reports from east London

---

[1] Longmate, pp. 8-9, 58, 86, 95-6; *Annual Register*, 1832.
[2] Longmate, pp. 90-1; 2 William IV, c. 10.

a few members of the Privy Council had been given a brief glimpse of the appalling sanitary and social conditions prevalent there, but for the general public the *Annual Register* could report that the alarm had been 'infinitely greater than the danger; and when the disease gradually disappeared in the course of the autumn [of 1832], almost every one was surprised that so much apprehension had been entertained'. In 1834 a Select Committee of the House of Commons again enquired into the metropolitan sewers, but although the 'want of system or combination' between the various authorities was criticized, members were still content merely to 'regret that it should not be in their power to suggest any practicable mode of correcting' such deficiencies.

In this same year, however, the passing of the Poor Law Amendment Act inaugurated a new era in the history of public administration. The haphazard methods of poor relief hitherto practised by the parish authorities were superseded by a central Poor Law Commission, from whose offices at Somerset House in London all the activities of the new local Boards of Guardians of the Poor were to be controlled. Generally, each Board was to be in charge of a group or Union of parishes; they were to provide workhouses for the reception of the poor, and the old system of 'outdoor' relief for the able-bodied was to be replaced (except in temporary emergency) by 'indoor' relief within the workhouse. There the new principle of 'less eligibility' was to be rigorously applied, to ensure that the lot of the pauper within the workhouse was always 'less eligible' than that of the poorest labourer outside.

The architect of the new Poor Law was Edwin Chadwick, the friend and disciple of the aged Jeremy Bentham. While still only in his early thirties he had written the crucial sections of the report on which the Poor Law Act was based, including those on 'less eligibility' and on the functions of the central Commission and the local boards, and later, as the salaried secretary of the Commission, he largely controlled this formidable new administrative machine in its early years. He became one of the most unpopular men in the whole country, detested alike by the poor for his abolition of the old allowance system in favour of the 'workhouse test' and by the vestrymen and the Boards of Guardians for the detailed central direction to which he ruthlessly subjected them. Intellectually hard and logical, and altogether lacking in a sense of the ridiculous, he was inexhaustibly industrious, the supreme organizer of vast masses of social information. Touchy and resentful of criticism, intolerant of opposition and utterly convinced that he could never be wrong, he devoted his whole life to what he conceived to be the limitless possibilities of social improvement through Benthamite administrative action. It was therefore natural that the knowledge and experience which he gained at the Poor Law Commission should lead him on to the still largely unexplored fields of sanitation and public health, which he dominated throughout the pioneer years from 1838 until his downfall in 1854.

In 1837–8 an epidemic of typhus was ravaging London and thousands of its victims were applying for poor relief. In order to remove the decaying refuse and stinking pools of sewage where the disease was thought to breed, the Boards of Guardians in east London spent public money in prosecuting neglectful landlords. The auditors disallowed this expenditure, and the matter was therefore referred to the Poor Law Commission at Somerset House for consideration.[1]

To Chadwick, disease was not only an expense; it was often also preventable by administrative action. Confronted with this argument, that prevention might actually prove to be an economy, the Poor Law Commissioners agreed to his demand for an enquiry, and three distinguished doctors set to work to investigate the problem in the East End in particular, as well as in London generally.

The three physicians had of course been carefully chosen by Chadwick for their interest in preventive medicine. Dr Neil Arnott had already 'paid attention to the circumstances governing the public health', while Dr James Kay had concerned himself with sanitary conditions in Manchester before becoming one of the salaried assistant Poor Law Commissioners; now better known as Sir James Kay-Shuttleworth, his later work in the field of education has already been described in Chapter 6. Arnott and Kay jointly concerned themselves chiefly with Wapping, Ratcliffe and Stepney, while Dr Southwood Smith, physician to the London Fever Hospital in Islington, examined Bethnal Green and Whitechapel.

Southwood Smith's report, presented early in May 1838, was entitled 'On some of the Physical Causes of Sickness and Mortality to which the Poor are particularly exposed, and *which are capable of removal by Sanatory Regulations*'. He showed that in many parts of Bethnal Green and Whitechapel fever 'of a malignant and fatal character is always more or less prevalent'. The streets, courts, alleys and houses where fever first broke out, and where it proved most fatal, were invariably in the immediate

---

[1] The following account is based on *Fourth Annual Report of the Poor Law Commissioners*, 1838, Appendix A, pp. 93–153, and *Fifth Annual Report*, 1839, Appendix C, pp. 160–71.

neighbourhood of uncovered sewers, stagnant ditches and ponds, gutters full of putrefying matter, nightmen's yards and privies, the soil of which lay openly exposed and was seldom if ever removed. 'It is not possible,' he wrote, 'for any language to convey an adequate conception of the poisonous condition in which large portions of both these districts always remain, winter and summer, in dry and in rainy seasons, from the masses of putrefying matter which are allowed to accumulate.' On a tour of inspection of Bethnal Green he noted dozens of examples of such conditions. For a mile between Virginia Row and Shoreditch 'all the lanes, courts and alleys pour their contents into the centre of the main street, where they stagnate and putrefy. Families live in the cellars and kitchens of these undrained houses, dark and extremely damp.' In Bethnal Green and Whitechapel alone, he estimated that nearly £2,500 per annum was being spent on the relief of the poor stricken with fever, and local fever hospitals for both the poor and 'the industrious classes' were desperately needed. But there would be no end to the expenditure of money in relieving individual cases of fever until the cause that produced the malady was removed. 'It becomes, then,' he concluded, 'a question whether, setting aside all higher considerations, it is not expedient, even on the ground of economy, to appropriate a part of the money expended on the poor in protecting them from fever, by removing from the immediate proximity of their dwellings the main cause that produces it, rather than by relieving a few individuals after they become affected with the disease.'

The report by Arnott and Kay was entitled 'On the prevalence of certain Physical Causes of Fever in the Metropolis, *which might be removed by proper Sanatory Measures*'. They divided the causes of fever among the poor into two categories, those 'arising independently of their habits' and those 'originating to a considerable extent in their habits'. In the first class they listed lack of sewers and drains, the existence of open stagnant ditches filled with decomposing animal and vegetable matter, unemptied cesspools and privies, accumulations of decaying refuse, inadequate ventilation in narrow courts and alleys, and the situation and condition of slaughterhouses and public burial grounds in densely populated districts. The second class of causes included overcrowded conditions of living, particularly in the common lodging-houses, dirtiness of person, intemperance and the neglect of vaccination.

Like Dr Southwood Smith they produced detailed evidence in support of their contentions, but Arnott and Kay took the argument a stage further when they set out the remedial measures needed. The first of these was 'A perfect system of sufficiently sloping drains or sewers, by which from every house and street all fluid refuse shall quickly depart by the action of gravitation alone.' This would need, secondly, 'A plentiful supply of water to dilute and carry all such refuse, and to allow of sufficiently washing of streets, houses, clothing, and persons.' An effective scavenging service was also needed for the removal of refuse, and all courts and alleys as well as main streets must be paved. Proper ventilation must be provided, and the situation and condition of cattle markets, slaughter houses, cow-houses, tripe-shops, gasworks and burial grounds must be regulated by 'competent authorities'. Greatly daring, they even suggested that the local Poor Law Boards of Guardians should be given power to discharge many of these functions. However it might all be done, they had 'no doubt that by proper sanatory police regulations, such as a public Board of Health might decide upon, the typhoid fevers of London and other places might be made to disappear, and we think the remedial measures would cost less than it now costs to parishes and public charities to take care of the sick, and to provide for the helpless widows or orphans of those who die'.

These two reports, drawn up within the brief space of a single month, provided the blue-prints for the mid-nineteenth-century sanitary move-ment. There had never been an official enquiry like this before, and hence-forth the problem of public health could never be conveniently forgotten, as it had largely been after the cholera outbreak of 1831–2. When Lord Normanby, a member of the government, had read the reports, he was incredulous that such conditions could exist, but after he had visited Bethnal Green with Dr Southwood Smith he admitted that 'so far from any exaggeration having crept into the descriptions which had been given, they had not conveyed to my mind an adequate idea of the truth'.[1]

The two reports provided Chadwick with his life's main work. Owing to personal animosities between himself and the Poor Law Commissioners he had by 1838 been deprived of much of his power as secretary to the Commission, and an enormous new field in which to exert his restless energies was just what he needed. He published the doctors' investigations as appendixes to the Commission's annual report for 1838, and he even induced the Commissioners themselves to say a few cautious words in favour of the need for sanitary legislation. In 1839 Dr Southwood Smith

[1] Quoted in Finer, p. 161.

S

produced another report, on the prevalence of fever in twenty metropolitan districts. 'These neglected places are out of view, and are not thought of,' he wrote; 'their condition is known only to the parish officers and the medical men whose duties oblige them to visit the inhabitants.'[1] Soon Chadwick was to make their condition known all over the country through a vast programme of systematic investigation. But first he had to obtain parliamentary authority to undertake this work. He began by having seven thousand copies of the reports printed and circulated, and in August 1839, at Chadwick's instigation, Bishop Blomfield successfully moved in the House of Lords that enquiry should be made as to the extent to which the conditions already described by the three doctors in London might 'prevail also among the labouring class in other parts of England and Wales'.[2]

This first general enquiry occupied Chadwick for nearly three years and was eventually published in 1842 under the title of *An Inquiry into the Sanitary Condition of the Labouring Population of Great Britain*. Its main objects were to dispel the almost universal ignorance which then prevailed about the living conditions of the working class, and to establish the relationship between dirt and overcrowding on the one hand and disease on the other – something so obvious now that it is hard to realize that it still needed proof in the early 1840s. Although mainly concerned with conditions in the provinces, the report nevertheless contained a mass of information about London as well, particularly about its drainage and water supply.

Metropolitan drainage was administered by eight independent Commissions of Sewers, whose members were mostly appointed by the Crown. Some of the Commissions still operated under the powers of an Act of Parliament of 1532, others under their own somewhat less antique local Acts; all of them discharged the contents of their sewers into the Thames. There was no co-operation between the different Commissions in the course, level, size, shape or mode of construction of their respective sewers, and when one Commission made improvements the increased flow might flood the sewers and even the houses within the jurisdiction of a neighbouring Commission, as had happened in the City itself in the early 1830s. Larger sewers were made to discharge into smaller ones, sewers with upright sides and circular crowns and inverts were connected with egg-shaped sewers, or the latter with the narrow part uppermost were connected with similar sewers having the smaller part downwards. In

[1] *Fifth Annual Report of the Poor Law Commissioners*, 1839, Appendix C, pp. 160–71.
[2] Finer, pp. 162–3.

some districts the Commissioners were even uncertain as to whether they had power to build new sewers at all. Jobbery, extravagance, inequitable rating assessment and gross technical incompetence were almost everywhere the rule.

The Commissioners of Sewers had for centuries been concerned solely with the disposal of surface water, and in Westminster until 1815, and in some other parts of London until later still, it was a penal offence to discharge sewage into the Commissioners' drains. In the Tower Hamlets area householders were permitted to make connections with the common sewers, but they had to pay a fine for so doing; otherwise, said James Peake, the Commissioners' surveyor, 'Every one would make a hole in the sewer' – i.e. everyone would use it. Thus throughout most of the first half of the nineteenth century cesspools were regarded as the proper receptacles for house drainage, and sewers as legitimate channels for carrying off the surface waters only.[1] London's subsoil became thickly studded with cesspools, and even within the area of the one relatively efficient metropolitan Commission, that of Holborn and Finsbury, only about one-third of all the houses in the 1840s had communications with the main sewers.[2]

What upset these arrangements in the first half of the nineteenth century was firstly the rapid rise of population, and secondly, the growing use of water closets. The amount of human waste matter, in both diluted and undiluted form, increased enormously. The cesspools overflowed, particularly in the poorer quarters where the cost of having them emptied was prohibitive or the landlord simply refused to act, and even where houses were connected to the sewers the unplanned levels often prevented a proper flow of liquid. Sometimes the common sewers were, indeed, nothing more than elongated cesspools, full of stagnant human excrement and not always even covered in.

In Chadwick's great report the clearest example of the prevailing ignorance of the connection between conditions of this kind and disease was provided by the unfortunate surveyor of the Tower Hamlets Commission. While being questioned he admitted that in certain streets in Whitechapel there were no sewers at all, that this district was, in his own words,

---

[1] P.P., 1842 (House of Lords), vol. xxvi, *Inquiry into the Sanitary Condition of the Labouring Population of Great Britain*, pp. 311–12; J. W. Bazalgette, 'On the Metropolitan System of Drainage and the Interception of Sewage from the River Thames', *Proceedings of the Institution of Civil Engineers*, vol. xxiv, 1864–5, pp. 1–2.

[2] P.P., 1844 (572), vol. xvii, *First Report of Royal Commission on the State of Large Towns and Populous Districts*, part II, p. 169.

'the filthiest place which can be imagined', and very densely populated. He was then asked 'Do you not think that the want of such provision is very injurious to the health of the inhabitants?', to which he replied, 'I do not think that sewers have the effect which is attributed to them.' Pressed next on whether he therefore disagreed with the doctors who thought that lack of underground drainage was prejudicial to the health of the inhabitants, he answered that he could not 'see how, if they have a good surface drainage, they can be improved by an underground drainage, in nine cases out of ten'. And finally, to the question 'Do you consider it your duty to alter a sewer, or carry up a sewer, with reference to the health of the inhabitants?', he replied, uncompromisingly, 'Certainly not.'[1]

The doctor employed by the Poor Law Guardians of Whitechapel Union to treat the sick poor there thought otherwise. For him the chief requisites for the prevention of fever and contagious diseases were 'the promotion of cleanly habits amongst the poor; the promotion of sewerage and drainage; having proper supplies of water laid on in the houses; the removal of privies from improper situations'. And to buttress these views Chadwick himself produced figures of the mortality in Whitechapel for the year 1838. These showed that whereas the average age at death of gentlemen or professional men and their families there was 45, for tradesmen and their families it was 27 years of age, and for mechanics, servants, labourers and their families it was only 22. In Bethnal Green for this last class it was even lower, the average age at death being a mere 16 years.[2]

But Chadwick's report did more than establish the relationship between dirt and disease. It also showed that the victims of the social evils which it described could not remove these evils by their own unaided efforts, and that public action on an unprecedentedly large scale would be needed. This unpalatable revelation was bad enough, but it also presented a tremendous challenge to existing vested interests, to the indifference and inefficiency of landlords, local vestries, paving boards, Commissioners of Sewers, and above all to the water companies.

Chadwick had found that in Holborn and Finsbury, where there was a very able surveyor, John Roe, the Commissioners had built their sewers with curved sides and semi-circular bottoms instead of with the usual straight sides and flat bottoms. This practice was not only cheaper and stronger, but it also produced a much more powerful flow of water in the sewers. By installing cast-iron flushing gates across the sewers the flow

---

[1] P.P., *Sanitary Condition of the Labouring Population*, p. 312.
[2] P.P., *Sanitary Condition of the Labouring Population*, pp. 148, 159–60.

could be held back until enough water had accumulated to sweep away all solid obstructions when the gates were opened. It was no longer necessary to break up the streets to get at obstructed sewers, and the sewers themselves – hitherto so large that in Westminster the Commissioners had 'walked in procession' down them – if cleansed by water, could be made smaller and therefore more cheaply.[1]

In Edinburgh Chadwick had also discovered that the farmers nearby had greatly improved the value of their land by diverting the contents of the town ditch to the irrigation and manuring of their fields. Thus there emerged in Chadwick's mind the idea of the arterial system of drainage, whereby with a plentiful water supply the sewers could be made self-cleansing and their contents sold for agricultural uses. The trouble was, of course, that the supply of water was not plentiful. Often it was only turned on at certain times of the day, and in the filthy courts and alleys where it was most needed it was not piped into the houses at all but had to be fetched in pails from one shared cock outside. The installation of water closets was therefore impossible and the water laboriously carried by hand was used over and over again. 'They merely pass dirty linen through very dirty water,' said the medical officer of Whitechapel Poor Law Union when describing the habits of the residents there. Washing, whether of human bodies or of clothes or of houses, was at a premium, and the final discouragement was the absence of any proper means for the final disposal of the water. 'If I cast my eye over the whole district at this moment,' said the same witness, 'I do not think that one house for the working classes will be found in which there is such a thing as a sink for getting rid of the water.'[2]

The water companies, therefore, as well as the landlords, the vestries and the Commissioners of Sewers, were to be among the objects of the sustained offensive which Chadwick was planning. The report itself, when published in July 1842, produced a sensation, more copies being sold than of any government publication hitherto.[3] It revealed the general drift of Chadwick's thinking, that the arterial system of drainage would remove the principal causes of dirt and disease, and hence that the whole problem was one for the engineers rather than the doctors; that new administrative machinery must be devised to implement the vast works

[1] P.P., *Sanitary Condition of the Labouring Population*, pp. 373–9.
[2] P.P., *Sanitary Condition of the Labouring Population*, pp. 48–9, 64.
[3] R. A. Lewis, *Edwin Chadwick and the Public Health Movement 1832–1854*, 1952, p. 60.

required, and that the cost must be spread over a number of years.[1] But there was as yet no attempt to apply such revolutionary ideas in detail, and after a year the government appointed a Royal Commission to investigate (in practice under Chadwick's guidance) 'the State of Large Towns and Populous Districts', and to recommend the means needed for improvement.

During this interim twelve-month period Chadwick had prepared another report, at the request of the Home Secretary, on the Practice of Interment in Towns. Most people were still buried in churchyards or in the burial grounds of the Nonconformist sects. These graveyards had become so overcrowded that in recent years eight commercial cemeteries had been established by joint stock companies on the outskirts of London for the more decent accommodation of the bodies of those whose relatives could afford to pay the higher fees. But by the early 1840s the growth of population, and therefore of the dead too, had rendered all these arrangements totally inadequate. Every year some 44,000 new bodies were packed into the 218 acres of ground comprised within the intramural burial grounds. In some of these grounds there were already over 3,000 bodies to each acre, and the average annual number of new burials per acre stood at 203. In the course of one generation, Chadwick estimated, over a million new bodies had been buried in London. Each layer of bodies required some seven years in which to decompose. But in many burial grounds the rate of new interments exceeded the rate of decay. The height of the ground rose, and hideous means were employed by the gravediggers to provide space for new intakes. To the mental distress and abhorrence excited by such barbarous conditions was added the physical nausea induced by the stench which pervaded not only the graveyards themselves but the surrounding streets as well.[2]

This terrible catalogue did not end here. Chadwick, of course, was a convinced miasmatist, who believed that the inhalation of odours caused by decaying animal matter provided means for the spread of many fatal diseases. He therefore showed at some length that the stench of death exerted its malign influence in the homes of the poor as well as in and around the graveyards. In a large proportion of cases the labouring classes had only one room. 'It is their bed-room, their kitchen, their wash-house, their sitting-room, their dining-room; and, when they do not follow any

[1] Finer, pp. 225–8.
[2] P.P., 1843 (509), vol. xii, Report on the Practice of Interment in Towns, pp. 27, 133.

out-door occupation, it is frequently their work-room and their shop. In this one room they are born, and live, and sleep, and die amidst the other inmates.' Here the body remained, often for up to twelve days, while funds for the funeral were assembled. Over a quarter of the £24 million deposited in savings banks was intended for funeral expenses, and the London undertakers were adept at playing up and exploiting the pathetic wish of distressed relatives to provide a decent burial. Meanwhile the life of the family went on with the body still in the room. The smell became intolerable, the coffin had to be tapped to release the liquid matter, and maggots were often to be seen 'crawling about the floor of a room inhabited by the labouring classes, and about the tressels on which the tapped coffin is sustained'. The danger of such conditions for the health of the survivors needs no explanation. But Chadwick did nevertheless explain it, and added, with unexpected compassion, that 'the evidence of the mental pain and moral evil generally attendant on the practice of the long retention of the body in the rooms in use and amidst the living . . . is yet more deplorable.'

The remedies which he proposed were drastic and simple. All burials in towns must cease, and even the new joint stock cemetery companies 'ought to be abandoned'. In their place there should be 'national cemeteries', and mortuaries for unburied bodies. In order to abate the 'oppressive charges' of the undertakers, the officers of these new establishments should provide funerals at reasonable prices, and fully qualified medical officers of health should be appointed to certify the causes of all deaths.[1]

As with his Sanitary Report of 1842, these recommendations challenged many vested interests – the clergy, to whom the closure of the ancient burial grounds would mean a severe loss of income, the Nonconformists, who would demand new ground outside London, the cemetery companies, which were to be dispossessed, and above all, the undertakers, who would lose their business. All this, plus the assumption of public responsibility for the provision and management of new cemeteries, was too much for the government in the 1840s. No action followed – yet.

By the time that this report was published in December 1843 Chadwick was already at work, at Gwydyr House in Whitehall, with the Royal Commission on the State of Large Towns and Populous Places. This enquiry covered much of the ground which he had already traversed in his Sanitary Report of 1842. It heard evidence relating to London from

[1] P.P., *Interment in Towns*, pp. 31, 39, 44, 199-200; Lewis, p. 70.

Dr Southwood Smith on the causes of disease and the need for sanitary regulations, from Dr Arnott on the evils arising from want of drainage, ventilation and cleanliness, and from the medical officer of the Whitechapel Union on the condition of the dwellings of the poor. It looked into the removal of street refuse and it pilloried the Commissioners of Sewers all over again, the chief victim on this occasion being Richard Kelsey, surveyor to the Commissioners of the City of London. He did, indeed, possess a map of the sewers in his district, but Chadwick revealed that it had one important defect. When asked, 'Can you tell, in inspecting the map, which way the water falls in all the drains represented?' he replied, 'I could tell, because I know it; but no stranger could tell.' He had large maps showing the direction of flow, but this particular map had only been made 'for the general use of the Commissioners'. To provide such information for them 'would lead to confusion', and it had not occurred to him to include it. And so on.[1]

But where the Royal Commission did break important new ground so far as London was concerned was in the matter of water supply. At the beginning of the nineteenth century most well-to-do Londoners had obtained their water from joint stock companies through whose leaky wooden pipes there dribbled, on alternate days, enough water, drawn unfiltered from the Thames or the Lea, to fill a cistern in the basement. Other Londoners relied on wells or rain-water butts, while the poor obtained their water from the companies' communal cocks in the alleys where they lived, or from wherever else they could get it. But with the manufacture of cheap metal water pipes and improved methods of steam pumping, which enabled water to be supplied at first- and even second-storey level to satisfy the inexorable demands of the water closet, a number of new companies were formed in the first two decades of the century. Fierce competition had ensued, prices had been reduced and ultimately peace had been restored by agreement between the companies to restore rates and apportion areas of supply. When a Select Committee of the House of Commons looked into the subject in 1821 all the chief protagonists in the struggle for a pure and plentiful water supply, which was to last for over eighty years until the formation of the Metropolitan Water Board in 1902, were already in the field. First there were the companies – on the north side of the river the two old ones, the New River (1609), drawing its water from Amwell in Hertfordshire, and the Chelsea (1723), plus the three new ones, the West Middlesex, the East London and the Grand Junction, while to the south

[1] P.P., *First Report on State of Large Towns*, part II, pp. 207–8.

of the river there were the Southwark, the Lambeth and the Vauxhall companies. Next there were the parish vestries and paving trusts, always at war with the companies over the incessant depredation of street pavements for the laying and repairing of pipes, and sometimes advocating the establishment of a municipally-owned water supply in place of the hated companies. And lastly there were the consumers, who grumbled and paid.[1]

No general Act regulating the metropolitan water supply was passed in the first half of the nineteenth century; the problems were too numerous and too baffling. First there was the question of control and ownership – how, in the absence of real competition after about 1820, to compel the companies to spend the large sums required to provide an adequate supply of water in all parts of London while maintaining a reasonable return on the shareholders' investment? What, indeed, was an adequate supply? The amount of water being supplied was constantly increasing, in terms of individual consumption per head as well, of course, as in terms of the rapidly growing population, but so, too, was the use of the water closet. By the 1840s, for instance, this invaluable appliance had been installed in one-third of all the houses supplied by the New River Company, and still the clamour was for more water. The supply was still only intermittent, not continuous, and in the overcrowded houses of the poor, where a piped supply was most needed but only very seldom found, the facilities for the storage of water, which an intermittent system demanded, were often virtually non-existent. And then there was the question of quality. Most of the companies drew their water from the Thames between Chelsea and London Bridge. In the days when the Commissioners of Sewers were only concerned with surface water drainage, and house sewage reposed in cesspools, this arrangement had not been challenged. But when both house drains and the overflow pipes from the cesspools were connected to the common sewers, which discharged into the same stretch of the river, widespread pollution of the water supply became inevitable. As early as 1827 a parliamentary enquiry had condemned the quality of Thames water, and in the following year the Chelsea Company had introduced filter-beds. But the experts disagreed about what, if any, remedial measures were required, and so, despite more inconclusive enquiries in the early 1830s, nothing was done.[2]

This was the situation with which the Royal Commission of 1843 was

[1] T. F. Reddaway, 'London in the Nineteenth Century: The Fight for a Water Supply', *The Nineteenth Century and After*, vol. 148, 1950, pp. 118–30.

[2] Reddaway, pp. 118–30.

confronted. It found that in one single area of London, that supplied by the Southwark Water Company, there were some 30,000 inhabitants without access to piped water even at communal cocks. Where communal stand-pipes did exist, the labour and loss of time involved in fetching water prevented its use in adequate quantity. 'I have seen as many as from 20 to 50 persons with pails waiting round one or two stand-pipes,' said one water engineer. 'Then there is quarrelling for the turn; the strongest pushing forward, and the pails, after they are filled, being upset.' Often the supply was only turned on during the hours when the residents were out at work, and in winter the cocks froze. Everybody agreed that a supply piped into the houses of the poor was desirable, but there were formidable obstacles. The advantage of communal cocks, another engineer remarked, was that they could not be stolen, but if pipes were installed in each house the 'pipe would be there in the evening, but it would be gone in the morning'. The companies had no obligation to provide a piped supply into the houses of the poor, and without adequate security on their capital outlay they had no financial inducement either. Most landlords refused to spend money on such improvements; besides, they thoughtfully added, 'we have no drains to carry off the waste. If we have more water brought into the premises, we shall only have more damp, and rot the floors, and make the houses more untenantable.'[1]

Evidence of this kind confirmed the vicious circle which Chadwick had begun to investigate in his report of 1842, and which his arterial system of drainage would break. The more detailed enquiries made under his aegis by the Royal Commission proved to him that a plentiful and constant supply of water piped into all houses would provide the motive power for the removal of domestic sewage by the natural flows within a properly constructed network of sewers, and that these liquids could be profitably used as agricultural manure. From the symmetrical simplicity of the whole conception, so irresistible to his orderly mind, he moved naturally to the conviction that in London there should be a single Crown-appointed Commission to provide and administer drainage, paving, street cleansing and even water.[2]

This was not to be. Perhaps the idea was too far ahead of its time, for it has recently been revived again.[3] The Royal Commissioners, at all events,

---

[1] P.P., *First Report on State of Large Towns*, part II, pp. 23, 116, 124; *Second Report*, 1845 (610), vol. xviii, part I, p. 93.

[2] Finer, p. 309.

[3] See *The Sunday Times*, 7 September 1969.

were more cautious. They were concerned with all large towns, not just with London, and in their thirty recommendations, published in February 1845 and covering the fields of drainage, paving, cleansing, nuisances, water, ventilation, lodging-houses, medical officers and financial cost, they referred over and over again to 'the local administrative body' which, subject to central supervision, was to direct 'the works required for sanatory purposes'. But in London no such 'local administrative body' existed, except in the City. The duties of sewering, paving and cleansing, let alone supplying water, were not there combined under one management, as they were in almost all other towns, and the Commissioners therefore appended to their recommendations 'some remarks on those distinctions that exist between the local laws generally in operation in the provincial towns, and those that are in force in the Metropolis.' In fourteen devastating pages they proceeded to expose once more to the public view the terrible deficiencies of the metropolitan drainage and water supply; but they made no recommendations as to how the remedies which they proposed for the provincial towns might be applied in London.[1]

In the same month, February 1845, as the publication of the Commissioners' recommendations, the Queen's Speech announced the government's intention to introduce a Bill for 'promoting the Health and Comfort of the Poorer Classes'. Seven years had already passed since the publication of the Poor Law doctors' reports on conditions in the East End. Now another three years were to elapse before any remedial legislation actually reached the statute book (apart from the not very successful Metropolitan Buildings Act passed in 1844). This was partly because the responsibility for promoting such legislation was in the hands of a minor and inappropriate member of the government, the First Commissioner of Woods and Forests, and partly because of Parliament's preoccupation with other matters, notably the repeal of the Corn Laws and the great famine in Ireland. When a Public Health Bill was at last introduced in 1847, London was excluded from its scope, and the Bill was eventually withdrawn.[2]

But the mid-1840s were not entirely wasted, for public demand for sanitary action was being gradually mobilized. The Metropolitan Association for Improving the Dwellings of the Industrious Classes had been founded as early as 1841, and in 1844, after the publication of the first

[1] P.P., *Second Report on State of Large Towns*, part I, pp. 10–137.
[2] Finer, p. 295.

report of the Royal Commission on the State of Large Towns and Populous Places, both the Society for the Improvement of the Condition of the Labouring Classes and the Health of Towns Association were established. The latter was a frankly propagandist body, formed 'for the purpose of diffusing among the people the information obtained by recent enquiries' into sanitary conditions. It produced reports and organized lectures, and its comprehensive membership, which included both Whig and Tory politicians as well as clergy and doctors, gave added weight to its activities.[1] By the end of 1847 the government could dilly-dally no longer; cholera was on the march once more in the Orient and had already reached Moscow. Public opinion, as voiced by a well-organized minority, demanded action. In September 1847 Chadwick was put in charge of yet another Royal Commission, to enquire into 'what special means may be requisite for the Health of the Metropolis', and in February 1848 the government introduced another Public Health Bill to deal with the rest of the country.

The next eight years, 1848 to 1855, were crucial in the history not only of the public health movement throughout the whole country, but of the local government of London as well. In London the fight for improved sanitation necessarily involved the reform of the whole field of metropolitan administration. The struggle between the supporters of Chadwick's programme of centralized control by nominated Commissioners and the anti-centralization school, led by the City Corporation and backed by the local vestries and a powerful lobby both in and out of Parliament, resulted in the victory of the latter. The precedents set by Peel's Metropolitan Police Act of 1829 and the Municipal Corporations Act of 1835 were followed again. The City was not assimilated. Against all odds it justified its continuance as a separate sanitary authority, thanks wholly to its first Medical Officer of Health, John Simon, while Chadwick's attempts to obtain central control over metropolitan drainage, water supply and burial grounds collapsed. In 1854 Chadwick was forced into retirement, and when the local government of London was at last reformed in the following year, the establishment of the Metropolitan Board of Works marked the triumph of the City, the vestries, the water companies and the anti-centralizers. During the thirty-four years of its career the Board did not prove a success, except in the matter of main drainage, and it finally collapsed in ignominy and corruption in 1889.

[1] Finer, pp. 237–9.

Within this wider conflict over the whole future shape of metropolitan local government there also existed an inner confrontation over the future shape of public health administration. Here the final outcome was not so clear-cut. Chadwick's erroneous devotion to the theory of 'epidemic atmosphere', that smell meant disease, demanded a programme of sanitary engineering for the removal of the smells. His arterial system of drainage, based on a plentiful water supply and small earthenware pipes to provide a flow of liquid powerful enough to make the drains largely self-cleansing, provided the solution for the hitherto baffling problem of urban drainage. But his passionate desire to exploit the commercial possibilities of the resultant liquid manure for agricultural purposes proved wrong-headed. So too, more significantly, did his contempt for the contribution which preventive medicine could make in the improvement of public health. He represented engineering and centralized administration, while Simon in the City represented preventive medicine and local management. Time was to show, after many years of endeavour, that it was only through the combination of these two approaches, and after a great extension of medical knowledge, that any substantial fall would occur in the remorseless incidence of death.

The battle over all these various conceptions began in November 1847, when, within less than two months of its appointment, Chadwick's Royal Commission on the Health of the Metropolis presented its first report. Under the terrifying threat of another attack of cholera it recommended that as a stop-gap measure all the Crown Commissions of Sewers in London should be revoked and superseded by a single new Commission for the whole metropolitan area. Within a fortnight this had been done – such was the sense of urgency – and the thousand members of seven separate Commissions were replaced by twenty-three Commissioners responsible for all London except the City, where the old Commission survived because it was not a Crown appointment. Most of the new Commissioners were chosen for their compliance with Chadwick's views, but a few representatives of the old régime were included as a sop to the local vestries. The new Commissioners forthwith started on an energetic programme of flushing out the sewers with water in order to disperse the smells which supposedly propagated cholera and other zymotic diseases.[1]

The anti-centralizers were alarmed. But they were still more enraged

[1] P.P., 1847–8(888), vol. xxxii, *First Report of Royal Commission on Means for the Improvement of the Health of the Metropolis*; Lewis, pp. 156–7.

at the terms of the Public Health Bill which Lord Morpeth, the First Commissioner of Woods and Forests, introduced early in 1848. When this Bill became law in August it established a General Board of Health consisting of three members, with the First Commissioner of Woods and Forests as president. The Board could initiate sanitary measures in any locality where the death rate reached 23 per 1,000, or upon receipt of a petition from one-tenth of the ratepayers. In either of these cases a local Board of Health was to be established by Order in Council with wide powers over drainage, building regulation, nuisance removal and water supply. Town councils could exercise these powers in places where they already existed, subject to the same conditions. Money for capital works such as drainage could be raised by mortgaging the rates, subject to the General Board's consent. The Act did not apply to London, and it was limited to five years' duration.[1]

The Public Health Bill, and the promise that it would shortly be followed by a similar measure for London, evoked passionate hostility in many quarters. It was a threat to local freedom and a dangerous extension of bureaucracy. 'The principles of the Bill,' it was said, 'would breed a revolution even in Russia, if attempted there.'[2] In London and in Parliament itself this opposition was led by the City, and violent pamphlet war ensued between the champions of local elective sanitary administration, who claimed that the existing arrangements were perfectly satisfactory, and the critics, led by the Health of Towns Association, who claimed that the City Commission of Sewers was 'the most inefficient and the most wasteful in the country'. The City enjoyed the vociferous support of the local vestries and pavement trusts. Since the radical agitation of 1828–30 against the select vestries, most vestrymen were small tradesmen and shopkeepers whose sole concern, to keep the rates down, had produced a régime of contemptibly petty meanness. Their very existence was now threatened by the possibility of a Crown-appointed Commission on Chadwickian lines; while the alternative, an elected municipality for the whole of London, was equally repulsive to Parliament, where it was thought that the influence of the City Corporation, representing only a tiny fraction of the whole metropolitan area, was already powerful enough.

The impasse was finally resolved by a 'deal' made between the Corporation and the government. In order to prevent the absorption of its own

[1] Lewis, pp. 172–6.

[2] Quoted in Asa Briggs, 'Public Health: The Sanitary Idea', in *The Origins of the Social Services*, published by *New Society*, 1968.

independent Commission of Sewers, as envisaged in the government's impending sanitary Bill for London, the City Corporation had promoted a rival Bill of its own, enlarging the powers of its Commission. In the summer of 1848 the government agreed to allow the City's Bill to proceed, on condition that the Corporation sent representatives to the government's Metropolitan Commission of Sewers whenever main drainage was to be discussed. The City thus maintained its independence and abandoned its discreditable allies in opposition, the suburban vestries and paving trusts, whom the government could now afford to defy. By the autumn both Bills had become law.[1]

So by the end of 1848 the entire sanitary landscape had been refashioned. First there was the General Board of Health, whose three members were Lord Morpeth, Lord Ashley (better known as Lord Shaftesbury), and Chadwick himself, with powers in the provincial towns. Next there was the new Metropolitan Commission of Sewers, equipped by the government's Act with extensive new powers over the drainage of all London except the City and dominated by Chadwick, who was a member of it and who was determined that in the next parliamentary session it should absorb street paving and cleansing and even the water companies. Lastly there was the City Commission of Sewers, also equipped with a new Act, but which provided for the appointment of a new-fangled person called a Medical Officer of Health. Soon the rival authorities in London were to be put to the test by the worst attack of cholera ever experienced in Britain.

The City of London in 1848 had changed little during the previous fifty years. Its wealthier inhabitants were moving out to the suburbs, as they had begun to do before 1800, and poorer people were moving in. The population reached its maximum nineteenth-century figure of 129,128 in 1851, and thereafter declined rapidly. But in 1848 the extensive displacement of houses and tenements by new warehouses, offices and banks had hardly begun. The City was still, as it had been for centuries, an overcrowded place where people lived at or near their work. The Corporation had triumphantly survived an abortive Royal Commission of Inquiry in 1837, and still presided without any outside interference whatever over its vast inherited revenues, powerful, extravagant, smug and perhaps corrupt.

The City Commission of Sewers was an autonomous body comprising

[1] Finer, pp. 328-9.

the Lord Mayor, Aldermen and one Common Councilman from each ward. Over the years it had built some forty-four miles of huge sewers, and compared with the rest of London, or with the large provincial towns, it had reason to be proud of its record. But less than half the 16,000 separate buildings in the City were as yet connected to the sewers, and within the square mile there were over 5,400 cesspools. Housing conditions in the peripheries, in the filthy dilapidated tenements off Bishopsgate, Aldgate and Farringdon, were as bad as any in the whole of London. Water was scarce, thousands of sheep and cattle still fouled the streets on their way to Smithfield Market, and some 1,800 bodies were still being buried each year in the eighty-eight ancient parish graveyards. Until 1848 the City authorities had made no attempt to deal with any of these problems. They were indeed unaware that a sanitary problem existed.[1]

It is therefore not surprising that the City Sewers Act of 1848, which had only been promoted as a means to preserve the City's independence, was largely copied from a provincial exemplar, Liverpool's Sanitary Act of 1846, with some clauses taken from Lord Morpeth's Public Health Act of 1848. But this Act was none the less an enduring landmark. All sewers were vested in the Commissioners, and no new houses were to be built without drains connected to the street sewers (if any such existed). The Commissioners could compel the owners of property within fifty feet of a sewer to make a connection with it, and they were given full power to control private cesspools. All new houses were to have water cisterns, while the owners of existing buildings could be compelled to provide them. But the Act went further, for it permitted the Commissioners to enter houses and cleanse them if there was reason to believe that their filthiness constituted a threat to public health; and in the case of common lodging-houses which the Medical Officer of Health considered to be overcrowded or diseased, the Commissioners could even decide what number of lodgers should be accommodated there in future.

The effectiveness of the Act would depend largely upon the calibre of the Medical Officer, for many of the powers granted were only permissive, not obligatory. Even the appointment of a Medical Officer at all was discretionary, and as at that time there was only one such person in all England – Dr W. H. Duncan, appointed at Liverpool in 1847 – the City Commissioners of Sewers would probably have spared themselves the expense, had it not been for the impending threat of another outbreak of

[1] Royston Lambert, *Sir John Simon 1816-1904 and English Social Administration*, 1963, pp. 74-88, an outstanding work to which I am heavily indebted.

cholera. So they decided to have a temporary, part-time M.O., and in October 1848 they chose Dr John Simon.[1]

Simon was to become the leading figure in the second generation of sanitary reformers, just as Chadwick had been the pioneer in the early years. He was now aged thirty-two, with a growing private practice outside the City. But it was in the City that he was to win fame, and paradoxically it was at least in part because his appointment there was only part-time that he was able to maintain a position of personal independence from the Corporation which would have been impossible if he had been a salaried full-time official.

During the eight short months between his appointment and the appearance of cholera in the City in June 1849 he built the framework of an entirely new local medico-sanitary administration. He organized weekly returns of all deaths, and, with more difficulty, of pauper sickness too, while the City police were employed to provide reports of street nuisances. On the basis of this information Simon was able to send out the four City Inspectors of Nuisances to compel the cleansing of privies, the suppression of cesspools and the removal of dung and excrement. He persuaded the New River Company to supply water twice instead of only once a day in some of the filthiest alleys. His office became the hub of sanitary information and sanitary action. He battled with his masters, the Commissioners of Sewers, to whom he reported weekly, and many of whom regarded his activities at first with suspicion and then with hostility. Above all, he showed that he was a man who could not be ignored.

When the cholera arrived the City police were used to inspect all the houses in the poorer districts, and when their constant reports of nuisances inundated the Inspectors of Nuisances, Simon persuaded the Commissioners to treble the number of inspectors. The wholesale compulsory removal of filth probably reduced the spread of the disease by contact, but the frequent flushing of the sewers, which Simon, like Chadwick, believed would remove the supposedly infectious smells, had a fatally adverse effect, and in August 1849 the epidemic became water-borne. The mortality rate in the City leapt up to one hundred victims a week. The incidence of the disease, hitherto largely confined to the filthy poor, now became indiscriminate and attacked everyone drinking infected water, whatever their social class might be.

As the deaths mounted Simon extended his activities from the field of prevention to that of treatment. He tried to persuade the Poor Law

[1] Lambert, pp. 88–109.

T

Guardians of the three Unions within the City to provide cholera wards in their workhouses, temporary accommodation to which the inhabitants of cholera-infested houses might retreat, and medical house-to-house visitation of the poor districts to find and treat new cases of cholera in their early stages. Two of the Unions partially complied, but the third refused to do anything. At last the Corporation itself agreed to act, prompted by the bitter criticism of *The Times*. A committee consisting of Simon and the Poor Law Medical Officers (who had previously refused to help in the organization of preventive measures) was set up to visit every substandard house, and five thousand families were visited daily. By this time, however, the epidemic was declining, and by the middle of October 1849 it was over. During the previous three months 854 people had died of cholera in the City alone.[1]

'The cholera is the best of all sanitary reformers,' commented *The Times*, 'it overlooks no mistake and pardons no oversight.' In the City it gave Simon an opportunity to expose the full extent of the sanitary problem in the most uncompromising terms, and it provided him with powerful allies. First there were the Poor Law Medical Officers, who now co-operated in providing him with weekly information about sickness prevalent among the poor. On the Corporation itself he had won the ardent support of a small group of active sanitarians among the Councilmen, while the 'dirty party' (whose leader was impolitely nicknamed the 'Defender of the Filth') was in disarray, at least for the moment. Most important of all, *The Times* took up the cause of sanitary reform in the City, and launched a series of bitter attacks on the complacency and obscurantism of the Corporation. With the backing of public opinion, Simon could now go over to the attack.[2]

This he did in November 1849, when he presented the Corporation with his first annual report, a classic document in the history of nineteenth-century sanitary improvement. He began by confronting his readers with the stark fact that the annual death rate in the City, at 30 per 1,000 living, was nearly three times as great as in the metropolitan suburbs with the lowest mortality. In some sub-districts of the City inhabited by the poor the rate reached higher still, to 36 and even 40 per 1,000. From these indisputable facts he went on to analyse the causes of this appalling waste of life. There were six headings – defective house drainage, inadequate water supply, offensive trades and occupations, intramural burials, houses 'absolutely unfit for habitation', and 'the personal habits of the lowest

[1] Lambert, pp. 113–31.   [2] Lambert, pp. 131, 139–41.

classes, and the influence of destitution in increasing their mortality'. 'Animals will scarcely thrive in an atmosphere of their own decomposing excrements,' the Corporation was informed, 'yet such, strictly and literally speaking, is the air which a very large proportion of the inhabitants of the City are condemned to breathe.' Water supply must 'be looked at almost as though it were today broached for the first time', the 138 slaughterhouses within the City must be abolished, and all burials must cease. In the poorer quarters the Corporation should buy and demolish whole series of courts and alleys where the existing houses were beyond redemption, and it should build model dwellings and lodging-houses and provide public baths and laundries. 'The poor of a Christian country can no longer, in their own ignorance and helplessness, be suffered to encounter all the chances which accompany destitution, and which link it often indissolubly, to recklessness, profligacy, and perdition. Never, he concluded, in all its long history, 'has the Corporation had so grand an opportunity as now for the achievement of an unlimited good'. To it, now, 'the Country looks for the perfection of a sanitary scheme which shall serve as model and example to other municipal bodies undertaking the same responsibility'.[1]

The Corporation had never had a report like this before – none of their officers, indeed, had ever hitherto thought of presenting an annual report at all. After so recent and so terrible a visitation of cholera, sanitary matters were very much in the news, and the London newspapers printed the report in full, all seventy-one pages of it. Simon and the City Medical Officership of Health became famous all over the country. But the impact of the report was not merely a legacy of the cholera. What gave it its peculiar force was that it emanated not from Chadwick, the arch-centralizer, and the General Board of Health in Whitehall, already the source of many sanitary reports, but from an officer of the City Corporation itself, the arch-protagonist of the cause of local self-government.[2]

For by this time Chadwick and centralized administration had suffered a severe set-back in London. The General Board of Health still stood high in public estimation, but the unified Metropolitan Commission of Sewers was in disgrace.

In the autumn of 1848, with cholera imminent, an Act rushed through

[1] John Simon, *Reports relating to the Sanitary Condition of the City of London*, 1854, pp. 1–71.
[2] Lambert, p. 143.

Parliament had conferred emergency powers on the new General Board, authorizing it to give directions to the local authorities, including the Boards of Guardians, for the removal of nuisances and the prevention of disease. The Board's original three members, Lord Morpeth, Lord Ashley and Chadwick, all devoted sanitarians, had now been reinforced by a fourth, medical, member, Dr Southwood Smith. They had forthwith issued directions about what should be done, but almost everywhere the local Poor Law Guardians refused to obey, and the Act had been so hurriedly drawn that the General Board had no powers of compulsion. In Whitechapel, on the day on which the first case of cholera occurred, the Guardians decided that the General Board's directions 'need not be acted on in this Union'. In St Pancras the Guardians refused to appoint the extra staff needed for the house-to-house visiting demanded by Chadwick, while in Bethnal Green, where mortality was particularly high, the Guardians declined to provide either dispensary or hospital, or to cleanse infected houses. At the notorious Tooting 'baby farm', where some 1,400 pauper children were boarded out by the Metropolitan Guardians, there were 300 cases of cholera, 180 of them fatal, before the remaining children were withdrawn. Chadwick, by contrast, as soon as he heard that the sewer there was a stagnant open ditch, at once sent a platoon of fifty navvies to construct emergency drains. But with an exiguous staff, inadequate powers and charged with the direction of operations all over the country, not just in London, the task was quite beyond the General Board. Even the minutes of meetings were not kept, such was the pressure of business, and both the staff and all the members of the Board were ill at one time or another – even Chadwick himself, at last. But they had at least shown where the fault lay.[1]

The record of the Metropolitan Commission of Sewers was very different. It will be recalled that in December 1847, with cholera impending, one small unified Commission for the whole of London except the City had been appointed. In the autumn of 1848 the new Commission was granted extensive new powers over London's drainage, and with Chadwick and his allies in control of the Commission the moment for far-reaching action appeared to have arrived at last. But the opportunity was wasted. Chadwick himself was overwhelmed with work at the General Board of Health and at the Commission's offices in Greek Street, Soho, he insisted, probably rightly, that the building of a new system of main drainage could not begin until the Ordnance Survey had made detailed maps. For this delay he was assailed by his enemies on the Commission,

[1] Lewis, pp. 188, 201, 205–6; Finer, pp. 344, 349.

a minority drawn from the London vestries, the permanent staff became involved in the Commissioners' dissensions, and when in the spring of 1849 the general principles of drainage for the whole of London, and of Westminster in particular, could at last be considered, rival schemes were promoted, exacerbated by personal animosities. With cholera at its height in the summer, squabbling of this kind, much of it retailed in *The Times*, did not present an edifying spectacle.[1]

On one subject, however, Chadwick had had his way, and this proved to be disastrous. As a dedicated miasmatist he had insisted that the sewers should be systematically flushed. Excrement infected with cholera was poured into just those stretches of the Thames from which several of the water companies drew their supplies, and in July 1849 the epidemic became water-borne. The deaths in London rose from 246 in June to 6,644 in September; and just at this very moment a young doctor, John Snow, published a short pamphlet, based on his work in Southwark and Wandsworth, in which he asserted that cholera was not inhaled through the air, but swallowed with water contaminated by infected excreta.[2]

Flushing the sewers was at last stopped, but with the onset of colder weather the epidemic was already on the decline. Some 14,000 people had died in London alone and in the whole of England and Wales since September 1848, some 53,000 – probably an under-estimate. The Metropolitan Commission of Sewers had been totally discredited, and in September 1849 Chadwick himself, the arch-flusher, was removed from it. Even without him it was to prove no more effective during the remaining six years of its existence, and the construction of London's main drainage system had to wait until the new Metropolitan Board of Works took it in hand in 1855.[3]

Thus by the end of 1849 Chadwick and his fellow sanitarians at the General Board of Health had lost their grip on London. Sewers, the central feature of Chadwick's arterial system of drainage, had been removed from their authority, but there still remained two subjects to which the Board could address itself in London – the burial grounds, under the powers of a Nuisance Removal Act passed in August 1849, and the water supply, the investigation of which had devolved upon the Board from the now defunct Royal Commission of 1847 on the Health of the Metropolis.[4] In London,

[1] Finer, pp. 355–75.　　　　　　　　　　[2] Finer, p. 347; Longmate, p. 183.
[3] Finer, pp. 346, 349, 376–7; Longmate, p. 180.
[4] P.P., 1850, vol. xxii, *Report of the General Board of Health on the Supply of Water to the Metropolis*, p. 2; Lewis, p. 238.

from which it was in all other matters now excluded, these two subjects now engaged the whole attention of the Board. A general mêlée ensued between the Board, the Metropolitan Commission of Sewers, the vestries, the water companies and the Government, in which the principal casualties were the Board itself and the efficient progress of metropolitan sanitary administration.

For the London burial grounds Chadwick already had a scheme ready, based on his report of 1843. All the ancient intramural churchyards and burial grounds were to be closed and new national cemeteries were to be established outside the built-up area under the management of a public Burial Board. In order to make the scheme financially self-supporting this Board was to have a complete monopoly of all burials, and therefore the eight recently formed joint stock cemetery companies must be compulsorily acquired. A large initial loan would be required, which would be paid off in due course from the Board's receipts.[1]

The Bill to establish this scheme became law, amazingly, in August 1850, with the General Board of Health acting as the Burial Board. It evoked widespread hostility, particularly from the vestries, the clergy and the undertakers, and just at this moment the strength of the Board was greatly impaired by the retirement of Lord Morpeth, who had recently succeeded to the Earldom of Carlisle. His successor, Lord Seymour, was obstructive to the whole idea of sanitary reform and often absent from the Board's meetings. The financial viability of the whole scheme depended on the establishment of the public monopoly of burials, but the Treasury would only agree to advance the capital for the initial purchase of one or two of the joint stock cemetery companies, and money was not to be had from commercial sources in the City because the General Board of Health could not offer adequate security, its statutory life being limited to five years from 1848. Eventually only one of the eight cemeteries – that at Brompton – was bought, and after eighteen months none of the festering old graveyards had been closed. In 1852 the Act of 1850 was repealed. The vestries were empowered to provide their own new grounds outside the built-up area, and the Home Secretary was authorized to close down the old ones piecemeal. It was left to Lord Palmerston, who happened to be Home Secretary from 1852 to 1855, to execute this long-awaited reform with his usual jaunty efficiency.[2]

[1] P.P., 1850 (1158), vol. xxi, *Report on a General Scheme of Extra-Mural Sepulture*, pp. 115–16.

[2] Finer, pp. 401, 413, 422, 456.

Here at least there was progress, despite rather than because of the General Board of Health, but over water supply the outcome was not so fortunate. With incredible rapidity the Board had in May 1850 produced a three-hundred-page report on the metropolitan water supply, plus as many pages of appendixes. It demanded that the use of Thames water should cease in favour of new sources, pure and filtered, to be drawn from the Farnham area of Surrey. The eight existing companies should be amalgamated and a high-pressure, constant supply be everywhere provided. Lastly, it was absolutely necessary 'to consolidate under one and the same management, the whole works for the supply of water, and for the drainage of the metropolis'.[1]

This was carrying war into the enemy's camp with a vengeance. The vestries, the Metropolitan Commission of Sewers and the water companies were all up in arms, and a formidable opposition was mounted. An Association of Parochial Representatives was formed to press for the parochial management of both water and the nominated Commission of Sewers. With the vestries in full cry, with growing doubts about the viability of providing water from Farnham, and with a hundred water-company shareholders in the House of Commons, Lord John Russell's government wavered. Then early in 1852 it fell and was replaced by a short-lived minority administration under Lord Derby. This was not the time to challenge such a formidable array of vested interests, and so the Metropolitan Water Act of 1852, which settled the subject in broad outline for the next fifty years, contained no provision for the unified administration of water and drains, or even for the amalgamation of the various water companies. By 1855-6 the companies were to cease drawing any supplies from the Thames below Teddington. They were to cover their reservoirs and 'effectually' filter their water, and within five years they were to provide a constant supply if four-fifths of the consumers in any district demanded it. The Board of Trade was given general powers of supervision, but the companies' charges were not limited and their monopoly was in effect confirmed.[2]

So ended the last chance to establish a single authority for the administration of metropolitan water and drainage. The Metropolitan Commission of Sewers proceeded on its ineffective course, now dominated by the civil engineers and men of practical affairs – Thomas Cubitt, Robert

[1] P.P., *Report on the Supply of Water to the Metropolis*, pp. 312–25.
[2] Reddaway, pp. 129–30; Finer, p. 403.

Stephenson, Sir Morton Peto and Philip Hardwick, the last three of whom had all been concerned in the building of the London and Birmingham Railway. They were used to building bricklined railway tunnels, so they naturally favoured large-bore brick-lined sewers, but the sewer which they started to build on these lines in the new Victoria Street promptly collapsed. Shortly afterwards Chadwick published a statement again advocating the use of small-bore earthenware pipes, but even he was confounded (for the moment) when a virulent outbreak of fever at Croydon in November 1852 was attributed to the defective working of the small-bore arterial system of drainage which had very recently been installed there. By 1853 London was exasperated beyond endurance at the interminable bickering and the almost total lack of progress.[1]

But there had been progress in one part of London – in the City. There the new Medical Officer of Health had not been able to achieve all the objectives which he had set before the astonished Corporation in his first annual report in 1849, but he had gone some way. Another City Sewers Act, passed in 1851, had put the Medical Officership on a permanent basis and greatly enlarged the City Commission's powers, notably in the control of markets, noxious trades and slum housing. Simon had established permanent administrative machinery for the systematic visitation of the dwellings of the poor, and had won the support of most of the Councilmen, who controlled the City's purse. During the rumpus caused in 1850 by the appointment of a Royal Commission to enquire into Smithfield Market Simon had kept tactfully in the background. The Commission had recommended the removal of the live-cattle market, and the Corporation had decided to retain it. It was no doubt due to Simon's influence that this decision was subsequently reversed, and by 1855 the live market had been moved to Islington. Over sixty churchyards were closed for burials, and it was Simon who persuaded the Corporation to establish its own cemetery at Manor Park, Essex, opened in 1856 and still in use. In his fifth annual report, presented in November 1853, he was already looking out from the new model which he had built in the City towards the wider horizons of the still disorganized sanitary landscape of London as a whole.[2]

It was at this moment that cholera returned to England once more. When it reached London in the summer of 1854 it attacked its usual haunts in the poorest districts of Southwark and Lambeth, and also in the closely packed district of Soho, where Dr John Snow lived. Here, in an area only some 250 yards wide, over 500 people died within ten days. Most

[1] Finer, pp. 380, 441–8.   [2] Lambert, pp. 161, 188, 191, 197–8.

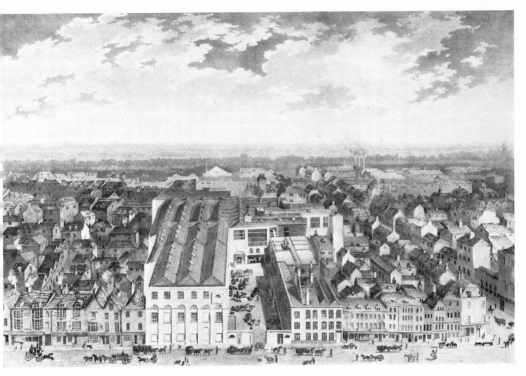

25 Brown and Parry's Brewery in Golden Lane, 1807

26 Entrance to the Regent's Canal at Limehouse

27 Thomas Cubitt's yard and works, Pimlico, looking west, *c.* 1845–50

28 The West India Docks from the south-east, c. 1830

29 Unloading a collier

of the residents obtained their water from a single pump in Broad Street, and when Snow was able to persuade the local Board of Guardians to prevent the use of this source by chaining up the handle of the pump, the outbreak ended with the same dramatic suddenness as it had begun. But in the City Simon at least was ready. Of the 10,738 fatal cases in the whole of London, only 211 were in the City. Whereas in 1849 the City's victims had amounted to one-twentieth of the total metropolitan deaths, now they amounted to less than one-fiftieth.[1]

It was at this moment, too, when the London reputation of Chadwick and the General Board of Health and all that they stood for was at its lowest, while that of the City stood high, that the whole future shape of metropolitan administration was about to be decided for the next thirty-five years. The statutory limit to the life of the Board, as provided in the Public Health Act of 1848, was about to expire. In July 1854 Palmerston proposed that the Board should be placed under the control of the Home Secretary and its existence continued for another two years. But there was a formidable opposition afoot, amounting, in Professor Finer's opinion, to 'a conspiracy of "interests"'. The agitation was largely a London affair, got up by the water companies with the backing of the vestries and the engineers for the maintenance of their vested interests under the high-sounding pretext of the defence of local self-government against un-English centralization. A 'Private Enterprise Society', which produced a series of pamphlets purporting to defend the public interest, was in reality got up by the water companies, and its sparsely-attended meetings were only attended by the companies' adherents. In Parliament the lobbies were crowded with water engineers, while the members themselves were either indifferent, or absent or water-company shareholders. Sir Benjamin Hall, one of the members for Marylebone and the spokesman of the re-doubtable vestry there, carried all before him. Chadwick was a dangerous and unscrupulous man, his ideas were 'mischievous vagaries and extrava-gances', and he and Dr Southwood Smith must go. 'For God's sake,' he concluded, pay them their salaries 'and send them about their business if you believe they have been of service to the State; but it is impossible to get on with them'.[2]

Even Palmerston could not withstand such a concerted onslaught. Reluctantly, he asked Chadwick to resign, and Lord Shaftesbury and Southwood Smith at once followed him out. But even then, with cholera raging in London, Palmerston's Bill for the temporary continuance of the

[1] Lambert, pp. 204–5; Longmate, p. 192.   [2] Finer, pp. 462–7.

General Board of Health was defeated in what he afterwards described as 'the foulest vote I have ever known in all my parliamentary experience'. The age of Chadwick was over; the anti-centralizers and the vested interests had won at last after six years of struggle; and their triumph was complete when in August 1854 it was announced that the President of the newly-constituted Board of Health which was quickly established was to be no less a person than Sir Benjamin Hall himself.[1]

Nearly twenty years had now elapsed since the Municipal Corporations Act of 1835 had reformed the administration of all the principal towns throughout the country. Only London, by far the largest city of all, remained unprovided for, the City Corporation itself still unreformed and the rapidly proliferating suburbs as chaotic as ever. In 1835 the government had promised a Bill to reform the City, but in 1852, when this promise was still unfulfilled, a Royal Commission had been established to enquire again into the state of the City Corporation. By this time even such an ardent defender of the established order as Joshua Toulmin Smith could declare without exaggeration that 'the present condition of this huge metropolis exhibits the most extraordinary anomaly in England. Abounding in wealth and intelligence, by far the greater part of it is yet absolutely without any municipal government whatever.'[2]

The Royal Commission reported in 1854. It advocated far-reaching reform of the Corporation, including the abolition of the Courts of Aldermen and Common Hall and the amalgamation of the City police with the metropolitan force. But it jibbed at the extension of the City's boundaries on the grounds that 'a municipal administration of an excessive magnitude' would be created. Instead, it recommended for the suburbs the establishment of seven new municipal councils for the seven existing metropolitan parliamentary boroughs, and a Metropolitan Board of Works for the whole London area, to be composed of representatives chosen by the seven new councils and the City Corporation. In March 1855 the Home Secretary stated that a Bill for the reform of the City Corporation founded on these recommendations was in preparation, but that the Bills then being drafted by Sir Benjamin Hall for the whole metropolitan area should be considered first.[3]

---

[1] Finer, pp. 468–73.

[2] Joshua Toulmin Smith, *The Metropolis and the Municipal Administration*, p. 6.

[3] P.P., 1854 (1772), vol. xxvi, *Report of Royal Commission on the existing State of the Corporation of the City of London*, pp. xxxv–xxxviii; *Hansard, Third Series*, vol. 137, 6 March 1855, col. 190.

But once again the City Corporation survived, for the Bill which the Home Secretary did introduce in 1856 never reached the statute book. The opportunity for the comprehensive reform of metropolitan local government was missed, for Sir Benjamin Hall's Bill for the suburbs fell far short of even the tentative recommendations made by the Royal Commission. Today Sir Benjamin is much more widely remembered for his connection with the great bell erected in the clock tower of the new Houses of Parliament, which was at once nicknamed Big Ben, than as a founding father of efficient metropolitan administration.

As finally enacted after prolonged debate, the Metropolis Management Act of 1855[1] applied to an area of some 74,000 acres – an area which remained substantially unchanged until the establishment of the Greater London Council in 1965. Instead of the Royal Commission's seven municipal councils Sir Benjamin Hall set up thirty-eight units of metropolitan administration. In the twenty-three largest parishes, such as Kensington or Islington, the ancient vestries were retained in reconstituted form, the vestrymen being elected for three years by all householders rated for the poor rate at not less than £40, or in poorer districts £25. The remaining smaller parishes, such as St Paul's, Covent Garden, were grouped together in fifteen district boards, whose members were to be elected not directly by the electors but by each constituent parish vestry. These thirty-eight bodies plus the Common Council of the City Corporation were in their turn to elect the members of a new central body, the Metropolitan Board of Works. The Common Council elected three members, the six largest vestries elected two each, and the remainder were chosen by the other seventeen vestries and the district boards. One-third of the members of the Metropolitan Board were to retire each year.

The main function of the Metropolitan Board of Works was to design and construct 'a system of sewerage which should prevent all or any part of the sewage within the metropolis from passing into the Thames in or near the metropolis'. The building and maintenance of local sewers was to be the responsibility of the vestries and district boards, but the Metropolitan Board was to have powers of general control. It could also make or widen highways to improve communication between one part of London and another, and under a separate Act also passed in 1855 it acquired extensive powers for the regulation of buildings, some of which had hitherto been exercised since 1844 by the Office of Metropolitan Buildings. All these powers were supplemented by the duty to make bye-laws

[1] 18 and 19 Vict. c. 120.

for the regulation of sanitation, new streets and general standards of building.

The vestries and district boards were to manage local sewage and drainage. They could compel owners of existing houses to construct drains into the common sewer, and no new houses were to be built without proper drains and 'sufficient' sanitary conveniences. They were to be responsible for street paving, lighting and cleansing, and they could make local street improvements. They were to regulate underground vaults and cellars, remove projections and obstructions and enforce the cleansing of houses. They were designated as the metropolitan authorities for the enforcement of an important new Nuisances Removal Act[1] applicable to the whole country, and each one of them was to appoint its own Medical Officer of Health and Inspectors of Nuisances.

The Metropolis Management Act of 1855 was a turning-point in London's complicated sanitary history. It put an end to both select and open vestries, to innumerable *ad hoc* paving and lighting trusts and commissions, and it gave London a sanitary code roughly analogous to that of the rest of the country. It was indeed the first legislative attempt to tackle the problem of metropolitan local government as a whole – or at any rate, almost as a whole, for the City was still virtually exempt. But it nevertheless contained very considerable shortcomings. With thirty-eight district authorities still in existence, metropolitan administration was, on the one hand, still absurdly fragmented, while on the other hand the system of indirect election to the Metropolitan Board, coupled with the continuing existence of the City Corporation, provided insuperable obstacles to the Board's becoming the focal point of any metropolitan feeling of municipal pride and enterprise analogous to that later achieved in Birmingham by Joseph Chamberlain. The Board's powers were, moreover, extremely limited. It had no power to appoint a Medical Officer of Health to advise on matters affecting the health of London as a whole, and worse still, it was unable to compel negligent vestries and district boards either to execute their statutory duties or to enforce the Board's own bye-laws.[2] In the course of time it did acquire important additional powers in the fields of slum clearance and the formation of parks and open spaces, and in 1866 it took over control of the fire brigade. But throughout its whole career the Board was often handicapped by inadequate power, notably in the field of slum

[1] 18 and 19 Vict. c. 121.

[2] William A. Robson, *The Government and Misgovernment of London*, 1948 edn, p. 61.

clearance, where it could only sell or lease ground for the erection of labouring-class accommodation but had no power to spend money itself for this purpose, and where until 1884 it was obliged to sell all surplus lands acquired for street improvements within ten years of the completion of the works.[1] Yet even such exiguous powers as it did possess were regarded as excessive by some Members of Parliament, one of whom, during the debates of 1855, denounced 'this system of centralization' as 'repugnant to our principles and our taste, which have hitherto always encouraged local self-government'.[2]

The inadequacy of the Board's powers was the chief reason for more delay over the construction of the main drainage system. The Act of 1855 required the Board to submit its plans for the approval of the Chief Commissioner of Works. In May 1856 the Board did so, the plans having been prepared by (Sir) Joseph Bazalgette, who had been chief engineer of the Metropolitan Commission of Sewers before being appointed to the same post under the Board. The Chief Commissioner, Sir Benjamin Hall, objected to parts of the scheme and referred the whole matter to three consulting engineers. In July 1857 they condemned the Board's proposals and produced alternative designs of their own, the estimated cost of construction of which was £5,437,265, more than double that for Bazalgette's scheme. The Board naturally refused to adopt these proposals, and in its turn referred them to consulting engineers, who reported in April 1858 that the true cost would be between £7,000,000 and £11,000,000, and that anyway the whole scheme 'might be regarded as impracticable'. Thus after nearly two and a half years of bickering no progress whatever had been made.[3]

But Parliament itself was being inconvenienced by its own dilatoriness. With the continued presence of vast masses of untreated sewage in the river, the Thames stank unbearably in hot weather, and not even the windows of the splendid new Houses of Parliament could keep out the smell. In July 1857 Sir Benjamin Hall was asked 'whether he has any plan for the prevention of the pestilential stench which comes every evening into every window on the river front of the Houses of Parliament'.[4] Sir Benjamin had

---

[1] *Survey of London*, vol. xxxi, 1963, pp. 69, 71.

[2] *Hansard, Third Series*, vol. 138, 14 May 1855, col. 570.

[3] P.P., 1861 (476), vol. viii, *Third Report of Select Committee on Metropolis Local Taxation*, p. x.

[4] *Hansard, Third Series*, vol. 147, 30 July 1857, col. 709.

indeed got a plan – he would refer the matter to Mr (later Sir) Golds-
worthy Gurney, the distinguished inventor, for his consideration; and in
due course Mr Gurney reported. All London's sewage, he considered,
should be discharged into the Thames *within* the metropolis.[1] In April
1858 this surprising conclusion was referred to a Select Committee of the
House of Commons. Summer stinks would soon be returning; the matter
was urgent. But even so the Committee spent nearly three months in
collecting some three hundred pages of evidence before reporting that it
could not recommend Mr Gurney's plan. But the Committee did excogi-
tate one massive piece of common sense, for it stated that 'the expediency
of applying a system of deodorization to the sewage of the metropolis
belongs rather to the functions of the Metropolitan Board of Works
than to those of a Committee of the House of Commons, and the
Metropolitan Board of Works have ample means of making all necessary
enquiries on that subject without the assistance of a Committee of the
House of Commons.'[2]

Lord Derby's government had already come to the same view, but
before a Bill could be prepared the summer stinks had come again, with
dramatic results. On 30 June 1858 officers in one of the corridors of the
Houses of Parliament

> were suddenly surprised by the members of a committee rushing out
> of one of the rooms in the greatest haste and confusion . . . foremost
> among them being the Chancellor of the Exchequer [Disraeli], who,
> with a mass of papers in one hand and with his pocket handkerchief
> clutched in the other, and applied closely to his nose, with body
> half bent, hastened in dismay from the pestilential odour, followed
> closely by Sir James Graham, who seemed to be attacked by a sudden
> fit of expectoration; Mr Gladstone also paid particular attention to
> his nose, while . . . the other members of the committee also pre-
> cipitately quitted the pestilential apartment, the disordered state of
> their papers, which they carried in their hands, showing how impera-
> tively they had received notice to quit.[3]

A fortnight later Disraeli introduced the government's Bill, without
even waiting for the publication of the report on Mr Gurney's scheme,

[1] P.P., 1857–8 (21), vol. xlviii, *Mr Gurney's Report to the First Commissioner of Works
on the State of the Thames in the Neighbourhood of the Houses of Parliament*, pp. 423–30.
[2] P.P., 1857–8 (442), vol. xi, *Report of Select Committee to consider Mr Gurney's
Report on the State of the River Thames*, pp. 361–621.
[3] *The Times*, 3 July 1858.

although he doubtless knew of its contents. The Thames, he said, was 'a Stygian pool reeking with ineffable and intolerable horrors'. There was 'a pervading apprehension of pestilence in this great city', and the question which everybody was asking was 'Is this a local or a national business?' The government, he continued, had decided that it was a local affair – a very convenient decision, incidentally, for it absolved the Treasury of any responsibility for providing the money – but in conferring certain duties on the Metropolitan Board of Works the House of Commons had not 'combined with those duties the power adequate to their due discharge'. Now at last the matter was to be put right, at any rate so far as stinking drains were concerned.[1] The Board was to be absolved from the duty to obtain the First Commissioner's approval for their plans, and was to construct whatever system of main drainage it thought fit 'with all convenient speed'. It could raise a loan of £3,000,000 and levy a 3*d*. main drainage rate for forty years. And so far as its other public works not connected with drainage were concerned, the tiresome clauses in the Metropolis Management Act of 1855, whereby the Board was compelled to submit plans to the First Commissioner of Works for all schemes costing over £50,000 and to Parliament itself for schemes of over £100,000, were both to be repealed. Within eighteen days of its first reading the Bill had become law.[2] At last the building of the main drains could begin – no less than eleven years after the establishment of the first Metropolitan Commission of Sewers for this very purpose.

The existing sewers discharged into the Thames. Bazalgette's scheme provided for the building of main sewers extending from west to east across London, which would intercept the contents of the old sewers and allow it to flow into the Thames far below the built-up area. By making use of the natural configuration of the land the flow within the interceptor sewers was to be mostly by gravitation, but some pumping was necessary.

On the north side of the river a high-level sewer extended from Hampstead through Hackney to Abbey Mills, Stratford. There it was joined by the middle-level sewer, which began at Kensal Green. The flow in both these sewers was by gravitation, but the contents of the low-level sewer, beginning at Chiswick, had to be pumped up at Pimlico. From thence it flowed beside or near the river to the Tower, and from there to Abbey Mills, where after being pumped up again it met the other two sewers, and flowed by gravity to the Northern Outfall Works at Barking Creek. There the sewage was discharged via a nine-acre reservoir into the river, also by gravity.

[1] *Hansard, Third Series*, vol. 151, 15 July 1858, col. 1508.   [2] 21 and 22 Vict c. 104.

On the south side of the Thames the lie of the land presented greater problems. There were only two main intercepting sewers, one at a high level extending from Balham to Deptford and the other at a lower level from Putney to Deptford; in both of these the flow was by gravity. Near Nine Elms, Battersea, a pumping station lifted the contents of the Effra River (or ditch) into the low-level sewer, and at Deptford there was another lift, of eighteen feet, into the outfall sewer. There was also a short branch sewer for the low-lying districts of Bermondsey and Rotherhithe, and here too the sewage had to be pumped up into the outfall sewer. From Deptford all the sewage of south London flowed by gravity for nearly eight miles to the Southern Outfall Works at Crossness in the Erith Marshes, where it was pumped up into a six-acre reservoir to await discharge into the river. At both the Northern and Southern Outfall Works discharging normally took place only at or near the time of high water, and the sewage, still totally untreated, was then carried downstream on the ebb tide for some twenty-six miles below London Bridge.

Although now largely forgotten because few people ever see it, Bazalgette's main drainage system was one of the greatest engineering feats in a great age of engineering. His sewers, eighty-two miles in length, were built in or tunnelled beneath a densely built-up area, and they carried away, largely by gravity, all the sewage generated in London, as well as most of the rainwater which fell there. They were built of brick, most of them being circular in shape and varying from four to twelve feet in diameter, but others were egg-shaped with the narrow part downwards to achieve the maximum velocity when the flow was light. The greater part of the system was completed by 1865, at a cost of over £4 million, and was capable of channelling away some 420 million gallons of sewage and rainwater daily. Formidable difficulties had been mastered – the underpinning of innumerable houses, an aqueduct over the Metropolitan Railway at Sloane Square (still to be seen there), a tunnel underneath the Deptford Creek and an enormous raised embankment for most of the way from Abbey Mills to Barking. The report of the Royal Commission on the drainage of the metropolis published in 1884 testified to the complete success of Bazalgette's system; much of it is indeed still in use today.[1]

[1] J. W. Bazalgette, 'On the Metropolitan System of Drainage and the Interception of the Sewage from the River Thames', *Proceedings of the Institution of Civil Engineers*, vol. xxiv, 1864–5; A. F. Green, 'The Problem of London's Drainage', *Geography*, vol. XLI, 1956, pp. 147–54.

The second achievement of the Metropolitan Board of Works was in the building of a large number of new main streets. We have already seen in Chapter 3 that in the first half of the nineteenth century the government itself, in the absence of any adequate metropolitan municipal authority, had performed this duty in London. Under the auspices of the Commissioners of Woods and Forests Regent Street, New Oxford Street, Victoria Street and a number of other thoroughfares had been built, as well as two large parks – Victoria Park in Hackney and Bethnal Green, and Battersea Park. But despite the reports of a dozen parliamentary Select Committees between 1832 and 1851, the impetus of improvement had weakened during the 1830s and 1840s, and few schemes had been implemented, largely owing to the lack of an adequate and appropriately metropolitan source of revenue to meet the high costs involved. In 1855 the Metropolitan Board of Works became the authority responsible for important London street improvements, but incredible as it may seem, the Board was not given any powers for the purchase of land or property by compulsion. In 1862 the Board was at last granted very limited compulsory powers, but in practice it still had to apply to Parliament, in almost every case of important improvement, for a special Act authorizing the work. Progress was therefore slow, at least at first.[1]

The only scheme to be completed before 1862 was the formation in 1861 of Garrick Street, where almost all the land required belonged to one owner, the Duke of Bedford, a willing seller anxious to improve access to his Covent Garden Market. After 1862 progress was more rapid, and in the next ten years the following improvements were finished: Burdett Road, Stepney, 1862; Southwark Street, 1864; High Holborn, widening, 1867; High Street, Kensington, widening, 1869; Commercial Road, Whitechapel, westward extension, 1870; Hamilton Place, Hyde Park Corner, widening and extension, 1871; and Queen Victoria Street, City, 1871. The Board also paid part of the costs of a number of local improvements sponsored by the vestries and district boards.[2]

Much the most important improvement made by the Board in these years was, however, the embankment of nearly 3½ miles of land beside the Thames at a cost of some £2,500,000. The government, acting through the Office of Works and Public Buildings, had already embanked the long stretch from Millbank to Chelsea Hospital in 1854, and after the 'Great

[1] Percy J. Edwards, *History of London Street Improvements, 1855–1897*, 1898, pp. 10–11.

[2] Edwards, *passim*.

U

Stink' of 1858 Parliament had felt a strong desire to get rid of the offensive mud-banks which disfigured the shores of the river, particularly between Westminster and Waterloo Bridges. In 1860 a Select Committee of the Commons recommended an embankment all the way from Westminster to Blackfriars, to be constructed by the Metropolitan Board of Works, but in the following year a Royal Commission recommended that the work should be entrusted to a body of Special Commissioners instead – another very striking instance of parliamentary reluctance to allow the Board to be an effective master within its own house. In this case Parliament relented after a strong protest from the Board, and it was the Board which successfully built the Victoria Embankment – a very difficult job involving the reclamation of 37 acres of ground from the river and the construction of the low-level main sewer and the Metropolitan District Railway below ground as well as a wide new road on the surface. In these same years, too, the Board also embanked the Surrey side of the river between Westminster Bridge and Vauxhall, this stretch being completed in 1869 and named the Albert Embankment, and the Middlesex side from Chelsea Hospital to Battersea Bridge, which was completed in 1874. These three embankments provide the most enduring visible monument to all the various labours of the Metropolitan Board of Works.[1]

These improvements were matched in the City by others executed by the Corporation – the lengthening of Cannon Street (1854), the rebuilding of Billingsgate Market (1852) and Blackfriars Bridge (1869), the formation of Farringdon Road (1856) and the erection of a dead-meat market (1868) on part of the site vacated by Smithfield cattle market. The last two schemes were associated with the largest project of all, the building of Holborn Viaduct, nearly a quarter of a mile in length, across the deep valley of the now enclosed River Fleet at a cost of some £2,500,000 (1869).[2] During the 1860s an immense amount of rebuilding was taking place in the City, much of it occasioned by the incursions of the underground railways and the London, Chatham and Dover Railway, by a rapid rise in land values and by the continuing migration of many of its well-to-do inhabitants to the suburbs.

The City Corporation was, in fact, having to set about putting its house in order, goaded now to action, as its Commissioners of Sewers had already been by John Simon, by the constant threat of parliamentary legislation.

[1] Edwards, pp. 125–9.

[2] Charles Welch, *Modern History of the City of London*, 1896, pp. 202, 206, 210, 257, 261–2.

After the failure of his Bill of 1856 for the reform of the Corporation, Sir
George Grey, the Home Secretary, had introduced another Bill in 1858.
Lord Palmerston's ministry had resigned soon afterwards, however, but
the incoming Tory administration at once announced an intention to
'legislate for the City' in the next session. By 1859 Palmerston was back
again, and in both this year and in 1860 his Home Secretary, Sir George
Cornewall Lewis, sponsored Bills for 'the better regulation of the City of
London'. Neither of them became law, and in 1861 the Commons were
busy investigating local taxation in London. Two years later Sir George
Grey, now Home Secretary again and in the light of previous experience
evidently willing to settle for something less than complete reform, put
forward a Bill for the amalgamation of the City police.[1] In 1866–7 another
Commons enquiry into metropolitan local government recommended that
most of the members of the Metropolitan Board of Works should be
elected directly by the ratepayers, that the vestries and district boards
should be superseded by larger local Common Councils, and that the whole
of London should have its own separate Commission of the Peace.[2] How
the City Corporation was to be fitted into this new framework was not
made clear, and the government took no action. After 1870, when three
abortive private Bills for the reform of metropolitan local government were
sponsored, the whole subject was dropped for a while. The only results
of all these attempts to reform the Corporation were the Thames Conservancy Act of 1857, which compelled the Corporation to share its hitherto
sole responsibilities for the control of the river, and an Act of 1867 extending the right to vote in the election of members of the Common
Council, previously confined to the freemen, to all £10 ratepayers. The
latter was indeed the only significant change made in the constitution of
the Corporation during the whole of the nineteenth century.[3] Few things
are more remarkable in the history of London during this period than on
on the one hand the reluctance of successive governments to endow the
capital with appropriate municipal institutions, and on the other hand, the
extraordinary powers of survival of the unreformed City Corporation.

We may now turn to the work of the vestries and district boards in the
fields of sanitation and general improvements. Under the Metropolis

[1] Welch, pp. 215, 219, 222–3, 235.

[2] P.P., 1867 (268), vol. xii, *Second Report of Select Committee on Metropolitan Local
Government*, pp. v–vii.

[3] Welch, pp. 211–12, 264; Robson, p. 30.

Management and the Nuisances Removal Acts of 1855 they had been charged, in effect, with the duty of cleansing the Augean stable of London sanitation, and by the standards of the time, they had been endowed with considerable powers. Above all, the principle of inspection, first applied in London by John Simon in the City, had been recognized by the requirement that each vestry or district board was to appoint a Medical Officer of Health and one or more Inspectors of Nuisances.

In the cleansing and lighting of their streets, and under the supervision of the Metropolitan Board of Works in the building of local sewers and in the filling in of thousands of cesspools, the metropolitan local authorities made progress, particularly after the completion of the main drainage system in 1865. But in other fields the annual reports of their Medical Officers show that they lacked the will or the ability to attack private vested interests. The exercise of many of their powers was optional, not mandatory, and even when they were obliged to act, as in the appointment of Nuisance Inspectors, evasion was still possible. In Bethnal Green, for instance, where there were over 14,000 houses, there was only one Inspector. The adulteration of food, the practice of noxious trades, the stink of the river and the appalling pollution of the atmosphere by smoke and industrial vapours were all beyond the power or the capacity of the local authorities to remedy. The Medical Officers' calls to action fell on deaf ears. 'The right of life stands before the right of property,' wrote the Medical Officer of St James's. 'Should less care be bestowed upon our fellow creatures than is daily afforded the lower animals?' asked his colleague in the Strand District. 'To permit such grievous evils as are to be seen in the worst localities of this great city is a contradiction to the teaching of Christianity,' echoed St Martin in the Fields. But it was all in vain. London's new municipal institutions were still totally inadequate for the herculean tasks which confronted them; and even the economic argument for action, that disease and sickness entailed heavy expenditure of public money through the poor rates, received little public recognition.[1]

The heart of the problem of the terrible conditions in which the poor of mid-Victorian London lived lay in the pitiful shortage of housing and in the gross overcrowding to which this gave rise. This was the period when demolitions in the central area, for railways, docks, warehouses and street improvements, were at their height. Over 4,000 poor were, to use the

---

[1] This and the following paragraphs are based on the account in Henry Jephson, *The Sanitary Evolution of London*, 1907.

contemporary phrase, 'displaced', for the Holborn Valley scheme alone, and the various agencies responsible for this mass destruction were as yet under no obligation to provide alternative accommodation. High rents, the imperative need to live near the source of employment, and the ceaseless arrival of fresh immigrants all aggravated the situation. In one wretched district of Mile End Old Town the population increased by 3,094 between 1851 and 1861, yet only 84 new houses were built. 'In many of the districts of the metropolis,' wrote the Medical Officer of St George the Martyr, Southwark, 'between 60 and 70 per cent of the population are compelled to live in one small overcrowded room, and in which every domestic operation has to be carried on; in it birth and death takes place; there plays the infant, there lies the corpse; it is lived in by day, and slept in by night.' And the result was that in Christian London of little more than a century ago there were 'swarms of men and women who had yet to learn that human beings should dwell differently from cattle, swarms to whom personal cleanliness was utterly unknown, swarms by whom delicacy and decency in their social relations were quite unconceived . . .'. No wonder that drunkenness and delinquency were rife, or that deaths among children under five accounted for almost half of all the deaths throughout the whole of London.[1]

Until the closing years of the nineteenth century the London vestries and district boards made little effort to get to grips with the frightful problem of housing. The regulation of common lodging-houses for the labouring class was, it is true, not within their purview, for Lord Shaftesbury's Act of 1851[2] had placed the registration, inspection, cleansing and limitation of overcrowding in these establishments in the capable hands of the Metropolitan Police. But under another Act of the same year, also sponsored by Lord Shaftesbury, the London local authorities had been empowered to buy, lease or build lodging-houses.[3] Yet none of them had adopted the Act, and only a handful of them established public baths and wash-houses under powers granted in an Act of 1846. More important, perhaps, were the powers contained in the Nuisances Removal Act of 1855, by which a vestry or district board could take proceedings for the abatement of overcrowding in a house occupied by more than one family. In 1866 these powers were greatly enlarged by a general Sanitary Act,[4] which enabled the vestries and boards to make regulations for all houses let in lodgings or occupied by more than one family, including the limitation of

[1] Jephson, pp. 108, 120, 164–7. [2] 14 and 15 Vict. c. 28.
[3] 14 and 15 Vict. c. 34. [4] 29 and 30 Vict. c. 90.

the number of occupants and the enforcement of cleansing and lime-washing. Yet here again there was virtually no effective action, except in Chelsea and Hackney, and in 1884–5 a Royal Commission reported that this section of the Act was 'likely to remain a dead letter in many districts of the metropolis, until some improved means be devised for putting it in action'.[1] The author of a report addressed in 1865 to John Simon, now Medical Officer of Health of the Privy Council, put his finger on the nub of the problem when he wrote that:

> There is no authority which can deal with London in these matters as a whole, and they are matters in which uniform treatment is quite necessary. The local authority which finds the whole of its district overcrowded, naturally hesitates before beginning action which may relieve one house only to overfill the next, and may reasonably think that such action, unless done thoroughly, not only through the district, but through the whole capital, might prove hurtful.[2]

Yet prosperous respectable Victorians were not callous or indifferent to human suffering. The trouble was that they were generally ignorant of its vast extent, and sometimes, perhaps, even of its very existence. The provision of working-class housing, they were at first convinced, was a job for commercial builders, and the function of philanthropy was merely to lead the way by demonstrating that the thing could be done at a profit. Thus the aim of the pioneer organization in this field, the Metropolitan Association for Improving the Dwellings of the Industrious Classes, founded in 1841, was to provide 'the labouring man with an increase of the comforts and conveniences of life, with full compensation to the capitalist'. The Association was to be self-supporting, the dividend payable to the shareholders was to be limited to 5 per cent, and any surplus profits were to be used to enlarge the Association's work. By 1850 it had housed 216 families in three blocks of tenements, two in Spitalfields and one in St Pancras, and its rent-roll yielded over £3,300. Very similar, too, was the Society for Improving the Condition of the Labouring Classes, with Lord Ashley as its chairman and the Prince Consort as its president. By 1851 it had built dwellings at Bagnigge Wells near Gray's Inn Road, and in Streatham Street, Bloomsbury, and established a model lodging-house in

[1] London County Council, *The Housing Question in London 1855–1900*, 1900, pp. 3, 71.

[2] Quoted in Jephson, p. 186.

the rookery of St Giles. It had spent some £23,000 and claimed a net return of 6 per cent.[1]

In later years this semi-philanthropic, semi-commercial approach was followed by Alderman Sydney Waterlow, a wealthy printer and stationer. He began in 1862 by building four blocks of dwellings in Mark Street, Finsbury, at his own expense, and went on to establish the Improved Industrial Dwellings Company in 1863, with a capital which eventually reached £500,000. But as a practical man of affairs he soon realized that the problem of working-class housing was so enormous that public intervention would be needed, and perhaps his own most important work was in promoting this end. In 1862–3 he persuaded the City Corporation to spend some £20,000 on the erection of artisans' dwellings in Farringdon Road, and a few years later he propelled the government into empowering the Public Works Loan Commissioners to grant loans upon mortgage of lands and houses used for working-class housing.[2]

Much less concerned with the profit and loss side of the business were two munificent benefactors, Angela Burdett-Coutts, the fabulously wealthy daughter of Sir Francis Burdett and grand-daughter of Thomas Coutts of Coutts' Bank, and George Peabody, an American merchant long resident in London. Angela Burdett-Coutts' principal foray into the field of housing occurred in 1860–2, when she built four Gothic blocks of dwellings, known as Columbia Square Buildings, in Bethnal Green at a personal cost of £43,000 – a project which housed 183 families and yielded a return of only 2½ per cent. Peabody's donation of £150,000, made in 1862 and later increased to £500,000, was administered by trustees, who within six years had built four groups of dwellings and housed nearly 2,000 people – a figure which by 1897 had risen to nearly 20,000.[3]

Another pioneer, Octavia Hill, had a different contribution to make. As the grand-daughter of Chadwick's devoted colleague, Dr Southwood Smith, she put her inherited philanthropic concern to good use when she persuaded John Ruskin in 1864 to finance the purchase of a few tumbledown houses in Paradise Place, St Marylebone. She believed that the repair of old dwellings should be accompanied by the gradual reformation of the habits of the occupants, and the agency for the achievement of this object was to be regular visitation of the tenants by voluntary rent-

[1] David Owen, *English Philanthropy 1660–1960*, 1965, pp. 374–8.
[2] George Smalley, *The Life of Sir Sydney H. Waterlow, Bart.*, 1909, pp. 72–3; Welch, p. 237.
[3] Owen, pp. 378, 381.

collectors. Gradually she became responsible for the repair and management of a large number of old houses scattered throughout the poorest parts of London, and the chief limitation to the growth of her work proved to be lack of capable voluntary workers rather than lack of capital. She herself described her system as: 'Repairs promptly and efficiently attended to, references completely taken up, cleansing sedulously supervised, overcrowding put an end to, the blessing of ready-money payments enforced, accounts strictly kept, and above all, tenants so sorted as to be helpful to one another.' Her recipe was imitated in many provincial towns, and even in Europe and America, and she can indeed be regarded as the first teacher of many of the basic precepts of modern local authority housing management.[1]

So by the mid-1860s there was a wide variety of semi-philanthropic agencies engaged in the improvement of working-class housing. But they were encountering formidable difficulties – the very high cost of sites in the central areas, the near impossibility of earning a profit comparable with that to be obtained by ordinary commercial investment, and above all the problem, perhaps only truly faced by Octavia Hill, of providing for the very poorest class of all, for whom the rents charged by the Peabody Trust or the Improved Industrial Dwellings Company were too high. The existence of these numerous well-publicized agencies nevertheless salved the public conscience; something was being done, and the fact that the full extent of their efforts only touched the fringe of the problem passed largely unnoticed. In 1875, for instance, the total number housed during the previous thirty years (26,000) amounted to only half the regular annual increase in the population of London,[2] and the main value of all this philanthropic work lay rather in the stimulus which it gave to the need for public action than in its actual achievements measured in terms of bricks and mortar. But within the period up to 1870 which is covered by this book, legislative progress was pitifully slow, and the principal housing Act of the 1860s was sponsored not by the government, but by a private member, William Torrens, M.P. for Finsbury. His Act of 1868 enlarged the power of local authorities to compel owners to maintain their property in decent order, but it only applied to individual houses, not to the whole areas which were usually involved, and was in practice of little value.[3] The day for effective large-scale public action was still far away.

Private philanthropy was more effective in another branch of public

---

[1] Owen, pp. 388–9; *Dictionary of National Biography*, Octavia Hill.
[2] Owen, p. 385.   [3] L.C.C., *The Housing Question*, pp. 4–5.

health – the provision of hospitals. Here, in the words of Professor David Owen, 'the humanitarian concern of the Victorians and their confidence in science as an agent of human progress joined in beneficent alliance.[1]' After the foundation of the Middlesex Hospital in 1745 there had been a long pause before another general hospital was established. The year 1818 saw the inauguration of the West London (now Charing Cross) Hospital, and in 1833 and 1839 respectively the two teaching hospitals at University College and King's College were founded. Between 1800 and 1861 another four general hospitals were established, bringing the total number in London up to fourteen, with a total annual income in 1861 from voluntary contributions of £58,000, plus another £127,000 from land or investments. But with the gathering momentum of medical advance this was *par excellence* the great age of special hospitals. In 1800 there were only twelve such institutions in London; by 1861 there were no fewer than sixty-six, mostly receiving in-patients. Among the more famous of these new foundations were those later known as the Royal London Ophthalmic Hospital, Moorfields (1804), the Royal Orthopaedic Hospital (1838), the Hospital for Consumption and Diseases of the Chest (1841), the Hospital for Sick Children, Great Ormond Street (1851), and the National Hospital for Nervous Diseases, Queen Square (1859). In 1861 these sixty-six hospitals received an income from voluntary sources of nearly £74,000, with another £81,000 from property and dividends. For the outdoor medical care of the sick poor there were also thirty-nine dispensaries, twenty-nine of them established since 1800.[2] Yet even here, where the scale and scope of Victorian philanthropy is perhaps seen at its best, voluntary effort was not enough. The sick still died in uncounted thousands in the prison-like conditions of the general mixed workhouses, and it was not until 1867, with the establishment of the Metropolitan Asylums Board, that the provision of a public hospital system began. When the Board's first hospital was opened in 1870, admission was restricted to paupers suffering from certain specified infectious diseases such as smallpox or scarlet fever, but over the course of years the range of diseases treated was greatly enlarged and free admission was no longer restricted to the poor. By the early twentieth century many of these new publicly supported hospitals had surpassed the older voluntary foundations in quality of both buildings and equipment,[3]

---

[1] Owen, p. 170.

[2] Sampson Low, *The Charities of London*, 1867, p. vii.

[3] Sidney and Beatrice Webb, *English Poor Law History*, Part II, *The Last Hundred Years*, 1929, pp. 321, 575; Jephson, p. 210.

and provided yet another example of the mounting scale of state action in the provision of social services.

The slowness of this process, and the cost of this slowness in terms of loss of human life, are nowhere more clearly illustrated than in the history of London's water supply. We have already seen that a Select Committee of the House of Commons had enquired into this subject as long ago as 1821, but that despite incessant criticism of both the quantity and the quality of the supply, no general legislation had ensued for more than thirty years. The Metropolitan Water Act of 1852 had at last required the companies within five years to cease drawing any supplies from the Thames below Teddington, and to filter their water 'effectually', but in all other respects the Act had proved a 'wretched sell-out to vested interests',[1] and even its two important requirements were not always observed. We must now examine the consequences of this negligence.

Cholera had yet one more terrible lesson to inflict, perhaps the most terrible of all, for there had been ample opportunity to learn it before the the last major attack occurred in London in 1866. The first cholera death was reported on 18 July, from Poplar. Within three days it became apparent that an alarming proportion of all cases within London were in the East End. In the week ending 28 July the deaths in all London from cholera and diarrhoea had reached 1,253, of which 924 were in Bethnal Green, Whitechapel, St George in the East, Stepney, Mile End Old Town and Poplar. The London Hospital in Whitechapel was already full, despite the readiness of a large new wing which was to have been opened on 27 July by Mrs Gladstone. The opening ceremony was hastily abandoned, and Mr and Mrs Gladstone made themselves responsible for thirty small boys orphaned by the cholera, for whom they provided a house on the family estate at Hawarden. The suddenness and virulence of the outbreak were terrifying. In Bow the victims included both the local Medical Officer of Health and the Clerk to the District Board of Works, whose name still appeared on the placards announcing precautionary measures to be taken. 'The people are falling ill every hour,' wrote Dr William Farr, the principal statistician in the Registrar-General's office.

You see them of all ages, children and adults, lying about their beds like people under the influence of a deadly poison, some acutely suffering, nearly all conscious of their fate and of all that is going on

[1] Lambert, p. 269.

around them. Here the doctor is drawn in by the husband to see the wife now attacked; there the husband lies in spasms; here is an old woman seated dead, with eyes wide open; there lies a fine four-year old child, his curly head drooping in death. . . . The people themselves are most patient; most willing to help each other, the women always in front, and none shrinking danger. There is no desertion of children, husbands, wives, fathers, or mothers from fear.[1]

None of this appalling suffering should ever have occurred. In his return of births and deaths in London for the week ending 28 July Dr Farr pointed out an interesting fact – that the area where most of the slaughter was taking place was supplied with water by the East London Water Company from the River Lea. The Company was outraged at the inference evidently intended to be drawn from this statement, and its engineer, Mr Charles Greaves, wrote a letter to *The Times*, published on 2 August, asserting that 'not a drop of unfiltered water has for several years past been supplied by the Company for any purpose'. But when this letter was reprinted in *The East End News* two East Enders wrote to say that they had each found a dead eel stuck in the water pipes of their houses. In one of these cases, where the writer had subsequently lost two of his children from cholera, the eel had been fourteen inches in length. 'It was in a *putrid* state, and the stench arising from it was most *fearful*.'[2]

The truth was out; the East London Water Company had been supplying unfiltered water, in flagrant breach of the Act of 1852.

The total mortality from cholera in all London in 1866 was 5,915, of which no less than 4,276 occurred in the eastern districts and the adjacent suburban districts of West Ham and Stratford. In the inquiry which subsequently took place into the conduct of the East London Water Company the engineer admitted that unfiltered water had in fact been supplied, and the government inspector concluded that this profligate and criminal negligence had been the cause of the outbreak of cholera in East London. Yet the difficulty of legal proof was so great and the maximum penalty provided in the Act of 1852 was so small (a fine of £200) that no prosecution ever took place.[3]

[1] *Registrar General's Weekly Return of Births and Deaths in London*, vol. xxvii, 1866, No. 30; John Simon, *Public Health Reports*, 1887, vol. II, p. 276; Longmate, pp. 219–20.

[2] *Registrar General's Weekly Return*, 1866, No. 30; *The Times*, 2 August 1866; Longmate, p. 217.

[3] Simon, *Health Reports*, vol. II, 288–9, 408.

Once again, as in 1848, it had been demonstrated that the threat of cholera had no rival as a force to compel governments to act in the field of sanitary reform. The general Sanitary Bill of 1866 was prepared in May, when the epidemic was expected, and discussed and enacted in the very weeks when the disease was rampaging through the East End. We have already seen that this Act greatly enlarged the powers of local authorities, and, more importantly, it also enlarged the powers of the central government over the local authorities.[1] It came none too soon for the health of Londoners, for despite all the sanitary efforts of the last two decades the death rate for the whole of London was soon to show a rise, from 23·6 per 1,000 living for the years 1850–9 to 24·3 per 1,000 for 1860–9. And even now, after the fearful lesson so brutally imposed in 1866, another London water company – the Southwark and Vauxhall – was still from time to time in 1868 drawing water from the prohibited stretch of the Thames at Battersea Reach. What might have been the result of this callous and flagrant defiance of the law, if cholera infection had at the time been present in London, is too frightful even to imagine.[2]

[1] Lambert, pp. 382–9.
[2] Simon, *Health Reports*, vol. II, pp. 410–11.

8

The Radical
Politics
of London

THE RISE of a predominantly urban and industrial society in
nineteenth-century Britain was based upon a parallel transformation in the position and organization of the labouring population.
The periodic short-lived political pressure exercised by the eighteenth
century 'mob' was gradually displaced by the continuous and far more
effective pressure of the new industrial working class, partially equipped
at last, after many abortive experiments, with small but stable trade unions
and, after the Reform Act of 1867, with the more direct instrument of the
parliamentary vote. In the achievement of this long and painful social
revolution the London radical reformers occupied a position of strategic
national importance, close to the seat of national power and surrounded
by the largest concentration of working men in the whole country. Yet
despite these great advantages London did not provide the seemingly
natural focal point for the multifarious activities of the social and political
reform movement. As the Chartists were to discover, London's population
was too large and too diffuse in its social and occupational structures for
its full influence to be effectively brought to bear in any sustained effort
such as that of the Manchester-based Anti-Corn Law League. London's
influence was, indeed, far greater as a centre of political and social ideas,
such as the People's Charter itself, which was written and first published
in London, than as a rallying ground for practical action; and only on
two or three brief occasions, in May 1832, in the last Chartist crisis in
1848, and perhaps in the events leading up to the second Reform Act of
1867, did London exert a direct influence over immediate events.

In the closing years of the eighteenth century the ideals of revolutionary France and the writings of Tom Paine had redoubled the vigour of the popular demand for reform, which had reached a great crescendo in the mid-1790s before suffering almost total extinction at the hands of William Pitt's administration. In the early years of the nineteenth century there was a slow and painful recovery in which a new pattern gradually evolved. London provided several of the strands in this new pattern, for sheer size and social complexity prevented the emergence of any generally acknowledged metropolitan leadership.

In Westminster the revival began with the victory of the two radical candidates at the general election of 1807. Westminster was one of the few parliamentary constituencies with a large franchise, consisting of some 18,000 electors who included many shopkeepers, small master-craftsmen and even some journeymen. Hitherto its two members had been either Whigs or Tories, often acting in collusion to share the two seats. After the death of Charles James Fox, Westminster's Whig member, in 1806, the Duke of Northumberland's son, Lord Percy, was elected with the aid of copious largesse provided by the Duke. Francis Place, the radical tailor whose shop at Charing Cross stood near Northumberland House, was outraged to see the electors of Westminster scrimmaging for the lumps of bread and cheese thrown to them by the Duke's liveried flunkies, and when a general election took place in the following year Place and a few friends formed a committee to sponsor a radical candidate. Sir Francis Burdett, recently displaced from Middlesex, where he had spent a fortune at successive elections, agreed to stand, but refused to appear at the hustings or to contribute a farthing to the expenses of his election. His victory was therefore entirely due to the assiduous canvassing organized by Place's committee of tradesmen, whose exiguous financial resources precluded all bribery and treating. Another Radical, Lord Cochrane, was elected to the other seat, and thenceforward Westminster remained for many years the principal stronghold of parliamentary radicalism in London.

But this triumph had its limitations. Although it was engineered by more democratic methods than those previously employed by Wilkes and Burdett himself in Middlesex, the Westminster members were still gentlemen, socially quite distinct from their committee of supporters. Soon there was also a marked divergence of opinion between the members and their supporters, for the intensity of Burdett's radicalism diminished so greatly that eventually, after thirty years as one of the members for Westminster, he crossed the floor of the House of Commons and represented Wiltshire as a Tory for the last seven years of his life (1837–44). Neither he nor John Cam Hobhouse, who became the other member for Westminster in 1820, proved energetic enough to lead the small group of reformers in the House of Commons. Place, on the other hand, soon became disillusioned with both Burdett himself and with the possibility of organizing effective action on Wilkite lines, for even the golden opportunity presented by the Commons' committal of Burdett to the Tower in 1810 for contempt had only produced much noise and confusion. He fell increasingly under the influence of Jeremy Bentham and James Mill, and became an ardent proponent of utilitarian social economy and political action through the middle classes. The mood of democratic protest in which the Westminster committee had originated in 1807 was largely lost, and although it was periodically revived at subsequent elections it was never strong enough to command the radical aspirations of all London.[1]

The revival in Westminster did, nevertheless, mark a shift of emphasis away from the City, which until Pitt took office in 1784 had been the most continuously articulate centre of London political protest. After Pitt's death in 1806 and the Westminster election of 1807 the City abandoned its long alliance with the mainly Tory governments of the last twenty years and reverted to its more customary posture of opposition. This return to opposition began in 1808, when the Court of Common Council protested at the Convention of Cintra, and in the following year criticized the conduct of the Walcheren expedition and accused the Duke of York of corruptly disposing of army commissions. After the committal of Sir Francis Burdett to the Tower in 1810 the Court of Common Hall, always the most radical of the City's various assemblies, revived its ancient demands for parliamentary reform in a violently worded petition in which members of the House of Commons were reminded that so far from representing the people, they were known to have been selected 'by the absolute nomination or powerful influence of about 150 peers and others'. This was followed, in 1812, by an address from the Common Hall to the Prince Regent on the same subject, backed this time by a similar address from the Common Council. Only the Court of Aldermen remained aloof from this reviving mood of protest, but even here a gradual shift of opinion was visible, eight of the fourteen vacancies on the aldermanic

[1] J. M. Main, 'Radical Westminster, 1807–1820', *Historical Studies, Australia and New Zealand*, vol. 12, 1965–7, Melbourne, pp. 186–204; E. P. Thompson, *The Making of the English Working Class*, Pelican edn, 1968, pp. 504–13, 670–1.

bench between 1807 and 1820 being filled by Whigs against only five by Tories, plus one unknown.

But the stream of hostile petitions and addresses which was now beginning to flow out once more from the Guildhall seldom possessed the force which widespread popular support had conferred in the days of Wilkes. During the discussion of the Corn Law Bill in 1815 the old tacit alliance between the City and the London crowd was, it is true, temporarily revived, the protests of both the Common Council and the Common Hall being reinforced during four days and nights by bands of men roaming through the streets of the West End and attacking the houses of ministers and unpopular members. But neither the Common Council's repeated demands during the next five years for parliamentary reform, nor its opposition to the suspension of Habeas Corpus in 1817 and to the Six Acts of 1819 evoked any further popular response of this kind. The days of the riotous Wilkite crowd were over, and the days of the independent working-class political movement had not yet arrived.[1]

During this long period of transition the labouring population gave widespread support to a few leaders of national stature, of whom William Cobbett, Major John Cartwright and Henry Hunt were the most important. None of them was specifically a London figure, but their influence in London forms another strand in the complicated pattern of metropolitan radicalism. Cobbett first produced his weekly *Political Register* in 1802, and continued to publish a regular commentary until his death in 1835. He made himself the most powerful political journalist of his time, and his successful evasion of the stamp duty laws by the publication of his famous 'Twopenny Trash' in 1816 greatly enlarged his circulation and marked the first beginnings of the popular radical press. Cartwright was the doyen of the group, already seventy-two years old at the formation in 1812 of the London Hampden Club, on which he based his nation-wide campaign for the revival of the parliamentary reform movement; while Hunt was the great orator, vain and demagogic, yet also persistent and brave, who spoke both at the Spa Fields meetings in London in 1816 and at St Peter's Fields, Manchester in 1819.[2]

Cobbett and Hunt both disseminated much more extreme ideas than either Burdett or Place or the City's Court of Common Hall, but they were constitutionalists none the less, who stopped short of treason. Others were

[1] Reginald R. Sharpe, *London and the Kingdom*, 1895, vol. III, pp. 270, 272, 277–9, 294–311; Alfred B. Beaven, *The Aldermen of the City of London*, 1913, vol. II, pp. 141–2.
[2] Thompson, pp. 665–6, 679, 686–7.

not so cautious, and there was also in London a small group centred round Dr James Watson, his son of the same name, and Arthur Thistlewood, who maintained the tradition of violent conspiracy for which the unfortunate Colonel Despard had been hanged in 1803. They envisaged London's part in terms of Paris and the *coup d'état*, and Thistlewood also eventually paid for his ineffective determination with his life.

But some, at least, of London's labouring population had more immediately useful tools of self-protection than those provided by any of these varied elements of political radicalism. These were the 'society men', a small proportion of the most skilled of London's 100,000 artisans, who were organized in small and highly exclusive trade clubs. In a period of frequent under-employment, when new skills engendered by the progress of industrial technology were constantly appearing, and when old skills were as constantly losing their value, these clubs existed as much to protect their members from the competition of the unskilled as from the oppressiveness of their employers – as William Lovett found in 1821 when he tried to obtain work as a cabinetmaker without having served an apprenticeship.

Despite the Combination Laws of 1799–1800 many such clubs flourished openly during the early years of the nineteenth century. The London master printers still negotiated with their men, and so did the master coopers, while the brushmakers had 'A List of Prices agreed upon between the Masters and Journeymen', and the London Cabinetmakers' Union was not afraid to publish its book of prices in 1811. Nevertheless the threat of prosecution always existed, as the case of some of the journeymen printers employed by *The Times* in 1810 demonstrated, and even the non-skilled, outside the clubs, suffered under the Combination Laws, for union discipline became stricter and admission more difficult. Through the concerted opposition which it provoked, the repeal in 1814 of the apprenticeship clauses of the Elizabethan Statute of Artificers temporarily increased the power of the London clubs, and such trades as the hatters, coopers, curriers, compositors and shipwrights were able to maintain earnings at as high a level as 30*s*. to 50*s*. a week. Sidney and Beatrice Webb even state that the skilled trades had 'never been more completely organized in London than between 1810 and 1820'.[1]

The history of the decade after the end of the French wars in 1815

---

[1] Sidney and Beatrice Webb, *The History of Trade Unionism*, 1920 edn, pp. 74–8, 83, 85; William Lovett, *The Life and Struggles of William Lovett in his Pursuit of Bread, Knowledge and Freedom*, 1876, pp. 30–1.

shows the interplay of all these disparate facets of London radicalism. During the first five years of peace both the money wages and the real wages of London artisans were falling,[1] and unemployment and hunger, or the fear of them, provided the main impulse of protest. This protest was expressed in the powerful new dimension created by Cobbett, Tom Paine and French Jacobinism, and backed, often, by far more widespread support than in earlier years. We have already seen the spontaneous support which the City's petitions against the Corn Law of 1815 received from the London crowd, and at the end of the following year, when the appearance of 'Twopenny Trash' had greatly extended Cobbett's influence, three great demonstrations were held in Spa Fields, Islington. The main speaker on all three of these occasions was 'Orator' Hunt, but at the second meeting, on 2 December, the two Watsons, Thistlewood and a few of their followers attempted an insurrection. The Tower and the Bank of England were to be seized at the outset, and for several months previously Thistlewood had frequented the guard-rooms and barracks of London attempting to suborn the troops. At last he was satisfied that he had won their support, and the assembly of a large peaceable crowd waiting for Hunt's arrival provided a suitable opportunity to inaugurate the *coup*. Suddenly the Watsons and a few followers appeared, bearing tricolor flags; they mounted a waggon, delivered 'a very inflammatory harangue to the surrounding populace' and then marched off towards Clerkenwell, followed by a few of the crowd. At Snow Hill they raided a gunsmith's shop (where an astonished bystander was shot after boldly telling them 'to go about their business') and they then proceeded down Cheapside towards the Bank, near to which, at the Royal Exchange, they were met by the Whig Lord Mayor, Matthew Wood, and a party of the City constabulary. Three of them had been artfully trapped inside the Exchange, none of the canny citizens showed any disposition to join them, so they moved off towards the Minories, the centre of the London gunsmiths' trade, where they seized the contents of several shops and even possessed themselves of two small brass field-pieces. Here they remained for some hours, while parties of soldiers began to surround them, until in the early dusk of winter they began to disperse in small bands. There was to be no revolution after all, and 'the evening and the night were rendered tranquil by numerous patroles of horse, and all disorder subsided with the day'.[2]

[1] Rufus S. Tucker, 'Real Wages of Artisans in London 1729–1935', *Journal of the American Statistical Association*, vol. 31, 1936, pp. 73–84.

[2] *Annual Register*, 1816.

Thistlewood and the Watsons were indicted for high treason. They and a few of their followers had been captured, but the younger Watson escaped and later made his way to America. They were lodged in the Tower, but the government was overplaying its hand and Watson senior was acquitted of treason, although he would certainly have been convicted on a charge of riot. After this setback no evidence was offered against Thistlewood, who by the autumn of 1817 was already planning to blow open the Bank and start another rising at Smithfield during the confusion of St Bartholomew's Fair.

The Spa Fields gatherings were the first mass reform meetings to be held in the capital since 1795, and they demonstrated the ineffectiveness of London's radical leadership. They threw Major Cartwright's meeting of Hampden Club delegates, summoned to meet in London in January 1817, into confusion, and Burdett refused to attend. After a weekend of indecisive debates over the merits of manhood or household suffrage the Hampden convention, which was to have provided the climax for Cartwright's missionary activity in the provinces, broke up in confusion, while a few weeks later the government suspended Habeas Corpus and passed a Seditious Meetings Act. In March 1817 Cobbett retreated to America, and the London reform movement collapsed.[1]

The focus of attention now shifted to the provinces. London became a centre of journalistic propaganda rather than of effective action, and even the sense of outrage engendered by the Peterloo massacre outside Manchester in August 1819 only produced a short-lived unity among the metropolitan leaders, which was exemplified at several large demonstrations. Peterloo was followed by the Six Acts in December, and by this time it was clear that Orator Hunt, the hero of Peterloo, was too pusillanimous to exploit the opportunity of the moment. The constitutional movement had failed, and conspiracy reasserted itself in London once more.

After the Spa Fields insurrection in 1816 Thistlewood and the elder Watson had resumed their plotting in the pot-houses of London's radical underworld, where their every move was watched by government spies. In 1818 Thistlewood had been in prison again for a short while for threatening a breach of the peace by challenging the Home Secretary, Lord Sidmouth, to a duel, but by the summer of 1819 he was out again. Within a few months the lack of any effective response to Peterloo and the Six Acts had driven him to desperation. Some sort of underground

[1] Thompson, pp. 691–702.

organization was formed, very possibly with provincial ramifications, but it was penetrated by an *agent provocateur*, George Edwards, who became Thistlewood's innermost confidant. It was Edwards, evidently, who suggested that the entire government cabinet should be assassinated while dining at Lord Harrowby's house in Grosvenor Square. Thistlewood took a lease of a stable and loft in Cato Street, a dilapidated court off the Edgware Road not far from Grosvenor Square, and here he and his confederates, now some twenty-five or thirty in number, assembled with their arsenal of pistols, cutlasses, bayonets, bombs and grenades. But ministers knew every detail of the plot, and the stable had been watched during all these elaborate preparations. At eight-thirty on the evening of 23 February 1820, when the conspirators in the loft were buckling on a fearsome array of accoutrements, a party of Bow Street Runners rushed up the narrow ladder and attempted to arrest them. The lights were instantly put out and a desperate struggle began. Within a minute the police were reinforced by thirty Coldstream Guards who had been waiting nearby, but with some fifty or more men shooting and fighting in the inky blackness of a small hayloft most of the conspirators escaped, Thistlewood among them. Nine of them were taken off to Bow Street under heavy guard; one of the Runners was killed, and there were several wounded on both sides.

Thistlewood, who was captured a short while later, and a number of his followers were convicted of high treason. He and four others were hanged outside Newgate on 1 May 1820, and their bodies were afterwards publicly decapitated. Thistlewood died with the same defiance as he had shown at the end of his trial, when he had proclaimed that 'Albion is still in the chains of slavery. I quit it without regret. My only sorrow is that that soil should be a theatre for slaves, for cowards, for despots.'[1]

The Cato Street conspiracy marked the end of the post-war reform agitation. Despite its failure, the whole movement had been founded upon the new ideas of popular sovereignty and the rights of man, rather than, as hitherto, upon loyalty to individuals – hence the ineffectiveness of Burdett compared with Wilkes. Its national collapse in 1820 was therefore only temporary. Shortly after the government's Draconian legislation of 1819 there was a marked improvement in the real wages of London artisans,

[1] *Dictionary of National Biography*, Arthur Thistlewood; *Annual Register*, 1820.

which continued (except during the financial crisis of 1825) until 1831. This took the steam out of the mass popular agitation, and the political initiative reverted for a while to the City.[1]

The parliamentary election of 1818, when the City returned three Whigs and one Tory, was the first general election since 1784 at which more than one Whig candidate had been successful there. At the election of 1820, held shortly after the Cato Street conspiracy, there was a brief return to the old pattern of Tory predominance, but this was finally broken in 1826, when three of the four successful candidates were Whigs, and from then until 1874 the City's parliamentary representation remained as over-whelmingly Whig or Liberal as it was thereafter to be overwhelmingly Conservative.[2] A new generation of leaders was emerging in the City, of whom Alderman Matthew Wood, first returned at a by-election in 1817, and Alderman Robert Waithman, first chosen in 1826, were the most notable, and in 1820 Alderman Wood was particularly well placed to exploit the opportunity of the moment, for he was the friend and counsellor of Queen Caroline.

The Queen's return, in June 1820, from seven years of gallivanting on the Continent presented ribald Londoners with a golden chance to ridicule the ministers at whose hands they had suffered so much in preceding years, and the City's Court of Common Council was quick to give them a lead. Alderman Wood had escorted her in her triumphal progress from Dover. 'Deptford and Greenwich poured out in indiscriminate concourse all ranks and conditions of their inhabitants; Blackheath resembled some great continental fair; and at Shooter's Hill were drawn up an array of barouches, chaises, and other vehicles filled with respectable and decent women.' After a short rest at the Green Man inn she had driven on to London, across Westminster Bridge, where the ladies testified their enthusiasm 'by every demonstration not unbecoming the delicacy of their sex', past Carlton House itself, where the sentries presented arms 'in a manner indicating that some reserve and embarrassment extended even to their humble stations', and at last to Alderman Wood's house in South Audley Street, where she was to stay for a while.

For the the next fourteen months the Queen's affairs – so romantic, so scandalous and so delightfully embarrassing for the King and the government – 'excited and absorbed the public attention to a degree unparalleled perhaps by anything in our history'. Cato Street and Spa Fields were

[1] George Rudé, *The Crowd in History*, 1964, p. 234; Tucker, p. 79.
[2] Beaven, vol. I, pp. 282-5.

forgotten in an orgy of illuminations and carefully selected window-breaking. There were endless congratulatory addresses – from the City Court of Common Council, of course, from the County of Middlesex, from 'the mechanics of the metropolis', from the inhabitants of Hammersmith, where the Queen was now living, and from countless others too. There was the 'trial' for adultery, by a Bill of Pains and Penalties in the House of Lords, during which she excursed about London amid universal applause; there was the breakdown of the trial, followed by three nights of illuminations, with all the opportunities thereby presented for the erection of such cryptic banners as 'May the Queen stand like the oak, and may her enemies fall like the leaves'; there was another flood of congratulatory addresses, to which she responded in just the way that the sponsors of the addresses had hoped she would – 'The people have made many sacrifices for me, and I will live for the people,' she told the Court of Common Council of 'the first city in the world'. And then in 1821 there were debates in the Commons about the exclusion of her name from the liturgy of the Church, about the grant of an annuity for her maintenance, and even about her right to participate in the impending coronation ceremony – a claim which the King and government had already refused. Finally, and worst of all, there was her public exclusion from Westminster Abbey, where she had presented herself on the morning of the coronation on 19 July 1821.

Three weeks later she was dead. But even now the tragi-comic carnival of the last months of this ill-starred, ill-advised, ill-treated and ill-behaved woman's life was not quite over. She had died at her house at Hammersmith, but she was to be buried in her native Germany, and somehow or other her body had to be conveyed to the port of embarkation at Harwich. The King, who fortunately for himself was out of London and on his way to Ireland for a state visit, ignored the Court of Common Council's request that the funeral procession should go through the City, from which his deceased consort had derived so much of her support, and decided that it should proceed around the northern outskirts of London instead. But the Queen's adherents were determined that her remains should pass through the City, and through the City they therefore went. At eight o'clock in the morning the procession moved off from Hammersmith in pouring rain, intending to turn left at Kensington, up Church Street into the Bayswater Road. But Church Street was found to be blocked with a barricade of waggons. There was a halt for an hour and a half. Then the escorting squadron of Life Guards, led by Sir Robert Baker, the chief

Bow Street magistrate, moved off westward along Kensington Gore. But the park gates were found to be locked or barred by determined men bawling 'To the City! the City!', and so too was Park Lane. The horses were turned about, an unlocked gate was found and the cavalcade proceeded apprehensively through Hyde Park at a brisk, unfunereal trot. Cumberland Gate (now Marble Arch) was blocked now, and Edgware Road. A scuffle began, stones were thrown and shots fired, and several people were killed before the north-west passage was forced. Eastward again into the Marylebone Road swung the procession, now somewhat battered and begrimed, but at the junction with Tottenham Court Road it encountered an impenetrable barrier of densely packed carts and vociferating men. There was only one way for the distracted cortège to go – south to the Strand, with no left turn unclosed en route, and thence eastward under Temple Bar and through the City, with the Lord Mayor at its head.[1]

The agitation in support of the Queen was a short-lived and predominantly middle-class affair. It was matched by the much longer, vastly more important and in the main working-class struggle for the freedom of the press. At the beginning of the nineteenth century the publication of anything with a malicious intention of causing a breach of the peace was a criminal libel. This could be construed to include virtually any criticism of the existing social and political order, and the law, although haphazardly administered, could therefore be applied to the news-sheets and political pamphlets which proliferated during the mass reform movement of the early years of peace. Prosecutions could be brought by the Home Office, by the magistrates or by bodies like the Society for the Suppression of Vice, the victim could be kept in prison for many weeks without trial until the prosecutor chose to proceed, and at the trial juries were often packed. Nor were these the only obstacles to the spread of popular radical literature, for the newspaper stamp duties added an enormous financial burden.

These archaic limitations on the political freedom of the press were to a large extent ended between 1817 and 1825 by the courage and persistence of a handful of London working printers, booksellers and journalists. We have already seen that in November 1816 William Cobbett, who had previously been imprisoned for two years (1810–12) for attacking the flogging of militiamen by German mercenaries, began to publish the 'leading article' contained in each number of his weekly *Register* as a separate item. This

[1] *Annual Register*, 1820, 1821; Sharpe, vol. III, pp. 318–19.

famous 'Twopenny Trash' soon enjoyed such an enormous circulation that when Cobbett withdrew to America a few months later his successful experiment was instantly copied by T. J. Wooler, a printer, whose weekly *The Black Dwarf*, published every Sunday morning in Finsbury, contained pungent attacks on government ministers. At about the same time William Hone, a bookseller off Ludgate Hill, produced a ribald political parody of Anglican religious doctrine. In 1818 John Hunt started a short-lived fourpenny *The Yellow Dwarf* to which his brother Leigh Hunt and William Hazlitt both contributed, and during the general election of that year John Wade, formerly a journeyman wool-sorter, inaugurated the first penny paper, *The Gorgon*, primarily devoted to the achievement of universal suffrage 'for the whole biped race'. And 1819, the year of Peterloo, saw the appearance of many other ephemeral publications of the same genre.

Both Wooler and Hone were prosecuted, the former for defamatory libel on the ministers and the latter for blasphemous libel. Wooler was found guilty, but in circumstances which produced a reform of the City of London Special Jury list, while Hone's acquittal, after seven months' imprisonment and a three-day trial in which he most ably conducted his own defence, ensured that no Attorney General would ever prosecute a witty parodist again. But while Hone was in gaol the most formidable of all the champions of the free press appeared – Richard Carlile, a journeyman tin-plate worker who, 'being fired by the political publications of the day', bought a hundred copies of Wooler's *The Black Dwarf* and succeeded in placing orders for them in a number of shops scattered throughout London. Soon he too was imprisoned, for eighteen weeks without trial for re-publishing Hone's parodies, but when he came out he established himself in a shop in Fleet Street and began to re-publish the works of Tom Paine. For this offence he was in 1819 sentenced to a fine of £1,500 and three years' imprisonment, and was bundled off to Dorchester gaol, where through his refusal to pay the fine he was to remain for nearly six years.[1]

But the widespread publicity of his trial only served to enlarge the sales of forbidden works at Carlile's shop, where his place at the counter was taken by his equally formidable wife. In January 1821 she was sentenced to two years' imprisonment and joined her husband in Dorchester gaol, but in Fleet Street she was succeeded by Carlile's sister, who by the end of the year had also been sent to Dorchester, for twelve months. The business

[1] William H. Wickwar, *The Struggle for the Freedom of the Press, 1819–1832*, 1928, pp. 19–71, 95, 263.

was subsequently continued by a succession of volunteer assistants, recruited through the medium of *The Republican*, the weekly which Carlile himself edited from his cell in Dorchester gaol, and in which he published accounts of every fresh trial for libel. There were repeated arrests, many of them instigated by the 'Constitutional Association for opposing the Progress of Disloyal and Seditious principles', and many of the volunteers also went to prison.

But by 1824 a general change of public attitude was beginning to make itself felt. Juries could no longer be relied upon to convict, the lawyers were becoming impatient with the law, the funds of the Constitutional Association were exhausted, the Society for the Suppression of Vice was in little better shape, and even the Home Office was beginning to despair. Meanwhile the circulation of 'libellous' radical publications had increased by leaps and bounds, and the reports of each new trial only enlarged it still further. At last a truce was called, and when Carlile himself, now bad-tempered and in ill health, mounted the coach to leave Dorchester in November 1825, the prosecutions had already ceased. They were later revived for a short while in 1830–1, when Carlile served another three years' imprisonment. The libel laws were not altered for many years, and the campaign for the abolition of the stamp duties was yet to come, but the substance of victory in the struggle for the free press had already been won.[1]

The free press, free to question and deride the claims of the established order, and free to discuss any methods for the reconstruction of that order, provided the means for the widespread dissemination of the plethora of new ideas which appeared in the 1820s. The immensely varied literature which poured out from the London printing presses was passed from hand to hand and from group to group in the taverns, trade clubs and wherever else working men congregated together, extending its influence far wider than its sales figures – 12,000 copies, for instance, in the case of *The Black Dwarf* – might suggest. There was an insatiable appetite for knowledge – Cobbett's *Grammar of the English Language* sold over 100,000 copies in the fifteen years after its first publication in 1818 – and a willingness to experiment with new notions, often of the most impractical nature. Through the free press working men were becoming more articulate and more aware of their own rapidly emerging social ethos, distinct from that of the middle class, from which many of their leaders had hitherto been drawn. But in these early steps towards independence and self-reliance

[1] Wickwar, pp. 209–43.

they were still uncertain which path to tread, and this uncertainty reflected itself in the unsteady and irresolute progress of the working-class
movement.

Carlile, the principal hero in the struggle for the free press, maintained
to the end of his life in 1843 the traditions of individualism and free thought
enshrined in the writings of Tom Paine. But by 1831, when he had
hired the Rotunda, a large hall in Blackfriars Road, for a series of secu-
larist lectures, he was to find that the discussions provided by the new
National Union of the Working Classes were more closely in tune with the
prevailing mood during the Reform Bill crisis. Radical interests had
greatly enlarged themselves since he had first gone to prison in 1817. As
long ago as 1818 *The Gorgon*, with which Place had been associated, had
concerned itself with Benthamite political economy and the social conditions of working men as well as with the achievement of universal suffrage.
Place, too, had been largely responsible for engineering the repeal of the
Combination Laws in 1824, which, contrary to his own expectations, had
been followed by numerous strikes, notably, in London, among the
shipwrights and the coopers. The Thames-side shipwrights' leader was
John Gast, who had played a prominent part in a strike there as long ago
as 1812, and who had been connected with the formation in 1818 of the
Philanthropic Hercules, the first short-lived attempt at a general union of
trades. In 1825, when there was a possibility that the Combination Laws
might be re-enacted, representatives of a number of trades gathered in
London to concert their opposition. From this there emerged the *Trades
Newspaper*, a weekly sevenpenny stamped paper, managed by a committee
of delegates from different trades, and of which Gast was chairman. Its
motto, 'They helped every one his neighbour', proclaimed its trade-union
inspiration, and under its editor, J. C. Robertson, it preached unfamiliar
new ideas such as the antagonism between capital and labour. New trade
clubs proliferated, strength through union being their common object.
One of these, the Friendly Society of Operative House Carpenters and
Joiners, was formed at a meeting of delegates held in London in 1827,
and its first rules asserted that 'for the amelioration of the evils attendant
on our trade, and the advancement of the rights and privileges of labour',
it was 'absolutely necessary that a firm compact of interests should exist
between the whole of the operative carpenters and joiners throughout the
United Kingdom of Great Britain'.[1]

[1] Thompson, pp. 838–55; Webb, pp. 104, 110–11; G. D. H. Cole, *Attempts at
General Union. A Study in British Trade Union History, 1818–1834*, 1953, pp. 10–11.

But this thrusting, unstable trade unionism, equally antipathetic to both Carlile and Place, was not the only source of new ideas in the 1820s. Ever since 1817, when Robert Owen had attended a meeting of wealthy London merchants at the George and Vulture tavern to explain his proposals for 'Villages of Unity and Mutual Co-operation', the idea of planting new self-supporting communities outside the existing social structure had gripped the imagination of many working men. William Lovett, who was one such, says in his autobiography that 'This notion has a peculiar attraction for the plodding, toiling, ill-remunerated sons and daughters of labour.' In 1821 George Mudie, a Scots disciple of Owen, established such a 'Co-operative and Economical Society' in Spa Fields, where some twenty-one mainly working-class families took up residence. Each family paid a fixed charge for maintenance, and meals, education and recreation were all provided communally. Some members worked outside for wages which they pooled, while others worked inside. This experiment seems only to have lasted for some three years, but its failure did not prevent the establishment of the London Co-operative Society in 1824, recruited largely from the artisan class, with its own journal, *The Co-operative Magazine*, founded two years later. Soon the Society had plans for a new community based on co-operative principles which would guarantee the full benefits of their labour for its members. But several thousand pounds were needed to establish the community, and through the lack of such resources the co-operators' aims were soon reduced to amassing the necessary funds by co-operative buying and selling. The middlemen's profits were to be eliminated by the establishment of 'Labour Exchanges' where members could sell the produce of their labour and buy the produce of other members, all profits being set aside for the subsequent formation of self-supporting independent communities.[1]

The working classes were, in fact, 'to form themselves into joint stock associations of labour, by which (with industry, skill, and knowledge) they might ultimately have the trade, manufactures, and commerce of the country in their own hands'. By the end of the 1820s there were several hundred co-operative societies in existence, of which a few were in London, and in 1829 William Lovett was one of the leaders in the formation in London of the British Association for Promoting Co-operative Knowledge.

[1] Lovett, p. 43; W. H. G. Armytage, *Heavens Below. Utopian Experiments in England 1560–1960*, 1961, pp. 92–5; Sidney Pollard, 'Nineteenth-Century Co-Operation: From Community Building to Shopkeeping', in *Essays in Labour History*, ed. Asa Briggs and John Saville, 1960, pp. 79–80.

In September 1832 a 'Labour Exchange' was opened under Owen's auspices in Gray's Inn Road, most of its members being artisans who could exercise their skills without large means – furniture-makers, shoe-makers, hatters, tailors and glaziers for instance. In 1833 the London United Trades' Association was established to buy materials wholesale for unemployed members and set them to work co-operatively in the production of goods for the exchange. Existing trade unions were also encouraged to bring their members' goods, and so by the early 1830s the co-operative and trade union movements were beginning to coalesce in the building of a new system of production and distribution which, it was intended, should ultimately take over the regulation of the industrial out-put of the whole nation. In the mood of bitter disappointment prevalent among the working population after the passing of the Reform Act in 1832, this recipe for the millennium had an irresistible attraction which led two years later, to the spectacular rise and fall of the Grand National Consolidated Trades' Union.[1]

The struggle for the Reform Bill was thus fought out against the back-ground of all these new ideas which had increasingly engaged the attention of working men in London during the 1820s. And there were other forces at work – the example of the revolution in France in July 1830, the mount-ing agitation against the metropolitan select vestries, and the widespread dislike and distrust of Peel's new police force. It was at about this time, too, that the struggle for a free press was resumed, now directed against the stamp duty on newspapers. The pioneer was Henry Hetherington, a printer, who in October 1830 began to issue unstamped *Penny Papers for the People*. In the following year these became *The Poor Man's Guardian*, which carried on its front page the challenge 'A weekly newspaper for the people, established contrary to "Law", to try the power of "Might" against "Right".' Hetherington was soon imprisoned, but (as in the days of Richard Carlile) the paper continued to appear in defiance of the law, supported by a new generation of men later to become leaders in the Chartist movement – James Bronterre O'Brien, who edited it, and William Lovett, John Cleave, Julian Hibbert and James Watson the publisher, who organized its distribution and a 'Victim Fund' for the maintenance of imprisoned vendors. Other unstamped papers soon began to appear, and

[1] Lovett, p. 41; Pollard, pp. 80–8; W. H. Oliver, 'The Labour Exchange Phase of the Co-Operative Movement', *Oxford Economic Papers, New Series*, vol. 10, 1958, pp. 355–67.

in the five years 1830–5 over five hundred people went to gaol for offences against the stamp laws. In 1834 *The Poor Man's Guardian* itself was declared to be legal after all, and in 1836 the stamp duty was reduced from 4*d*. per copy to 1*d*.[1]

So when George IV died in 1830 and a general election was held, radical London was already seething with excitement and expectation. Within a month of the accession of William IV the City's Court of Common Hall drew up an address demanding parliamentary reform, but the Duke of Wellington remained obdurate. Through his uncompromising opposition to reform he suddenly became the most unpopular man in the kingdom. In November 1830 the Lord-Mayor Elect warned the Duke that danger might beset him if he accompanied William IV to a banquet at Guildhall, and in the event both he and the King decided to forgo their visit. The effect of this cancellation 'upon the minds of the citizens was beyond description. Men hastened to purchase arms and to secure the fastenings of their houses, as if the banner of rebellion had been actually displayed in the streets.' Consols fell about 3 per cent, and alarm grew when inflammatory handbills were found in the streets. One of these stated that 'all London meets on Tuesday – come armed – we assure you, from ocular demonstration, that 6,000 cutlasses have been removed from the Tower, for the immediate use of Peel's bloody gang. . . . These damned police are now to be armed. Englishmen, will you put up with this?' This, in fact, was the explanation of the Cabinet's decision to prevent the King's visit to the Guildhall – there was no conspiracy, but simply a fear on the part of the government that the new police, only established fourteen months previously, might not be able to control the situation. The ministry suddenly became ridiculous, and within a week a defeat in the Commons was followed by their resignation on 16 November 1830.[2]

'This is the first time,' Place recorded, 'that apprehension of violence by the people against an administration has induced them openly to change their plan of proceeding.' But after this initial impetus from the capital it was Birmingham, not London, which assumed the leading role throughout most of the campaign for the Reform Bill. In this great industrial town, with a population of nearly 150,000 but as yet without either its own municipal council or its own Member of Parliament, Thomas Attwood, a much-respected banker, had already, in January 1830, established the first of the Political Unions which were to play such a vital part in the crisis. The first and principal object of the Union was the reform of the

[1] Lovett, pp. 59–65.   [2] Sharpe, vol. III, p. 328; *Annual Register*, 1830.

House of Commons; for seven hours a huge audience had listened to the endless speeches, and soon other unions on the Birmingham model were being set up in many other large towns. But Attwood and his friends in Birmingham retained the leadership of all the political unions through-out the two-year struggle. 'What passed at Birmingham immediately determined the issue of this mighty contention,' Harriet Martineau subsequently wrote. 'Birmingham was at that time looked upon as the headquarters of reform', and Lord Durham, a member of the Reform ministry, declared a few days after the Bill had finally received the royal assent that it was to Birmingham that the country owed its salvation.[1]

In London there was no Political Union until as late as November 1831 – nearly two years after Birmingham had given the lead – and even then it did not become really effective until almost the very last weeks of the struggle, in May 1832. Lord Grey's ministry, which took office in November 1830, enjoyed the active backing of the Courts of Common Council and Common Hall (though not of the Court of Aldermen), but the lack of any powerful, spontaneously formed, articulate metropolitan body of opinion in support of the Bill left a gap which was quickly penetrated by working-class organizations. The National Union of the Working Classes, formed in May 1831 at a meeting of delegates at the Bazaar Coffee House, Castle Street, St Marylebone, was the political arm of the Owenite British Association for Promoting Co-operative Knowledge, which William Lovett had helped to form two years earlier. Its chief objects were 'the Protection of Working Men; the Free Disposal of the Produce of Labour; and Effectual Reform of the Commons' House of Parliament; the Repeal of all Bad Laws; the Enactment of a Wise and Comprehensive Code of Laws . . .'. Branches of the Union were established throughout London, and 'class leaders' managed the meetings, at which there were political discussions and readings from the newspapers. At Richard Carlile's Rotunda in Blackfriars Road there were weekly debates, which were fully reported in *The Poor Man's Guardian*. The Union seems to have drawn its main strength from London's radical artisans, and it included Hetherington, Lovett, Watson and Cleave among its members, plus a more extreme wing which favoured violence and secret conventions. But it did not enjoy any widespread support among the still inarticulate mass of un-skilled labourers. The Rotundanists' debates were nevertheless important

[1] Graham Wallas, *The Life of Francis Place 1771–1854*, 1925 edn, p. 249; Conrad Gill, *History of Birmingham*, vol. I, pp. 206, 209 n.; J. R. M. Butler, *The Passing of the Great Reform Bill*, 1964 edn, p. 385.

because many of the ideas later to be embodied in the Chartist movement were discussed and clearly articulated here, either by or in the presence of men who later became prominent in metropolitan Chartism. The National Union naturally declared for universal suffrage, annual parliaments and vote by ballot, but more important for the future was the heightened sense of divergence of interest between the middle and working classes. The Whigs' Reform Bill excluded the working class, and was intended to be a permanent settlement of the suffrage question. In the eyes of the National Union the promoters of the Bill merely intended to consolidate their power by recruiting the support of the middle classes, while working men were to be for ever excluded from the pale of the constitution. *The Poor Man's Guardian* summed the matter up for the Rotundanists when it stated that: 'The only difference between the Whigs and the Tories is this – the Whigs would give the shadow to preserve the substance; the Tories would not give the shadow, because stupid as they are, the millions will not stop at shadows but proceed onwards to realities.'[1]

Francis Place expressed the same equation in different terms when he wrote that 'the difference between the political Unions [on the Birmingham model] and the Unions of the Working Classes was that the first desired the Reform Bill to prevent a revolution, the last desired its destruction as a means of producing a revolution'. In reality, however, class loyalties were not yet clear-cut except among a very small proportion of the working class, and the great orderly procession which followed the House of Lords' first rejection of the Bill in October 1831 must have contained within its ranks many Londoners to whom the Bill would not give the vote. This crisis revealed the absence in London of the steadying influence of a well-organized Political Union such as those of Birmingham and other towns, for in the three days between the rejection of the Bill and the day of the procession there had been numerous rowdy meetings in the parks, and the police had had to prevent a large crowd of Rotundanists from marching on the Palace of Westminster. The procession itself, consisting mainly of 'shopkeepers and superior artisans', was assembled by the parish reform associations, some of which had probably evolved from the agitation against the select vestries. It numbered some 70,000 men, and included many who wore the white scarves of the Rotundanists. Its leaders carried an address to the King at St James's Palace, where they were received by the Home Secretary, Lord Melbourne.[2]

---

[1] Cole, p. 39; Lovett, pp. 68–9; Thompson, p. 893.   [2] Butler, pp. 292–3, 382 n.

This procession was the first mass gathering in London since the beginning of the Reform Bill crisis, and it showed that well-conducted men who were not usually concerned with politics were willing to take an active part in supporting the Bill. It also showed the ambivalent attitude of the working men towards the Bill, for while some of them had supported the address to the King, others of the National Union, now led by Lovett and Watson, planned to hold their own meeting on 7 November at White Conduit House, Islington, to ratify a 'bill of rights' demanding universal suffrage, annual parliaments, vote by ballot, and the abolition of all hereditary distinctions of birth. In order to forestall this projected polarization of working-class loyalty, and to establish if possible a union of middle- and working-class opinion, Francis Place and the Westminster Reform Committee contrived a public meeting in Lincoln's Inn Fields on 1 November for the inauguration of a National Political Union on the Birmingham model. Sir Francis Burdett took the chair at what turned out to be a stormy occasion, for a large body of Rotundanists, headed by Lovett and Cleave, appeared and demanded that some members of the council of the new union should be chosen from the working classes. To this Burdett unconvincingly replied that 'they all formed only one class, the people of England'. But the workers were not to be satisfied, one of them vociferating amidst the mounting uproar that 'The middle classes merely wish to make us the tools of their purposes; we are not even to have votes, and they tell us it would be impolitic now to demand that. There is no use in preaching up policy and patience when we are starving; it is a mockery of us.' They did indeed succeed in securing half the places on the council, but they seem to have played no further part in its affairs. And so Place was left in control of the National Political Union, which in his hands was certain to play its part at the next crisis. The Rotundanists' meeting at Islington was abandoned in face of threats from the government.[1]

Meanwhile there was an interval of five months before the last great climax, during which the new National Political Union did not greatly distinguish itself. In February 1832, when the Bill was going through the Commons for the last time, it held its first general meeting for the purpose of presenting a petition in support of the measure. There was a dispute about the wording and Burdett, who was chairman, flounced off in a huff – 'I tell you what,' he had already confided to Hobhouse, 'the more I see, the more I am convinced that there is no having to do with any but gentlemen; that is, with men of education.' This contrasted oddly with

[1] Butler, p. 305; Lovett, pp. 72–7; *Annual Register*, 1831.

Birmingham, where on the very same day, 2 February 1832, the Union, now 27,000 strong, presented an address pledging their continuing support for their leader, Attwood.

London's ineffectiveness was again shown on 21 March, which the King had proclaimed as a day of general fast on account of the cholera then prevalent in the capital. The occasion was soon referred to as the day of general farce, and the National Political Union decided to hold aloof from it. But the National Union of the Working Classes decided to assemble in Finsbury Square, according to the newspapers, for 'the distribution of bread and meat amongst the lower orders'. A crowd variously estimated at between 25,000 and 100,000 assembled, but the occasion merely degenerated into an affray with the police. And when the National Political Union next met again in full conclave on 4 May to petition the Lords, who were about to consider the Bill in the crucial committee stage, it was only to be once again outshone by a vast assembly of 200,000 people at Birmingham.

On the very day of this great Birmingham meeting, 7 May 1832, the tactics of the opposition in the committee of the House of Lords compelled Lord Grey to threaten resignation unless the King promised to create at least fifty new peers. The King refused, and on 9 May all the ministers resigned. For the next eleven days the country hovered on the brink of revolution, and it was now at last that London belatedly assumed the role of the capital city in the great national struggle. For the first six days, until 15 May, during which the Duke of Wellington was attempting to form a ministry, there were feverish meetings all over London – meetings of unions, parishes, wards, trades and vestries, all demanding that the Lords should pass the Bill. In the City the Court of Common Council urged Members of Parliament to vote no supplies until the Bill had been secured, and a joint committee of all the aldermen and commoners was appointed to sit from day to day until this object had been achieved. There were resolutions to pay no taxes, and placards on walls and in windows openly announced this determination – welcomed even by the men of the Rotunda, who in other respects now stood aloof from what they regarded as no concern of theirs. At last, too, the National Political Union came into its own with a great meeting on 9 May at which it was decided to petition the Commons to refuse supplies, and another on the following day to denounce the King – 'false, fleeting, perjured Clarence'.[1]

[1] Butler, pp. 305, 339–40, 350–1; Gill, p. 209; *Annual Register*, 1832; Sharpe, vol. III, p. 341.

Y

But while all these outward demonstrations were maintaining pressure on the King and Parliament and preventing any risk of public apathy, far more important arrangements were being made in semi-private. Communications had been established with the leaders of the Political Unions in a number of provincial towns, and on 11 May a deputation from Birmingham arrived, authorized to pledge its Union to a rising. 'The means of organizing the people for effectual resistance' were discussed, as Francis Place subsequently related, 'there was a general agreement that Birmingham was the place in which to hoist the standard of revolt, and it was understood that the first hostile defence against the Duke of Wellington's administration should be made there', while in London there should be demonstrations of sufficient scale to prevent the dispatch of troops to the Midlands. On the next day, 12 May, a council of union deputies from many parts of the country was held at a tavern in Covent Garden at which it was agreed that if the Duke succeeded in forming a ministry, 'open resistance should at once be made'. Lists of names and addresses 'of persons in every part of the country likely to be useful' were made, proclamations and handbills were prepared for the printers, towns would 'be barricaded – new municipal arrangements will be formed by the inhabitants, and the first town which is barricaded shuts up all banks'.

This threat of financial dislocation probably had more effect upon the Duke than any amateur military plans. On 13 May placards with the simple message, 'To stop the Duke go for gold', suddenly appeared all over London, and large parcels of these bills were already on their way by coach and carrier to all parts of the country. In a single day the Bank of England alone paid out £307,000 in specie, and it at once became probable that the run on gold would quickly drain every banker in the kingdom. Two days later, on 15 May, Wellington abandoned his attempt to form a ministry, and Lord Grey and the Whigs returned, though still without a promise from the King to create peers. The final climax was not reached until 18 May, when the Cabinet, fully aware through Hobhouse of all the semi-secret preparations for resistance, at last demanded a firm pledge from the King. In the course of the afternoon the obstinate old man reluctantly gave way; the demand for gold at once ceased, and the terrible tension began to relax.[1]

The influence of London on the whole two-year struggle is difficult to assess. When compared with Birmingham, a town with less than one-tenth of the population of the metropolis, the impact of London on the course

[1] Wallas, pp. 298–315; Butler, pp. 405, 410–11.

of events seems to have been relatively small, at least until the very last days, when it was perhaps decisive. London had given no lead; the working classes as yet possessed no stable organization, either in London or elsewhere, and so far as the middle classes were concerned Francis Place, though cool, efficient and resourceful, was a back-stage wire-puller, not a leader. London the great city has indeed always lacked leaders. Place himself, writing some years later to Richard Cobden about the lack of support in London for the Anti-Corn Law League, described the difficulties.

London differs very widely from Manchester, and, indeed, from every other place on the face of the earth. It has no local or particular interest as a town, not even as to politics. Its several boroughs in this respect are like so many very populous places at a distance from one another, and the inhabitants of any one of them know nothing, or next to nothing, of the proceedings in any other, and not much indeed of those of their own. London in my time, and that is half a century, has never moved [politically]. A few of the people in different parts have moved, and these, whenever they come together, make a considerable number – still, a very small number indeed when compared with the whole number – and when these are judiciously managed, *i.e.* when they are brought to act together, not only make a great noise, which is heard far and wide, but which has also considerable influence in many places. But, isolated as men are here, living as they do at considerable distances, many seven miles apart, and but seldom meeting together, except in small groups, to talk either absolute nonsense on miserable party politics, or to transact business exclusive of everything else, they will tell you they have no time to give to the Association to help repeal the Corn Laws, while the simple fact is that, with the exception of the men of business (and even they lose much time), four-fifths of the whole do nothing but lose their time.[1]

Sheer size, then, was already a problem, and so, too, was the presence of the central government, constantly drawing away to the general affairs of the nation the men who in the provinces would have first established themselves on a local pre-eminence. London in the first seventy years of the nineteenth century never had its Attwood or its Chamberlain or its Bright or its Cobden – for Sir Francis Burdett can hardly stand comparison with them – and its influence was correspondingly diminished.

[1] Wallas, pp. 393–4.

Yet London remained the stage where the national drama was enacted, and during the passage of the Reform Bill the possibility that her citizens might become overmighty was often expressed. 'They had, unfortunately, heard too much of Paris being France,' exclaimed an apprehensive M.P. during one of the innumerable debates on the Bill; 'Let them, therefore, take warning lest they made London England.'[1] The warning proved unnecessary, but it is easy to imagine that London in 1832 might have followed the example of Paris in 1830 if the parish constables and watchmen had not been recently superseded by Peel's new police.

Under the terms of the Reform Act the number of M.P.s representing the whole metropolitan area was increased from ten to twenty-two.[2] This was a substantial increase, but in the reformed House of Commons there were 658 members (including the Irish M.P.s), so that London's share in the representation was still only about one-thirtieth of the whole – far below its true share, whether calculated in terms of wealth or population. But even this increased representation was hotly opposed in the Commons, both on the grounds that it was an 'extension of that system of centralization in all things, the growing influence of which it was their duty, as it was the interest of the country at large, to endeavour to counteract, rather than to extend', and also (by Sir Robert Peel) because the metropolitan M.P.s would be unduly subjected to the 'ill-considered commands of their constituents'. Young Mr Macaulay, later to achieve immortality as a historian, was probably nearer the mark when he asserted that 'as long as regular Government existed, the metropolis was, in fact, weak; but when the course of regular Government was disturbed, the metropolis possessed, and could employ, a vast and overwhelming force'.[3]

The passing of the Reform Bill left the working men of London, and indeed of the whole country, in a state of profound disillusionment. Those who had supported the Bill felt that they had been betrayed, while those who had been hostile or indifferent were now ready to assert themselves by industrial rather than political means. By 1833 the National Union

[1] *Hansard, Third Series*, vol. 10, 1832, cols. 923–4.

[2] Before the Reform Act the City of London returned four M.P.s, and Middlesex, Westminster and Southwark two each. The Act established the parliamentary boroughs of Marylebone, Finsbury, Tower Hamlets, Lambeth and Greenwich, each with two seats. The County representation of Surrey was also increased from two to four, and the new Eastern Division formed part of the southern outskirts of London.

[3] *Hansard, Third Series*, vol. 10, 1832, cols. 931, 946, 954.

of the Working Classes was already in decline, and its London membership amounted to only about three thousand. In May it held its last great public assembly, in Cold Bath Fields, where about eight hundred people met to prepare for a national convention; but the sole result was another affray in which the police 'made a furious onslaught upon the assembled multitude, knocking down, indiscriminately, men, women, and children'. One constable lost his life, but feeling against the police was so intense that the inquest jury returned a verdict of justifiable homicide. [1] This was the last of the series of sizeable physical contests in which the new police were engaged during the early years of their existence; and it also marked, for practical purposes, the end of the National Union.

In this mood of embittered disappointment working men began to feel that the way to gain power was not by political action, either with or without the middle classes, but by a mass union of all productive workers, which would lead quickly and inevitably to a peaceful take-over of the entire affairs of the nation. In 1833 one hundred thousand men were said to be 'walking about London in want of employment', [2] and in such a field of suffering ideas of this kind found a perfect breeding ground. This was particularly the case with the skilled artisans, who had provided the main strength of the now moribund National Union of the Working Classes, and to whom the Owenite labour exchanges and ideals of co-operative socialism made a particularly strong appeal.

The Grand National Consolidated Trades Union of Great Britain and Ireland was established at a meeting of union delegates in Robert Owen's Institute in Charlotte Street, Fitzroy Square, in February 1834. Unlike the slightly earlier Operative Builder's Union, which had temporarily federated the unions of the seven different trades involved in the building industry, the Grand National drew a large proportion of its support from the London craftsmen and made little impact on the factory workers of the north. A national union of all the trades had been much discussed for some months previously, and the determination of the silk weavers of Derby to inaugurate a workers' co-operative in defiance of their employers provided the occasion for the formation of the Grand National. The skilled

---

[1] Lovett, p. 82; see also Gavin Thurston, *The Clerkenwell Riot. The Killing of Constable Culley*, 1967. The jurymen were subsequently fêted as heroes, and a procession was organized in their honour. The great silk banner made for this occasion has survived, and is now in the London Museum. It is inscribed 'In Honour of the Independent & Heroic 17 Jurymen who in Defiance of Tyrannic Dictation Returned an Honest Verdict'.

[2] *Annual Register*, 1833.

London tradesmen, particularly the tailors and the cordwainers, dominated the union, but the tailors themselves were almost immediately involved in a ruinous strike, and the builders (who stood aloof from the National) soon afterwards in a lock-out. Many provincial craft unions quickly affiliated themselves, but there was never any stable central organization. Letters remained unanswered, policy undecided. Disintegration set in within a few months, and the Grand National was eventually wound up in August 1834, after a career of barely six months' duration. It had excited considerable public alarm, for a strike of the London gasworkers had plunged Westminster into partial darkness for a few nights, and the great procession in April of 40,000 men, marching from Copenhagen Fields to Whitehall, with Robert Owen himself on horseback at its head, to protest against the savage sentences recently imposed on the Dorchester unionists (better known as the Tolpuddle Martyrs), had put *The Times* into a great state of excitement.[1]

Yet despite the brevity of its existence and the pitiable collapse of the millennarian hopes which it had inspired, the Grand National had more lasting results. The London artisans and craftsmen had failed in their attempt at national leadership. They would be unlikely to repeat such an attempt *en masse*, and their brothers in the provinces would be still less likely to follow them again. So Chartism, which, unlike the Grand National, was soon to cause prolonged and widespread fear, was primarily a provincial movement, and except perhaps in 1848 never possessed a mass support in London; in time this lack of strength in the capital was to be one of the main causes of the failure of the whole Chartist effort.

By the mid-1830s the pattern of London radicalism was taking a new form. The City's Courts of Common Council and Common Hall were no longer presenting addresses and petitions on national affairs with quite such frequency as hitherto, and after 1837 elections to the Court of Aldermen were no longer conducted on open party lines. In Westminster the enormous parliamentary franchise had been greatly diminished by the Reform Act, and at the first election held afterwards the number of votes cast there was only about half the average number in the 1820s. At this first general election to the reformed House of Commons all of the twenty-two metropolitan members were either Whigs or Radicals, and this clean sweep at the hustings reflected the victory of the middle-class Benthamite philosophy of reform. But even now only about one in every eighteen of all the

---

[1] W. H. Oliver, 'The Consolidated Trades Union of 1834', *Economic History Review*, *Second Series*, vol. 17, 1964–5, pp. 77–95.

inhabitants of London had the parliamentary vote, and after the collapse of the Owenite trade-union bubble in 1834 working men turned once more to the extension of the suffrage as a more reliable means to achieve their social and political aims.[1]

Once again it was the skilled men who provided the leaders, but from 1832 to 1835 the real wages of London artisans were rising, and support was at first extremely small. Towards the end of the successful campaign against the stamp duty on newspapers a committee composed chiefly of working men had been formed to pay off the fines imposed on John Cleave and Henry Hetherington. Lovett was one of the secretaries of this group, and it was probably due to him that 'the question arose among us, whether we could form and maintain a union formed exclusively of this class. . . . We were the more induced to try the experiment as the working classes had not hitherto evinced that discriminating and independent spirit in the management of their political affairs which we were desirous to see.' From these deliberations there emerged the London Working Men's Association, formed in 1836 with Lovett as its secretary and Hetherington as its treasurer.

The first object of the Association was: 'To draw into one bond of *unity* the *intelligent* and *influential* portion of the working classes in town and country.' It was not, in fact, intended to have an unlimited appeal like that of the London Corresponding Society in 1792, and its London membership never exceeded a few hundreds. Self-instruction was to be the chief instrument in the achievement of the association's second aim, which was 'To seek by every legal means to place all classes of society in possession of their equal political and social rights.' The collection of information, 'especially statistics regarding the wages of labour, the habits and condition of the labourer, and all those causes that mainly contribute to the present state of things', meetings to digest and publish this information, the formation of a library and 'the education of the rising generation' – these were the patient, cautious methods which the new Association intended to pursue.

The Association established itself in premises off Gray's Inn Road. In November 1836 it sent an address to the working men of Belgium – claimed by Lovett to have been the first such international working-class communication – and soon afterwards it published its first educational pamphlet, entitled *The Rotten House of Commons*. In February 1837 it

[1] Beaven, vol. II, p. 145 n.; Henry Stooks Smith, *The Parliaments of England*, 3 vols. 1844-50.

convened a public meeting at the Crown and Anchor Tavern in the Strand, the venue for many radical meetings in the 1830s and 40s, to prepare a petition to Parliament for what were soon to become the famous six points of the People's Charter – universal suffrage, vote by ballot, equal electoral districts, annual parliaments, no property qualification for membership and payment of M.P.s. Resolutions on these lines were unanimously adopted, and in May the support of the small group of radical M.P.s (several of them representing London constituencies) was being canvassed. At this point the general election caused by the death of William IV provided the Association with an opportunity to put out all over the country an address announcing the preparation of a Bill to be entitled 'The People's Charter'. The Charter itself was published on 8 May 1838, and the Bill founded upon it was written by Lovett, with assistance from Francis Place and John Roebuck.[1]

Thus within less than two years of its foundation the London Working Men's Association had embarked on the stormy waters of a far-reaching programme of political reform. It had sent missionaries out to preach in the provinces, some of whom, like Henry Vincent and Richard Hartwell, both printing compositors, expounded far less cautious views than those originally proposed, and soon there were several hundred affiliated working men's associations scattered up and down the country. For a few months the London Association was the leader of a widespread movement of working-class opinion. But much of this support was in reality engendered by growing unemployment and hatred of the New Poor Law, grievances of terrible immediacy which Feargus O'Connor, with his vague threats of physical force, was soon able to exploit in the midlands and the north. And even in London there were divisions of opinion within the parent association, which resulted in the resignation in 1837 of a number of members led by George Julian Harney, and the formation of a rival society, the East London Democratic Association.[2]

Within a few months of its publication the Charter commanded the loyalty of a large section of the working class throughout the country, but the London Working Men's Association which had originated it had

---

[1] Lovett, pp. 91–121, 164–5; Mark Hovell, *The Chartist Movement*, 1925 edn, pp. 60, 62; Tucker, pp. 73–84. For the origins of the L.W.M.A. and the authorship of the 'People's Charter' see also D. J. Rowe, 'The London Working Men's Association and the "People's Charter",' *Past and Present*, no. 36, 1967, pp. 73–86, and I. Prothero's reply, *Past and Present*, no. 38, pp. 169–73.

[2] Lovett, p. 181; Hovell, pp. 67, 71, 75; A. R. Schoyen, *The Chartist Challenge. A Portrait of George Julian Harney*, 1958, p. 14.

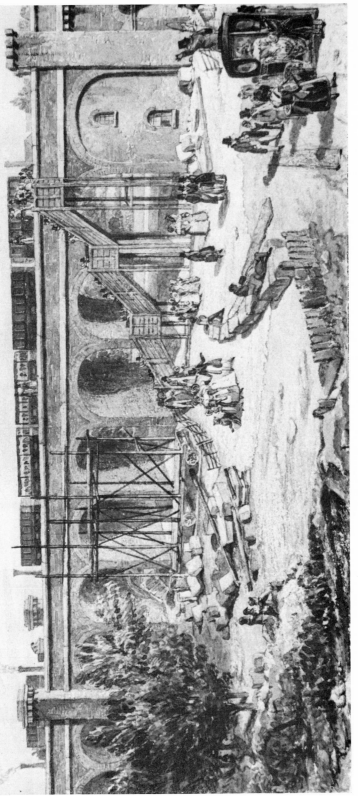

30 The London and Greenwich Railway, *c.* 1840

(*over leaf*) 31 London *c.* 1874–8

32 (*top*) The London and Croydon Railway, 1838. Greenwich Railway in background

33 (*bottom*) Building the Stationary Engine House, Camden Town, on the London and Birmingham Railway, 1837

been engulfed in the process. In September 1838 it held a great public meeting at the very doors of Parliament in Palace Yard to elect the metropolitan delegates for the national convention to be held in the following February. Chartism had assumed an independent existence of its own, and it carried with it many of the seeds of its ultimate decay. The original long-term educational aims of the London Working Men's Association had been swamped by the desire for quicker action through a petition to Parliament, and the question of what to do if the petition were rejected was never resolved. In London itself, the seat of government where the success or failure of such a movement would ultimately be largely decided, Chartism was still weak. To the London artisans, with their long and varied radical traditions, Chartist ideas were not new, and they therefore made relatively little immediate impact there. When in 1841–2 Chartism did begin to command wider support in London it encountered difficulties peculiar to the metropolis. Because of the enormous variety of trades and occupations practised in London, the impact of trade depression there was not as universally disastrous as it was in areas of less diversified employment. Even when times were bad, London was too big and too diverse for mass fervour to flourish as it did in many northern towns under O'Connor's auspices. The East London Democratic Association, for instance, failed to recruit a mass following in its chosen area; despite changing its name to the London Democratic Association, thus including the whole of the capital, its membership only amounted to some 3,000; and the difficulty of kindling a general emotional ardour within the vastness of London helps to explain why even among the Spitalfields weavers, who undoubtedly did plumb the full depths of social misery, Chartism evoked little response.[1]

London was none the less inevitably the scene of the three great climaxes of the Chartist movement, when the presentation of a monster petition to Parliament was preceded by a meeting of a national convention of delegates. The first convention, consisting of fifty-three members, met on 4 February 1839 at the British Coffee House in Cockspur Street, from which it soon removed to a hall in Bolt Court, off Fleet Street. A quarter of the delegates were Londoners, and Lovett himself was elected secretary, but many of the provincial delegates were greatly struck by the general lack of support among the London working men. Efforts were made to

[1] D. J. Rowe, 'Chartism and the Spitalfields Silk-weavers', *Economic History Review, Second Series*, vol. 20, 1967, pp. 482–93; I. Prothero, 'Chartism in London', *Past and Present*, no. 44, 1969, pp. 76–101.

arouse them, and to obtain more signatures for the petition throughout the whole country, while in the meantime the convention discussed the 'ulterior measures' to be adopted if the petition were rejected. Harney's faction, backed by the London Democratic Association, advocated direct action, but there was no mass metropolitan support for a militant policy, and in May the convention adjourned to the less isolated environment of Birmingham, where it reassembled on 1 July. Four days later a posse of Metropolitan Police which had been sent down to assist the local magistrates broke up a peaceful Chartist meeting there, and Lovett was arrested soon afterwards. On 9 July the convention returned to London for the great climax of the House of Commons' debate on the motion to take into consideration the National Petition, and after the inevitable rejection of the motion, the rump of the convention voted, on 16 July, for a 'sacred month' or national holiday, to begin on 12 August. This decision was subsequently rescinded, and in September the convention dissolved.[1]

This marked the end of the first phase of Chartism, which had been inaugurated in London. At first glance, the capital's part in the movement now appears to have declined. In April 1840 Hetherington (one of the few prominent Chartists not to have been imprisoned in the aftermath of the débâcle of 1839) was the leading figure in the formation of a short-lived Metropolitan Charter Union on much the same lines as the old London Working Men's Association. But in July 1840 London ceased for a time to be the headquarters of the movement when the National Charter Association was set up in Manchester. Harney, the founder of the now moribund London Democratic Association, migrated first to Scotland and then to Yorkshire, and it was not until after Lovett's release from gaol that London Chartism showed any outward sign of revival. From his unsuccessful bookshop in Tottenham Court Road he sponsored in 1841 his National Association of the United Kingdom for Promoting the Political and Social Improvement of the People, but for thus supposedly challenging the ascendancy of the National Charter Association he was violently attacked by the O'Connorite newspaper the *Northern Star*. Lovett gained no general support among the provincial Chartists, and within a few months he found himself virtually excluded from further participation in the movement. O'Connor had, in fact, established himself as the demagogic hero of working-class Chartism, as the middle-class leaders of Birmingham's Complete Suffrage Union also discovered early in 1842. 'London is rotten,' O'Connor had declared in 1840, and under his banners there

1 Schoyen, pp. 54–86; Hovell, pp. 116–73; Lovett, pp. 201–25.

was no place for the idealism and serious endeavour of the original founders of the movement.

But despite these quarrels and rivalries of the national leaders there is good reason to believe that Chartism was in reality gaining support in London during the years 1841–2. This support expressed itself in the formation of local branches of the National Charter Association, and of Chartist trade associations, chiefly among the tailors, shoe-makers, hatters and stonemasons. By 1842 there were nearly forty Chartist societies scattered throughout London, led by a new generation of working men with a growing awareness of class consciousness and fully alive to the need for the co-ordination of all these various local Chartist bodies now flourishing within the whole gigantic metropolitan area.

London Chartism reached its climax in April 1842, when a convention assembled to arrange for the presentation of the second National Petition. This convention sat for only three weeks, compared with the seven months' session of the first. The petition itself contained over three million signatures, and was carried to Parliament on 2 May in a procession whose great size demonstrated the scale of the support which Chartism now possessed in London, as too did the series of open-air meetings and the sporadic outbreaks of violence which followed the inevitable rejection of the petition.[1]

By 1843 Chartism was in rapid decline. It had failed to secure the widespread middle-class support which it needed for the achievement of its political aims, and now improved economic conditions were beginning to diminish the fervour of even its working-class supporters. At this late stage the whole movement became London-based once again. In 1843 the headquarters of the National Charter Association was removed from Manchester to London, and in the following year the *Northern Star* left Leeds for the same destination, perhaps because London was now the principal centre of Chartist support, or perhaps to suit the convenience of O'Connor, who now lived in London. Here Lovett was already consorting with a number of European political refugees, of whom Mazzini was one, and had formed a short-lived international society, the Democratic Friends of All Nations. Chartist leaders and erstwhile leaders were beginning to drift along new channels, and when Harney came south again with the *Northern Star*, he too plunged into the society of exiled revolutionaries

[1] Schoyen, pp. 100, 105; Hovell, pp. 195–6, 205–8, 230–58; D. J. Rowe, 'The Failure of London Chartism', *The Historical Journal*, vol. xi, 1968, pp. 472–87; Prothero, 'Chartism in London'.

living in London, and in 1845 established the Fraternal Democrats, a communistic 'assemblage for mutual information'. He became acquainted with Friedrich Engels, and as its editor he was able to use the *Northern Star* to propagate new ideas of international working-class solidarity.[1]

The abdication of Louis Philippe in February 1848 and the proclamation of a republic, closely followed by other revolutionary outbreaks elsewhere in Europe, therefore evoked great excitement in London Chartist circles. A meeting held on 6 March in Trafalgar Square, originally intended for the irreproachable purpose of protesting against the income tax, was converted through mismanagement by the police into a popular émeute. To the Chartists the long-sought victory seemed imminent at last, for a national convention was due to meet in London within a few days, and another petition, bigger yet than any of its predecessors, was already being prepared.[2]

The convention, consisting of forty-four representatives from thirty-six towns, assembled at a hall in John Street, Fitzroy Square, on Monday, 3 April. It announced that the petition, which was said to bear nearly six million signatures, would be presented on the following Monday, when there would be a mass rally on Kennington Common to form up the procession to Westminster. In the meantime the convention spent the week of waiting in debating the old subject of what should be done if the petition were again rejected, and ultimately it was decided that a national assembly should be convened which should memorialize the Queen and remain in permanent session until the Charter had somehow or other become the law of the land. The effect of this decision was, of course, to postpone once more the hour for the outbreak of the revolution – the testing-point which the French and other Continentals seemed able to pass with such ease, but which in England still presented such a formidable obstacle.

The government, however, displayed no such irresolution during this fateful week. The Whig Prime Minister, Lord John Russell, who had been Home Secretary at the time of the first Chartist petition in 1839, called in the Tory Duke of Wellington, still commander-in-chief though now nearly eighty years old, to arrange the defences of the capital. This he did with his customary efficiency, but the first line of defence was a civilian one, and during the week some 170,000 special constables were sworn in to assist the police. On the Thursday Rowan and Mayne, who

[1] Schoyen, pp. 124, 134–42; Hovell, pp. 268–9; Prothero, 'Chartism in London'.
[2] Hovell, pp. 287–8.

were still, after nearly twenty years, the joint Commissioners of the Metropolitan Police, publicly announced by numerous placards that no procession would be permitted to pass from Kennington Common to the Houses of Parliament.

Early on the morning of Monday 10 April 1848 – a warm and sunny day – large bodies of troops, horse, foot and artillery, were stationed at strategic points along the south bank of the river, near Blackfriars, Waterloo and Westminster Bridges. Reserve forces were kept on the north side, at Millbank Prison, the Horse Guards, in the City and at the Tower, and specially chartered steamers waited at the numerous piers to transport them to any spot where serious danger might arise. All the armed forces were, however, carefully kept so far as possible out of sight, and the streets were lined by the police and the special constables. At about nine o'clock the Chartists began to assemble at various points – Russell Square, Finsbury Square, Clerkenwell Green and Whitechapel – and in the course of the morning they passed over Blackfriars and London Bridges in good order, the members of the convention seated in a great car drawn by six horses, and the petition itself reposing in another adorned with appropriate devices.

Kennington Common is now known as Kennington Park, a respectable public garden with its shrubberies, children's playground and all the usual impedimenta provided by a benevolent municipality. In 1848 it was still a dismal place, its tired grass 'soiled by a troop of cows' and its ditches full of stagnant excreta and dead cats and dogs, while a nearby vitriol factory gave off a constant stream of black sulphurous vapour. Here the Chartists began to assemble in the latter part of the morning, but only some 25,000 of them, not nearly as many as had been expected. As soon as the convention's car arrived a police inspector 'of gigantic stature and good-natured aspect' advanced through the crowd to summon O'Connor to the Horns Tavern, where Commissioner Mayne was waiting for him. Meekly O'Connor obeyed, and at the Horns he was told that the meeting would not be interfered with so long as it remained peaceful, but that a return across the river in procession would be prevented at all hazards.

The Chartists had indeed been out-manoeuvred. They had marched to the wrong side of the river, and now there were only two equally unattractive alternatives – to fight or to disperse. They chose to disperse. The banners and flags were folded away, the trimmings and decorations on the convention's car were dismantled and the car itself was removed to a neighbouring stable yard. The petition was divided into four portable bundles and with half-a-dozen of the delegates in attendance it was conveyed across Westminster Bridge in three hired cabs to the indifferent House of Commons. By a quarter past two Kennington Common had resumed its normal depressing aspect; only about one hundred people remained, and 'a stranger to the day's proceedings would never have guessed, from the appearance of the neighbourhood, that anything extraordinary had taken place'.[1]

So ended the last attempt by Englishmen to overawe the established government by sheer weight of numbers. 'My poor friends, you know as much about starting a riot as the Italians about writing a symphony,' commented the French composer Hector Berlioz, who had witnessed the day's proceedings.[2] In the event it was the government which had overawed the demonstrators by the sheer weight of its supporters, and to this success was later added the triumph of ridicule. The petition was found, on examination by the clerks of the House of Commons, to bear less than two million signatures, and the appearance of such unexpected names as 'Victoria Rex, April 1', the Duke of Wellington and Sir Robert Peel, or even 'Pugnose' and 'No Cheese', aroused doubts about the authenticity of the rest of the document. Chartism had been decisively discredited, and although it struggled on for another ten years, it no longer excited fear. The nation's capacity for the peaceful resolution of political crises, already exemplified in 1832, was fortified in 1848, the year of violent reckoning in Europe, and became a matter of pride, even for some men still without the vote, many of whom must have enrolled themselves in the civilian army of special constables.[3]

Middle-class consciousness had, indeed, proved to be the decisive political factor in London. In its latter stages, under the leadership of O'Connor, Chartism had lost most of its middle-class support, and its failure showed that working men, although capable of organizing an independent movement of their own, were still not powerful enough to obtain political power without middle-class help. For many years after 1848 this help was not forthcoming, the antagonism between the Manchester School economics of the middle-class Radicals on the one hand and the collectivist

[1] *Annual Register*, 1848; *The Illustrated London News*, 15 April 1848, p. 241; *Survey of London*, vol. xxvi, 1956, p. 33.

[2] *The Memoirs of Hector Berlioz*, trans. and ed. David Cairns, 1969, p. 44. I owe this reference to the kindness of Mr R. F. Sheppard.

[3] In 1848 the total electorate of the metropolitan area was still far below 170,000.

ideas of the trade unions and the increasingly socialist remnants of Chartism on the other being too strong to permit any enduring alliance. But with increasing prosperity this antagonism gradually subsided. The need for economic revolution became less strong, its possibility more hopeless. The trade unions no longer sought to challenge the foundations of the existing social order, and sought instead to promote the interest of their members within its framework. On the other hand the Radicals' need for working-class co-operation gradually overcame their fear of working-class power, and from the uneasy alliance which emerged in the 1860s there finally resulted the second Reform Act of 1867.

In London the more practical aims of trade unionism had first been seen in 1845 with the formation of the National Association of United Trades for the Protection of Labour. The aims of the Association were 'to protect the interests and promote the well-being' of the trades which affiliated to it, but unlike the Owenite Grand National Consolidated of 1833–4 the National Association proved moderate and cautious. The idea of co-operative production still persisted, but only in the form of union workshops which were to provide a productive alternative to the payment of strike money, and conciliation and arbitration were whenever possible to take the place of strikes. Unauthorized strikes did nevertheless occur in the provinces in 1846–7, which the London executive was unable to support. At the second conference, held in Manchester in 1846, the Association claimed to represent 40,000 members, but it soon ceased to have any practical importance. Its existence nevertheless marks a transitional phase between the fragile general unionism of the 1830s and the enduring trade unions which were to emerge in the 1850s and 1860s.

These unions were numerically still extremely small. They were only to be found among the skilled trades, and as they came to accept the fact that wages were related to supply and demand, so they became more concerned with the limitation of the supply of skilled labour. Their object was, in fact, the creation of an aristocracy of labour, equipped with bastions against invasion from outside as well as with weapons for assaulting the employers. Their members were disillusioned with Owenite ideas of a general union of all trades, but the societies were still too small and minutely subdivided to exert effective pressure. This was particularly clear in the field of engineering, largely concentrated in the two great centres of London and Lancashire, where a multiplicity of little local societies represented the five trades of mechanics, smiths, moulders, engineers and millwrights. As early as 1844 members of the London societies had discussed the need for a national amalgamation, and at last, after seven years of negotiation, this was achieved in 1851 with the formation of the Amalgamated Society of Engineers.[1]

The leading figure in this great consolidation was William Newton (1822–76), an engineer who after being dismissed from his job through his union activity had taken a public house in Ratcliffe, Stepney. At the general election of 1852 he stood unsuccessfully for the Tower Hamlets division against the two sitting members, both Radicals, thereby establishing the claim to have been the first independent 'labour' candidate, and subsequently he became a prominent member of the Metropolitan Board of Works. Just as he himself represented something new in working-class history, so too did the Amalgamated Society of Engineers. Its 11,000 members each paying one shilling per week provided it with an annual income of £28,600; within ten years its membership had doubled and its accumulated balance had reached £73,398. It was by far the largest trade society of the time, and with its salaried officials, London headquarters and well-organized provincial branches it represented not only a potent new force but a model to be copied by other trades.

The Amalgamated Society was at once involved in a struggle with the employers when it attempted, in 1852, to impose the abolition of overtime and piecework. The employers replied with a lock-out, and then 'presented the Document', whereby written renunciation of union membership was required from every man as a condition of return to work. After three months many of the men were nearing destitution, despite payments of over £43,000 by the union, and in April they returned to work on the employers' terms. But they regarded their signature of 'the Document' as a contract extorted under duress whose obligations they were therefore entitled to ignore, and the union survived this hated challenge, which had hitherto been always successful in destroying the men's organization.

The widespread public attention focused upon the engineering lock-out did nothing to promote harmony between the middle and working classes. Only the small group of Christian Socialists had supported the men, and middle-class susceptibilities were also offended in the early 1850s by the programme of social reform then being advocated by the National Reform League for the Peaceful Regeneration of Society, of which Bronterre O'Brien was a leading member. Between 1848 and 1855 a body known as the Metropolitan Trades' Delegates issued a series of addresses in support of such alarming aims as manhood suffrage, state-

[1] Webb, pp. 186–96, 202–12.

supported secular education and the nationalization of the land, while Ernest Jones, now the leader of the Chartist rump, repeatedly denounced all attempts at alliance with the middle classes.[1]

In the summer of 1855 a series of disturbances in Hyde Park still further discredited working men in middle-class eyes. A private member's Bill to prevent Sunday trading in London resulted in the assembly, on four consecutive Sundays, of large crowds in the park 'to see how the aristocrats kept the Sabbath'. On the second Sunday, 1 July, 150,000 people, mostly from the East End of London, gathered to watch the *beau monde* drive in their carriages beside the Serpentine, and to salute them with hisses and yells and cries of 'Go to church.' The windows of fashionable houses in Belgravia were smashed, without discrimination between supporters and opponents of the Bill, and at a subsequent enquiry the police were severely criticized for using unnecessary violence in subduing the multitude.[2]

In the early 1850s an entente between the middle and working classes was still impossible, as the failure of the National Parliamentary and Financial Reform Association, formed in London in 1849 and dissolved in 1855, clearly indicated. The only successful example of such co-operation in these years was provided by the Association for the Repeal of the Taxes on Knowledge, which had originated as a quasi-Chartist organization sponsored by such old stalwarts as Lovett, Hetherington and James Watson. In alliance after 1851 with Richard Cobden it had achieved the repeal first of the advertisement duty in 1853, then of the remaining newspaper tax in 1855, and lastly of the paper duty in 1861, thus finally completing the long campaign for a free press – a campaign of enduring achievement largely conducted by London working-men over a period of more than forty years.[3]

In the years after the Crimean War London was the scene of one of the great industrial disputes of the nineteenth century – the builders' strikes of 1859–61. The financial crisis of 1857, when Bank rate rose to 10 per cent, threw many building employees out of work, and a group of them organized a mass meeting at Smithfield. Here a short-lived National Association of Unemployed Operatives was formed, one of its objects being to press for a reduction in hours of labour. At this time it was not unusual

[1] Webb, pp. 206, 213–16, 226; Frances Elma Gillespie, *Labor and Politics in England 1850–1867*, 1927, pp. 38–41, 67–71, 100.

[2] *Annual Register*, 1855.

[3] Gillespie, pp. 68–9, 86–110; Thomas Kelly, *A History of Adult Education in Great Britain*, 1962, pp. 162–3.

Z

for the building operatives to work from 6 a.m. to 5.30 p.m. on five days of the week, with some slight shortening on Saturdays, and previous efforts made by the still small societies of London carpenters and stonemasons to obtain a reduction had all failed. In 1858 representatives of the societies of the principal building trades formed the Conference of the United Building Trades to press for a nine-hour day, the leading member of the Conference being George Potter, a young man of twenty-seven who was chairman of a small London society of carpenters and joiners. The Central Association of Master Builders rejected the Conference's claims, and in July 1859 Messrs Trollope of Pimlico, one of the largest London firms, dismissed one of the workers' spokesmen. A strike at once ensued, to which all the London master builders employing over fifty men retorted with a lock-out, followed by presentation of the hated 'Document', and by August 225 firms had closed and some 24,000 men were out of work.

The challenge of 'the Document' united the whole trade-union world, both in London and throughout the country, and provided an opportunity to demonstrate the new strength of the movement. Delegates of the London trades not connected with the builders organized financial support; the London pianoforte makers, for instance, contributed £300, the Amalgamated Society of Engineers proved the strength of their unity by three successive weekly payments of £1,000 each, and altogether some £23,000 was subscribed by societies as far afield as Manchester, Glasgow and even Paris. Backed by this unprecedented support the building workers hung on throughout the winter of 1859–60, despite the intense suffering of their members. The demand for a nine-hour day was wisely withdrawn in order to concentrate the issue solely upon the employers' challenge to the very existence of trade unions, and at last, in February 1860, 'the Document' was withdrawn. The masters' attempt to destroy the unions had failed.[1]

But the men had not won the nine-hour day, and this struggle was therefore renewed under Potter's leadership in 1861. On this occasion the men were no longer united, and they were outwitted by the large London employers, who announced that they would in future pay their men by the hour instead of by the day. They claimed that each man would be able to choose for himself how long he would work, but in reality this method meant (in the words of Sidney and Beatrice Webb) 'a total abandonment of the

[1] Gillespie, pp. 131–2; Webb, pp. 228–31; *Journal of the Statistical Society of London*, vol. XXIV, 1861, pp. 604–5; *London Trades Council 1860–1950, A History*, Foreword by Julius Jacobs, 1950, pp. 3–5. See also Raymond Postgate, *The Builders' History*, 1923.

principle of Collective Bargaining'. The stonemasons and bricklayers stood out against the new system, but the other trades reluctantly returned to work, and the strike dragged on indecisively into 1862, the men's only gain being the ending of work at one o'clock on Saturdays.[1]

The builders' strikes of 1859–61 showed how far the trade-union movement had progressed since the days of Robert Owen and the Grand National Consolidated of 1833–4, but they had also shown that many weaknesses still existed. So after these years of bitter strife there followed a period of consolidation, in which important improvements in organization were made. The strikes had shown that among the London building operatives the stonemasons were the only trade with a stable union, while the strength of the other trades was still dissipated among innumerable small and often short-lived benefit clubs, of which George Potter's Progressive Society of Carpenters and Joiners was a typical example. Immediately after the strike representatives of these two trades met to discuss the formation of a national union, and in June 1860 the Amalgamated Society of Carpenters and Joiners was established on lines consciously imitating the successful example of the Amalgamated Society of Engineers. Two years later the new society appointed Robert Applegarth, then the secretary of a small carpenters' union in Sheffield, as its general secretary, and its progress was so rapid that within a short while it had become one of the strongest unions in the country, second only to the engineers. In 1866 this example was followed by the tailors, and in many other trades the process of amalgamation and absorption went on apace.

The builders' strikes had also shown the value of support from other trades. During previous strikes temporary committees of men from trades not directly involved had often been formed to give aid and comfort to the strikers. But the scale of the support given during the strife of 1859–61 had been far greater than ever before, and from this effort there emerged in 1860 a permanent multi-trade organization, the London Trades Council, which still exists after more than a century of busy endeavour. The members of its first executive were mostly drawn from the small societies still prevalent among such trades as the rope-makers or the hatters, but the large unions such as those of the engineers and the carpenters and joiners soon came in, each affiliated society paying two shillings per hundred members per year. The revenues of the London Trades Council were

[1] Webb, pp. 245–6; Jacobs, 17–18; Stephen Coltham, 'The *Bee-Hive* Newspaper: Its Origin and Struggles', *Essays in Labour History*, ed. Asa Briggs and John Saville, 1960, pp. 178–80; *Statistical Society*, vol. XXIV, 1861.

therefore comparatively small, but its function was to guide and co-ordinate the individual London trade societies, not to take them over. It was 'to watch over the general interests of labour, political and social, both in and out of Parliament; to use their influence in supporting any measure likely to benefit Trades Unions', and to decide whether strikes in which individual member-societies might become involved should be supported by other London societies.[1]

The emergence of this new brand of trade unionism, moderate, well-informed and well-organized on the secure foundation of national support, was largely the work of a small group of labour leaders in London. Of these the most prominent were William Allen, secretary of the engineers, Robert Applegarth, secretary of the carpenters and joiners, Edwin Coulson, secretary of the London Order of Bricklayers, and George Odger, a member of a small society of makers of ladies' shoes. They were cautious empiricists, preferring to build up the strength of their members by the accumulation of large bank balances, and to negotiate whenever possible for improved conditions, rather than to indulge in expensive strikes. All of them, and others like them, were members of the executive of the London Trades Council, one of whose first successes, in 1861, was to persuade the government to withdraw soldiers lent to replace builders on strike at Chelsea barracks. As members or officers of their own trade societies, which now often possessed nation-wide ramifications, they were well able to adjudicate on the merits of requests for support from individual unions engaged in industrial disputes, and during the 1860s the London Trades Council granted credentials or support not only to London societies but to others all over the country, extending even as far as Tyneside. Its headquarters at the Bell Inn, Old Bailey, became, in fact, for a few years, the cabinet-room of the whole trade-union movement.

The trade unions were also beginning to look overseas and to be influenced by events there. During the American Civil War the London Trades Council organized a great meeting at St James's Hall, Piccadilly, in support of the North, and a few days later a deputation called upon the American ambassador to present an address to Abraham Lincoln. In the same year, 1863, members of the Council organized another meeting at the same place to urge the government to intervene in the Polish revolution. French delegates attended this meeting, and after another conclave at the Bell Inn an address 'on behalf of the working men of England' was sent to Paris, urging regular interchange of ideas between working men of all

[1] Webb, pp. 224, 231–2, 242–5; Jacobs, pp. 5–6.

nations. From these cordial relations there emerged in 1864 the International Working Men's Association – the First International, established at St Martin's Hall on 28 September, with Odger as president of its provisional council. Karl Marx, who had been living in poverty in London since 1849, was also a member of the first council, and it was he who prepared the Association's manifesto, unanimously adopted, which declared that 'the subjection of the man of labour to the man of capital lies at the bottom of all servitude, all social misery, and all political dependence'. At that time, probably, few English working men understood the full implications of statements of this kind, their main concern being with such matters as wages, hours and conditions of employment, but large numbers of them, including Applegarth, nevertheless joined the International, as well as some fifty trade unions by affiliation. Within a few years, however, the Association was disrupted by internal disputes, and the Paris Commune which followed the Franco-Prussian War greatly discredited it in England. After the removal of its headquarters from London to New York in 1872 it ceased to have any influence in England, and it was dissolved in 1876.[1]

But the greatest working-class enthusiasm was reserved for Garibaldi, the hero of middle-class Victorian liberalism, whose visit to England in 1864 was to exert a powerful influence over the events of the London reform movement three years later. When he arrived in the capital he was greeted by a procession organized by the London Trades Council of some fifty thousand men, which escorted him with trade banners flying to Stafford House, St James's. When similar demonstrations were planned for him in thirty provincial towns, the government took fright and asked him to leave the country, which he did. This at once provoked a demonstration of protest held on Primrose Hill under the joint auspices of the London Workingmen's Reception Committee and a middle-class radical Garibaldi committee headed by Edmond Beales. The violent dispersal of this meeting by the police called in question the public right to peaceful open-air meetings in the parks, and a deputation to the Home Secretary subsequently organized by the joint sponsors of the meeting only elicited an unsatisfactory answer. The matter was not allowed to rest, and from this unexpected challenge on Primrose Hill there emerged next year the Reform League.

So by the middle of the 1860s London working men, and indeed working men all over the country, were beginning once more to take a

[1] Webb, p. 235 n.; Gillespie, pp. 215–26; Jacobs, pp. 32–3.

growing interest in politics, so long avoided after the Chartist collapse. As early as 1861 the London shoemakers, always one of the most politically conscious of the skilled trades, had two Reform Associations of their own, and soon afterwards Applegarth and Odger were among a group of union leaders who formed the Manhood Suffrage and Vote by Ballot Association. Men such as they were realizing that political power was necessary for the achievement of their social aims in such matters as the law of master and servant, and of trade-union law in general. Confronted with the continuing indifference of the trade-union rank and file to political action, they used the London Trades Council and the similar councils which were formed in many towns in the 1860s as instruments of political pressure. In this they were unintentionally assisted by George Potter, the leader of the London builders' strike, who in 1861 had founded the *Bee-Hive*, a weekly newspaper conducted 'in the interests of the working classes'. He was the rogue-elephant of the trade-union world in the 1860s, sometimes accused and sometimes accepted by the cautious men of the London Trades Council, and the possessor of wide influence in the political and industrial fields, which he always exerted in favour of the active assertion of working-class claims.[1]

This, then, was the situation in 1864 when Gladstone stated to a deputation from the London Trades Council that 'the franchise ought to be extended to the working classes'. By this time John Bright had made himself the leader of the middle-class demand for parliamentary reform, and ever since his election as M.P. for Birmingham in 1857 Birmingham had been the centre of gravity of this demand, as it had been in 1830–2, and as Manchester had later been of the Anti-Corn Law movement. On practical grounds Bright had proclaimed for a rate-paying household suffrage. He admitted that he had no objection to a much wider extension, but in the existing climate of opinion he thought this would be impossible to achieve. In London his programme had little appeal, either to the middle or the working classes, for there a large proportion of householders already possessed the vote under the £10 qualification of 1832, and even household suffrage would not enfranchise the artisans, most of whom were lodgers, not householders. The way was therefore clear for London to become the centre of the more radical demand for manhood suffrage and vote by ballot. But London had no leader of Bright's stature, and in its early stages the movement was led by Ernest Jones, who had suffered greatly for his devotion to the Chartist cause. By 1857 he was advocating

[1] Gillespie, pp. 204, 210–19.

an entente between the Chartists and the middle classes, from which there emerged in 1858 the Political Reform Union, one of the forerunners of the Reform League of 1865–7. Its principal plank was manhood suffrage, and it therefore received little middle-class support, many of its leading members being ex-Chartists such as Holyoake and Harney, or the new generation of trade unionists, such as Newton and Allan.

The two abortive parliamentary reform Bills introduced by Disraeli and Lord John Russell in 1859 and 1860 respectively, both proposing very modest extensions of the franchise, had evoked little support in London. Disraeli's, indeed, was greeted by numerous hostile working-class demonstrations in Hyde Park and elsewhere, and at the general election of 1859 the boroughs of Finsbury, Tower Hamlets, Southwark and Marylebone maintained their radical allegiance. The builders' strike was in progress, and this was not the moment for a class rapprochement. In Parliament itself deadlock prevailed, and no futher progress was made until the conversion of Gladstone to the cause of reform in 1864 and the death of the Prime Minister, Lord Palmerston, in 1865.[1]

It was in these two years that all the disparate elements of the demand for parliamentary reform were gathered together within three new bodies, the National Reform Union, founded at Manchester in 1864, the Reform League, founded in London also in 1864, and the London Working Men's Association of 1865. The Reform Union was modelled on the Anti-Corn Law League, its principal supporters being the mercantile middle classes of radical Lancashire and the industrial north, and its objects being severely practical. It was for this reason that its leaders avoided the term 'manhood suffrage', which was the principal aim of the London-based Reform League. The president of the League was Edmond Beales, an elderly barrister who later became a county-court judge. After the dispersal of the Garibaldi protest meeting on Primrose Hill in 1864 he had been concerned to vindicate the right of peaceful public meeting in the parks, and when the League was formed a year later this object was very much in the minds of its leaders. These included a few middle-class intellectuals, but they were mostly drawn from the trade unions, and included Odger, Applegarth, Coulson and Potter, although the last soon left after a quarrel and founded his own London Working Men's Association. The League's support came very largely from working men, either individually or by affiliation through the unions, and it stood for manhood suffrage and the ballot. So too did Potter's breakaway association,

[1] Gillespie, pp. 151, 160–3, 180–6, 243.

which also campaigned for a lodger qualification, of vital significance in London.[1]

These were the forces already in array when the crisis of the second Reform Bill began in June 1866 after the defeat of Gladstone's very moderate proposals. The crisis – if indeed it can truly be termed a crisis at all – lasted for a little more than one year. There was never anything like a revolutionary situation, for although the demands of the Union, the League and the L.W.M.A. were all more extreme than either political party was prepared to grant, all three bodies were ready to accept less than they demanded. Moderation was therefore the hallmark of this 'crisis', but this is perhaps more apparent in retrospect than it was at the time, for labouring men were showing their strength more clearly than ever before, and how far they were prepared to use it was as yet unknown. Economic conditions were uncertain. In May 1866 there was the dramatic crash of Overend and Gurney in the City. During the winter unemployment caused acute distress in the East End, in January 1867 there were bread riots in Deptford and Greenwich, and the London tailors were on strike. Middle-class fear of working-class power had recently been inflamed by a number of trade-union outrages at Sheffield, yet the unions were once again increasing their strength by the success of their agitation, in 1867, for the amendment of some of the injustices of the old law of master and servant – their first victory in the province of legislation. The unions, too, felt themselves threatened when the court case of Hornby *v.* Close, decided in January 1867, deprived their funds of the security which they had hitherto enjoyed, and when in the following month the government announced the appointment of a Royal Commission to investigate their workings, the unions became thoroughly alarmed. The situation seemed to have all the makings of a class clash.[2]

But nobody wanted this to happen, as events in London were to prove. For nearly a year a series of massive demonstrations took place in the capital under the auspices of the League, the unions and Potter's L.W.M.A. All of them were peaceful and well managed, arms were never carried, processions were controlled by the organizers' own marshals, and even hissing in Pall Mall opposite the Carlton Club was successfully prohibited. The only significant outbreak of violence, in Hyde Park on 23 July 1866, appears to have been accidental. Widespread violence would merely have

[1] Gillespie, pp. 243–59; Maurice Cowling, *1867. Disraeli, Gladstone and Revolution. The Passing of the second Reform Bill*, 1967, pp. 242–5.

[2] *Annual Register*, 1867; Webb, pp. 253, 259–60; Gillespie, p. 275.

antagonized the government. Peaceful, unremitting pressure was a much more effective instrument, and although even this probably had little effect on the course of events in Parliament, it nevertheless successfully maintained the momentum of the demand for reform and ensured that at last something was placed on the statute book. Working men could no longer be almost wholly excluded from the affairs of the nation, and by their responsible conduct they were now to prove to the rest of the community that they had acquired the middle-class virtues deemed requisite for a place within the pale of the constitution.

The first demonstration was the most famous. Soon after Lord Derby's minority Tory government came to power in June 1866, Disraeli stated in the Commons that the new ministry would not pledge itself to deal with the question of parliamentary reform in the next session. The Reform League at once announced its intention to hold a great meeting in Hyde Park on 23 July. With the rapid outward growth of London the traditional venues for such occasions – Cold Bath Fields, St George's Fields or Spa Fields, for instance – had been covered with bricks and mortar, and the only large centrally situated open spaces left were the royal parks. The right of public assembly there had first been called in question after the Sunday trading demonstrations in 1855. The law officers of the Crown had decided that the Crown had the right to close the gates, and the Home Secretary, Spencer Walpole, now decided to exercise this right. On being informed of this the leaders of the League decided nevertheless to march to Hyde Park, and if prevented from entering, to proceed to Trafalgar Square. Printed leaflets to this effect were distributed in large numbers. When the leaders of the procession reached Marble Arch they found the gates closed and a large body of police assembled. After being refused admission by the police commissioner, Sir Richard Mayne, Beales and the crowd near him left for Trafalgar Square. But other processions were still arriving, control broke down, and soon a densely-packed mass of men were pressing against the railings. The railings and stonework were old and weak, and breach after breach was quickly made along Park Lane and the Bayswater Road. The police resisted these incursions, and scuffling broke out, but many thousands of people were now inside the park, and even a company of the Grenadier Guards, whose arrival was loudly cheered, could not oust the invaders except by the use of firearms. After an hour or two of cheerful speechifying darkness began to fall, and the crowd dispersed voluntarily.[1]

[1] *Annual Register*, 1866.

This event discredited the government, but it cannot have greatly alarmed ministers, for Parliament was prorogued from August until early in February 1867, and Derby and Disraeli both spent most of this time at their country houses, Derby's being in faraway Lancashire. During this period a series of demonstrations were held up and down the country, those in London, on 8 August at the Guildhall and on 3 December at Beaufort House, Kensington, being notable for the prominence of trade unionists. The meeting in the grounds of Beaufort House was indeed an almost exclusively unionist affair, attended by some 25,000 men. The organizers had originally intended to meet in Hyde Park, but they accepted the government's refusal to allow this, and Lord Ranelagh had then granted them the use of his own private park instead. The police were kept in the background, and the trade societies' own marshals, led by a group of mounted farriers, had preserved perfect order.

The reassembly of Parliament in February 1867 was greeted by a great League procession from Trafalgar Square to the Agricultural Hall in St Pancras. The terms of the projected reform were now being debated, and more meetings were held to pass resolutions demanding a low borough-franchise qualification and the inclusion of a lodger clause. The last great London assembly took place on 6 May, when the extent of the reform to be granted was quivering in the balance of parliamentary discussion. The Reform Union and the League were now at last in alliance, and the unions fully aroused by the recent appointment of the Royal Commission. The whole movement was for a brief moment united, and the League announced that it would once again assert its right to meet in Hyde Park. This time the Home Secretary wavered; he merely issued a proclamation stating that the 'meeting is not permitted' and warning the public not to attend. The gates were not closed, however, and over 200,000 people surged in to listen to speeches delivered from ten separate platforms. Hardly a policeman was to be seen, although a large number were held in unobtrusive reserve nearby. The meeting concluded with three cheers for the Queen, and it was claimed that in the park 'not a plant was disturbed, nor a leaf or a flower touched'.[1]

By August the crisis was over and the Bill had received the royal assent. In the boroughs the Act conferred the vote on all male ratepaying occupants and upon all lodgers who had rented their lodgings, of a yearly value of £10 or over, continuously for not less than twelve months. It did not grant either of the two points most strenuously advocated by both the

[1] *Annual Register*, 1867.

League and the trade unionists – manhood suffrage and the ballot – yet it nevertheless gave more than most working men had probably expected, and more than most other members of the community had wished.

What effect did the Act have on the parliamentary representation of London? The Reform Act of 1832 had increased the number of M.P.s for the whole metropolitan area from 10 to 22. The Act of 1867 established two new boroughs, Hackney and Chelsea, each with two members, and in Surrey half the eastern division was split off to form a new western constituency. Thus the total representation rose from 22 to 28, plus one new seat for London University. In 1866 the total electorate for the 22 metropolitan seats had been 179,607. In 1868 the electorate for the 28 seats covering the same area had risen to 304,416 but the ultimate increase was probably rather larger, for the registration of new voters had not been completed by 1868. These figures, for what they are worth, show that the London electorate increased by only some 41 per cent, compared with the national increase of 82·5 per cent in the total electorate of the whole country. The key factor in London, the lodger franchise, proved ineffective in practice, for working men experienced great difficulty in registering their right to vote. Votes in London continued to be scarce, the proportion of the metropolitan electorate to that of the whole country actually declining slightly, from some 13 per cent in 1866 to 12 per cent in 1868. And the metropolitan representation remained sparse too, for whereas the 304,416 London voters elected 28 M.P.s, the twenty-three smallest provincial boroughs, with a total electorate of only about 28,000, still returned 45 members in 1868.[1]

Since the Reform Act of 1867 the trade unions have played a continuous rôle in the political life of the nation. The period of cautious self-imposed withdrawal from active political participation was over. Their leaders vindicated themselves during their evidence before the Royal Commission, and in 1868 they obtained statutory protection of their funds from embezzlement by defaulters. In the same year the Trades Union Congress was established in Manchester. Within eight years of the second reform of Parliament, the whole field of trade-union law was revised, ultimately, after a sharp struggle, to the great advantage of the unions, the right to collective bargaining being finally recognized. In the political field voting by secret ballot was enacted in 1872, and at the general election of 1874

[1] P.P., 1866, vol. lvii, *Electoral Returns;* 1877, vol. lxviii, *Electoral Returns,* no. 432; F. B. Smith, *The Making of the Second Reform Bill,* 1966, pp. 236, 239.

there were a dozen trade-union candidates for Parliament, including Odger, unsuccessful at Southwark. London working-men had travelled far since the days when the Duke of Northumberland could command a seat in the House of Commons by corrupting the electors with lumps of cheese and other largesse, contemptuously distributed to the rabble by his servants at the door of his mansion at Charing Cross.

9

Living in Mid-Nineteenth-Century London

I N THE middle years of the nineteenth century there lived in London two incomparable observers of the metropolitan social scene – Charles Dickens and Henry Mayhew. Dickens's descriptions of London, particularly those in *Bleak House* and *Our Mutual Friend*, are so well known, and so many books have already been written around them, that they have been intentionally omitted here. Mayhew's work, on the other hand, after enjoying a great success in the 1850s and 60s, was largely forgotten until it recently became a favourite quarry for social and economic historians. In the latter part of the 1840s, Mayhew had contributed a number of articles to the London daily press, and in 1851 he collected them together into two volumes, published under the title of *London Labour and the London Poor*. He had set out to discover how the poor lived, and to this task he brought the qualities of an indefatigable sociologist and a highly gifted journalist, as well as the profound concern of a true philanthropist. No detail of human circumstance or quirk of human behaviour seems to have escaped his notice in his endless peregrinations through the darkest quarters of London, and because he enjoyed the complete confidence of everyone he spoke to, he was able to reproduce the living speech of the costermongers, beggars, mud-larks, dustmen, crossing-sweepers, coal-heavers and all the other unfortunates who struggled to make a living by one means or another in mid-Victorian London.

Mayhew's factual records often convey a sense of actuality almost equal to that which Dickens conjured from his imagination.

'Bless your heart the smell's nothink,' said the man who searched in the sewers for anything saleable, 'it's a roughish smell at first, but nothink near so bad as you thinks, 'cause, you see, there's sich lots o' water always a-coming down the sewer. . . . The rats is wery dangerous, that's sartin, but we always goes three or four on us together, and the varmint's too wide awake to tackle us then, for they know they'd git off second best. . . . The reason I likes this sort of life is, 'cause I can sit down when I likes, and nobody can't order me about. When I'm hard up, I knows as how I must work, and then I goes at it like sticks a-breaking; and tho' the times isn't as they was; I can go now and pick up my four or five bob a day, where another wouldn't know how to get a brass farden.'

Or the coster-girl on the advantages of marriage over living in sin:

'If parties is married, they ought to bend to each other; and they won't, for sartain, if they're only living together. A man as is married is obligated to keep his wife if they quarrels or not; and he says to himself, says he, "Well, I may as well live happy, like." But if he can turn a poor gal off, as soon as he tires of her, he begins to have noises with her, and then gets quit of her altogether.'

And so one could go on, through page after page and even volume after volume, for in the 1860s new editions and supplementary volumes of Mayhew's work were issued, all piling more and more detail on to the enormous mound of social minutiae which he had accumulated.

One of these supplementary volumes, entitled *The Criminal Prisons of London and Scenes of Prison Life*, contains, by contrast, Mayhew's impressions of London as a whole. For a brief moment he stood back to take in the entire picture at a glance, and what struck him first and hardest was the sheer size of the capital. In his boyhood (he was born in 1812) cities with a population of over 100,000 had still been something of a novelty, and now here was London with over 2,800,000 people in 1861. He at least realized that a new form of human civilization was arising all around him, and having examined London 'below the moral surface, as it were', he determined to see it from above as well, and so he took a trip in a balloon to observe the view. There, far below

lay the Leviathan Metropolis, with a dense canopy of smoke hanging over it, and reminding one of the fog of vapour that is so often seen steaming from the fields at early morning. It was impossible to tell where the monster city began or ended, for the buildings stretched not only to the horizon on either side, but far away into the distance, where, owing to the coming shades of evening and the dense fumes from the million chimneys, the town seemed to blend into the sky, so that there was no distinguishing earth from heaven.

Very uncharacteristically he omitted to record where or how he descended, but whatever the circumstances may have been, he had seen that London was not a city or a province but a world of its own, with Belgravia and Bethnal Green as its poles, 'the one icy cold from its exceeding fashion, form, and ceremony, and the other wrapt in a perpetual winter of withering poverty', with Temple Bar its equator, and great suburban continents like Paddington or Lambeth sprawling out as far as the eye could see: such was mid-Victorian London to this intrepid and percipient man – 'The Great World of London'.

To a modern aeronaut, accustomed to skim across the world in the pampered luxury of an airliner from one great city to another, the size of London no longer provokes astonishment. But Mayhew was also impressed by something more terrible than mere magnitude. For him London was a world of its own, not only through its size but also because it possessed contrasts of the same order as did the wider expanse of the world itself. The antitheses which existed within the peoples of the metropolis, between the lackadaisical dandy at Almack's and the Billingsgate porter, or between the judges presiding at the courts in Westminster and the Jewish 'fences' of Petticoat Lane, were to him hardly less marked than those distinguishing the various ethnic groups of the whole human race. In their modes of speech too, where the young man of fashion talked of 'taking – aw – his afternoon's *w*ide – aw – in *W*otton *W*o – aw – aw or of going to the Ope*w*a', and the thieves and beggars each had their own private linguistic codes, it was much the same. He noted also the extraordinary range of the metropolitan charities and set this off against the criminality of another section of the population. But above all he was struck by the contrast between the riches and the poverty of London. Here the very extremes of society were to be seen in greater force than anywhere else. 'This constitutes, as it were, the topographical essence of the Great Metropolis – the salient point of its character as a Capital – the distinctive mark which isolates it from all other towns and cities in the world.' And if Mayhew was impressed by this antithesis, how much the more should we be in our egalitarian times today.

For foreign visitors, London's almost unbelievable size was the thing which always struck them most. 'It is absolutely impossible to communicate to one who has not seen it any just idea of it,' wrote Henry Colman, a companionable American who spent some time in England in the 1840s. For him, as for Mayhew, London was 'a world within itself', or rather 'the heart of the great world, where gather, and are sent out, and then return again, all the mighty circulations of the social and political body, and whose pulsations are felt in every extremity'. But, again, like Mayhew, the more discerning foreigners also commented on the extremes of human condition to be found there. How, Colman asked himself, could these be reconciled with the kindness and generosity of the English, which he had everywhere encountered? He was stunned and baffled by the magnitude of the problem, and he returned to it again and again: 'In the midst of the most extraordinary abundance, here are men, women, and children dying of starvation; and running alongside of the splendid chariot, with its gilded equipages, its silken linings, and its liveried footmen, are poor, forlorn, friendless, almost naked wretches, looking like the mere fragments of humanity.'[1]

Descriptions of this kind were not exaggerated. The occupants of these 'gilded equipages' were for the most part the members of the great landed aristocratic families, slightly over three hundred in number,[2] whose fortunes enabled them to run both a country mansion and either a large town house or even another mansion in London. Their annual incomes ranged from a few thousands up to such enormous sums as the £85,000 gross enjoyed by the sixth Duke of Bedford in 1816,[3] £10,000 per annum being generally reckoned to be adequate for 'a man who only wanted all the conveniences and comforts that London and the country could give'.[4] This was the class which formed the core of fashionable London society, and which owned the great private palaces of the West End such as Spencer House, Northumberland House, Grosvenor House or Devonshire House, to name but a few.

But this class, though numerically small, was not an exclusive caste. Many of the 7,000 persons who did not belong to it but who, with the

[1] Henry Colman, *European Life and Manners*, 1849, vol. I, pp. 2, 151, 155.

[2] F. M. L. Thompson, *English Landed Society in the Nineteenth Century*, 1963, p. 25.

[3] *Survey of London*, vol. xxxvi, 1970, p. 41.

[4] Thompson, pp. 25–6.

landed aristocracy, between them owned four-fifths of all the land in the United Kingdom, also took part from time to time in the multifarious activities of metropolitan society. They might not be able to afford such *éclat* as Londonderry House in Park Lane, which cost nearly £250,000 in the 1820s, or even as Bridgwater House in Cleveland Row (cost around £50,000), but many could manage to own a handsome house in one of the fashionable squares, or at least to rent one occasionally for perhaps a thousand pounds a year. Even bankers and successful men of business such as Thomas Coutts, who lived off Piccadilly and whose daughter married Sir Francis Burdett, were to be seen within the charmed circle with increasing frequency, particularly after the value and power of land had begun to decline; while on the peripheries there hovered uncertainly a host of people well endowed with commercial wealth and aspiring social ambitions, living in Marylebone perhaps, or Brompton, and able to join the fashionable throng at the Opera or in their carriages in drives in the Park, yet neither wholly within society nor wholly outside it.[1]

The sum total of the social *divertissements* of these various groups together made up the London 'season', which extended from March or April through to July, when everybody with any social pretensions went off to the country, for to be seen in London in late summer or autumn was not the thing at all. But during the season everybody who mattered was in London. In the words of Professor F. M. L. Thompson, 'This was the world of politics and high society, of attendance at the House and gaming in the clubs, the place where wagers were laid and race meetings arranged, the source of fashion in dress and taste in art, the place where portraits were painted and galleries visited, as well as being the world of drawing rooms and *levées*, glittering entertainments and extravaganzas, *soirées*, balls and operas.' It was also the principal marriage market for the upper classes, and the innumerable dynastic alliances which were made in London during the season often provided both the incentive for anxious titled parents to come up to town and (sometimes at least) some consolation for the colossal cost; the annual town expenses of Earl Fitzwilliam in 1810–14 amounted, for instance, to between £2,000 and £3,000, and of the Duke of Northumberland in the 1840s to some £20,000 or more.[2]

High society in London had reached its zenith in the years of the Regency and the reign of George IV. This was the age of the dandy, of Beau Brummell and Count D'Orsay, of huge wagers at Crockford's and of

---

[1] Thompson, pp. 27, 104–5; *Survey of London*, vol. xxx, 1960, pp. 496–7.
[2] Thompson, pp. 104, 106.

A A

duelling with firearms at dawn in the royal parks. It was also the great age
of the fashionable *salons*, of Lady Holland at Holland House or of Lady
Blessington at Gore House, where the guests included writers, painters
and actors as well as aristocrats and, sometimes, the latest fashionable
charlatan too. To gain admission to Almack's assembly rooms in King
Street, St James's, was 'the seventh heaven of the fashionable world',
from which even the Duke of Wellington himself was on one occasion
denied entrance because he was incorrectly dressed, while the Argyll
Rooms in Regent Street were hardly less exclusive. Even the Opera
House in the Haymarket, where interminable financial difficulties had
for over twenty-five years prevented the completion of rebuilding after the
fire of 1789, was at last provided by John Nash with a handsome colon-
naded façade appropriate to the glitter and beauty of its aristocratic patrons.
And this long-awaited consummation was only a small part of the gigantic
backcloth which the royal improvements in the West End were providing
for the playground of the *beau monde*.

But after the death of George IV in 1830 changes gradually became
apparent. The royal Court itself, which set the tone, became dull under
William IV and strait-laced under Victoria and Albert. Young peers, like
Lord Ashley, later seventh Earl of Shaftesbury, might now be earnest in
religion, whereas their fathers in Regency days had often not greatly concerned themselves in such matters. With the exacerbation of political
strife in the early 1830s conflicting party loyalties undermined personal
relationships, at least for a while, and the importance of the private
salons declined. Almack's lost its pre-eminence around 1835, although the
assemblies were still held for some thirty more years until the rooms were
finally turned over to dinners, concerts and public meetings. Few splendid
new town mansions were built; Stafford (now Lancaster) House, originally
intended for Frederick, Duke of York, Bridgwater House and Dorchester
House were among the last of the long line of private palaces which wealthy
aristocrats had built in London since the sixteenth century. They had
always regarded their country seats as their real homes, and twenty years
of isolation from Europe during the Napoleonic wars had broken the
cultivated tradition of the Grand Tour. Their interests were directed more
towards the stables and the hunting field and less towards the arts and the
muses than hitherto, and the need to make a splash in London was correspondingly diminished.

They still came for the season, of course, but by the middle years of
the century 'society' had become much diluted and therefore enlarged. The

days of huge private receptions were over, Lady Palmerston's at her house in Piccadilly (now the Naval and Military Club, or 'In and Out') in the 1850s and 1860s being the last to unite under one roof all of society's now widely diverging elements. The season was becoming a hectic social whirl, as William Prescott, the American historian, discovered during a visit in 1850:

> I took a long range among people of rank & fashion of both sexes, whom I chased round in a succession of lunches, dinners, afternoon breakfasts, balls and routs, with a perseverence and power of endurance quite astonishing to myself. I had a dozen invitations for a single day, and was booked up in the way of dinners for more than a month in advance. I had the satisfaction of dining with Sir Robert Peel, though only a week before his death. Five times I was obliged to decline the invitation of the premier, Lord John Russell, and was invited to dine with five of the mitred nobles, including the Archbishop of Canterbury, I was at court several times, and had three invitations to the palace. . . .[1]

The need for masculine refuge from this exhausting social turmoil was perhaps one of the causes for the great proliferation of gentlemen's clubs in the nineteenth century. The convivial tradition inaugurated in the coffee-houses of St James's Street and Pall Mall in the days of Addison, Steele and Swift had been maintained throughout the eighteenth century by the great proprietary clubs like White's, Brooks's and Boodle's, and was now to take on a more sedate and imposing aspect appropriate to the new age. In the words of Mr P. A. Bezodis, the old proprietary subscription clubs were 'augmented by or transformed into clubs owned and run by the members themselves. Usually larger than the eighteenth-century clubs, they resembled them in that they often catered for the needs of officers of a post-war era or of participants in the increasingly organized party conflicts of the Victorian age.' The establishment of the first of the members' clubs, Arthur's in 1811, was followed within the generation after the return of peace in 1815 by the building of a dozen great new houses in Pall Mall and its vicinity. The United Service, the Athenaeum, the Travellers' and several others each provided luxurious *rendez-vous* for groups of gentlemen united by common tastes and social background,

---

[1] *The Literary Memoranda of William Hickling Prescott*, ed. C. Harvey Gardiner, 1961, vol. 2, p. 195.

but the Carlton (founded in 1832) and the Reform (1834) were also the private headquarters of the two rival political parties. To quote Mr Bezodis again, these foundations gave and still give the Pall Mall area 'its most striking single type of building, which conveys forcibly to the eye its character as the stronghold of masculine society at a period of great national power'.[1]

Foreign visitors were always greatly impressed by the West End clubs. 'These impregnable fortresses play a most important part in an Englishman's life,' wrote Monsieur Wey, a rather sour Frenchman who was invited to dine at the Reform in the 1850s. The comfort, the privacy, the good talk and even the *cuisine* (presided over by the famous French chef, Alexis Soyer) had all aroused his admiration, and he had reluctantly concluded that English clubs were 'a perfect substitute for the *café*, the reading-room and the restaurant'.[2] But they were, of course, exclusively for men, and the popularity of club-life undoubtedly aggravated the masculine selfishness and arrogance so prevalent in society circles. 'The ladies are obliged to study the tastes and pursuits of the gentlemen, in order to find favour in the eyes of these lords of creation,' complained Lady Blessington. 'Is not this a dreadful degradation to our sex? Only fancy women talking of horses, and not only talking of, but visiting them in their stables!' Clubmen, she continued, 'prefer a well-dressed dinner to the best-dressed woman in the world', and were 'well aware that the *recherché* repasts, with "all appliances to boot", to be obtained at clubs, at a price within their reach, would be totally unobtainable in a ménage of their own, except by relinquishing some other extravagance'.[3] And Monsieur Wey noticed the same thing, though from a different angle, when to his astonishment he was invited to accompany the beautiful daughter of an English friend for a drive in Hyde Park – without a chaperone! Their carriage took its place in the rolling stream of vehicles. They watched the riders cantering by; they alighted by the Serpentine and joined the fashionable throng listening to the band. 'There is no exaggeration in the much-vaunted beauty of English women,' he noted to himself, but he was dumbfounded to observe that the men 'pass them by with lowered lids, apparently quite indifferent to their charms'. And when his companion politely asked him what had struck him most in London he could only reply 'the coldness of your compatriots towards the fair sex and the warmth

---

[1] *Survey of London*, vol. xxix, 1960, pp. 10–11.

[2] Valerie Pirie, *A Frenchman sees the English in the 'Fifties*, 1935, pp. 50–63.

[3] Quoted in Mark Edward Perugini, *The Omnibus Box*, 1946, pp. 254–7.

of their passion for horses'. In France, he concluded, 'we find husbands for our daughters; here they have to do so for themselves'.[1]

But both the clubs and (as we have already seen) the parades in the Park had a unifying social influence as well. In the saloons and coffee-rooms of Pall Mall clubmen who possessed wealth or intellectual distinction but neither land nor lineage could meet the greatest aristocrats in the kingdom on equal terms, and in the Park any of London's 80,000-odd 'carriage folk' could fancy that they were at any rate within bowing distance of the *beau monde*. There were, in fact, tenuous cultural links between the residents of Mayfair and Belgravia on the one hand and the far more numerous peoples of St John's Wood, Tyburnia and Kensington on the other. But there was also a fundamental difference of attitude to London itself between these two groups. For the latter, as for their neighbours in St Pancras or Camberwell or a dozen other new suburbs, London was not merely the place to be visited in the season; it was their sole and permanent home. What had it to offer to them?

Behind the impassive brick or stuccoed fronts of countless Victorian terraces and villas, within the privacy of lace curtains and a plethora of heavy mahogany furniture, middle-class domestic life in London differed little from its counterpart in numerous provincial towns. There was more of it, of course, in terms of numbers, and after the flight from the over-crowded conditions of City residence had begun, the scale of living was more often grand and luxurious. But in general the pattern of home life in London was much the same as elsewhere. In many households there were family prayers, dutifully attended by the servants, and family meals when the children had outgrown the nursery; there was the governess or the spinster's private school-room round the corner; there was sewing and dressmaking to be done, afternoon calls to be paid and visiting cards to be left, and annual visits to the country or the seaside to be arranged. The rooms were often filled with either the vacuous gossip of women with time on their hands, or with the pompous pronouncements of masculine outward pre-eminence; and always there were the servants, servants scrubbing, polishing and dusting, servants with cans of hot water and pails of bedroom slop, servants carrying up the coals for the fires whose smoke enveloped the air with grime and fog, servants endlessly trudging up and down the stairs.

There was, to be sure, an almost infinite range of minute gradations in

[1] Pirie, pp. 161–7.

both the style and the scale of living, for anyone with an annual income of upwards of £150 probably regarded himself as middle-class. But despite this variety there was also a more potent underlying homogeneity of outlook, which was most clearly to be seen in times of crisis such as the great Chartist assemblies of 1848; in more normal times it manifested itself in the domestic orderliness and the formality and reserve of even the closest family relationships which prevailed in so many well-to-do Victorian households, and which seldom failed to catch the notice of foreign observers.

Within the citadels of the home the garrisons of London lived, in fact, the same sort of life as they might have lived in many other places. Even in the great metropolis entertaining still took place in the home, for only a very few restaurants had yet appeared in London, and apart from a few small hotels in the West End, such as Long's in Clifford Street, where Sir Walter Scott stayed in 1815, chop-houses, coffee-houses or coaching inns – all unsuitable for ladies – were the only places where one could eat out. It was not until the building of large hotels at some of the principal railway termini, and of the Langham Hotel at the south end of Portland Place in the 1860s, followed around 1870 by the slow discovery of the gastronomic delights of Soho, that this depressing state of affairs began to change.

But outside the home, London had much to offer – shopping boulevards and bazaars of unrivalled splendour, parks and pleasure gardens, galleries and museums, concerts and theatres, all in a profusion unknown in any other English town and all contributing to that sense of being at the centre of affairs which citizens of any great capital city always possess, and which citizens of provincial towns often find so exasperating. And if the enjoyment of these amenities required respectable people to leave the refuge of their homes and expose themselves to the scenes of vice and depravity in the streets which foreigners often remarked upon – 'however rigid English prudery may be in the home circle, it is shocked by nothing in the street, where licentiousness runs riot,' was Monsieur Wey's comment[1] – Londoners themselves seem to have been oblivious of the contrast.

Shoppers had never hitherto been so well served as they were in the mid-nineteenth century. Shops were still small and independent, owned and run by the shopkeeper, who kept his door open to all hours, allowed credit and was always ready to deliver. He had to provide keen service in order to stay in business, for he found formidable competition from the street hawkers – 13,000 of them, according to Mayhew – and in the food trade,

[1] Pirie, p. 41.

from the retail street markets, today almost extinguished by the supposedly more important requirements of motor traffic, but enjoying their hey-day in mid-Victorian times. Bakers' shops were not so common as they were later to become, for bread was still often baked at home; fruit and vegetables were usually bought in the markets, and milk and dairy produce were delivered by the roundsman, who called twice daily. But still, food shops were the most numerous, followed by the haberdashers and linen drapers, whose trade in materials rather than in finished articles shows the importance of domestic sewing and needlework in the days before the mass-production of ready-made garments. Only in the tailors' and shoemakers' shops were the traditional direct contacts between maker and purchaser still to some extent maintained.

But change was coming, reflecting the vast increase in the population of London. The drapers had led the way in the more intensive use of capital, concentrating on low profits and a quick turnover; it was they, for instance, who had in the 1820s first used price labels on the goods exhibited in their windows. The centre of gravity of their fashionable trade was moving from the City and Fleet Street to the West End, particularly to Oxford Street and Regent Street, where there was space for larger shops like Swan and Edgar's, equipped with the great plate-glass windows first used by Francis Place at his tailor's shop at Charing Cross, and now brilliantly illuminated by gaslight. Henry Colman thought that one of the most beautiful sights he had seen in London had been 'on a ride down Regent Street, on the box-seat of an omnibus, in the evening, when the streets are crowded with people elegantly dressed, and the shops in long ranges, with their illuminated windows of immense length, and their interior, exhibiting an almost indefinite perspective, are in all their glory'.[1]

In the second half of the century the pace of change increased. Bigger shops and more pushing business methods produced great armies of shop assistants and very long hours of work. A few West End drapers again led the way by enlarging their shops into department stores offering a very wide range of goods, Debenham's, Swan and Edgar's and Dickins and Jones being pioneers in this field. But this process was not restricted to the West End, for prosperous suburbs were generating new shopping centres of their own in such places as High Street Kensington and Knightsbridge, where Barker's and Harrod's quickly rose from small beginnings to departmental status. Harrod's was originally a grocer's, and it was chiefly the

[1] Colman, vol. I, p. 120.

grocers who were to initiate another revolution in retailing by the introduction of multiple shops, the leader here being John Sainsbury, who
opened his first shop in 1869 in Drury Lane. By the 1880s John Barker of
Kensington was combining grocery and drapery, and he already employed
400 hands. He closed at between 6.30 p.m. and 8 p.m., depending on the
time of year, but some shops nearby stayed open until 10 p.m. or even
midnight on Saturdays, and many shop assistants worked 80 or 90 hours a
week.[1]

But almost all shops – except those kept by the Jews – did shut on
Sundays, and Sunday was therefore the most popular day for a family
excursion to the parks. The royal parks open to wheeled traffic – Kensington Gardens, Hyde Park and Regent's Park – were the most popular, and
the Green Park and St James's were convenient for the West End. Many
people often came to these oases from a considerable distance, for elsewhere in London many traditional open spaces such as Spa Fields had
recently been covered with bricks and mortar, and the municipal authorities had not yet started to establish new parks. The only new parks formed
in London before the establishment of the Metropolitan Board of Works
in 1855 were therefore formed by the government, acting through the Commissioners of Woods and Forests. Besides Regent's Park there were Victoria Park, Hackney, opened in 1845, and Battersea Park (1858), where
the marshy nature of the ground had required the deposit of a million
cubic feet of earth excavated during the building of the Victoria Docks
at Blackwall. In 1852 Kennington Common, where the Chartists had held
their last great rally in 1848, was emparked, but on the commons at
Blackheath, Clapham and Wandsworth building encroachment continued
until the Metropolitan Commons Act of 1866 forbade any further enclosures within a radius of fourteen miles of Charing Cross.[2] Ultimately
the remains of these and other once wide expanses of common land were
vested in public ownership of one kind or another. By the 1870s the
Metropolitan Board of Works was beginning to take an interest in the
matter, Finsbury Park (opened in 1869) being its first important achievement, followed by the acquisition of Hampstead Heath in 1872.

The lack of public open spaces in many parts of mid-nineteenth-century
London helps to explain the continuing popularity of the privately owned
pleasure gardens to be found in many of the suburbs. The pleasure garden,

---

[1] Dorothy Davis, *A History of Shopping*, 1966, *passim.*; P.P., 1866, vol. xii, *Report of
Select Committee on Shops Hours Regulation Bill*, pp. 163–5.

[2] J. J. Sexby, *The Municipal Parks, Gardens and Open Spaces of London*, 1898, p. 381.

with its pavilions and its groves of trees for polite promenading to the soft sound of the music of a string band, was an essentially eighteenth-century form of diversion. In the first half of the nineteenth century many of these resorts were engulfed in the outward march of the suburban frontier, particularly in the 1840s and 1850s, when Bagnigge Wells, Islington Spa, White Conduit House and Copenhagen House all closed their doors, the last in 1852 to make way for the new Metropolitan Cattle Market. Yet elsewhere new gardens were opening, often in the grounds of a popular tavern, and the successful adaptation of old traditions gave this form of recreation a new lease of life which enabled it to survive into the late 1870s. Sadler's Wells, indeed, where the theatre built in the original pleasure garden became first a music hall and then after rebuilding a home for opera and ballet, survives to this day.

The nineteenth-century pleasure gardens ceased to have any pretensions to fashion and catered instead for the less sophisticated tastes of a middle-class clientèle. This was so even at Vauxhall, the most famous of the eighteenth-century resorts, which survived until 1859, and where in 1833 as many as 27,000 people crowded in on a single day. Everywhere the formality of the traditional eighteenth-century fare was supplemented by new attractions – by fireworks, by displays of juggling, conjuring or acrobatics, by dioramas or balloon ascents, or indeed by any novelty which would draw custom. At the Red House, Battersea, there were pigeon-shooting matches and boat races, while on the outskirts of north and east London wrestling, dog-fights and rat-killing were favourite sports. But everywhere the soot and grime of the smoke-laden atmosphere – hard even to imagine in the mid-twentieth century – was slowly moving all these diversions indoors, to improvised saloons and halls and theatres like the Grecian Saloon in the City Road, the offspring of the garden at the Eagle tavern, or the Surrey Music Hall, built in the grounds of the Surrey Zoological Gardens at Walworth.

The most famous of the nineteenth-century resorts was Cremorne Gardens, which occupied twelve acres of ground in Chelsea between the river and the King's Road. For some years after its opening in 1832 Cremorne had flourished as a private sports club with facilities for archery and golf, but in the mid-1840s a new owner opened the grounds to the public (subject to payment for admission, of course) and after a flamboyant advertising campaign he drew large crowds to a miscellany of diversions which included balloon ascents and a mock tournament. The gardens and the dancing were the main attractions for the 'students and shop girls, soldiers and civilians, dissipated young bloods, paterfamilias with their better halves, schoolboys and children's nurses' who patronized Cremorne, but in the course of time the proprietors' endless search for novelty produced little more than a vulgar pastiche and a great deal of noise. The Chelsea Vestry and the residents of the new streets which had been built around the grounds protested at the rowdyism and the drunkenness, the prosperity of the place declined, and within a year or two of its closure in 1877 most of the site was covered with houses – the inevitable ultimate fate of almost all the London pleasure gardens. The urban *al fresco* tradition of the eighteenth-century gardens was indeed dead at last.[1]

But indoors it was already branching out into a new form of entertainment, the music hall, as essentially Victorian as the pleasure gardens had previously been so characteristically Georgian. With the inexorable outward advance of the built-up area the pleasure gardens had retreated beyond convenient walking-distance of central London, and so to meet the demand there for eating, drinking, light music and popular entertainment, numerous song and supper rooms had arisen in the 1840s and 1850s. The first and most famous of these were in or near Covent Garden, at Evans's in King Street, at the Coal Hole in the Strand and the Cider Cellars in Maiden Lane. But with the decline of the pleasure gardens the song and supper rooms had soon spread to such suburbs as Whitechapel, Hoxton and Lambeth. The proprietors were usually licensed victuallers, whose principal source of revenue was the sale of drink. At first the singing and entertainment was provided by the customers themselves, but soon professionals were hired, a platform at one end of the hall was constructed for them, and a small entrance fee of perhaps sixpence was levied. From there it was only a short step to the full-blown music halls. Among the earliest were the Canterbury Hall in Upper Marsh, Lambeth (1852) and the Oxford Music Hall in Oxford Street (1861). The former was built on the site of a skittle alley at the back of the Canterbury Arms tavern, the latter in the yard of an old coaching inn. Sites such as these provided a home for many of the forty-odd music halls which existed in London by 1868, many of them in the suburbs, but including also such famous West End names as the London Pavilion and the Alhambra.[2]

Besides the pleasure gardens and the music halls there was an extraordinary variety of other entertainments to be had in mid-nineteenth-century

[1] E. Beresford Chancellor, *The Pleasure Haunts of London*, 1925, *passim*; Warwick Wroth, *Cremorne and the Later London Gardens*, 1907, p. 22.

[2] Raymond Mander and Joe Mitchenson, *British Music Hall*, 1965, pp. 9–19.

London. There was a circus at Astley's Amphitheatre, Westminster Bridge Road, a short-lived racecourse out at Notting Hill, a menagerie at Exeter Hall in the Strand and the gardens of the Zoological Society in Regent's Park. The wide desire for knowledge, as well as mere human curiosity, probably accounts for the immense popularity of exhibitions of all kinds. Madame Tussaud's waxworks were already famous, all the wonders of the world seemed to find their way to the displays at the Egyptian Hall in Piccadilly, and John Ruskin thought that the educational value of the beautifully painted panoramas exhibited at Burford's in Cranbourn Street was so great that the government ought to make a grant for the support of the place in its declining years in the 1860s. Until its destruction by fire in 1865 Savile House, a capacious old mansion in Leicester Square, became a favourite venue for innumerable exhibitions and lectures as well as other less respectable diversions, and for ten years Wyld's Great Globe, a gigantic model of the earth, was permitted to occupy the greater part of the open ground within the Square itself. The area round Piccadilly Circus and Leicester Square was in fact already becoming the acknowledged centre of London's entertainment world long before the building of half-a-dozen theatres nearby in Shaftesbury Avenue at the close of the century.

The London theatre as a whole was not enjoying one of its great periods during the first three-quarters of the nineteenth century. Until 1843 the two great theatres of Drury Lane and Covent Garden still in theory enjoyed the dual monopoly of theatrical rights which had been conferred upon Thomas Killigrew and Sir William Davenant and their heirs by royal letters patent in 1662–3. At the opening of the nineteenth century both these theatres were of enormous size; indeed they had to be in order to justify their claim that they could still meet the theatrical demands of the already vast population of London. But in 1808–9 both the patent theatres had been destroyed by fire. After rebuilding they were still uneconomically large and they entered on their new careers burdened with very heavy capital debts. They now found themselves beset by the competition of a rapidly growing number of minor theatres whose presentation of 'burlettas', or quasi-musical entertainments, successfully disguised the systematic evasion of the restrictions imposed by the royal patents of 1662–3. Whereas in 1800 there were fewer than half-a-dozen such rivals, including the Haymarket Theatre and the King's Theatre or Opera House, also in the Haymarket and both licensed by the Lord Chamberlain, by 1843 nearly forty new minor theatres had been established all over

London. Many of these newcomers were very short-lived, but a few survive to this day, notably the Adelphi and the Royal Coburg (now known as the Old Vic). The fiction of monopoly could no longer be maintained, and in 1843 it was finally abolished.

During these troubled years the London theatre was no longer fashionable. The aristocratic patrons who subscribed for the rebuilding of Drury Lane in 1810–12 soon lost interest; the behaviour of the audiences in the two patent theatres was sometimes riotous and debased and in the minor theatres coarse and disorderly. Only attendance at the opera retained any significance in the social season. By the 1820s, too, the evangelical moral code was already beginning to cast its baleful influence over the stage. The great writers of the time – even those such as Byron, Keats or Dickens, who were unaffected by this influence – devoted little or no time to writing for the stage, and although there were many great actors the size and bad acoustics of the two patent theatres forced them to vulgarize their techniques and encouraged excessive expenditure on splendid scenic spectacles. The star performers commanded such high fees for their services that there was little left for the playwrights, and apart from their frequent productions of Shakespeare the indifferent melodramas and extravaganzas which were so popular at this time were often unworthy of such great actors as Macready, the Keans or the Kembles.

There were, however, some hopeful signs. The introduction in some theatres of stall seats in place of the old disorderly pit, and of reserved seats, reduced rowdyism, and the use of gas light on the stage opened up a whole new field of scenic effect. The gradual removal of proscenium doors and of the stage apron was perhaps not so fortunate in the long run, for it divided the audience from the action and led on to the total separation imposed by the modern picture-frame proscenium. But in those days of insensitive audience behaviour this was perhaps a necessary phase of theatrical evolution, and no doubt contributed to the gradual emergence in the 1840s of a new playgoing public. In the early years of her reign Queen Victoria's frequent visits to the theatre encouraged quieter behaviour there, while less fortunate people whose recreational needs required an opportunity to make a noise as well as merely to listen tended to go to the new music halls. After the Act of 1843 ending the monopoly of the patent houses hardly any new theatres were built in London for over twenty years, and when another surge began in the mid-1860s even Drury Lane and Covent Garden (the latter rebuilt again in 1856–8 after another fire) were enjoying some share in the general rise of national prosperity.

Railways and omnibuses were making the theatre accessible to a far larger public than ever before. Ranting histrionics were giving place to more naturalistic acting, and under such new leaders as Squire Bancroft and W. S. Gilbert the modern director in charge of the whole production was superseding the confused and ill-rehearsed performances hitherto often prevalent.[1]

Music, or at any rate indigenous music, was at a low ebb after the great days of Handel and Arne. Despite the foundation of the (Royal) Philharmonic Society in 1813 London had no adequate concert hall until the building of the St James's Hall in Piccadilly in 1858, and at the King's Theatre in the Haymarket (renamed Her Majesty's in 1837) the management of opera was bedevilled by personal squabbles and by interminable legal and financial difficulties. Eventually the headquarters of opera in London was transferred to its modern home at Covent Garden Theatre in 1847, and twenty years later the destruction of Her Majesty's by fire proved the death knell of opera there. There were no English composers of note, and few native performers either, and all of the musical distinction of the period was imported from abroad in performances of opera by Mozart, Rossini and Donizetti, and in ballet, in the exquisite romantic dancing of Marie Taglioni.[2]

Painting and learning were beginning to be objects of public patronage and encouragement. This was the age of the foundation of the National Gallery in 1824 (in Pall Mall, until its removal to Trafalgar Square in 1837), of the National Portrait Gallery in 1856 and of the South Kensington Museum in 1857, from which later developed the Science Museum and the Victoria and Albert Museum. In 1867 the Royal Academy obtained possession of Burlington House and subsequently built extensive galleries on the site of the garden to the north. The British Museum was entirely rebuilt, its collections were greatly enlarged, notably by the acquisition of the King's Library, the Grenville Library and the Elgin Marbles, and the number of annual visitors leaped from about 13,000 in 1808 to nearly 900,000 forty years later. Yet few if any of these places were open on Sundays – the British Museum, for instance, not until 1896[3] – and

[1] Allardyce Nicoll, *Early Nineteenth Century Drama, 1800–1850*, 1955 edn.; Nicoll, *A History of Late Nineteenth Century Drama, 1850–1900*, vol. I, 1946; Raymond Mander and Joe Mitchenson, *The Theatres of London*, 1963 edn.; *Survey of London*, vol. xxxv, *The Theatre Royal, Drury Lane, and the Royal Opera House, Covent Garden*, 1970.

[2] Harold Rosenthal, *Opera at Covent Garden: A Short History*, 1967, pp. 17–30; Janet Leeper, *English Ballet*, 1944, pp. 5–6.

[3] Information kindly supplied by the Secretary of the British Museum.

their use was therefore restricted to persons of leisure, or (to quote the regulations of the British Museum in 1810) to 'persons of decent appearance'. At the more popular level, the ratepayers of the City voted twice, in 1855 and 1861, against the adoption of the Free Libraries Act, and although the Corporation eventually, in 1870–2, erected the building still used to house the splendid Guildhall Library, no progress was yet being made elsewhere in London in the provision of public libraries.[1]

But whatever its shortcomings and limitations might be, London was indisputably the cultural and intellectual capital of the nation. It was here that almost all of the societies which proliferated at this time had their origins and their headquarters – learned societies, professional societies, religious societies, philanthropic societies, well over a hundred of them dating from between 1810 and 1870, and many of them, such as the Howard League for Penal Reform or the Royal Society for the Prevention of Cruelty to Animals, now household names. In the world of the theatre London's pre-eminence was absolute. The residence there for substantial periods of many of the greatest writers, including Keats, Byron, Coleridge, Lamb, Carlyle, Thackeray, Browning, George Eliot, Macaulay and, of course, Dickens, demonstrates the capital's ascendancy in the field of letters. Many even of those writers who never lived there, such as Jane Austen or the Brontë sisters, nevertheless had business dealings with their publishers there, for only Edinburgh could rival London in the book trade. For the painters the position was, it is true, rather different, for London had nothing of visual interest for them in the age of the romantic revival. Yet despite frequent absences on provincial or foreign tours, most artists who exhibited at the Royal Academy had at least a *pied-à-terre* in London and often a studio or a house as well, usually in St Marylebone, or from about 1850 onwards, in South Kensington or Chelsea. The Pre-Raphaelites all had their headquarters in London, and even Constable spent many years there. Two of the very greatest painters of the time, Blake and Turner, were both Londoners by birth, and made their homes there throughout most of their lives.

So far we have been examining what London had to offer to those of her citizens with enough money, leisure and knowledge to make at least some use of the recreational and cultural facilities which existed in the metropolis. But what of the poor, the unleisured and the ignorant, whose ways of

[1] W. B. Boulton, *The Romance of the British Museum*, n.d., pp. 11–14; Charles Welch, *A Modern History of the City of London*, 1896, pp. 208, 228, 266, 277.

life absorbed the attention of Henry Mayhew? 'Go to the Court End of London,' wrote the American, Henry Colman, 'and nothing can exceed the splendor and gorgeousness of the display which you meet continually; but go into the low places of the town, and it is impossible to describe the wretchedness, dirt, and squalidness of thousands of famished and half-starved, drunken, dissolute vagabonds, who are there to be seen.'[1] What had London for them?

In previous chapters we have already seen some aspects of the way of life of what contemporaries described as 'the sunken sixth' of the people of London. We have seen how easily immigrants, in the bewilderment of their first arrival in London, could lose their previous norms of moral and domestic behaviour; how unemployment and destitution could reduce the labouring populace to living conditions of unimaginable filth and squalor, devoid of water or the basic necessities of sanitation, and exposed to correspondingly frightful rates of mortality; and we have seen how in the central districts of London extensive demolition of working-class housing for the building of railways and commercial undertakings was compressing the poor into ever more overcrowded slums, where all hope of escape to even the rudiments of civilized living was often forgotten. 'Nothing short of personal experience,' wrote George Godwin, who was not a sensationalist, 'would have led us to believe in the frightful amount of ignorance, misery, and degradation which exists in this wealthy and luxurious city.'[2]

Overcrowding was not new in London. The rookeries at St Giles in the Fields, or the valley of the Fleet, or Saffron Hill, or Whitecross Street, or Houndsditch, or in Spitalfields and Whitechapel, were already old at the beginning of the nineteenth century. But all these concentrations were either within the City itself or near to its boundaries. What was new in the nineteenth century was the great extension of overcrowding (though not always in such acute form as the word rookery suggests) to parts of Bethnal Green, St George's in the East, Bermondsey, Rotherhithe and Southwark, and even to Westminster (particularly around the Abbey), and to such outlying points as Lisson Grove in St Marylebone or Jennings Buildings in Kensington High Street. It was in areas such as these that the lodging-house keepers and the middlemen drove their prosperous trade; fourpence or threepence for a night's lodging with or without a bed

---

[1] Colman, vol. II, p. 380.

[2] George Godwin, *London Shadows: A Glance at the 'Homes' of the Thousands*, 1854, p. 32.

in a house with a total capacity of between forty and fifty persons produced an annual revenue of nearly £250. In 1852 nearly 50,000 people were nightly accommodated in common lodging-houses, while many of the families with a single room to themselves were in little better circumstance. The combined work of a whole family, including young children, might only bring in some 15s. a week, there was hardly any furniture to sell if no work was to be had, and the rent of 2s. or 3s. a week must be paid within two days of first demand on Monday. 'In the occupants of such places,' Godwin commented, '– men and women with bodies to suffer and souls to be lost – the feelings are blunted, the moral perceptions distorted; decency is out of the question, and degradation nearly certain. Goodness and virtue are sometimes to be found there, wonderful to say, but the majority have no hope; progress is impossible, the future a blank: in the dirt they are, and in the dirt they must remain.'[1]

The endless variety of ways by which these unfortunates tried to scrape a living is the principal subject of Mayhew's *London Labour and the London Poor*. It was from this great slough of human suffering that London drew the cheap unskilled or semi-skilled labour upon which so many of its trades and manufactures depended, and upon which, indeed, its whole prosperity was in considerable measure built. In page after page Mayhew enumerates trade after trade – the coal-heavers, the coal-barkers, the ballast-getters, the ballast-lightermen, the ballast-heavers and the lumpers, to mention only one of his groups – and piles detail upon detail until the reader is almost exhausted. His comparatively rare moments of more general observation are, indeed, often more illuminating, and in one of these, his description of labour recruitment at the docks, he conveys what work meant to the poor and the hungry. Anyone wishing to know, he wrote:

> should wend his way to the London Dock gates at half-past seven in the morning. There he will see congregated, within the principal entrance, masses of men of all ranks, looks, and natures. Decayed and bankrupt master butchers are there, and broken-down master bakers, publicans, and grocers, and old soldiers, sailors, Polish refugees, *quondam* gentlemen, discharged lawyers' clerks, 'suspended' government officials, almsmen, pensioners, servants, thieves – indeed everyone (for the work requires no training) who wants a loaf, and who is willing to work for it. The London Dock is one of the few places in

[1] Godwin, pp. viii, 15–21; Godwin, *Town Swamps and Social Bridges*, 1859, p. 28.

34 Building the Metropolitan Railway in Praed Street, *c.* 1866.
Paddington Station in background

35 Building Kensington High Street Metropolitan Railway Station, *c.* 1867

36 Paddington Station in 1862

37 Building St Pancras Station, 1868

38 Baker Street Metropolitan Railway Station, 1863

39 The Clerkenwell Tunnel on the Metropolitan Railway near Farringdon Street, 1868

40 Site clearance for the building of Queen Victoria Street and the District Railway, *c.* 1869

41 Building the District Railway along the Embankment in front of Somerset House, *c.* 1869

the Metropolis where men can get employment without character or recommendation.

As the hour approaches eight, you know by the stream pouring through the gates, and the rush towards particular spots, that the 'calling foremen' have made their appearance, and that the 'casual men' are about to be taken on for the day.

Then begins the scuffling and scrambling, and stretching forth of countless hands high in the air, to catch the eye of him whose nod can give them work. As the foreman calls from a book of names, some men jump up on the back of others, so as to lift themselves high above the rest and attract his notice. All are shouting, some cry aloud his surname, and some his christian name; and some call out their own names to remind him that they are there. Now the appeal is made in Irish blarney; and now in broken English.

Indeed, it is a sight to sadden the most callous to see thousands of men struggling there for only one day's hire, the scuffle being made the fiercer by the knowledge that hundreds out of the assembled throng must be left to idle the day out in want. To look in the faces of that hungry crowd is to see a sight that is to be ever remembered. . . . Until we saw with our own eyes this scene of greedy despair, we could not have believed that there was so mad an anxiety to work, and so bitter a want of it among so vast a body of men.[1]

Besides those who worked for a wage there were thousands of others who worked in equally various ways on their own account. For such people the public streets were the cheapest places to work in, for there there were no rents or rates to pay, nor heating or lighting, and in many trades the equipment required could be bought for a shilling or two. The streets of mid-nineteenth-century London bustled and rang with a quasi-nomadic economic life which has now almost completely disappeared. There were some 30,000 costermongers alone, dealing in fruit, vegetables and fish, either going their rounds with their barrows, or congregating at the street markets, particularly on Saturday nights and Sunday mornings when the poor did their shopping. But almost any article of food could be bought in the streets, delicacies such as hot eels, pickled whelks and sheep's trotters being included in the daily menu alongside such more common-place items as bread, milk, cats' meat and even water. Many small

[1] Henry Mayhew and John Binny, *The Criminal Prisons of London, and Scenes of Prison Life*, 1862, p. 35.

B B

manufactured articles were always on offer from itinerant salesmen – fusees, fly-papers, cutlery, old clothes, rat poison, toys and spectacles, for instance; there were dog-sellers, bird-sellers and goldfish-sellers, blind sellers of matches or needles, and in the poorer districts a living could be made (or at any rate attempted) by the writing of begging letters to individual customers' requirements. But the street was more than a place of business; the acrobats, jugglers, conjurers, singers, pavement artists, strong men, hurdy-gurdy men and Punch-and-Judy men made it a place of entertainment as well. Shoe-blacking or crossing-sweeping often provided children with a cheap mode of entry to the great world of street trade, and if all else failed, the destitute could resort to the collection of the very ordure of the streets – cigar-ends, the droppings of horses and even dogs, the last being sold by the pail-full to the tanneries.

The social costs of ways of living such as these were incalculable. Thomas Beames, a curate at St James's, Piccadilly, knew from first-hand experience that 'Rookeries hide the listlessness of departed hope, and the indolence of broken hearts. Compelled to herd with the worst of his species, because he cannot afford better lodging, the honest artisan is tempted to forget the lessons of his youth; and forced into precarious occupation, because his stated trade has failed him, he soon adopts it as his own.'[1] But the children born in the slums had never even had any lessons in their youth to forget, no standards of honesty or morality to abandon; and it was they who provided most of the recruits for the army of boys and girls, estimated at 100,000 in number in 1869, who wandered by day in London, 'destitute of proper guardianship, food, clothing, or employment . . . in fair training for the treadmill and the oakum shed, and finally for Portland and the convict's mark.'[2]

Nearly all criminals began their careers as urban juveniles. Boys as young as six or seven years of age, orphaned, perhaps, or deserted by their parents or forced daily into the streets to earn a few pence, would begin with petty theft – an apple off a stall or a tart from a pastrycook's. They would join a gang, or be conscripted into one, receive a systematic training in the arts of pocket-picking, and sally out on a life of deliberate crime, often at first under the aegis of an experienced adult, to whom a skilful child was a valuable asset. They became accepted members of the criminal fraternity, frequenting the flash-houses in much the same way as other

[1] Thomas Beames, *The Rookeries of London: Past, Present and Prospective*, 1850, p. 103.

[2] James Greenwood, *The Seven Curses of London*, 1869, p. 2.

differently situated Londoners might frequent the Athenaeum or any other club in Pall Mall, for refreshment, social conviviality or the discussion of business, which in their case meant the disposal of stolen goods. With girls it was much the same. Sexual promiscuity was widespread among juvenile delinquents from about the age of twelve upwards, and many girls moved on by natural progression from theft to prostitution. In 1859 there were 2,828 brothels and 8,600 prostitutes known to the police. These establishments were to be found all over London, for even Kensington, Hammersmith and Fulham had a dozen, with over a hundred practitioners in attendance there, and they catered for the full range of masculine taste and the masculine pocket. The main concentrations of the trade were in the East End and the older waterside districts south of the river, but in the West End there were fashionable marts like the Argyll Rooms, near Piccadilly Circus, or Cremorne Gardens at Chelsea, as well as the streets, where a less expensive girl could always be picked up. It was after a walk down the Haymarket and the Strand in the 1860s that the French historian Hippolyte Taine made one of the most terrible comments ever written by a foreign observer about nineteenth-century London: 'Every hundred steps one jostles twenty harlots; some of them ask for a glass of gin; others say, "Sir, it is to pay my lodging." This is not debauchery which flaunts itself, but destitution – and such destitution! The deplorable procession in the shade of the monumental streets is sickening; it seems to me a march of the dead. That is a plague-spot – the real plague-spot of English society.'[1]

Destitution, in fact, led many women to prostitution and many children to crime. Even in 1876, when the scale of juvenile delinquency in London had begun to decline, Dr Barnardo (who had opened his first orphanage six years earlier) estimated that some 30,000 children under sixteen years of age slept out on the streets, under the arches of railways or bridges, under waggons, in empty barrels, even in the heavy iron roller used in Regent's Park – anywhere. But after destitution had started a criminal career, drink provided much of the incentive for its continuance. Drinking often preceded and followed the committal of a crime, and much of the proceeds of crime was spent on drink. Drunkenness was certainly not confined to the poor, but between 1830 and 1869 beer-houses could be opened without a justices' licence, and the rapid proliferation of such

[1] I am much indebted to Dr J. J. Tobias's *Crime and Industrial Society in the 19th Century* for much of this paragraph; see also Greenwood, p. 282, and Hippolyte Taine, *Notes on England*, 1872, p. 36.

places provided a standing temptation to people for whom constructive forms of recreation were virtually impossible. Foreign visitors frequently commented on the terrible debauchery and violence to be seen outside the public houses of low districts on Saturday nights, while for many respectable middle-class Englishmen drunkenness was the vice of all others which was most frequently cast in the teeth of working men. Drunkenness seems to have affronted the Victorian conscience much more deeply than did such more deep-seated problems as bad housing or unemployment, and from the mid-1830s onwards innumerable temperance societies existed to put it down. By about 1870 a small decline in drinking had begun, thanks more, perhaps, to generally rising prosperity than to the efforts of the societies; but in 1868 there were still over 100,000 cases of drunkenness dealt with in the London courts.[1]

There was one large section of the labouring populace whose conditions of work placed its members apart from all the rest. These were the domestic servants, who purchased food and shelter at the price of the loss of a large measure of personal freedom. In 1851 there were nearly a quarter of a million domestic servants working in London. About one in every eleven of the entire metropolitan population spent his or her life in providing for the intimate daily needs, or supposed needs, of the other ten. In this particular trade women were more than five times as numerous as men. Domestic service was, indeed, by far the largest source of employment open to women, its requirements being almost twice as great as that of the clothing trade, and in 1851 it provided a subsistence for every sixth woman in London.

Domestic service must be one of the oldest occupations in the history of man, but in Victorian London its ramifications may perhaps have been more pervasive than ever before in England, for more and more people could afford to have a servant, just as in mid-twentieth-century London an ever growing number of people can afford to run a car. To employ a servant, and even in some cases, to *be* a servant, conferred respectability, and respectability extended throughout a wide range of the social spectrum. According to the authors of *A Practical Guide to the Peculiar Duties and Business of all Descriptions of Servants* (1825), who had themselves been 'Fifty years Servants in different Families', even 'a Widow or other unmarried Lady', with an income of only one hundred pounds per annum, 'may keep a Young Maid Servant at a low salary'. And from this humble

[1] Tobias, p. 180; Greenwood, p. 333.

foundation they went on to delineate the imposing domestic hierarchies appropriate to every income group, culminating in the splendid establish-ment suitable for a lady and gentleman blessed with some £5,000 a year – eleven female and thirteen male servants, comprising a housekeeper, cook, lady's maid, nurse, two house maids, laundry maid, still-room maid, nursery maid, kitchen maid and scullion, plus a butler, valet, housesteward, coachman, three grooms, two footmen, three gardeners and a labourer.

There was, in fact, an almost infinite variety of circumstance within the domestic world. The servant of all work, who according to the source already quoted, was 'usually taken from the industrious and labouring classes of the community, who are bred up with a view to the situation, having no other prospect or dependence', and whose wage might be as low as five guineas a year, stood almost as far beneath the housekeeper, with perhaps twenty-four guineas, as the housekeeper stood beneath her employer. Generally speaking, this wide range of personal skill and con-dition, plus the scattered nature of their employment, prevented the for-mation of trade clubs or societies among servants. They found work by personal enquiry or by answering advertisements in the newspapers. In such matters as wages, hours of work, annual holidays or board and lodging they had to a large extent to accept the conditions imposed by each individual householder. In return they were expected to display at all times the industry, truthfulness, virtue and humility of a saint. Religious faith was indeed held to be the means for the achievement of these rare attri-butes, as the authors of the *Practical Guide* automatically assumed in their 'Advice to Servants in General' when they wrote that 'The supreme Lord of the universe has, in his wisdom, rendered the various conditions of mankind necessary for our individual happiness: – some are rich, others poor – some are masters, and others servants. Subordination, indeed, attaches to your rank in life, but not *disgrace*.'

The extent of this subordination may be illustrated by the domestic conditions which prevailed in the early years of the nineteenth century in the household of Mrs Wollaston, wife of a merchant and banker engaged in trade with Genoa. At this time the Wollastons lived at Clapham; they had three or four young children, and kept six servants, all female. In reply to an application for the post of housemaid Mrs Wollaston wrote that the person required must be

a very trustworthy woman and perfectly able to take a housemaid's place in a large and very regular gentleman's family where only one [housemaid] is kept. As the family is extremely particular and very quiet and regular, none but a very steady, orderly, and quiet servant who does all her work very thoroughly would suit Mrs Wollaston. No perquisites of any sort allowed and everything included; the wages are £14 the first year and, if mutually satisfied, £15 the second. She must dress very plain and will be required to attend family prayers daily and church every Sunday (morning service one Sunday and afternoon the other) and assist in the nursery on a Sunday when the nurse or nursery maid are at church. She will have to get up with the laundrymaid to wash at 1 a.m. every Monday morning and wash till 5 or 6 a.m. according whether it is summer or winter, and whether there are grates to clean. Then comes in to do her housework which employs her till 10.30 a.m. or 11 a.m. when she returns to the washing till 9 p.m. She has nothing more to do with the linen or the getting it up, but twice a year helps the laundrymaid wash beds and other furniture. She washes her own things every four weeks in summer and every three weeks in winter, and it must be got up and quite finished in the day. The servants all go to bed at 10 p.m. and rise at 6 a.m. but in winter the housemaid goes to bed at 9 p.m. and rises at 5 a.m. as there are two fires and two rooms to be done by 7.30 a.m. The rest of her housework (when there is no scrubbing) generally employs her till 10.30 a.m. or 11 a.m. when she cleans herself and sits down to needlework till 8 p.m. Mrs Wollaston does not keep any lady's maid, consequently the little waiting upon she wants is done by the housemaid. She must be an active, diligent woman and do her business very thoroughly as Mrs Wollaston very much dislikes things done in a slovenly way, and she must be a good plain needlewoman. When she occasionally wants to go out, it must be on a weekday as the servants never go out for the day on a Sunday, and as the employments are very regular and there is a large family, it is not convenient to Mrs Wollaston to let the maid go out often.[1]

Conditions such as these were probably common in many London households throughout much of the nineteenth century. In practice they were often softened by the normal workings of human affection. This at any rate was certainly the case in the household of the Thornton family of

---

[1] Unpublished 'History of the Wollaston Family', 1960, by W. H. Wollaston, to whom I am much indebted for permission to quote the above passage.

bankers living at Battersea Rise. In her recollections of her childhood Marianne Thornton, who was born in 1797, records that:

> Nothing could exceed the kindness of my father and mother to all their servants and their families. They objected strongly to the usual restriction of 'no followers allowed' and used to say that a servant who would consent to cut all connection with her friends and relations could not be worth having. They were told when and how they could see their friends, and were encouraged to tell all their family circumstances. Many a country girl was allowed to invite her old father and mother to stay for a few days, and a present made towards their journey. Many a younger sister has come to our house to find a place and remained till she could hear of a promising one.

Nurse Hunter, who served the Thorntons for fifty-two years, the 'personification of a nurse, never weary, never irritable, never overdone by the sick babies by night, or the well ones by day', naturally enjoyed first place in the family affections. But Mr and Mrs Thornton also 'paid peculiar attention to the lower servants, such as the underhousemaid and the kitchen maid, the helper in the stables and washer woman in the laundry, fancying these were often overworked and tyrannically treated by the upper servants'; and whenever a servant had a holiday or was unable to get to London by the public coach, 'it seemed a natural arrangement that the carriage should take her'.[1]

Such were often, no doubt, the feelings of kindly families towards their domestic dependents. But how, on the other side of the green baize door, the servants felt towards their employers, their work and the world at large, has only been rarely recorded. The diary (already mentioned in Chapter 1) which was kept in 1837 by a twenty-nine-year-old footman, William Tayler, has a critical, appraising tone about it which is perhaps more familiar to modern ears than either the meticulous routine of Mrs Wollaston or the benevolent paternalism of the Thorntons.[2] Tayler's place with Mrs Prinsep, the widow of a wealthy East India merchant living in Great Cumberland Street, near Marble Arch, was comfortable and well paid (£42 a year). In addition to Tayler himself there were three maids, 'very quiet good sort of bodys', to minister to the requirements of Mrs

[1] E. M. Forster, *Marianne Thornton 1797–1887. A Domestic Biography*, 1956, pp. 31–4.

[2] *Diary of William Tayler, Footman, 1837*, ed. Dorothy Wise, 1962, St Marylebone Society Publications.

Prinsep and her unmarried daughter. His work was not hard, although it must have involved endless running up and down stairs, and when he stood behind the ladies' carriage during their frequent drives in the Park he sometimes got very cold. Often he had no need to get up before eight o'clock in the morning, yet he was usually free to go out on his own account by eleven, provided that he was back in time to wait at table for dinner. He fed extremely well, and when off duty could and often did entertain his friends and relations in his own private pantry, 'a very comfortable room'.

Yet despite these advantages he clearly had little or no warm personal feeling for either Mrs Prinsep or her daughters and grandchildren – why, indeed, should he? – and when his mistress was gravely ill he only hoped for her recovery because he did not wish to lose his place through the break-up of the household which her death would entail. In his view Mrs Prinsep thought 'of little else but playing cards and paying visets all the time', her friends 'talked about every bodeys buisness but their own', and on a Sunday when he went up to take lunch away he noticed that 'she was reading a novel with the Bible laying by her, ready to take up if any body came in'. Miss Prinsep, aged about forty, was 'an old maid', and the grandsons who strewed the house 'with spanish liquris and barly sugar and and such rubish' on their holiday visits were nothing but 'cattle'. Extravagant parties sometimes excited his sense of injustice – 'This is the way the gentry spend the money which ort to be given to the poor' – but what seems to have angered him most were the conversations so thoughtlessly carried on in his presence.

> There ar a sertain sort of old wimen that meet to drink tea with each other. They does nothing else but talk about the cheapest tradespeople and scandaliseing each others servants [and] backbiteing their neighbours. . . . And if a servant girl happen to be in the famley way, her character is rueind at once, and no lady will take them after and would think it quite shocking to have such a person in their house. . . . Axidents of this kind happens to young wimen in high life as well as to those in lower life, only the higher ones have a better chance of hiding these matters.

Here follows copious chapter and verse in support of this assertion, and the conclusion that 'It mite not happen once in twenty famleys, but it do happen and they are very fond of exposeing the lower classes when it takes place amongst them, therefore I think it's only fair to expose the upper classes in returne. . . . Now I leave the reader to judg whether the upper classes are not quite as bad as the lower classes.'

William Tayler only kept his diary for a single year. He had started it, full of good intentions, on 1 January 1837 for the purpose of improving his handwriting; but he had had much trouble and expense with his pens; and by the end of the year he was heartily sick of it. He was no doubt an out-of-the-ordinary servant in having kept a diary at all, yet the urge to self-improvement which inspired him to do so was probably often to be found on many London backstairs. He regarded himself as an aristocrat among servants, a 'gentleman's servant', very much more respectable than either mechanics or tradespeople or the servants of such people. In his own eyes, in fact, he liked to think that he had a certain status in the social hierarchy, yet he was well aware that this status was not always recognized by others. He was much vexed when he found himself touching his hat to a mere tradesman who tipped him half a crown, and childishly delighted when a gentleman mistook him for an army captain. The predicament of his own ambivalent situation, so painful to both himself and to sensitive modern readers, was summed up in the sad words of his penultimate entry, for 30 December. 'The life of a gentleman's servant is something like that of a bird shut up in a cage. The bird is well housed and well fed but is deprived of liberty, and liberty is the dearest and sweetes object of all Englishmen. Therefore I would rather be like the sparrow or lark, having less houseing and feeding and rather more liberty.' This, it may safely be surmised, was one of the principal causes for the almost complete disappearance of the ancient occupation of domestic service in modern England – a social revolution still unaccomplished when Tayler died in 1892.

Their peculiar problems and discontents placed domestic servants in a class apart. We may now return to those more numerous people who had 'less houseing and feeding and rather more liberty', and see how the community treated them when through whatever cause they fell below the minimum requirements of social behaviour.

Some went to gaol, some to the workhouse and some became the objects of charitable effort. It was, indeed, exceedingly easy to go to gaol in mid-nineteenth-century London. Until the 1850s when reformatory schools were established, boys of only eight years of age were frequently sent to prison; by the time that they had reached the age of twelve they had often served half-a-dozen or more sentences, and in 1828 there were some

170 boys under the age of fourteen on board the *Euryalis* hulk awaiting transportation.[1] In 1851, on the day of the census, the metropolitan gaols contained 6,188 prisoners, and it was estimated that in the course of every twelve months some 20,000 different individuals passed through them – figures equivalent to well over a quarter of the entire prison population of the whole of England and Wales.[2]

All prisons were in theory the King's, but at the opening of the nineteenth century almost all of them were in practice still administered locally, either by the County Justices of the Peace or the municipal authorities. In London, however, the position was complicated by the presence of the Royal Courts of Justice at Westminster, which had their own special prisons, those of King's Bench, the Marshalsea and the Fleet, chiefly used for debtors. In 1842 the Fleet and Marshalsea were closed, and after 1869 the Queen's Bench prison ceased to be used for debtors. The notion that the government had any responsibility for the establishment and maintenance of prisons for convicted criminals was, however, still comparatively new, and had indeed only arisen through force of circumstance when the American War of Independence had put a stop to the transportation of criminals across the Atlantic. As a temporary expedient prisoners had been confined in two old hulks moored in the Thames off Woolwich, pending the erection of a national penitentiary. This was ultimately realized at Millbank, on the site now occupied by the Tate Gallery, where the government built between 1812 and 1821 a gigantic 'model' prison at enormous expense. But with the increase of both population and crime the hulks were still also in use (until 1858), and when transportation to New South Wales was abandoned in 1840, a second government prison had to be built – at Pentonville, opened in 1842.[3]

Almost all the other London prisons were administered by the City Corporation and the Justices of the Peace for Middlesex and Surrey. The City Corporation was the greatest gaol-master in the whole country, with prisons at Newgate, Bridewell (in Bridge Street near Blackfriars), Giltspur Street (built in 1791 and closed in 1855), Whitecross Street (for debtors, built in 1813–15 and closed in 1870) and the Borough Comptor off Tooley Street in Southwark (closed in 1853). In 1852 this extensive accommodation was supplemented by a new House of Correction, built at Holloway, and in 1860 Bridewell was closed. The Middlesex Justices had their county gaol at Clerkenwell, rebuilt in 1846, and two Houses of Correction,

---

[1] Tobias, pp. 78–82.   [2] Mayhew and Binny, pp. 83–4.
[3] S. and B. Webb, *English Prisons under Local Government*, 1922, pp. 1, 43–8, 180–1.

one at Coldbath Fields to the east of Gray's Inn Road and the other at Tothill Fields, Westminster. Both these Houses of Correction had originally been established in the early seventeenth century, and both were now rebuilt, Coldbath Fields in 1794 with many later additions, and Tothill Fields in 1826–34 on a new site which is now occupied by Westminster Catholic Cathedral. Surrey County gaol, opened in 1798, was in Horsemonger Lane, off Newington Causeway, near the site now occupied by Newington Sessions House. In 1819–20 the Surrey Justices built a House of Correction at Brixton, and when this became inadequate they built another larger one at Wandsworth in 1849–51. Brixton prison was then closed, but due to the partial abolition of transportation in 1853 the government bought it for the confinement of convicted female prisoners. Lastly there were the private sponging-houses, or bailiffs' abodes, many of them round Chancery Lane, where debtors were detained in custody before being committed to prison.

From this brief conspectus it will be seen that the first half of the nineteenth century was a great age for prison building. The first impetus had been provided in the closing years of the eighteenth century, partly by the stoppage of transportation to America and partly by the philanthropic work of John Howard (d. 1790). But in the design of these new prisons, such as Newgate, rebuilt in the 1770s and 1780s, Howard's ideas had been ignored and the old abuses had been perpetuated. The convicted and the unconvicted were still herded together, no work was provided for the prisoners, the gaolers still made their living from the fees which they exacted and the provisions which they sold (at the King's Bench prison the profits from the sale of beer alone amounted to £800 per annum), and, above all, there was still no official prison inspectorate. During the long wars with France the reforming impulse died away, little having been achieved.[1]

Its renewal was largely due to the zeal of the Benthamite Radicals and the evangelical Christians, the latter led by Elizabeth Fry, whose visits to the women of Newgate, started in the winter of 1812–13, had awakened the conscience of such influential families as the Gurneys, the Buxtons, the Hoares and the Barclays. Even the City Corporation had been induced to make some short-lived improvements. But the Benthamite influence was to prove more enduring, for the government's new penitentiary at Millbank was derived from Bentham's own 'panopticon' scheme. There 1,200 convicts were accommodated in six pentagonal ranges which converged on the

[1] Webb, pp. 8–42.

chapel in the centre of the whole complex. Each prisoner had his own cell, where he slept and worked; reading matter was restricted to religious books and tracts. Here in this grim fortress the terrifying nineteenth-century theory of cellular isolation was first inaugurated, but even here it was not applied in its full rigour, for a small measure of communal work and exercise prevented the achievement of complete separation. There was worse to come.[1]

The change-over from the extremes of eighteenth-century brutality and promiscuity to the equally appalling extremes of the Victorian penal code took time, however. In 1815 the exaction of prison fees was abolished, but this reform did not apply in the three principal metropolitan debtors' prisons, where there was no fund from which to compensate the existing gaolers. Sir Robert Peel's Prison Act of 1823 – the first government-sponsored measure of penal reform – attempted to impose a code of administration on all prisons managed by the County Justices or the City Corporation, the classification of prisoners in productive labour being one of its main objects. The tread-wheel and the rule of silence became the vogue, the former being first introduced in London in the early 1820s at Coldbath Fields and the Surrey House of Correction at Brixton, sometimes for the grinding of corn but often too for the purposeless grinding of the empty air. But with no central inspectorate the prisons of the two most important authorities in the whole country, the City Corporation and the Middlesex Justices, remained 'pre-eminent in maladministration'. At Clerkenwell gaol, for instance, over 400 prisoners slept in only 32 rooms, and it was not until the appointment of four Home Office inspectors in 1835 that the new penology was widely applied.[2]

For the next forty years the County and Borough Justices continued to administer their gaols, but subject to ever growing Home Office regulation. The 'separate system' of cellular isolation, combined with absolute silence among the prisoners in association for work, became an article of faith which was now to be strictly enforced. This was, in the opinion of Sidney and Beatrice Webb, 'perhaps the most momentous official decision in English prison history'. At Millbank separation had already had to be modified because of increasing insanity among the prisoners, but when it was found that during periods of work in association complete silence could not be enforced, the remedy adopted at Pentonville (opened in 1842) was still greater stringency. There the prisoners worked in their cells, often on a new device, the crank, an iron drum which could be turned at

[1] Webb, pp. 71–2; Mayhew and Binny, pp. 235–6. [2] Webb, pp. 70, 97–9, 106.

1,200 revolutions an hour for over eight hours a day. All contact with other human beings, except the prison staff, was forbidden, and when convicts left their cells to visit the chapel or the exercise yard they wore masks with narrow eye-slits in order to prevent identification by their fellows. Here too the growing incidence of insanity compelled some modification of this frightful régime, but the enforcement for a fixed period (originally eighteen months) of cellular isolation and complete non-intercourse, followed by a period of associated labour in silence, was nevertheless the basis of the new penal servitude system established in the 1850s. This, in the Home Office view, was the only alternative to the old promiscuity, and this therefore was the objective towards which all convict prisons must move, whatever the effect on its victims might be. In the 1850s and 1860s the system was applied with unrelenting severity in the locally-administered prisons, many smaller establishments like Giltspur Street and the Borough Compter being closed in favour of large correctly designed new penal palaces such as Holloway. With the transfer of the management of all prisons to the Home Office in 1877 the building of the grim enduring edifice of the Victorian prison system was virtually complete.[1]

In the administration of poor relief there was a corresponding enlargement of state action, although in different form. Until the Poor Law Amendment Act of 1834 the relief of the poor was administered by the parish vestries. In London nearly all the vestries had their own workhouses, or rather poorhouses, for in many of them there was little attempt to make the inmates work. In the larger parishes, such as Islington, St Marylebone or St Pancras, these were institutions of great size, cost and administrative complexity, operated from day to day by salaried employees under powers conferred by special local Acts of Parliament. At St Marylebone, for instance, where there were over 1,100 paupers living in the workhouse in 1797 besides a large number on outdoor relief, there were eight separate departments. The superintendent's department was responsible for attending the meetings of the Directors and Guardians (i.e. the parish vestrymen), for the general management of the paupers in the house, the payment and visitation of the outdoor poor, and the execution of orders under the settlement laws for removal and apprehension. The steward's department managed provisions and stores, the matron's ran the domestic economy, and supervised the clothing, the kitchen, the nursery and the girls' school. There was also a medical department, responsible for all the

[1] Webb, pp. 114, 123, 128, 146, 180–200; Mayhew and Binny, pp. 114–15.

sick poor. The manufacturing department, the accountant's department, the clerk of the works' department and the boys' school completed the whole cumbrous mechanism.

During the first three decades of the nineteenth century some of the most extreme severities of the poor law were mitigated by a series of piece-meal reforms. The larger London parishes built infirmaries for the sick poor, at which a physician or an apothecary provided treatment and medicine; the apprenticing of children to chimney-sweeps was forbidden, and an Act of 1816 which forbade the apprenticeship of London children to masters farther than forty miles from the capital put an end to the hitherto common practice of carting off unwanted boys and girls to the voracious mills of Yorkshire and Lancashire. Even the terrible lot of the pauper lunatics, hitherto incarcerated in the workhouse or boarded out, often in the utmost squalor and degradation, at private madhouses, was at least slightly softened by Acts of 1808, 1815 and 1828. The Justices of the Peace could now build county lunatic asylums, and Middlesex acquired its first establishment of this kind in 1831, at Hanwell.

But the main problem of these years was the enormous increase in the number of able-bodied men and women wholly or partly dependent on poor relief for their very existence. At their famous meeting at Speen-hamland in 1795 the Berkshire magistrates had decided to grant outdoor relief from the poor rates as a supplement to the now totally inadequate wages of the labouring classes. This practice had quickly spread to other rural areas of southern England and to London. A temporary expedient became an accepted practice, and between 1802 and 1817 national expenditure on poor relief had doubled. In London the problem was aggravated by the presence of thousands of vagrants, most of whom came to the capital in search of work. They had no legal settlement there, and when they failed to find employment they were driven to begging in the streets. There they were often taken before a magistrate by the parish beadles, and after a few days' imprisonment were returned to their place of settlement. In Middlesex this passing was done on such a large scale that the conveyance of vagrants was farmed to a contractor, who in 1819–20 carted 7,000 paupers to the county boundary.

The extent to which in London wages were supplemented by doles from the poor rates is difficult to assess, but the practice never became so widespread as in many country districts. In 1797 it was already the custom in St Marylebone 'to make small allowances to be continued on application from time to time to such poor industrious persons as may appear thereby likely to maintain themselves and families out of the workhouse', and by 1817 there were 1,147 families, or about 3,500 people, receiving outdoor relief in this one parish. Except in the case of the aged and the sick, these doles were not intended to provide the recipients with full maintenance. 'They only have something in aid and assistance of what they do,' said a London witness at a parliamentary enquiry in 1817. At St George the Martyr, Southwark, the payments were only about 3s. per head per week in 1833, and they rarely exceeded 5s. anywhere. Some parishes no longer insisted on an applicant for relief selling his belongings to qualify for a dole, and in Spitalfields, where there was often extensive unemployment among journeymen and labourers, casual relief was freely given even to applicants who had no settlement there.[1]

For Edwin Chadwick, the architect of the Poor Law Amendment Act of 1834, outdoor relief for the able-bodied was anathema, whether as a supplement for inadequate wages or as a dole for unemployment. He found widespread fraud in the working of the old poor law in London – a man in receipt of 5s. a week for more than seven years had been in full work all the time, for instance – and London was therefore included in the Act of 1834, despite a half-hearted attempt to have the metropolis exempted.[2] A central Poor Law Commission, with offices at Somerset House in the Strand, was to control all the activities of the new local Boards of Guardians, who were to supersede the parish authorities. Generally, each Board was to be in charge of a group or Union of parishes; they were to provide workhouses for the reception of the poor, and outdoor relief for the able-bodied was to be replaced (except in temporary emergency) by indoor relief within the workhouse. There the new principle of 'less eligibility' was to be rigorously applied, to ensure that the lot of the pauper within the workhouse was always 'less eligible' than that of the poorest labourer outside.

We have already seen that the reform of London's police, sanitary administration and municipal institutions were all treated separately from that of the rest of the country. It is therefore remarkable that no separate provision was made in the case of poor relief in London, where many of the problems differed from those elsewhere. In the first place it proved impossible to prohibit outdoor relief even for the able-bodied in London

[1] F. H. W. Sheppard, *Local Government in St Marylebone 1688–1835*, 1958, pp. 218–44; J. H. Stallard, *London Pauperism amongst Jews and Christians*, 1867, p. 200.
[2] Thomas Mackay, *A History of the English Poor Law from 1834 to the Present Time*, 1899, p. 130.

and a number of other large towns where trade depression periodically threw vast numbers of men out of work. In the course of time it also proved impossible in London to refuse relief to able-bodied vagrants. Thousands of labourers, tramps, wayfarers and much of the displaced flotsam thrown up by rapid social and economic change drifted to London in search of work, food, shelter, and in some cases no doubt, of whatever they could could get by whatever means. There were great differences between one part of London and another in both the type and level of relief granted and in the extent of the financial burden on the ratepayers, and for more than thirty years the Poor Law Commission (or Board after 1848) was unable to exert full control over a number of large metropolitan parishes. The early years of the new poor law in London can, in fact, be viewed as the slow, inexorable recognition of the differentness of London, and the need for different policies there.

After the passing of the Act in 1834 the new poor law Unions of parishes were formed without much difficulty in London, despite a short-lived clamour from some of the vestries, and by 1838 thirteen had been set up, each with its own elected Board of Guardians. Elsewhere thirteen parishes, like Lambeth or Shoreditch, were deemed to be large enough to have their own Board of Guardians, and here the transfer of power from the old parish authorities to the new Boards excited some opposition. But the real difficulty came with those parishes which had hitherto managed the poor under their own local Acts. There were originally eight such places (five single parishes and three pairs); here the parish directorate remained in power, ignoring the new Poor Law Commissioners' regulations so far as possible, recalcitrant and unco-operative pockets of traditional local independence which were not finally extinguished until 1867.[1]

Doles in aid of wages were at once abolished everywhere in London, the change-over being helped by the abundance of provisions in 1835–6. But owing to the magnitude of the destitution which prevailed there in times of trade depression, outdoor relief to the able-bodied in London could not be totally prohibited. The Poor Law Commissioners therefore urged the local Guardians to establish labour yards in their workhouses, where applicants could be compelled to do a few hours' work (usually stone-breaking, wood-chopping or oakum-picking) before receiving a meal and a few halfpence in money. In 1845 the Commissioners made their first attempt to treat the whole of London as one unit, in this case for the relief of vagrancy, their intention being to build half-a-dozen special

[1] *Annual Reports of the Poor Law Commissioners*, 1835–8; Mackay, p. 492.

42 Workmen's Train arriving at the London, Chatham and Dover Railway Station
at Victoria, 1865

43 Metropolitan Railway Workmen's Train, *c.* 1872

44 Crank labour at Surrey House of Correction, Wandsworth

45 The Prison hulks off Woolwich

46 Picking oakum under the silent system at Coldbath Fields Prison

47 Tread-wheel and exercise yard, Coldbath Fields Prison

48 Holborn Viaduct, 1869

49 Building the Abbey Mills Main Drainage Pumping Station, West Ham, *c.* 1867

asylums for vagrants in the suburbs, near the principal roads entering London. This sensible scheme was to be paid for by contributions from all the metropolitan Boards of Guardians and the surviving separate parishes. It therefore met with strong opposition, particularly from the semi-independent parishes, and was abandoned. In 1850 there was still wide variation between one part of London and another in the treatment of both the settled poor and of vagrants.[1]

Within the London workhouses still lived the children and those of the aged and the sick who had no one to look after them or whose condition was too bad to enable them to live outside on a weekly allowance of a few pence. As an alternative to living in the workhouse some London pauper children had prior to 1834 been boarded out at contractors' farm schools in the suburbs. Two of these establishments have already been mentioned in previous chapters – those at Norwood, where Dr James Kay first introduced the pupil-teacher system, and at Tooting, where 180 children died of cholera in 1848-9. As with vagrancy so with the education of the workhouse children the Poor Law Commissioners had urged combined action by all the metropolitan poor law authorities. They wished to have special poor law schools (usually referred to as district schools) catering for all the children within large groups of Unions. But the Guardians had proved reluctant to pay for the heavy costs, and it was not until after Kay's success at Norwood and the disaster at Tooting that any progress was made. The contractors' schools came to a sudden end, and the London poor law authorities formed three school districts (later increased to five), each with its own school for all their pauper children. These gaunt, gigantic establishments were later stigmatized as 'Barrack Schools', no doubt for excellent reasons, but their foundation did nevertheless mark an important advance in the treatment of the unfortunate children concerned – an advance not yet matched by any corresponding improvement of the lot of the sick and the old within the workhouses.[2]

In the 1860s this matter, and indeed the whole question of poverty in London, became an object of widespread public attention. The *Lancet* ran a series of articles on the extremely defective care of the sick in the London workhouses, and parliamentary enquiries and debates revealed both inhumanity and neglect. According to the official figures the rate of metropolitan pauperism was actually falling, but there was a general

[1] *Poor Law Commissioners' Report*, 1836; Mackay, pp. 306, 373-4; S. and B. Webb, *English Poor Law History, Part II, The Last Hundred Years*, 1929, pp. 365-7.

[2] Webb, pp. 255, 263-4.

C C

belief at the time that it was rapidly rising. The absolute numbers of paupers in receipt of relief were certainly rising, from 93,495 on a one-day count in 1861 to 142,371 in 1871. Whatever the truth may have been, there were enormous variations in the incidence of the poor rates, ranging from over four shillings in the pound in parts of the East End down to fourteen pence in the pound in Kensington and Hampstead, and eight-pence in the City. Yet despite the high rates in East London the vast extent of destitution there meant that the average outdoor relief paid there was only eightpence or ninepence per head per week, much less than half the amount paid in many less poverty-stricken districts. A large part of the total cost of poor relief in London was in fact being paid for by the poor themselves. When no less than 27 per cent of the inhabitants of St George's in the East received relief on a single day, and the relief amounted to less than one penny per day for each man, woman and child, the case for a less inequitable distribution of the burden became irresistible.[1]

The first successful step in this direction came in 1864, when the Metro-politan Houseless Poor Act compelled the London Boards of Guardians to provide Casual Wards for destitute wayfarers, wanderers and foundlings. Thus ended in London the attempt to refuse lodging to able-bodied men, but more important in the long run, perhaps, was the fact that the cost of the relief given in these Casual Wards was made a common charge upon the whole of London. This precedent was followed shortly afterwards in the Metropolitan Poor Act of 1867, which provided for the creation of district asylums or hospitals for the sick poor, to be managed by a Metropolitan Asylums Board. The cost of these hospitals was to be met from the Metro-politan Common Poor Fund, also established by this Act, to which all the London poor law authorities were compelled to contribute in pro-portion to their rateable value. The sick poor were thus at last removed from the prison-like conditions of the general mixed workhouses to the 'magnificent hospital system' – the words of Sidney and Beatrice Webb – which was quickly developed by the Metropolitan Asylums Board.[2]

In describing these slow steps towards the partial alleviation of some, at any rate, of the worst severities of the poor law, it is easy to convey (unintentionally) an impression of the inevitable progress of public bene-ficence, and to overlook what life in the workhouse actually meant to its inhabitants, or how life was ever sustained at all by an unemployed man

---

[1] Stallard, pp. 187–8, 267; Webb, pp. 316–19; Charles Loch Mowat, *The Charity Organization Society 1869–1913. Its Ideas and Work*, 1961, p. 5.

[2] Webb, pp. 319–21, 406–7.

or woman with only one penny a day, many of whom undoubtedly died of starvation.[1] In order to correct this impression we may perhaps in conclusion turn to the words of James Greenwood, whose enquiries into poverty in London in the 1860s prompted him to disguise himself as an unemployed artisan and apply to the workhouse for relief. Even Mayhew had never done this, and afterwards Greenwood was often asked what had been his principal thought during so unusual an experiment. 'Nothing can be more simple or honest than my answer to that question,' he wrote.

This was it – *What if it were true*? What if, instead of your every sense revolting from the unaccustomed dreadfulness you have brought it into contact with, it were your lot to grow used to, and endure it all, until merciful death delivered you? What if these squalid, unsightly rags, the story of your being some poor devil of an engraver, who really could not help being desperately hard-up and shabby, were all *real*? And why not? Since in all vast commercial communities there must always exist a proportion of beggars and paupers, what have I done that I should be exempt? Am I – are all of us here so comfortably circumstanced because we deserve nothing less? What man dare rise and say so?[2]

The solid and seemingly unassailable comfortableness of mid-Victorian middle-class living was in some measure built upon the filth, insecurity, hunger and disease which formed an endemic feature of life for many of the urban poor, both in London and elsewhere. Too much, we may feel, of the profits of commerce and industry was distributed in the form of dividends or re-invested to produce further economic growth, and not enough was used to pay the higher wages which would have enabled the labouring populace to buy better housing, food and health. The whole process provides, indeed, at least in retrospect, a striking exemplification of the well-known observation that 'to him that hath shall be given, and from him that hath not shall be taken away'; and its social effects, even after the lapse of a century and more than sixty years of death duties, are still not quite exhausted, for many people are still bolstered by incomes derived from capital of Victorian origin.

How well-to-do, kindly and still mostly Christian Victorians reconciled the contrast between their own mode of living and that of the poor and the

[1] Stallard, pp. 257-9.   [2] Greenwood, pp. 432-3.

destitute provides one of the greatest problems of comprehension for the modern student of the nineteenth century. Much of the social evil of the times was still widely attributed to the personal inadequacy of the victims rather than to the force of circumstances outside their control, and it therefore followed that the remedy was thought of in personal terms rather than in the general reform of society by state action. A helping hand to the weak to enable them to stand on their own was what was needed, and all would then be well. In the 1850s and 1860s there was still little realization of the full magnitude of the social problems engendered by the nineteenth-century urban explosion; and private charity, prompted also by religious faith, human compassion and other motives, could therefore still be regarded as the principal means for their remedy.

The exuberant confidence of this belief is strikingly illustrated by the immense variety and resources of the charities of London. Many of these charities were of great antiquity; the City Livery Companies, soon to be investigated by a Royal Commission, with extensive lands as well as a total income from investments of some £750,000 and the City parochial charities are cases in point. But many more of them were of more recent origin, and those established during the first sixty years of the nineteenth century reflect the immense range of philanthropic concern for suffering of all kinds. This is clearly shown in the surveys made by Sampson Low in the 1850s and 1860s of the charitable resources of London, although his system of classification is somewhat confusing. In addition to the hospitals and dispensaries, which we have already discussed in a previous chapter, Low lists 16 societies for the relief of prisoners (including refuge and reformatory institutions), and 22 penitentiary homes for women, making for this field of activity a total of 38 agencies, of which 34 had been founded since 1800. Twenty-five of the 29 institutions for the relief of street destitution and all of the 21 homes for needlewomen and servants were of nineteenth-century origin, as were 10 of the 16 charities for the blind, deaf and dumb, 10 of the 14 orphanages, 25 of the 31 educational bodies, and 51 out of 56 of the Bible and home missionary societies. According to Low's calculations there were some 640 charitable agencies of all kinds in London in 1861, of which nearly a quarter had been founded during the previous decade alone, and in the eight years 1853–61 their combined annual income had also risen by about a quarter, from some £1,800,000 to £2,440,000. These figures include a few societies of national and not merely metropolitan scope, but on the other hand they exclude donations by private almsgiving. Whatever their limitations may be, Low's surveys demonstrate beyond question the enormous scale and scope of charitable activity in mid-nineteenth-century London.[1]

But towards the end of the period covered by this book the value of much of this immense effort was being questioned for the first time. We have already seen that in the 1860s it was widely believed that the rate of pauperism in London was increasing, and that because of the continuing growth of the overall metropolitan population the total number of paupers in receipt of relief was undoubtedly rising. From this depressing situation there now arose the conviction that, in the words of Beatrice Webb, 'the mass-misery of great cities arose mainly, if not entirely, from spasmodic, indiscriminate, and unconditional doles, whether in the form of alms or in that of Poor Law relief'.[2] To give was no longer enough; the spheres of public relief and private charity must be accurately defined to prevent wasteful overlapping; outdoor relief must be abolished, and private benevolence must be concentrated upon those destitute persons capable, by means of such help, of establishing themselves in self-supporting independence. Thus only the idle and the refractory would be subjected to the rigours of the workhouse, while detailed individual direction of private charity would put an end to the demoralizing effects of indiscriminate almsgiving.[3]

These ideas were advocated by the Charity Organization Society, whose foundation in London in 1869 marks the start of a new emphasis in the fields of both the poor law and of philanthropy. For some thirty or more years the C.O.S. enjoyed a considerable influence, but neither the more stringent administration of outdoor relief which was practised in many Unions during this period, nor the Society's own attempts to co-ordinate the charitable activities of London and other places proved successful. What did prove of enduring value in the Society's work was the great extension of accurate knowledge about the needs of the poor and the causes of poverty which its scientifically-organized casework gradually accumulated. The Society's district visitors were, in fact, the forerunners of the modern professional social workers. As their experience grew, so too came the gradual realization that private agencies would never be capable of remedying the huge, deep-seated social problems of London

[1] Sampson Low, *The Charities of London*, 1850, 1854, 1867 edns; see also David Owen, *English Philanthropy 1660–1960*, 1965, pp. 163–81.

[2] Beatrice Webb, *My Apprenticeship*, 1926, quoted in Owen, p. 217.

[3] S. and B. Webb, *English Poor Law History, Part II*, pp. 455–61.

and other large towns, and that the real need was for action on a scale which only the State could command.

Almost another century has now elapsed since this new conception of the rôle of the State began to make itself widely felt. Over the years the scale and scope and cost of state action in the field of social problems have inexorably advanced, until they have now reached dimensions which would have been inconceivable to our Victorian ancestors. Yet despite all the gigantic efforts made towards social amelioration, many of the principal problems of the nineteenth century appear to be as far from solution as ever, at least in any precise arithmetical sense. The situation described in the Milner Holland report of 1965 on housing in Greater London has much in common with the situation of the 1860s, and even in 1970 it has been estimated that throughout the whole nation five million people still live below the official poverty line.[1] Standards have of course risen greatly in both these fields, for in London rookeries, at least, no longer exist, and deaths from starvation are nowadays rare. Advances of this kind certainly appear on the credit side of the balance sheet, but plenty still remains on the debit side, and there are new entries there of twentieth-century origin, notably that of race relations, which are as baffling to us as any which confronted our Victorian progenitors.

In contemplating the failings and shortcomings of Victorian social attitudes and policies, we should, therefore, remember those of our own age as well, for theirs are perhaps no more striking to us than ours may appear to our descendants after the lapse of another hundred years. We may, indeed, do well to study our forebears with charity, and if possible with understanding. They were, after all, our own grandfathers and grandmothers, from whom we each derive in large measure our own individual temperaments, attitudes and even physical appearance, and to whom we are linked at only one remove by the closest ties of human kinship, so near are they to us even at this distance of time; so near and yet so irretrievably far.

[1] *The Times*, 23 January 1970, citing A. B. Atkinson, *Poverty in Britain and the Reform of Social Security*, 1970.

Appendix

The Distribution of Occupations and Social Classes in London in 1851

THE TWO tables printed below are the work of Professor Lynn Lees of Mount Holyoke College, South Hadley, Massachusetts, by whose kindness and generosity, so characteristic of American historians, I have been permitted to publish them here. They were compiled by Professor Lees for her at present unpublished Harvard University thesis 'Social Change and Social Stability among the London Irish, 1830–1870', which was presented in 1969. They are based on samples taken from the manuscript schedules for the census of 1851, which were then analysed by computer. In her thesis, which she hopes will be published shortly in modified form, Professor Lees fully explains the coding and classification schemes which she used, and states that the basis for her 'division of London occupations into industrial groups was the official census tabulation for 1851, combined with Charles Booth's occupational categories which he compiled from several British censuses'. (See Charles Booth, 'Occupations of the People of the United Kingdom, 1801–1881', *Journal of the Statistical Society*, vol. XLIX, 1886, pp. 414–15.)

DISTRIBUTION OF OCCUPATIONS: LONDON, 1851

| | Percentage of total male or female population | |
	Males	Females
Agriculture	2·06	0·12
Mining	0·01	0·00
Construction	6·27	0·01
Metal	3·13	0·06
Machinery	2·39	0·02
Ships	0·45	0·00
Gas	0·54	0·03
Glass	0·57	0·05
Textiles	2·07	1·34
Dress	5·89	8·61
Leather	1·19	0·09
Wood	3·17	0·26
Paper	1·33	0·40
Printing	1·87	0·24
Food	6·31	1·21
Transport		
(1) Dock, canal	2·17	0·01
(2) Railroad, road	1·39	0·00
(3) Goods	4·50	0·00
General labour	4·82	0·95
Commerce and finance	4·19	0·52
Service	0·65	0·97
Domestic service	2·96	16·05
Administration	1·21	0·06
Military	1·65	0·00
Police	0·57	0·00
Professions	2·11	0·00
Art, education, etc.	0·87	1·02
Other, unknown	1·22	1·42
Outside the labour market	34·27	66·40

Source: Census of England, 1851.

DISTRIBUTION OF SOCIAL CLASSES:
TOTAL POPULATION OF LONDON, 1851

Class	Percentage of total population
I. Professionals Rentiers Owners, managers	2·17
II. Sub-professionals Lower-level managers Annuitants	3·52
III. Employees, clerks	0·96
IV. Shopkeepers	4·80
V. Skilled labour	19·87
VI. Semi-skilled labour	11·97
VII. Unskilled labour	5·32
VIII. Agricultural self-employed tenants, labourers	0·26
IX. Outside the labour market	49·32
X. Others, unknown	1·77

Source: Census of England, 1851.

Bibliography

P.P. denotes Parliamentary Papers.

General Works
Annual Register
Besant, Sir Walter, *London in the Nineteenth Century*, 1909.
Brayley, E. W., Nightingale, Joseph, and Brewer, J. Norris, *London and Middlesex*, 1810–16, 4 vols.
George, M. Dorothy, *London Life in the XVIII Century*, 1925.
Knight, Charles (ed.), *London*, 1841, 6 vols.
Loftie, W. J., *A History of London*, 1883, 2 vols.
Robbins, Michael, *Middlesex*, 1953.
Sharpe, Reginald R., *London and the Kingdom*, 1894–5, 3 vols.
Smith, John Thomas, *An Antiquarian Ramble in the Streets of London*, 1846, 2 vols.
Thornbury, Walter, *Old and New London*, 1873, 6 vols.
Timbs, John, *Curiosities of London*, 1855.
Weale, John (ed.), *London Exhibited in 1851*.
Welch, Charles, *A Modern History of the City of London*, 1896.
Wheatley, Henry B., *London Past and Present*, 1891, 3 vols.

CHAPTER I

A. The People
Dyos, H. J., *Victorian Suburb. A Study of the Growth of Camberwell*, 1961.
Dyos, H. J., 'Railways and Housing in Victorian London', *Journal of Transport History*, vol. II, 1955.
Dyos, H. J., 'The Slums of Victorian London', *Victorian Studies*, vol. XI, 1967.
Friedlander, D. and Roshier, R. J., 'A Study of Internal Migration in England and Wales, Part I', *Population Studies*, vol. 19, 1965–6.
Glass, D. V., 'Some Indicators between Urban and Rural Mortality in England and Wales and Scotland', *Population Studies*, vol. 17, 1963–4.
Guy, W. A., 'Two Hundred and Fifty Years of Small Pox in London', *Journal of the Statistical Society*, vol. XLV, 1882.
Hibbert, Christopher, *The Making of Charles Dickens*, 1967.
Hobsbawm, E. J., 'The Nineteeth Century London Labour Market', in *London, Aspects of Change*, ed. Ruth Glass, 1964.

Jackson, John A., 'The Irish', in *London, Aspects of Change*, ed. Ruth Glass, 1964.

Jackson, John A., 'The Irish in East London', *East London Papers*, vol. 6, 1963.

Kellett, John R., *The Impact of Railways on Victorian Cities*, 1969.

Lees, Professor Lynn Hollen, 'Social Change and Social Stability among the London Irish, 1830–1870', unpublished Harvard University thesis, 1969.

Lovett, William, *The Life and Struggles of William Lovett in his Pursuit of Bread, Knowledge and Freedom*, 1876.

Mayhew, *London Labour and the London Poor*, 1861 edn.

McKeown, Thomas, and Record, R. G., 'Reasons for the Decline of Mortality in England and Wales during the Nineteenth Century', *Population Studies*, vol. 16, 1962–3.

P.P., 1865, vol. xiii, *Supplement to the Twenty-fifth Annual Report of the Registrar General*.

P.P., 1875, vol. xviii, part II, *Supplement to the Thirty-fifth Annual Report of the Registrar General*.

Price-Williams, R., 'On the Increase of Population in England and Wales', *Journal of the Statistical Society of London*, vol. XLIII, 1880.

Price-Williams, R., 'The Population of London, 1801–81', *Journal of the Statistical Society of London*, vol. XLVIII, 1885.

Redford, Arthur, *Labour Migration in England 1800–1850*, 1964 edn.

Shannon, H. A., 'Migration and the Growth of London, 1841–1891', *Economic History Review, First Series*, vol. 5, 1935.

Talbot Griffith, G., *Population Problems in the Age of Malthus*, 1967 edn.

Wise, Dorothy, and Cox-Johnson, Ann, (ed.), *Diary of William Tayler, Footman, 1837*, St Marylebone Society Publications, 1962.

Weber, A. F., *The Growth of Cities in the Nineteenth Century*, 1899.

B. Government

Briggs, Asa (ed.), *Chartist Studies*, 1959.

Brooke, James Williamson, *The Democrats of Marylebone*, 1839.

Browne, Douglas G., *The Rise of Scotland Yard*, 1956.

Butler, J. R. M., *The Passing of the Great Reform Bill*, 1914.

Cole, G. D. H., *Chartist Portraits*, 1941.

Critchley, T. A., *A History of Police in England and Wales, 900–1966*, 1967.

Gash, Norman, *Mr Secretary Peel*, 1961.

Hovell, Mark, *The Chartist Movement*, 1943 edn.

Maccoby, S., *The English Radical Tradition 1763–1914*, 1952.

Mather, F. C., *Public Order in the Age of the Chartists*, 1959.

Oliver, W. H., 'The Consolidated Trades Union of 1834', *Economic History Review, Second Series*, vol. 17, 1964–5.

Patterson, M. W., *Sir Francis Burdett and his Times*, 2 vols., 1931.

Radzinowicz, Leon, *A History of English Criminal Law and its Administration from 1750*, vol. II, 1956.

Reddaway, T. F., 'London in the Nineteenth Century: the Origins of the Metropolitan Police', *The Nineteenth Century and After*, vol. 147, 1950.

Reith, Charles, *A New Study of Police History*, 1956.
Sheppard, F. H. W., *Local Government in St Marylebone 1688–1835*, *A Study of the Vestry and the Turnpike Trusts*, 1958.
Wallas, Graham, *The Life of Francis Place, 1771–1854*, 1925 edn.
Webb, S. and B., *English Local Government: The Parish and the County, 1906; The Manor and the Borough*, 1908; *Statutory Authorities for Special Purposes*, 1922.
Webb, S. and B., *The History of Trade Unionism*, 1920 edn.

CHAPTER 2

The London Money Market
Ashton, J. S. and Sayers, R. S. (ed.), *Papers in English Monetary History*, 1953.
Bagehot, Walter, *Lombard Street. A Description of the Money Market*, introd. by Hartley Withers, 1931 edn.
Bolitho, Hector and Peel, Derek, *The Drummonds of Charing Cross*, 1967.
Clapham, J. H., *An Economic History of Modern Britain*, vol. I, *The Early Railway Age, 1820–1850*, 1926; vol. II, *Free Trade and Steel, 1850–1886*, 1932.
Clapham, J. H., *The Bank of England: A History 1694–1914*, 1944.
Duguid, Charles, *The Story of the Stock Exchange. Its History and Position*, 1901.
Fulford, Roger, *Glyn's 1753–1953. Six Generations in Lombard Street*, 1953.
Gregory, T. E., *The Westminster Bank Through A Century*, 1936, 2 vols.
Gregory, T. E. (ed.), *Select Statutes, Documents and Reports relating to British Banking, 1832–1928*, 1929, 2 vols.
Hoare's Bank. A Record 1672–1955, 1955.
J. R. T. Hughes, *Fluctuations in Trade, Industry and Finance. A Study of British Economic Development 1850–1860*, 1960.
King, W. T. C., *History of the London Discount Market*, 1936.
Jenks, Leland Hamilton, *The Migration of British Capital to 1875*, 1938 edn.
Martin, John Biddulph, *'The Grasshopper' in Lombard Street*, 1892.
Morgan, E. Victor and Thomas, W. A., *The Stock Exchange. Its History and Functions*, 1962.
Pressnell, L. S., *Country Banking in the Industrial Revolution*, 1956.
Price, F. G. Hilton, *A Handbook of London Bankers*, 1890–1.
Robinson, Ralph M., *Coutts'. The History of a Banking House*, 1929.
Roth, Cecil, *The Magnificent Rothschilds*, 1939.
Sayers, R. S., *Central Banking after Bagehot*, 1957.
Sayers, R. S., *Lloyds Bank in the History of English Banking*, 1957.
Scammell, W. M., *The London Discount Market*, 1968.
Shannon, H. A., 'The Coming of General Limited Liability', in *Essays in Economic History*, vol. I, ed. E. M. Carus-Wilson, 1954.
Shannon, H. A., 'The Limited Companies of 1866–1883', in *Essays in Economic History*, vol. I, ed. E. M. Carus-Wilson, 1954.
Supple, Barry, *The Royal Exchange Assurance. A History of British Insurance 1720–1970*, 1970.
Sykes, Joseph, *The Amalgamation Movement in English Banking, 1825–1924*, 1926.

Twining, Stephen H., *The House of Twining 1706–1956*, 1956.
Xenos, Stefanos, *Depredations; or, Overend Gurney, and Co., and the Greek and Oriental Steam Navigation Company*, 1869.

CHAPTER 3

The Growth of London before the Railways

Ashworth, W., 'Types of Social and Economic Development in Suburban Essex', in *London, Aspects of Change*, ed. Ruth Glass, 1964.
Barker, Ashley, 'Nineteenth Century Estate Development in South Kensington', *Annual Report of the Kensington Society*, 1967.
Barker, Ashley, 'The Nineteenth Century Development of Notting Hill', in unpublished typescript proceedings of the Kensington Society Conference on Town Planning and Housing in North Kensington, 9 October 1965.
Barker, T. C., and Robbins, Michael, *A History of London Transport*, vol. I, 1963.
Bellman, Sir Harold, *Bricks and Mortar. A Study of the Building Society Movement and the Story of the Abbey National Society 1849–1949*, 1949.
Bird, James, *The Geography of the Port of London*, 1957.
Bowley, Marian, *Innovations in Building Materials*, 1960.
Broodbank, Sir Joseph G., *History of the Port of London*, 2 vols., 1921.
Bryant, Arthur, *Liquid History*, 1960.
Cairncross, A. K., and Weber, B., 'Fluctuations in Building in Great Britain, 1785–1849', *Economic History Review, Second Series*, vol. 9, 1956.
Carter, Paul, 'St Katharine Docks', *The London Archaeologist*, vol. I, 1969.
Clapham, J. H., *An Economic History of Modern Britain*, vol. I, *The Early Railway Age, 1820–50*, 1926; vol. II, *Free Trade and Steel, 1850–1886*, 1932.
Cleary, E. J., *The Building Society Movement*, 1965.
Colvin, H. M., *A Biographical Dictionary of English Architects 1660–1840*, 1954.
Cooney, E. W., 'Long Waves in Building in the British Economy of the Nineteenth Century', *Economic History Review, Second Series*, vol. 13, 1960–1.
Cooney, E. W., 'The Origins of the Victorian Master Builders', *Economic History Review, Second Series*, vol. 8, 1955–6.
Coppock, J. T., and Prince, Hugh C. (ed.), *Greater London*, 1964.
Dyos, H. J., 'The Growth of a Pre-Victorian Suburb: South London, 1580–1836', *The Town Planning Review*, vol. xxv, 1954.
Dyos, H. J., 'The Speculative Builders and Developers of Victorian London', *Victorian Studies*, vol. xi, Supplement, 1968.
Dyos, H. J., *Victorian Suburb. A Study of the Growth of Camberwell*, 1961.
Hobhouse, Hermione, 'The Building of Belgravia', *Country Life*, 8 and 22 May 1969.
Imray, Jean M., 'The Mercers' Company and East London, 1750–1850', *East London Papers*, vol. 9, 1966.
Matthews, R. C. O., *A Study in Trade-Cycle History. Economic Fluctuations in Great Britain 1833–1842*, 1954.
Olsen, Donald J., *Town Planning in London, the eighteenth and nineteenth centuries*, Yale University Press, 1964.

P.P., 1828, vol. iv, *Report and Minutes of Evidence of Select Committee on the Office of Works and Public Buildings.*

P.P., 1833, vol. vi, *Report and Minutes of Evidence from the Select Committee on Manufactures, Commerce and Shipping.*

Parry Lewis, J., *Building Cycles and Britain's Growth*, 1965.

Port, M. H., 'The Office of Works and Building Contracts in Early Nineteenth Century England', *Economic History Review, Second Series*, vol 20, 1967.

Postgate, R. W., *The Builders' History*, 1923.

Price-Williams, R., 'On the Increase of Population in England and Wales', *Journal of the Statistical Society*, vol. XLIII, 1880.

Price-Williams, R., 'The Population of London, 1801–81', *Journal of the Statistical Society*, vol. XLVIII, 1885.

Price, Seymour J., *Building Societies, Their Origin and History*, 1958.

Price, Seymour J., *From Queen to Queen. The Centenary Story of the Temperance Permanent Building Society 1854–1954*, 1954.

Pugh, R. B., *The Crown Estate*, 1960.

Reddaway, T. F., 'London in the Nineteenth Century: the freeing of the bridges, 1800–1880', *The Twentieth Century*, vol. 151

Reeder, D. A., 'A Theatre of Suburbs: Some Patterns of Development in West London, 1801–1911', in *The Study of Urban History*, ed. H. J. Dyos, 1968.

Saunders, Ann, *Regent's Park. A Study of the Development of the Area from 1086 to the Present Day*, 1969.

Shannon, H. A., 'Bricks – A Trade Index, 1785–1849', *Economica*, 1934. Reprinted in *Essays in Economic History*, ed. E. M. Carus-Wilson, vol. III, 1962.

Shannon, H. A., 'Migration and the Growth of London, 1841', *Economic History Review, First Series*, vol. 5, 1935.

Stern, W. M., 'The first London Dock Boom and the Growth of the West India Docks', *Economica*, vol. XIX, 1952.

Summerson, John, *Georgian London*, Pelican edn, 1962.

Summerson, John, *John Nash, Architect to King George IV*, 1935.

Survey of London, vol. xxvi, 1956, *St Mary Lambeth, Southern Area.*
   vol. xxix, 1960, *St James, Westminster, South of Piccadilly.*
   vol. xxxii, 1963, *St James, Westminster, North of Piccadilly.*

Thompson, F. M. L., *Chartered Surveyors. The Growth of a Profession*, 1968.

CHAPTER 4

The Transport Revolution

Bagwell, Philip S., 'The Railway Interest: its Organisation and Influence 1839–1914', *Journal of Transport History*, vol. VII, 1965.

Bagwell, Philip S., 'The Rivalry and Working Union of the South Eastern and London, Chatham and Dover Railways', *Journal of Transport History*, vol. II, 1955.

Baker, C., *The Metropolitan Railway*, 1951.

Barker, T. C. and Robbins, Michael, *A History of London Transport*, vol. I, *The Nineteenth Century*, 1963.

Bellman, Sir Harold, *Bricks and Mortar. A Study of the Building Society Movement and the Story of the Abbey National Society 1849–1949*, 1949.

Clapham, J. H., *An Economic History of Modern Britain*, vol. I, *The Early Railway Age, 1820–1850*, 1926; vol. II, *Free Trade and Steel, 1850–1886*, 1932.

Cleary, E. J., *The Building Society Movement*, 1965.

Coleman, Terry, *The Railway Navvies*, 1965.

Coppock, J. T., and Prince, Hugh C., (ed.), *Greater London*, 1964.

Course, Edwin, *London Railways*, 1962.

Dyos, H. J., 'Railways and Housing in Victorian London', *Journal of Transport History*, vol. II, 1955.

Dyos, H. J., 'Some Social Costs of Railway Building in London', *Journal of Transport History*, vol. III, 1957.

Dyos, H. J., 'Urban Transformation. A Note on the Objects of Street Improvement in Regency and Early Victorian London', *International Review of Social History*, vol. II, 1957.

Dyos, H. J., *Victorian Suburb. A Study of the Growth of Camberwell*, 1966 ed.

Dyos, H. J., 'Workmen's Fares in South London, 1860–1914', *Journal of Transport History*, vol. i, 1953.

Dyos, H. J., and Aldcroft, D. H., *British transport: an economic survey from the seventeenth century to the twentieth*, 1969.

Helps, Arthur, *Life and Labours of Mr Brassey*, 1872.

Jackson, Alan A., *London's Termini*, 1969.

Kellett, John R., *The Impact of Railways on Victorian Cities*, 1969.

Kidner, R. W., *The South Eastern and Chatham Railway*, 1963.

Lee, Charles E., *Passenger Class Distinctions*, 1946.

Lee, Charles E., *The Metropolitan District Railway*, 1956.

MacDermot, E. T., *History of the Great Western Railway*, 1964 edn.

P.P., 1846, vol. xvii, *Report of Royal Commission on projects for establishing Railway Termini within the Metropolis*.

P.P., 1854–5, vol. x, *Report of Select Committee on Metropolitan Communications*.

P.P., 1863, vol. viii, *Third Report of Select Committee of House of Lords on Metropolitan Railway Communications*.

Pollins, Harold, 'Railway Contractors and the Finance of Railway Development in Britain', *Journal of Transport History*, vol. III, 1957.

Price, Seymour J., *From Queen to Queen. The Centenary Story of the Temperance Permanent Building Society, 1854–1954*, 1954.

Reeder, D. A., 'A Theatre of Suburbs: Some Patterns of Development in West London, 1801–1911', in *The Study of Urban History*, ed. H. J. Dyos, 1968.

Robbins, Michael, *The North London Railway*, 1946.

Robbins, Michael, *The Railway Age*, 1962.

Savage, Christopher I., *An Economic History of Transport*, 1959.

Simmons, Jack, 'Railway History in English Local Records', *Journal of Transport History*, vol. I, 1954.

Simmons, Jack, *The Railways of Britain. An Historical Introduction*, 1961.

Summerson, John, 'The London Suburban Villa', *The Architectural Review*, vol. 104, 1948.

Survey of London, vol. xxvi, 1956, *Southern Lambeth*.

White, H. P., *A Regional History of the Railways of Great Britain*, vol. II, *Southern England*, 1961; vol. III, *Greater London*, 1963.

Williams, R. A., *The London and South Western Railway*, vol. I, *The Formative Years*, 1968.

CHAPTER 5

Industry and Commerce

Alford, B. W. E., 'Government Expenditure and the Growth of the Printing Industry in the Nineteenth Century', *Economic History Review, Second Series*, vol. 17, 1964–5.

Ashworth, W., 'Types of Social and Economic Development in Suburban Essex', in *London, Aspects of Change*, ed. Ruth Glass, 1964.

Barnard, R. W., *A Century of Service. The Story of the Prudential 1848–1948*, 1948.

Chandler, Dean, and Lacey, A. Douglas, *The Rise of the Gas Industry in Britain*, 1949.

Clapham, J. H., *An Economic History of Modern Britain*, vol. I, *The Early Railway Age, 1820–1850*, 1926; vol. II, *Free Trade and Steel, 1850–1886*, 1932.

Clapham, J. H., 'The Spitalfields Acts, 1773–1824', *The Economic Journal*, vol. xxvi, 1916.

Clowes, W. B., *Family Business 1803–1953*, n.d.

Crory, W. Glenny, *East London Industries*, 1876.

Dickson, P. G. M., *The Sun Insurance Office 1710–1960*, 1960.

Dowling, S. W., *The Exchanges of London*, 1929.

Everard, Stirling, *The History of the Gas Light and Coke Company, 1812–1949*, 1949.

Fletcher, Joseph, 'Statistical Account of the Markets of London', in *Journal of the Statistical Society of London*, vol. x, 1847.

Fraser-Stephen, Elspet, *Two Centuries in the London Coal Trade. The Story of Charringtons*, 1952.

George, M. Dorothy, *London Life in the XVIII Century*, 1925.

Gibb, D. E. W., *Lloyd's of London. A Study in Individualism*, 1957.

Gibson, A. V. B., 'Huguenot Weavers' Houses in Spitalfields', in *East London Papers*, vol. 1, 1958.

Glover, John, 'On the Decline of Shipbuilding on the Thames', *Journal of the Statistical Society of London*, vol. XXXII, 1869.

Gosden, P. H. J. H., *The Friendly Societies in England, 1815–1875*, 1961.

Haber, L. F., *The Chemical Industry during the Nineteenth Century*, 1958.

Hall, P. G., 'The East London Footwear Industry. An Industrial Quarter in Decline', *East London Papers*, vol. 5, 1962.

Hall, P. G., *The Industries of London since 1861*, 1962.

Handover, P. M., *Printing in London from 1476 to Modern Times*, 1960.

D D

Howe, Ellic, *The London Compositor*, 1947.

Martin, J. E., *Greater London. An Industrial Geography*, 1966.

Mathias, Peter, *The Brewing Industry in England 1700–1830*, 1959.

Morrah, Dermot, *A History of Industrial Life Assurance*, 1955.

Musson, A. E., 'James Nasmyth and the Early Growth of Mechanical Engineering', *Economic History Review, Second Series*, vol. 10, 1957–8.

Musson, A. E., 'Newspaper Printing in the Industrial Revolution', *Economic History Review, Second Series*, vol. 10, 1957–8.

Oliver, J. Leonard, 'The East London Furniture Industry', *East London Papers*, vol. 4, 1961.

P.P., 1840, vol. xxiii, *Report from Assistant Hand-Loom Weavers' Commissioners*.

P.P., 1864, vol. xxviii, *Sixth Report of the Medical Officer of the Privy Council, Sanitary Circumstances of Tailors, Dressmakers and Needlewomen in London*.

Passingham, W. J., *London's Markets*, n.d. [*c*. 1934].

Petree, J. Foster, 'Henry Maudslay and the Maudslay Scholarship', *Journal of the Junior Institution of Engineers*, vol. 60, 1950.

Petree, J. Foster, 'Maudslay, Sons and Field as General Engineers', *Transactions of the Newcomen Society*, vol. XV, 1934–5.

Pollard, S., 'The Decline of Shipbuilding on the Thames', *Economic History Review, Second Series*, vol. 3, 1950–1.

Robertson, A. B., 'The Smithfield Cattle Market', *East London Papers*, vol. 4, 1961.

Rose, Millicent, *The East End of London*, 1951.

Rowe, D. J., 'Chartism and the Spitalfields Silk-weavers', *Economic History Review, Second Series*, vol. 20, 1967.

Sabin, A. K., *The Silk Weavers of Spitalfields and Bethnal Green*, 1931.

Scott, J. D., *Siemens Brothers 1858–1958*, 1958.

Smiles, Samuel, *Industrial Biography: Iron Workers and Tool Makers*, 1863.

Smiles, Samuel, *Men of Invention and Industry*, 1884.

Smith, Raymond, *Sea-Coal for London. History of the Coal Factors in the London Market*, 1961.

Spate, O. H. K., 'Geographical Aspects of the Industrial Evolution of London till 1850', *The Geographical Journal*, vol. 92, 1938.

'Trade Unions and London Shipping', *Journal of the Statistical Society of London*, vol. XXXI, 1868.

Victoria County History of Kent, vol. III, 1932.

Victoria County History of Middlesex, vol. II, 1911.

Victoria County History of Surrey, vol. II, 1905.

Whetham, E. H., 'The London Milk Trade, 1860–1900', *Economic History Review, Second Series*, vol. 17, 1964–5.

Wilson, Aubrey, *London's Industrial Heritage*, 1967.

Wilson, Charles, and Reader, William, *Men and Machines. A History of D. Napier and Son, Engineers, Ltd 1808–1958*, 1958.

CHAPTER 6

Church, School and State

Bacon, Ernest W., *Spurgeon, Heir of the Puritans*, 1967.

Barnard, H. C., *A Short History of English Education from 1760 to 1944*, 1947 edn.

Bellot, H. Hale, *University College London 1826–1926*, 1929.

Best, G. F. A., *Temporal Pillars. Queen Anne's Bounty, the Ecclesiastical Commissioners, and the Church of England*, 1964.

Best, G. F. A., 'The Religious Difficulties of National Education in England, 1800–1870', *The Cambridge Historical Journal*, vol. xii, 1956.

Blomfield, Alfred (ed.), *A Memoir of Charles James Blomfield, D.D.*, two vols., 1863.

British Association, *London and the Advancement of Science*, 1931.

Burgess, H. J., *Enterprise in Education. The story of the work of the Established Church in the education of the people prior to 1870*, 1958.

Census of Great Britain, 1851, Religious Worship: Report by Horace Mann, 1854.

Chadwick, Owen, *The Victorian Church*, 2 vols., 1966 and 1970.

Clapham and the Clapham Sect, published for Clapham Antiquarian Society, 1927.

Clark, G. Kitson, *The Making of Victorian England*, 1962.

Clarke, Basil F. L., *Church Builders of the Nineteenth Century. A Study of the Gothic Revival in England*, 1938.

Cowie, Leonard W., 'Exeter Hall', *History Today*, vol. xviii, 1968.

Hearnshaw, F. J. C., *The Centenary History of King's College London 1828–1928*, 1929.

Hennell, Michael, *John Venn and the Clapham Sect*, 1958.

Howse, Ernest Marshall, *Saints in Politics. The Clapham Sect and the Growth of Freedom*, 1952.

Inglis, K. S., *Churches and the Working Classes in Victorian England*, 1963.

Jones, R. Tudur, *Congregationalism in England 1662–1962*, 1962.

Kelly, Thomas, *A History of Adult Education in Great Britain*, 1962.

Kelly, Thomas, *George Birkbeck, Pioneer of Adult Education*, 1957.

The North London Collegiate School 1850–1950. A Hundred Years of Girls' Education. Essays in Honour of the Centenary of the Frances Mary Buss Foundation, 1950.

P.P., 1857–8, vol. ix, *Report of Select Committee of the House of Lords on the Deficiency of Means of Spiritual Instruction and Places of Divine Worship in the Metropolis and in other Populous Districts*.

P.P., 1861, vol. xxi, *Report of the Commissioners on the State of Popular Education in England*, 1861 (the Newcastle Commission), 6 vols. For London, see vols. I and III.

P.P., 1867–8, vol. xxviii, *Commission on the Education given in Schools not comprised within two former Commissions of 22 and 25 Vict.* (the Schools Inquiry or Taunton Commission), 9 vols. For London, see vols. I and IX.

Port, M. H., *Six Hundred New Churches. A Study of the Church Building Commission, 1818–1856, and its Church Building Activities*, 1961.

Reader, W. J., *Professional Men. The Rise of the Professional Classes in Nineteenth-Century England*, 1966.

'Reports on the State of Education in Westminster', *Journal of the Statistical Society of London*, vol. I, 1839.

'Reports on the State of Education in Finsbury and St Marylebone', *Journal of the Statistical Society of London*, vol. VI, 1843.

Reynolds, Michael, *Martyr of Ritualism. Father Mackonochie of St Alban's, Holborn*, 1965.

Sheppard, F. H. W., *Local Government in St Marylebone 1688-1835*, 1958.

Simon, Brian, *Studies in the History of Education 1780-1870*, 1960.

Smith, Frank, *A History of English Elementary Education 1760-1902*, 1931.

Smith, Frank, *The Life and Work of Sir James Kay-Shuttleworth*, 1923.

Smith, Warren Sylvester, *The London Heretics 1870-1914*, 1967.

Tait, A. C., *The Spiritual Wants of the Metropolis and its Suburbs*, 1863.

Tuke, Margaret J., *A History of Bedford College for Women 1849-1937*, 1939.

Victoria County History of London, vol. I, 1909.

Victoria County History of Middlesex, vol. I, 1969.

Welch, P. J., 'Bishop Blomfield and Church Extension in London', *Journal of Ecclesiastical History*, vol. 4, 1953.

Whitley, W. T., *The Baptists of London 1612-1928*, n.d.

Chapter 7

Public Health

Bazalgette, J. W., 'On the Metropolitan System of Drainage and the Interception of the Sewage from the River Thames', *Proceedings of the Institution of Civil Engineers*, vol. xxiv, 1864-5.

Edwards, Percy J., *History of London Street Improvements, 1855-1897*, 1898.

Finer, S. E., *The Life and Times of Sir Edwin Chadwick*, 1952.

Green, A. F., 'The Problem of London's Drainage', *Geography*, vol. xli, 1956.

Hennock, E. P., 'Urban Sanitary Reform a Generation before Chadwick?', *Economic History Review, Second Series*, vol. 10, 1957-8.

Jephson, Henry, *The Sanitary Evolution of London*, 1907.

Keith-Lucas, B., 'Some Influences affecting the development of Sanitary Legislation in England', *Economic History Review, Second Series*, vol. 6, 1953-4.

Lambert, Royston, *Sir John Simon 1816-1904 and English Social Administration*, 1963.

Lewis, R. A., *Edwin Chadwick and the Public Health Movement 1832-1854*, 1952.

London County Council, *The Housing Question in London 1855-1900*, 1900.

Longmate, Norman, *King Cholera. The Biography of a Disease*, 1966.

Low, Sampson, *The Charities of London*, 1867.

Owen, David, *English Philanthropy 1660-1960*, 1965.

P.P., 1837-8, vol. xxviii, *Physical causes of Fever in the Metropolis which might be removed by proper Sanitary Regulations*. Dr N. Arnott and Dr J. P. Kay in *Poor Law Commission, Fourth Annual Report, Appendix A, No 1, Supplement to No. 1*.

P.P., 1837–8, vol. xxviii, *Physical causes of Sickness and Mortality to which the Poor are particularly exposed and the present condition of Bethnal Green and Whitechapel*. Dr Southwood Smith in *Poor Law Commission, Fourth Annual Report, Appendix A, No. 1, Supplement No. 2, No. 3.*

P.P., 1839, vol. xx, *Fever in Metropolitan Unions*, Dr Southwood Smith's Report in *Poor Law Commission, Fifth Annual Report, Appendix C (2).*

P.P., 1842 (House of Lords), vol. xxvi, *Inquiry into the Sanitary Condition of the Labouring Population of Great Britain.*

P.P., 1843, vol. xii, *Report on the Practice of Interment in Towns.*

P.P., 1844, vol. xvii, *Royal Commission on the State of Large Towns and Populous Districts, First Report*, 1845, vol. xviii, *Second Report, Parts I and II.*

P.P., 1847–8, vol. xxxii, *Royal Commission on Means for the Improvement of the Health of the Metropolis, First, Second and Third Reports.*

P.P., 1850, vol. xxi, *Report on a General Scheme of Extramural Sepulture.*

P.P., 1850, vol.xxii, *Report of the General Board of Health on the Supply of Water to the Metropolis.*

P.P., 1850, vol. xxxi, *Royal Commission on Smithfield Market and the Markets in the City of London for the Sale of Meat.*

P.P., 1850, vol. xxi, *Report of the General Board of Health on the Epidemic Cholera of 1848 and 1849.*

P.P., 1854, vol. xxvi, *Royal Commission on the State of the Corporation of the City of London.*

P.P., 1857–8, vol. xi, *Report of Select Committee of the House of Commons to consider Mr Gurney's Report on the State of the River Thames.*

P.P., 1857–8, vol. xlviii, *Mr Gurney's Report to the First Commissioner of Works on the State of the Thames in the Neighbourhood of the Houses of Parliament.*

P.P., 1861, vol. viii, *Third Report of Select Committee of the House of Commons on Metropolis Local Taxation.*

P.P., 1867, vol. xii, *Second Report of Select Committee on Metropolitan Local Government.*

Reddaway, T. F., 'London in the Nineteenth Century: The Fight for a Water Supply', *The Nineteenth Century and After*, vol. 148, 1950.

Robson, William A., *The Government and Misgovernment of London*, 1948 edn.

Simon, John, *Reports relating to the Sanitary Condition of the City of London*, 1854.

Simon, John, *Public Health Reports*, 1887, vol. II.

Smalley, George, *The Life of Sir Sydney H. Waterlow, Bart.*, 1909.

Webb, Sidney and Beatrice, *English Poor Law History, Part II, The Last Hundred Years*, 2 vols., 1929.

Welch, Charles, *Modern History of the City of London*, 1896.

CHAPTER 8

The Radical Politics of London

Armytage, W. H. G., *Heavens Below. Utopian Experiments in England 1560–1960*, 1961.

Beaven, Alfred B., *The Aldermen of the City of London*, 2 vols., 1913.

Briggs, Asa, *The Age of Improvement*, 1959.

Briggs, Asa, *Victorian Cities*, 1963.

Briggs, Asa, *Victorian People*, 1954.

Butler, J. R. M., *The Passing of the Great Reform Bill*, 1964 edn.

Cole, G. D. H., *Attempts at General Union. A Study in British Trade Union History 1818–1834*, 1953.

Cole, G. D. H., *Chartist Portraits*, 1941.

Coltham, Stephen, 'The *Bee-Hive* Newspaper: Its Origin and Struggles' in *Essays in Labour History*, ed. Asa Briggs and John Saville, 1960.

Cowling, Maurice, *1867. Disraeli, Gladstone and Revolution. The Passing of the second Reform Bill*, 1967.

Gillespie, Frances Elma, *Labor and Politics in England 1850–1867*, 1927.

Hobsbawm, E. J., *Labouring Men. Studies in the History of Labour*, 1964.

Hovell, Mark, *The Chartist Movement*, 1925 edn.

London Trades Council 1860–1950, A History. Foreword by Julius Jacobs, 1950.

Lovell, John, and Roberts, B. C., *A Short History of the T.U.C.*, 1968.

Lovett, William, *The Life and Struggles of William Lovett in his Pursuit of Bread, Knowledge and Freedom*, 1876.

Maccoby, S., *English Radicalism 1786–1832*, 1955.

Maccoby, S., *English Radicalism 1832–1852*, 1935.

Maccoby, S., *English Radicalism 1853–1886*, 1938.

Maccoby, S. (ed.), *The English Radical Tradition 1763–1914*, 1952.

Main, J. M., 'Radical Westminster, 1807–1820', *Historical Studies, Australia and New Zealand*, vol. 12, 1965–7, Melbourne.

Oliver, W. H., 'The Consolidated Trades Union of 1834', *Economic History Review, Second Series*, vol. 17, 1964–5.

Oliver, W. H., 'The Labour Exchange Phase of the Co-Operative Movement', *Oxford Economic Papers, New Series*, vol. 10, 1958.

Pollard, Sidney, 'Nineteenth-Century Co-Operation: From Community Building to Shopkeeping', in *Essays in Labour History*, ed. Asa Briggs and John Saville, 1960.

The Poor Man's Guardian, 1831–1835, 4 vols., 1969. Introd. Patricia Hollis.

Postgate, R. W., *The Builders' History*, 1923.

Prothero, I., 'Chartism in London', *Past and Present*, no. 44, 1969.

Prothero, I., 'The London Working Men's Association and the "People's Charter"', *Past and Present*, no. 38.

Rowe, D. J., 'Chartism and the Spitalfields Silk-weavers', *Economic History Review, Second Series*, vol. 20, 1967.

Rowe, D. J., 'The Failure of London Chartism', *The Historical Journal*, vol. xi, 1968.

Rowe, D. J., 'The London Working Men's Association and the "People's Charter"', *Past and Present*, No. 36.

Rudé, George, *The Crowd in History*, New York, 1964.

Saville, John (ed.), *Democracy and the Labour Movement*, 1954.

Schoyen, A. R., *The Chartist Challenge. A Portrait of George Julian Harney*, 1958.

Sharpe, Reginald R., *London and the Kingdom*, 1895, vol. III.

Smith, F. B., *The Making of the Second Reform Bill*, 1966.
Thompson, E. P., *The Making of the English Working Class*, Pelican edn, 1968.
Thurston, Gavin, *The Clerkenwell Riot. The Killing of Constable Culley*, 1967.
Wallas, Graham, *The Life of Francis Place, 1771–1854*, 1925 edn.
Webb, R. K., *The British Working Class Reader 1790–1848*, 1955.
Webb, Sidney and Beatrice, *The History of Trade Unionism*, 1920 edn.
Wickwar, William H., *The Struggle for the Freedom of the Press 1819–1832*, 1928.

CHAPTER 9

Living in Mid-Nineteenth Century London
Beames, Thomas, *The Rookeries of London: Past, Present, and Prospective*, 1850.
Blunt, Anthony, and Whinney, Margaret (eds.), *The Nation's Pictures*, 1950.
Bosanquet, Charles B. P., *London: Some Account of its Growth, Charitable Agencies, and Wants*, 1868.
Boulton, W. B., *The Romance of the British Museum*, n.d.
Boulton, W. B., *The Amusements of Old London*, 2 vols., 1901.
Cecil, Evelyn, *London Parks and Gardens*, 1907.
Chancellor, E. Beresford, *The Literary Ghosts of London*, 1933.
Chancellor, E. Beresford, *The Pleasure Haunts of London*, 1925.
Chancellor, E. Beresford, *The West End of Yesterday and Today*, 1926.
Colman, Henry, *European Life and Manners*, 2 vols., 1849.
Compton-Rickett, Arthur, *The London Life of Yesterday*, 1909.
Davis, Dorothy, *A History of Shopping*, 1966.
Early Victorian England 1830–1865, 2 vols., 1934.
Forster, E. M., *Marianne Thornton 1797–1887. A Domestic Biography*, 1956.
Francis, Claude De La Roche, *London, Historic and Social*, 2 vols, 1902.
A Frenchman Sees The English in the 'Fifties, adapted from the French of Francis Wey by Valerie Pirie, 1935.
Garwood, John, *The Million-Peopled City, Or, One-half of the People of London made known to the other half*, 1853.
Gavin, Hector, *Sanitary Ramblings, Being Sketches and Illustrations of Bethnal Green*, 1848.
Godwin, George, *London Shadows; A Glance at the 'Homes' of the Thousands*, 1854.
Godwin, George, *Town Swamps and Social Bridges*, 1859.
Greenwood, James, *The Seven Curses of London*, 1869.
Hodgkinson, Ruth G., *The Origins of the National Health Service*, 1967.
Hollingshead, John, *Ragged London in 1861*, 1861.
Jefferys, James B., *Retail Trading in Britain 1850–1950*, 1954.
Kelly, Thomas, *A History of Adult Education in Great Britain*, 1962.
Leeper, Janet, *English Ballet*, 1944.
The London Theatre 1811–1866. Selections from the diary of Henry Crabb Robinson, ed. Eluned Brown, 1966.
Low, Sampson, *The Charities of London*, edns of 1850, 1854, 1867.
Mackay, Thomas, *A History of the English Poor Law from 1834 to the Present Time*, 1899.

Mander, Raymond, and Mitchenson, Joe, *British Music Hall*, 1965.

Mander, Raymond, and Mitchenson, Joe, *The Theatres of London*, 1963 edn.

Mayhew, Henry. *London Labour and the London Poor*, 1861 edn.

Mayhew, Henry, and Binny, John, *The Criminal Prisons of London, and Scenes of Prison Life*, 1862.

Marshall, Dorothy, *The English Domestic Servant in History*, 1949.

Mowat, Charles Loch, *The Charity Organization Society 1869–1913. Its Ideas and Work*, 1961.

Neate, Alan R., *St Marylebone Workhouse and Institution, 1730–1965*, 1967.

Nicoll, Allardyce, *A History of English Drama 1660–1900: Early Nineteenth Century Drama, 1800–1950*, 1955 edn.

Nicoll, Allardyce, *A History of Late Nineteenth Century Drama 1850–1900*, vol. I, 1946.

Owen, David, *English Philanthropy 1660–1960*, 1965.

Perugini, Mark Edward, *The Omnibus Box*, 1946.

Rice, Charles, *The London Theatre in the Eighteen Thirties*, 1950.

Rosenthal, Harold, *Opera at Covent Garden. A Short History*, 1967.

Sexby, J. J., *The Municipal Parks, Gardens and Open Spaces of London*, 1898.

Sheppard, F. H. W., *Local Government in St Marylebone 1688–1835*, 1958.

Stallard, J. H., *London Pauperism amongst Jews and Christians*, 1867.

Stuart, Dorothy Margaret, *The English Abigail*, 1946.

Survey of London, vol. xxxv, *The Theatre Royal, Drury Lane, and the Royal Opera House, Covent Garden*, 1970.

Taine, Hippolyte, *Notes on England*, trans. W. F. Rae, 1872.

Diary of William Tayler, Footman, 1837, ed. Dorothy Wise, 1962, St Marylebone Society Publications.

Thompson, F. M. L., *English Landed Society in the Nineteenth Century*, 1963.

Tobias, J. J., *Crime and Industrial Society in the 19th Century*, 1967.

Webb, Sidney and Beatrice, *English Poor Law History, Part I, The Old Poor Law*, 1927; *Part II, The Last Hundred Years*, 1929.

Webb, S. and B., *English Prisons under Local Government*, 1922.

Welch, Charles, *A Modern History of the City of London*, 1896.

Wroth, Warwick, *Cremorne and the Later London Gardens*, 1907.

Index